Sources of
THE MAKING OF THE WEST

PEOPLES AND CULTURES

Volume I: To 1740

Sources of
THE MAKING OF THE WEST

PEOPLES AND CULTURES

Volume I: To 1740

KATHARINE J. LUALDI

BEDFORD/ST. MARTIN'S   Boston ◆ New York

History Editor: Katherine E. Kurzman
Developmental Editor: Molly Kalkstein
Production Editor: Thomas P. Crehan
Production Supervisor: Catherine Hetmansky
Marketing Manager: Jenna Bookin Barry
Copyeditor: Barbara Sutton
Text Composition: Karla Goethe, Orchard Wind Graphics
Cover Design: Donna Lee Dennison
Printing and Binding: Malloy Lithography Inc.

President: Charles H. Christensen
Editorial Director: Joan E. Feinberg
Director of Editing, Design, and Production: Marcia Cohen
Director of Marketing: Karen Melton
Managing Editor: Elizabeth M. Schaaf

For information, write: Bedford/St. Martin's, 75 Arlington Street, Boston, MA 02116 (617-399-4000)

ISBN:0-312-18386-0

Preface

COMPILED SPECIFICALLY TO ACCOMPANY *The Making of the West: Peoples and Cultures*, *Sources of THE MAKING OF THE WEST* is intended to help instructors bring the history of Western civilization to life for students. The collection is organized chapter by chapter to parallel *The Making of the West* and thereby enrich the major issues, ideas, and events discussed therein with the thoughts and experiences of people living at the time. In this way, the documents offer instructors varied opportunities to ignite a dialogue in the classroom between the past and present.

Together, these primary source documents provide a colorful array of voices for such a dialogue within the thematic and chronological framework provided by *The Making of the West*. For example, while the textbook outlines the basic details concerning the European slave trade, students can see it for themselves in the document reader through the eyes of Olaudah Equiano, an African slave who survived to tell his story (Volume II, Chapter 18, Document 1). Facts and chronology thus come alive with the emotions, opinions, and observations of people living at the time, revealing that the study of history is not fixed but is an ongoing process of evaluation and interpretation. *Sources of THE MAKING OF THE WEST* provides the raw materials for this process.

The criteria governing the selection of documents reflect historians' changing understanding of Western civilization. Although traditional political sources are included in the collection, these views are broadened by less conventional documents illuminating not only social and cultural life but also Europe's increasing interconnectedness with the world beyond its borders. Women's voices were also granted a special place in the selection process because of their crucial and often underappreciated role in shaping the course of Western history from both within and outside the corridors of power. In Volume II, Chapter 20, for instance, students can hear the collective voice of the National Assembly as it launched the French Revolution (Document 2) alongside that of a female political activist, Olympe de Gouges (Document 3), and Toussaint L'Ouverture, a revolutionary leader in the French colony of St. Domingue (Document 4). Here as elsewhere in the collection, I chose documents that work well together to elucidate important events and opinions of a specific historical era. The documents were also selected based on their accessibility and appeal to students. For this reason, I have carefully edited each document to speak to specific themes without impairing its overall sense and tone.

To assist students with their journey into the past, I have provided a summary for every chapter that situates the documents within the broader historical context and addresses their relationship to one another. An explanatory headnote accompanies each document to provide fundamental background information on the author and the source while highlighting its significance. Discussion questions are also included to help students examine the key points and issues in greater depth. Finally, each chapter concludes with a few comparative questions intended to encourage students to see both the harmony and discordance among the documents. Although these editorial features intentionally strengthen the coherency of each chapter as a unit, they also allow instructors to choose documents and questions that best suit their specific teaching goals and methods.

Acknowledgments

I owe many people thanks for helping to bring this project to fruition. First among them are the authors of *The Making of the West*, Lynn Hunt, Thomas Martin, Barbara Rosenwein, R. Po-chia Hsia, and Bonnie Smith, who provided invaluable suggestions, advice, and insight. I would also like to thank Larissa Juliet Taylor, Julia O'Brien, Megan Armstrong, and David K. Smith for their help and encouragement, as well as my development editor, Molly Kalkstein, for her careful eye and enthusiasm. Those at Bedford/St. Martin's also helped make this book possible.

I also owe a debt of gratitude to the staff of the University of Maine library system who patiently endured my seemingly endless requests for books and articles. Without them, compiling this collection would not have been possible.

Lastly, I would like to thank my husband, John, for his sense of humor and understanding as I lost myself in books and Post-it notes.

Introduction

THE LONG HISTORY OF WESTERN CIVILIZATION encompasses a broad range of places and cultures. Textbooks provide an essential chronological and thematic framework for understanding the formation of the West as a cultural and geographical entity. Yet the process of historical inquiry extends beyond textbook narratives into the thoughts, words, and experiences of people living at the time. Documents expose this world so that you can observe, analyze, and interpret the past as it unfolds before you. History is thus not a static collection of facts and dates. Rather, it is an ongoing attempt to make sense of the past and its relationship to the present through the lens of historical documents.

Sources of THE MAKING OF THE WEST *provides this lens for you, with engaging firsthand accounts representing a wide range of sources—from Egyptian chronicles, to English feminist tracts, to Prussian political memoirs. When combined, the documents reflect historians' growing appreciation of the need to examine Western civilization from different conceptual angles (political, social, cultural, economic) and geographic viewpoints. The composite picture that emerges as a result reveals a variety of historical experiences shaping each era from both within and outside Europe's borders. Furthermore, the documents demonstrate that the most historically significant of these experiences are not always those of people in formal positions of power. Women, minorities, and everyday folk likewise influenced the course of Western history.

The sources in this reader were selected with an eye to their ability not only to capture the multifaceted dimensions of the past but also to ignite your intellectual curiosity. Each document is a unique product of human endeavor and as such is often colored by the author's personal concerns, biases, and objectives. Among the most exciting challenges facing you is to sift through such nuances for what they reveal about the source and its links to the broader historical context.

Understanding how each document is connected to its author and to larger historical issues is key to the study of history. To this end, as you read each document, you should keep a series of questions at the front of your mind, just like a reporter investigating a breaking news story: Who wrote the document, when, for whom, why, and where? Each of these questions represents a crucial piece of the puzzle of the past and is an essential means of charting change and continuity over time.

A Nazi propaganda pamphlet written in 1930 (Volume Two, Chapter 27, Document 1) offers an instructive example. The author of the pamphlet, Joseph Goebbels, was the propaganda chief of Adolf Hitler, the leader of the Nazi party.

Both men were bounded by similar political goals and beliefs, including virulent anti-Semitism. At the time Goebbels wrote the document, Germany was mired in economic recession. Capitalizing on the downhearted mood of the day with promises of a better life, he successfully used pamphlets such as this one to broaden the Nazis' popular support on the eve of Hitler's rise to power. All of these factors—Goebbels's position within the Nazi party, what he was writing, for whom, when, and why—shaped the document's content, and thus should inform your interpretation of what it suggests about the Nazis and Germany in this period. By contrast, the recollections of Jews who were the victims of this propaganda (Volume Two, Chapter 27, Document 3) offer a far different view of the Nazis and the human impact of their regime. This difference can be attributed not only to the nature of the sources themselves but also to the opposing perspectives they represent.

Mining documents for their multiple layers of meaning thus requires a careful balancing act between fact and interpretation, and between the content of the document and the larger historical backdrop. To aid you with this process, *Sources of THE MAKING OF THE WEST* is designed to be used alongside *THE MAKING OF THE WEST*. Each chapter in the collection contains four documents illustrative of the central ideas, issues, and events discussed in the corresponding textbook chapter. In addition, *Sources of THE MAKING OF THE WEST* includes a variety of useful editorial features that supplement the basic information found in the textbook. A summary linking the documents to the historical period in which they were written prefaces each chapter. Every document has an introductory headnote that provides essential information about the author and the source and why the document is historically significant. Finally, several questions conclude each document and chapter to help you probe beneath the surface to understand what each document says and means, and to see the similarities and differences among them.

The documents included in *Sources of THE MAKING OF THE WEST* invite you to become active participants in discovering how history was actually lived over time by an array of different people in an array of different places. In this way, the documents offer snapshots of the past that, when viewed and interpreted together within the broader historical context, will help you paint a colorful and interconnected picture of the development of Western values, traditions, and institutions.

Contents

Foundations of Western Civilization to 1000 B.C.

S U M M A R Y   The roots of Western culture cut across distant lands and ancient societies. The four documents in this chapter expose the fundamental features of these early civilizations as they developed between the eighteenth and tenth centuries B.C. The evidence reveals that on the one hand, peoples then living in the Near East, Africa, and the Mediterranean developed their own distinctive beliefs, customs, and sense of identity. On the other, they shared many attributes, such as large urban populations, the use of writing, devotion to religion, and economies based on trade and agriculture. This unique mixture of cross-cultural similarities and differences forged the path for the future.

Priest written code of which we are aware.

1
King Hammurabi
The Code of Hammurabi
Early Eighteenth Century B.C.

The law code promulgated by King Hammurabi (r.c. 1792–1750 B.C.) of Babylon elucidates the inner workings of Mesopotamian society, the cradle of the world's first civilization. The copy of the code excerpted here is inscribed on a stone pillar, crowned by a bas-relief depicting the god of justice commissioning Hammurabi to write the laws. This image embodies the Mesopotamian belief that kings were divinely appointed and thereby responsible for imparting justice and promoting their subjects' well-being. As a messenger of the divine will, King Hammurabi influenced both the public and private lives of his people. As the following selection reveals, he was especially concerned with protecting property rights and the social hierarchy, with slaves at the bottom and free persons at the top. By codifying laws in writing, Hammurabi helped set an enduring precedent in the Western tradition.

1

When lofty Anum,[1] king of the Anunnaki,[2]
(and) Enlil, lord of heaven and earth,
the determiner of the destinies of the land,
determined for Marduk,[3] the first-born of Enki,[4]
the Enlil functions over all mankind,
made him great among the Igigi,[5]
called Babylon by its exalted name,
made it supreme in the world,
established for him in its midst an enduring kingship,
whose foundations are as firm as heaven and earth—
at that time Anum and Enlil named me
to promote the welfare of the people,[6]
me, Hammurabi, the devout, god-fearing prince,
to cause justice to prevail in the land,
to destroy the wicked and the evil,
that the strong might not oppress the weak,
to rise like the sun over the black-headed (people),[7]
and to light up the land. . . .

(v)

When Marduk commissioned me to guide the people aright,
to direct the land,
I established law and justice in the language of the land,
thereby promoting the welfare of the people.
At that time (I decreed):

From *Ancient Near Eastern Texts Relating to the Old Testament,* ed. James B. Pritchard, 3d ed. (Princeton, N.J.: Princeton University Press, 1969),164–78.

[1]The sky-god, the leader of the pantheon, worshiped especially in the temple of Eanna in Uruk, along with the goddess Inanna.

[2]In this inscription the Anunnaki are the lesser gods attendant upon Anum, and the Igigi are the lesser gods attendant on Enlil.

[3]The storm-god, the chief executive of the pantheon, worshiped especially in the temple of Ekur in Nippur in central Babylonia, modern Nuffar.

[4]The son of Enki and consort of Sarpanit; the god of Babylon and in Hammurabi's time the god of the Babylonian Empire with the functions of Enlil delegated to him; worshiped especially in the temple of Esagila in Babylon.

[5]Lord of the earth and the mass of life-giving waters within it, issuing in streams and fountains; the father of Marduk; worshiped especially in the temple of Eabzu in Eridu, in southern Babylonia, modern Abu Shahrein.

[6]Lit., "to make good the flesh of the people.

[7]The late-Sumerian expression for men in general.

property owner

The Laws

If a seignior[8] accused a(nother) seignior and brought a charge of murder against him, but has not proved it, his accuser shall be put to death.[9]

If a seignior brought a charge of sorcery against a(nother) seignior, but has not proved it, the one against whom the charge of sorcery was brought, upon going to the river,[10] shall throw himself into the river, and if the river has then overpowered him, his accuser shall take over his estate; if the river has shown that seignior to be innocent and he has accordingly come forth safe, the one who brought the charge of sorcery against him shall be put to death, while the one who threw himself into the river shall take over the estate of his accuser.

If a seignior came forward with false testimony in a case, and has not proved the word which he spoke, if that case was a case involving life, that seignior shall be put to death. . . .

If a seignior has purchased or he received for safe-keeping either silver or gold or a male slave or a female slave or an ox or a sheep or an ass or any sort of thing from the hand of a seignior's son or a seignior's slave without witnesses and contracts, since that seignior is a thief, he shall be put to death.

If a seignior stole either an ox or a sheep or an ass or a pig or a boat, if it belonged to the church (or) if it belonged to the state, he shall make thirtyfold restitution; if it belonged to a private citizen, he shall make good tenfold. If the thief does not have sufficient to make restitution, he shall be put to death. . . .

If a seignior has stolen the young son of a(nother) seignior, he shall be put to death.[11]

If a seignior has helped either a male slave of the state or a female slave of the state or a male slave of a private citizen or a female slave of a private citizen to escape through the city-gate, he shall be put to death.

If a seignior has harbored in his house either a fugitive male or female slave belonging to the state or to a private citizen and has not brought him forth at the summons of the police, that householder shall be put to death. . . .

---

[8]The word *awēlum*, used here, is literally "man," but in the legal literature it seems to be used in at least three senses: (1) sometimes to indicate a man of the higher class, a noble; (2) sometimes a free man of any class, high or low; and (3) occasionally a man of any class, from king to slave. For the last I use the inclusive word *man,* but for the first two, since it is seldom clear which of the two is intended in a given context, I follow the ambiguity of the original and use the rather general term *seignior* in Italian and Spanish, to indicate any free man of standing, and not in the strict feudal sense, although the ancient Near East did have something approximating the feudal system, and that is another reason for using *seignior.*

[9]With this law and the three following, cf. Deut. 5:20, 19:16 ff.; Exod. 23:1–3.

[10]The word for "river" throughout this section has the determinative of deity, indicating that the river (the Euphrates) as judge in the case was regarded as god.

[11]Cf. Exod. 21:16; Deut. 24:7.

handwritten: private property = high value

4 FOUNDATIONS OF WESTERN CIVILIZATION, THE STONE AGE TO 1000 B.C.

If a seignior made a breach in a house, they shall put him to death in front of that breach and wall him in.[12]

If a seignior committed robbery and has been caught, that seignior shall be put to death.

If the robber has not been caught, the robbed seignior shall set forth the particulars regarding his lost property in the presence of god, and the city and governor, in whose territory and district the robbery was committed, shall make good to him his lost property.

If it was a life (that was lost), the city and governor shall pay one mina[13] of silver to his people. . . .[14]

If a seignior rented a field for cultivation, but has not produced grain in the field, they shall prove that he did no work on the field and he shall give grain to the owner of the field on the basis of those adjoining it.

If he did not cultivate the field, but has neglected (it), he shall give grain to the owner of the field on the basis of those adjoining it; furthermore, the field which he neglected he shall break up with mattocks, harrow and return to the owner of the field. . . .

If a shepherd has not come to an agreement with the owner of a field to pasture sheep on the grass, but has pastured sheep on the field without the consent of the owner of the field, when the owner of the field harvests his field, the shepherd who pastured the sheep on the field without the consent of the owner of the field shall give in addition twenty *kur* of grain per eighteen *iku* to the owner of the field. . . .

If a merchant lent grain, wool, oil, or any goods at all to a trader to retail, the trader shall write down the value and pay (it) back to the merchant, with the trader obtaining a sealed receipt for the money which he pays to the merchant.

If the trader has been careless and so has not obtained a sealed receipt for the money which he paid to the merchant, the money with no sealed receipt may not be credited to the account.

If a trader borrowed money from a merchant and has then disputed (the fact) with his merchant, that merchant in the presence of god and witnesses shall prove that the trader borrowed the money and the trader shall pay to the merchant threefold the full amount of money that he borrowed.

When a merchant entrusted (something) to a trader and the trader has returned to his merchant whatever the merchant gave him, if the merchant has then disputed with him whatever the trader gave him, that trader shall prove it against the merchant in the presence of god and witnesses and the merchant shall pay to the trader sixfold whatever he received because he had a dispute with his trader.

If a woman wine seller, instead of receiving grain for the price of a drink, has received money by the large weight and so has made the value of the drink less

---

[12]Cf. Exod. 22:2, 3a.

[13]A weight of about 500 grams, divided into 60 shekels.

[14]For this and the preceding law, cf. Deut. 21:1 ff.

than the value of the grain, they shall prove it against that wine seller[15] and throw her into the water.

If outlaws have congregated in the establishment of a woman wine seller and she has not arrested those outlaws and did not take them to the palace, that wine seller shall be put to death. . . .

If a seignior pointed the finger at a nun or the wife of a(nother) seignior, but has proved nothing, they shall drag that seignior into the presence of the judges and also cut off half his (hair). → *social identification*

If a seignior acquired a wife, but did not draw up the contracts for her, that woman is no wife.

If the wife of a seignior has been caught while lying with another man, they shall bind them and throw them into the water. If the husband[16] of the woman wishes to spare his wife, then the king in turn may spare his subject.[17]

If a seignior bound the (betrothed) wife of a(nother) seignior, who had had no intercourse with[18] a male and was still living in her father's house, and he has lain in her bosom and they have caught him, that seignior shall be put to death, while that woman shall go free.[19]

If a seignior's wife was accused by her husband,[20] but she was not caught while lying with another man, she shall make affirmation by god and return to her house.

If the finger was pointed at the wife of a seignior because of another man, but she has not been caught while lying with the other man, she shall throw herself into the river[21] for the sake of her husband.[22] *Yucky*

If a seignior was taken captive, but there was sufficient to live on in his house, his wife [shall not leave her house, but she shall take care of her person by not] entering [the house of another].[23]

If that woman did not take care of her person, but has entered the house of another, they shall prove it against that woman and throw her into the water.[24]

If the seignior was taken captive and there was not sufficient to live on in his house, his wife may enter the house of another, with that woman incurring no blame at all.

state protection of weak.

---

[15]This has also been translated as "they shall bind that wine seller."

[16]Lit., "owner, master."

[17]Lit., "his slave." With this law cf. Deut. 22:22.

[18]Lit., "had not known."

[19]Cf. Deut. 22:23–27.

[20]Lit., "If with respect to a seignior's wife (*casus pendens*) her husband accused her."

[21]I.e., submit to the water ordeal, with the river as divine judge; cf. note 10.

[22]Cf. Num. 5:11–31.

[23]I.e., in order to live there as another man's wife.

[24]I.e., to be drowned.

*patriarchal soc.;
patrilineal*

If, when a seignior was taken captive and there was not sufficient to live on in his house, his wife has then entered the house of another before his (return) and has borne children, (and) later her husband has returned and has reached his city, that woman shall return to her first husband, while the children shall go with their father.

If, when a seignior deserted his city and then ran away, his wife has entered the house of another after his (departure), if that seignior has returned and wishes to take back his wife, the wife of the fugitive shall not return to her husband because he scorned his city and ran away. . . .

If a seignior wishes to divorce his wife who did not bear him children, he shall give her money to the full amount of her marriage-price and he shall also make good to her the dowry which she brought from her father's house and then he may divorce her.

If there was no marriage-price, he shall give her one mina of silver as the divorce-settlement.

If he is a peasant,[25] he shall give her one-third mina of silver.

If a seignior's wife, who was living in the house of the seignior, has made up her mind to leave in order that she may engage in business, thus neglecting her house (and) humiliating her husband, they shall prove it against her; and if her husband has then decided on her divorce, he may divorce her, with nothing to be given her as her divorce-settlement upon her departure.[26] If her husband has not decided on her divorce, her husband may marry another woman, with the former woman[27] living in the house of her husband like a maidservant.

If a woman so hated her husband that she has declared, "You may not have me," her record shall be investigated at her city council, and if she was careful and was not at fault, even though her husband has been going out and disparaging her greatly, that woman, without incurring any blame at all, may take her dowry and go off to her father's house.

If she was not careful, but was a gadabout, thus neglecting her house (and) humiliating her husband, they shall throw that woman into the water. . . .

When a seignior married a woman and a fever[28] has then seized her, if he has made up his mind to marry another, he may marry (her), without divorcing his wife whom the fever seized; she shall live in the house which he built and he shall continue to support her as long as she lives.

If that woman has refused to live in her husband's house, he shall make good her dowry to her which she brought from her father's house and then she may leave.

If a seignior, upon presenting a field, orchard, house, or goods to his wife, left a sealed document with her, her children may not enter a claim against her

---

[25]The word is *muškēnum.*

[26]Lit., "her journey," a noun in the adverbial accusative of manner.

[27]Lit., "that woman."

[28]The exact meaning of the word used here, *la'bum,* is not known.

after (the death of) her husband, since the mother may give her inheritance to that son of hers whom she likes, (but) she may not give (it) to an outsider. . . .

If a seignior's wife has brought about the death of her husband because of another man, they shall impale that woman on stakes. . . . *ambiguous*

If, when a seignior acquired a wife, she bore him children and that woman has then gone to (her) fate, her father may not lay claim to her dowry, since her dowry belongs to her children.

If a seignior acquired a wife and that woman has gone to (her) fate without providing him with children, if his father-in-law has then returned to him the marriage-price which that seignior brought to the house of his father-in-law, her husband may not lay claim to the dowry of that woman, since her dowry belongs to her father's house. . . .

If a member of the artisan class[29] took a son as a foster child and has taught him his handicraft, he may never be reclaimed. . . .

If a son has struck his father, they shall cut off his hand.[30]

If a seignior has destroyed the eye of a member of the aristocracy,[31] they shall destroy his eye.[32]

If he has broken a(nother) seignior's bone, they shall break his bone.[33]

If he has destroyed the eye of a commoner or broken the bone of a commoner, he shall pay one mina of silver.

If he has destroyed the eye of a seignior's slave or broken the bone of a seignior's slave, he shall pay one-half his value.

If a seignior has knocked out a tooth of a seignior of his own rank, they shall knock out his tooth.[34]

If he has knocked out a commoner's tooth, he shall pay one-third mina of silver.

If a seignior has struck the cheek of a seignior who is superior to him, he shall be beaten sixty (times) with an oxtail whip in the assembly.

If a member of the aristocracy has struck the cheek of a(nother) member of the aristocracy who is of the same rank as[35] himself, he shall pay one mina of silver.

significance of "turn the other cheek" in NT

---

[29]Lit. "the son of an artisan," where "son" is used in the technical sense of "belonging to the class of, species of," so common in the Semitic languages.

[30]Cf. Exod. 21:15. For the whole collection of laws dealing with personal injuries (laws 195–214), cf. the similiar collection in Exod. 21:12–27.

[31]Lit. "the son of a man," with "son" used in the technical sense already explained and "man" clearly in the sense of "noble, aristocrat." Or it is possible that "son" here is to be taken in its regular sense to indicate a person younger than the assailant.

[32]Cf. Exod., 21:23–25.

[33]Cf. Lev., 24:19f.

[34]Cf. Deut., 19:21.

[35]Lit. "who is like."

If a commoner has struck the cheek of a(nother) commoner, he shall pay ten shekels of silver.

If a seignior's slave has struck the cheek of a member of the aristocracy, they shall cut off his ear.

If a seignior has struck a(nother) seignior in a brawl and has inflicted an injury on him, that seignior shall swear, "I did not strike him deliberately";[36] and he shall also pay for the physician.

If he has died because of his blow, he shall swear (as before), and if it was a member of the aristocracy, he shall pay one-half mina of silver.

If it was a member of the commonalty, he shall pay one-third mina of silver.

If a seignior struck a(nother) seignior's daughter and has caused her to have a miscarriage,[37] he shall pay ten shekels of silver for her fetus.

If that woman has died, they shall put his daughter to death.

If by a blow he has caused a commoner's daughter to have a miscarriage, he shall pay five shekels of silver.

If that woman has died, he shall pay one-half mina of silver.

If he struck a seignior's female slave and has caused her to have a miscarriage, he shall pay two shekels of silver.

If that female slave has died, he shall pay one-third mina of silver. . . .

If an ox, when it was walking along the street, gored a seignior to death,[38] that case is not subject to claim.

If a seignior's ox was a gorer and his city council made it known to him that it was a gorer, but he did not pad its horns (or) tie up his ox, and that ox gored to death a member of the aristocracy, he shall give one-half mina of silver.[39]

If it was a seignior's slave, he shall give one-third mina of silver. . . .

The Epilogue

The laws of justice, which Hammurabi, the efficient king, set up,
and by which he caused the land to take the right way and have good government.
I, Hammurabi, the perfect king,
was not careless (or) neglectful of the black-headed (people),
whom Enlil had presented to me,
(and) whose shepherding Marduk had committed to me;
I sought out peaceful regions for them;
I overcame grievous difficulties;
I caused light to rise on them.

---

[36]Lit. "while I was aware of (it)."

[37]Lit. "caused her to drop that of her womb (her fetus)." With this and the following five laws, cf. Exod. 21:22–25.

[38]Lit. "and has caused his death."

[39]Cf. Exod. 21:28–36.

With the mighty weapon which Zababa and Inanna entrusted to me,
with the insight that Enki allotted to me,
with the ability that Marduk gave me,
I rooted out the enemy above and below;
I made an end of war;
I promoted the welfare of the land;
I made the peoples rest in friendly habitations;
I did not let them have anyone to terrorize them.
The great gods called me,
so I became the beneficent shepherd whose scepter is righteous;
my benign shadow is spread over my city.
In my bosom I carried the peoples of the land of Sumer and Akkad;
they prospered under my protection;
I always governed them in peace;
I sheltered them in my wisdom.
In order that the strong might not oppress the weak,
that justice might be dealt the orphan (and) the widow,
in Babylon, the city whose head Anum and Enlil raised aloft,
in Esagila, the temple whose foundations stand firm like heaven and earth,
I wrote my precious words on my stela,
and in the presence of the statue of me, the king of justice,
I set (it) up in order to administer the law of the land,
to prescribe the ordinances of the land,
to give justice to the oppressed.

DISCUSSION QUESTIONS

1. What do the Prologue and Epilogue indicate about the status of Mesopotamian rulers?
2. What values or ideals governing the code do you see underlying these excerpts?
3. What does the code reveal in particular about women's position in Mesopotamian society?
4. Historians traditionally view cities, formal political systems, knowledge of writing, and diverse crafts as defining features of civilization. Which of these features are reflected in the code?

2

The Book of Exodus
Chapters 19–24
c. Tenth–Sixth Centuries B.C.

This excerpt from the second book of the Hebrew Bible, Exodus, exposes an important trait shared by Hammurabi's Code and other ancient laws: perpetrators of acts defined as unlawful must endure a specified punishment. In its account of the Hebrews' flight from Egypt in the thirteenth century B.C., the book of Exodus includes

*the first proclamation by their God, Yahweh, of the divine laws governing his rela-
tions with them and with one another. The Hebrews agreed to follow the rules in exchange for God's promise to make them his chosen people. Although they did not yet
deny the existence of other gods, their covenant with him was a crucial stage in the
development of monotheism. The biblical story casts the Hebrew leader, Moses, in
much the same role as that of Hammurabi in his code: both are agents of divine justice and protection.*

19 On the third new moon after the people of Israel had gone forth out of the
land of Egypt, on that day they came into the wilderness of Sinai. And when they
set out from Rephidim and came into the wilderness of Sinai, they encamped in
the wilderness; and there Israel encamped before the mountain. And Moses went
up to God, and the LORD called him out of the mountain, saying, "Thus you shall
say to the house of Jacob, and tell the people of Israel: You have seen what I did
to the Egyptians, and how I bore you on eagles' wings and brought you to myself.
Now therefore, if you will obey my voice and keep my covenant, you shall be my
own possession among all peoples; for all the earth is mine, and you shall be to
me a kingdom of priests and a holy nation. These are the words which you shall
speak to the children of Israel."

So Moses came and called the elders of the people, and set before them all
these words which the LORD had commanded him. And all the people answered
together and said, "All that the LORD has spoken we will do." And Moses reported
the words of the people to the LORD. And the LORD said to Moses, "Lo, I am coming to you in a thick cloud, that the people may hear when I speak with you, and
may also believe you for ever."

Then Moses told the words of the people to the LORD. And the LORD said to
Moses, "Go to the people and consecrate them today and tomorrow, and let them
wash their garments, and be ready by the third day; for on the third day the LORD
will come down upon Mount Sinai in the sight of all the people. And you shall
set bounds for the people round about, saying, 'Take heed that you do not go up
into the mountain or touch the border of it; whoever touches the mountain shall
be put to death; no hand shall touch him, but he shall be stoned or shot; whether
beast or man, he shall not live.' When the trumpet sounds a long blast, they shall
come up to the mountain." So Moses went down from the mountain to the people, and consecrated the people; and they washed their garments. And he said to
the people, "Be ready by the third day; do not go near a woman."

On the morning of the third day there were thunders and lightnings, and a
thick cloud upon the mountain, and a very loud trumpet blast, so that all the
people who were in the camp trembled. Then Moses brought the people out of
the camp to meet God; and they took their stand at the foot of the mountain.
And Mount Sinai was wrapped in smoke, because the LORD descended upon it in
fire; and the smoke of it went up like the smoke of a kiln, and the whole moun-

From *The Holy Bible, Authorized King James Version* (Oxford: Oxford University Press,
1960), 67–72.

tain quaked greatly. And as the sound of the trumpet grew louder and louder, Moses spoke, and God answered him in thunder. And the LORD came down upon Mount Sinai, to the top of the mountain; and the LORD called Moses to the top of the mountain, and Moses went up. And the LORD said to Moses, "Go down and warn the people, lest they break through to the LORD to gaze and many of them perish. And also let the priests who come near to the LORD consecrate themselves, lest the LORD break out upon them." And Moses said to the LORD, "The people cannot come up to Mount Sinai; for thou thyself didst charge us, saying, 'Set bounds about the mountain, and consecrate it.'" And the LORD said to him, "Go down, and come up bringing Aaron with you; but do not let the priests and the people break through to come up to the LORD, lest he break out against them." So Moses went down to the people and told them.

20 And God spoke all these words, saying,

ı "I am the LORD your God, who brought you out of the land of Egypt, out of the house of bondage.

"You shall have no other gods before me.

ʅ "You shall not make yourself a graven image, or any likeness of anything that is in heaven above, or that is in the earth beneath, or that is in the water under the earth; you shall not bow down to them or serve them; for I the LORD your God am a jealous God, visiting the iniquity of the fathers upon the children to the third and the fourth generation of those who hate me, but showing steadfast love to thousands of those who love me and keep my commandments.

ɜ "You shall not take the name of the LORD your God in vain; for the LORD will not hold him guiltless who takes his name in vain.

Ч "Remember the sabbath day, to keep it holy. Six days you shall labor, and do all your work; but the seventh day is a sabbath to the LORD your God; in it you shall not do any work, you, or your son, or your daughter, your manservant, or your maidservant, or your cattle, or the sojourner who is within your gates; for in six days the LORD made heaven and earth, the sea, and all that is in them, and rested the seventh day; therefore the LORD blessed the sabbath day and hallowed it.

Ƽ "Honor your father and your mother, that your days may be long in the land which the LORD your God gives you.

ᵛ "You shall not kill.

˥ "You shall not commit adultery.

ȣ "You shall not steal.

ⴹ "You shall not bear false witness against your neighbor.

ıₒ "You shall not covet your neighbor's house; you shall not covet your neighbor's wife, or his manservant, or his maidservant, or his ox, or his ass, or anything that is your neighbor's."

Now when all the people perceived the thunderings and the lightnings and the sound of the trumpet and the mountain smoking, the people were afraid and trembled; and they stood afar off, and said to Moses, "You speak to us, and we will hear; but let not God speak to us, lest we die." And Moses said to the people, "Do not fear; for God has come to prove you, and that the fear of him may be before your eyes, that you may not sin."

And the people stood afar off, while Moses drew near to the thick cloud where God was. And the LORD said to Moses, "Thus you shall say to the people of Israel: 'You have seen for yourselves that I have talked with you from heaven. You shall not make gods of silver to be with me, nor shall you make for yourselves gods of gold. An altar of earth you shall make for me and sacrifice on it your burnt offerings and your peace offerings, your sheep and your oxen; in every place where I cause my name to be remembered I will come to you and bless you. And if you make me an altar of stone, you shall not build it of hewn stones; for if you wield your tool upon it you profane it. And you shall not go up by steps to my altar, that your nakedness be not exposed on it.'

21 "Now these are the ordinances which you shall set before them. When you buy a Hebrew slave, he shall serve six years, and in the seventh he shall go out free, for nothing. If he comes in single, he shall go out single; if he comes in married, then his wife shall go out with him. If his master gives him a wife and she bears him sons or daughters, the wife and her children shall be her master's and he shall go out alone. But if the slave plainly says, 'I love my master, my wife, and my children; I will not go out free,' then his master shall bring him to God, and he shall bring him to the door or the doorpost; and his master shall bore his ear through with an awl; and he shall serve him for life.

When a man sells his daughter as a slave, she shall not go out as the male slaves do. If she does not please her master, who has designated her for himself, then he shall let her be redeemed; he shall have no right to sell her to a foreign people, since he has dealt faithlessly with her. If he designates her for his son, he shall deal with her as with a daughter. If he takes another wife to himself, he shall not diminish her food, her clothing, or her marital rights. And if he does not do these three things for her, she shall go out for nothing, without payment of money.

"Whoever strikes a man so that he dies shall be put to death. But if he did not lie in wait for him, but God let him fall into his hand, then I will appoint for you a place to which he may flee. But if a man willfully attacks another to kill him treacherously, you shall take him from my altar, that he may die.

"Whoever strikes his father or his mother shall be put to death.

"Whoever steals a man, whether he sells him or is found in possession of him, shall be put to death.

"Whoever curses his father or his mother shall be put to death.

"When men quarrel and one strikes the other with a stone or with his fist and the man does not die but keeps his bed, then if the man rises again and walks abroad with his staff, he that struck him shall be clear; only he shall pay for the loss of his time, and shall have him thoroughly healed.

"When a man strikes his slave, male or female, with a rod and the slave dies under his hand, he shall be punished. But if the slave survives a day or two, he is not to be punished; for the slave is his money.

"When men strive together, and hurt a woman with child, so that there is a miscarriage, and yet no harm follows, the one who hurt her shall be fined, according as the woman's husband shall lay upon him; and he shall pay as the judges determine. If any harm follows, then you shall give life for life, eye for eye, tooth for tooth, hand for hand, foot for foot, burn for burn, wound for wound, stripe for stripe.

"When a man strikes the eye of his slave, male or female, and destroys it, he shall let the slave go free for the eye's sake. If he knocks out the tooth of his slave, male or female, he shall let the slave go free for the tooth's sake.

"When an ox gores a man or a woman to death, the ox shall be stoned, and its flesh shall not be eaten; but the owner of the ox shall be clear. But if the ox has been accustomed to gore in the past, and its owner has been warned but has not kept it in, and it kills a man or a woman, the ox shall be stoned, and its owner also shall be put to death. If a ransom is laid on him, then he shall give for the redemption of his life whatever is laid upon him. If it gores a man's son or daughter, he shall be dealt with according to this same rule. If the ox gores a slave, male or female, the owner shall give to their master thirty shekels of silver, and the ox shall be stoned.

"When a man leaves a pit open, or when a man digs a pit and does not cover it, and an ox or an ass falls into it, the owner of the pit shall make it good; he shall give money to its owner, and the dead beast shall be his.

"When one man's ox hurts another's, so that it dies, then they shall sell the live ox and divide the price of it; and the dead beast also they shall divide. Or if it is known that the ox has been accustomed to gore in the past, and its owner has not kept it in, he shall pay ox for ox, and the dead beast shall be his.

22 "If a man steals an ox or a sheep, and kills it or sells it, he shall pay five oxen for an ox, and four sheep for a sheep. He shall make restitution; if he has nothing, then he shall be sold for his theft. If the stolen beast is found alive in his possession, whether it is an ox or an ass or a sheep, he shall pay double.

"If a thief is found breaking in, and is struck so that he dies, there shall be no bloodguilt for him; but if the sun has risen upon him, there shall be bloodguilt for him.

"When a man causes a field or vineyard to be grazed over, or lets his beast loose and it feeds in another man's field, he shall make restitution from the best in his own field and in his own vineyard.

"When fire breaks out and catches in thorns so that the stacked grain or the standing grain or the field is consumed, he that kindled the fire shall make full restitution.

"If a man delivers to his neighbor money or goods to keep, and it is stolen out of the man's house, then, if the thief is found, he shall pay double. If the thief is not found, the owner of the house shall come near to God, to show whether or not he has put his hand to his neighbor's goods.

"For every breach of trust, whether it is for ox, for ass, for sheep, for clothing, or for any kind of lost thing, of which one says, 'This is it,' the case of both parties shall come before God; he whom God shall condemn shall pay double to his neighbor.

"If a man delivers to his neighbor an ass or an ox or a sheep or any beast to keep, and it dies or is hurt or is driven away, without any one seeing it, an oath by

[margin note, handwritten: moral responsibility of animals...?]

the LORD shall be between them both to see whether he has not put his hand to his neighbor's property; and the owner shall accept the oath, and he shall not make restitution. But if it is stolen from him, he shall make restitution to its owner. If it is torn by beasts, let him bring it as evidence; he shall not make restitution for what has been torn.

"If a man borrows anything of his neighbor, and it is hurt or dies, the owner not being with it, he shall make full restitution. If the owner was with it, he shall not make restitution; if it was hired, it came for its hire.

"If a man seduces a virgin who is not betrothed, and lies with her, he shall give the marriage present for her, and make her his wife. If her father utterly refuses to give her to him, he shall pay money equivalent to the marriage present for virgins.

"You shall not permit a sorceress to live.

"Whoever lies with a beast shall be put to death.

"Whoever sacrifices to any god, save to the LORD only, shall be utterly destroyed.

"You shall not wrong a stranger or oppress him, for you were strangers in the land of Egypt. You shall not afflict any widow or orphan. If you do afflict them, and they cry out to me, I will surely hear their cry; and my wrath will burn, and I will kill you with the sword, and your wives shall become widows and your children fatherless.

"If you lend money to any of my people with you who is poor, you shall not be to him as a creditor, and you shall not exact interest from him. If ever you take your neighbor's garment in pledge, you shall restore it to him before the sun goes down; for that is his only covering, it is his mantle for his body; in what else shall he sleep? And if he cries to me, I will hear, for I am compassionate.

"You shall not revile God, nor curse a ruler of your people.

"You shall not delay to offer from the fulness of your harvest and from the outflow of your presses.

"The first-born of your sons you shall give to me. You shall do likewise with your oxen and with your sheep: seven days it shall be with its dam; on the eighth day you shall give it to me.

"You shall be men consecrated to me; therefore you shall not eat any flesh that is torn by beasts in the field; you shall cast it to the dogs.

23 "You shall not utter a false report. You shall not join hands with a wicked man, to be a malicious witness. You shall not follow a multitude to do evil; nor shall you bear witness in a suit, turning aside after a multitude, so as to pervert justice; nor shall you be partial to a poor man in his suit.

"If you meet your enemy's ox or his ass going astray, you shall bring it back to him. If you see the ass of one who hates you lying under its burden, you shall refrain from leaving him with it, you shall help him to lift it up.

"You shall not pervert the justice due to your poor in his suit. Keep far from a false charge, and do not slay the innocent and righteous, for I will not acquit the wicked. And you shall take no bribe, for a bribe blinds the officials, and subverts the cause of those who are in the right.

reflects custom of hospitality (climate induced)

"You shall not oppress a stranger; you know the heart of a stranger, for you were strangers in the land of Egypt.

"For six years you shall sow your land and gather in its yield; but the seventh year you shall let it rest and lie fallow, that the poor of your people may eat; and what they leave the wild beasts may eat. You shall do likewise with your vineyard, and with your olive orchard.

"Six days you shall do your work, but on the seventh day you shall rest; that your ox and your ass may have rest, and the son of your bondmaid, and the alien, may be refreshed. Take heed to all that I have said to you; and make no mention of the names of other gods, nor let such be heard out of your mouth.

"Three times in the year you shall keep a feast to me. You shall keep the feast of unleavened bread; as I commanded you, you shall eat unleavened bread for seven days at the appointed time in the month of Abib, for in it you came out of Egypt. None shall appear before me empty-handed. You shall keep the feast of harvest, of the first fruits of your labor, of what you sow in the field. You shall keep the feast of ingathering at the end of the year, when you gather in from the field the fruit of your labor. Three times in the year shall all your males appear before the Lord God.

"You shall not offer the blood of my sacrifice with leavened bread, or let the fat of my feast remain until the morning.

"The first of the first fruits of your ground you shall bring into the house of the Lord your God.

"You shall not boil a kid in its mother's milk.

"Behold, I send an angel before you, to guard you on the way and to bring you to the place which I have prepared. Give heed to him and hearken to his voice, do not rebel against him, for he will not pardon your transgression; for my name is in him.

"But if you hearken attentively to his voice and do all that I say, then I will be an enemy to your enemies and an adversary to your adversaries.

"When my angel goes before you, and brings you in to the Amorites, and the Hittites, and the Perizzites, and the Canaanites, the Hivites, and the Jebusites, and I blot them out, you shall not bow down to their gods, nor serve them, nor do according to their works, but you shall utterly overthrow them and break their pillars in pieces. You shall serve the Lord your God, and I will bless your bread and your water; and I will take sickness away from the midst of you. None shall cast her young or be barren in your land; I will fulfil the number of your days. I will send my terror before you, and will throw into confusion all the people against whom you shall come, and I will make all your enemies turn their backs to you. And I will send hornets before you, which shall drive out Hivite, Canaanite, and Hittite from before you. I will not drive them out from before you in one year, lest the land become desolate and the wild beasts multiply against you. Little by little I will drive them out from before you, until you are increased and possess the land. And I will set your bounds from the Red Sea to the sea of the Philistines, and from the wilderness to the Euphrates; for I will deliver the inhabitants of the land into your hand, and you shall drive them out before you. You shall make no covenant with them or with their gods. They shall not dwell in your land, lest they make you sin against me; for if you serve their gods, it will surely be a snare to you."

24 And he said to Moses, "Come up to the Lord, you and Aaron, Nadab, and Abihu, and seventy of the elders of Israel, and worship afar off. Moses alone shall come near to the Lord; but the others shall not come near, and the people shall not come up with him."

Moses came and told the people all the words of the Lord and all the ordinances; and all the people answered with one voice, and said, "All the words which the Lord has spoken we will do." And Moses wrote all the words of the Lord. And he rose early in the morning, and built an altar at the foot of the mountain, and twelve pillars, according to the twelve tribes of Israel. And he sent young men of the people of Israel, who offered burnt offerings and sacrificed peace offerings of oxen to the Lord. And Moses took half of the blood and put it in basins, and half of the blood he threw against the altar. Then he took the book of the covenant, and read it in the hearing of the people; and they said, "All that the Lord has spoken we will do, and we will be obedient." And Moses took the blood and threw it upon the people, and said, "Behold the blood of the covenant which the Lord has made with you in accordance with all these words."

Then Moses and Aaron, Nadab, and Abihu, and seventy of the elders of Israel went up, and they saw the God of Israel; and there was under his feet as it were a pavement of sapphire stone, like the very heaven for clearness. And he did not lay his hand on the chief men of the people of Israel; they beheld God, and ate and drank.

The Lord said to Moses, "Come up to me on the mountain, and wait there; and I will give you the tables of stone, with the law and the commandment, which I have written for their instruction." So Moses rose with his servant Joshua, and Moses went up into the mountain of God. And he said to the elders, "Tarry here for us, until we come to you again; and, behold, Aaron and Hur are with you; whoever has a cause, let him go to them."

Then Moses went up on the mountain, and the cloud covered the mountain. The glory of the Lord settled on Mount Sinai, and the cloud covered it six days; and on the seventh day he called to Moses out of the midst of the cloud. Now the appearance of the glory of the Lord was like a devouring fire on the top of the mountain in the sight of the people of Israel. And Moses entered the cloud, and went up on the mountain. And Moses was on the mountain forty days and forty nights.

Discussion Questions

1. What does God mean by his "covenant," and what is its significance for the Hebrew people?

2. What do the Ten Commandments and the other laws delineated here reveal about the Hebrews' way of life?

3. How does the Book of Exodus cast light on the development of Hebrew monotheism?

3
Egyptian Scribal Exercise Book
Twelfth Century B.C.

In the fourth and third millennia B.C., another great civilization emerged to rival that of Mesopotamia: Egypt. Guided by a succession of powerful kings, Egypt became a prosperous, unified state. Many of its features—from the belief that the king was a god in human form to its rigid social hierarchy—have been preserved, thanks to scribes who recorded both official and everyday affairs in a variety of different scripts developed for that purpose. Egyptians thus enriched the technology of writing invented earlier by the Sumerians. Scribes learned their trade using books such as the one excerpted here. A high-ranking scribe, frustrated by his apprentice's poor performance, contrasts the prestige and comfort of the scribal profession to other forms of employment. Although the text is clearly biased in favor of scribes, it provides insight into their special status in Egyptian society and thus into the power that knowledge of the technology of writing conveyed.

Title

(1,1) [Beginning of the instruction in letter-writing made by the royal scribe and chief overseer of the cattle of Amen-Re, King of Gods, Nebmare-nakht] for his apprentice, the scribe Wenemdiamun.

The Idle Scribe is Worthless

The royal scribe and chief overseer of the cattle of Amen-Re, King of Gods, Nebmare-nakht, speaks to the scribe Wenemdiamun, as follows. You are busy coming and going, and don't think of writing. You resist listening to me; (3,5) you neglect my teachings.

You are worse than the goose of the shore, that is busy with mischief. It spends the summer destroying the dates, the winter destroying the seed-grain. It spends the balance of the year in pursuit of the cultivators. It does not let seed be cast to the ground without snatching it in its fall. One cannot catch it by snaring. One does not offer it in the temple. The evil, sharpeyed bird that does no work!

You are worse than the desert antelope that lives by running. It spends no day in plowing. Never at all does it tread on the threshing-floor. It lives on the oxen's labor, without entering among them. But though I spend the day telling you "Write," it seems like a plague to you. Writing is very (4,1) pleasant!------.

From *Ancient Egyptian Literature: A Book of Readings*, ed. Miriam Lichtheim, vol. 2 (Berkeley: University of California Press, 1976), 168–72.

All Occupations Are Bad Except That of the Scribe

See for yourself with your own eye. The occupations lie before you.

The washerman's day is going up, going down. All his limbs are weak, [from] whitening his neighbors' clothes every day, from washing their linen.

The maker of pots is smeared with soil, like one whose relations have died. His hands, (4,5) his feet are full of clay; he is like one who lives in the bog.

The cobbler mingles with vats. His odor is penetrating. His hands are red with madder, like one who is smeared with blood. He looks behind him for the kite, like one whose flesh is exposed.

The watchman[1] prepares garlands and polishes vase-stands. He spends a night of toil just as one on whom the sun shines.

The merchants travel downstream and upstream. They are as busy as can be, carrying goods from one town to another. They supply him who has wants. But the tax collectors carry off the gold, that most precious of metals.

The ships' crews from every house (of commerce), they receive their loads. (5,1) They depart from Egypt for Syria, and each man's god is with him. (But) not one of them says: "We shall see Egypt again!"

The carpenter who is in the shipyard carries the timber and stacks it. If he gives today the output of yesterday, woe to his limbs! The shipwright stands behind him to tell him evil things.

His outworker who is in the fields, his is the toughest of all the jobs. He spends the day loaded (5,5) with his tools, tied to his tool-box. When he returns home at night, he is loaded with the tool-box and the timbers, his drinking mug, and his whetstones.

The scribe, he alone, records the output of all of them. Take note of it!

The Misfortunes of the Peasant

Let me also expound to you the situation of the peasant, that other tough occupation. [Comes] the inundation and soaks him-, he attends to his equipment. By day he cuts his farming tools; (6,1) by night he twists rope. Even his midday hour he spends on farm labor. He equips himself to go to the field as if he were a warrior. The dried field lies before him; he goes out to get his team. When he has been after the herdsman for many days, he gets his team and comes back with it. He makes for it a place in the field. (6,5) Comes dawn, he goes to make a start and does not find it in its place. He spends three days searching for it; he finds it in the bog. He finds no hides on them; the jackals have chewed them. He comes out, his garment in his hand, to beg for himself a team.

When he reaches his field he finds [it] broken up. He spends time cultivating, and the snake is after him. It finishes off the seed as it is cast to the ground. He does not see a green blade. He does three plowings with borrowed grain. His

---

[1]The word is obscure but the context suggests a man who guards and cleans the temple at night and makes it ready for the morning service. [— Ed.]

wife (7,1) has gone down to the merchants and found nothing for barter. Now the scribe lands on the shore. He surveys the harvest. Attendants are behind him with staffs, Nubians with clubs. One says (to him): "Give grain." "There is none." He is beaten savagely. He is bound, thrown in the well, submerged head down. His wife is bound in his presence. His children are in fetters. His neighbors (7,5) abandon them and flee. When it's over, there's no grain.

If you have any sense, be a scribe. If you have learned about the peasant, you will not be able to be one. Take note of it!

Be a Scribe

The scribe of the army and commander[2] of the cattle of the house of Amun, Nebmare-nakht, speaks to the scribe Wenemdiamun, as follows. Be a scribe! Your body will be sleek; your hand will be soft. You will not flicker like a flame, like one whose body is feeble. For there is not the bone of a man in you. You are tall and thin. If you lifted a load to carry it, you would stagger, your legs would tremble. You are lacking in strength; (8,1) you are weak in all your limbs; you are poor in body.

Set your sight on being a scribe; a fine profession that suits you. You call for one; a thousand answer you. You stride freely on the road. You will not be like a hired ox. You are in front of others.

I spend the day instructing you. You do not listen! Your heart is like an [empty] room. My teachings are not in it. Take their [meaning] to yourself!

The marsh thicket is before you each day, as a nestling is after its mother. You follow the path of (8,5) pleasure; you make friends with revellers. You have made your home in the brewery, as one who thirsts for beer. You sit in the parlor with an idler.[3] You hold the writings in contempt. You visit the whore. Do not do these things! What are they for? They are of no use. Take note of it!

The Scribe Does Not Suffer Like the Soldier

Furthermore. Look, I instruct you to make you sound; to make you hold the palette freely. To make you become one whom the king trusts; to make you gain entrance to treasury and granary. To make you receive the ship-load at the gate of the granary. To make you issue the offerings on feast days. You are dressed in fine clothes; you own horses. Your boat is on (9,1) the river; you are supplied with attendants. You stride about inspecting. A mansion is built in your town. You have a powerful office, given you by the king. Male and female slaves are about you. Those who are in the fields grasp your hand, on plots that you have made. Look, I make you into a staff of life! Put the writings in your heart, and you will be protected from all kinds of toil. You will become a worthy official.

---

[2] A joking alteration of the teacher's title.

[3] Literally "He whose back is turned to his job."

Do you not recall the (fate of) the unskilled man? His name is not known. He is ever burdened [like an ass carrying] in front of the scribe who knows what he is about.

Come, [let me tell] you the woes of (9,5) the soldier, and how many are his superiors: the general, the troop-commander, the officer who leads, the standard-bearer, the lieutenant, the scribe, the commander of fifty, and the garrison-captain. They go in and out in the halls of the palace, saying: "Get laborers!" He is awakened at any hour. One is after him as (after) a donkey. He toils until the Aten sets in his darkness of night. He is hungry, his belly hurts; he is dead while yet alive. When he receives the grain-ration, having been released from duty, it is not good for grinding.

He is called up for Syria. He may not rest. There are no clothes, no sandals. The weapons of war are assembled at the fortress of Sile. (10,1) His march is uphill through mountains. He drinks water every third day; it is smelly and tastes of salt. His body is ravaged by illness. The enemy comes, surrounds him with missiles, and life recedes from him. He is told: "Quick, forward, valiant soldier! Win for yourself a good name!" He does not know what he is about. His body is weak, his legs fail him. When victory is won, the captives are handed over to his majesty, to be taken to Egypt. The foreign woman faints on the march; she hangs herself [on] (10,5) the soldier's neck. His knapsack drops, another grabs it while he is burdened with the woman. His wife and children are in their village; he dies and does not reach it. If he comes out alive, he is worn out from marching. Be he at large, be he detained, the soldier suffers. If he leaps and joins the deserters, all his people are imprisoned. He dies on the edge of the desert, and there is none to perpetuate his name. He suffers in death as in life. A big sack is brought for him; he does not know his resting place.

Be a scribe, and be spared from soldiering! You call and one says: "Here I am." You are safe from torments. Every man seeks to raise himself up. Take note of it!

Discussion Questions

1. What specific examples does the teacher give of a scribe's place in Egypt's political, religious, and economic life?
2. As described here, what sets the scribe apart from the other trades and professions identified in the document?
3. What does this document reveal about the structure of both the Egyptian economy and society at the time?

4

Daily Prayer of the Hittite King
1750 b.c.

Even after the emergence of great civilizations in Mesopotamia and Egypt, new societies that also left enduring legacies took root in the Mediterranean. This document concerns the most ambitious of these newcomers, the Hittites. By around 1750 b.c., they had forged a powerful and wealthy kingdom in Anatolia. Like Egyptians and

Mesopotamians, Hittites believed that their success depended on the goodwill of the gods, whom they honored with ceremonies, rituals, and temples. Recited daily in the name of King Mursili II (r. 1321–1295 B.C.), this prayer addressed to the god Telepinus reveals how Hittite rulers played a preeminent role in this regard. The prayer also exposes the centrality of religious concerns to early civilizations.

Entreaty

The scribe reads this tablet addressing the deity daily; he praises the deity (saying):

Telepinus, a mighty (and) noble deity art thou. Mursilis, the king, thy servant, and the queen, (5) thy handmaid, have sent me (with the request): "Go! entreat Telepinus, our lord, the guardian of our persons!"

Whether thou art in heaven above among the gods, noble Telepinus; whether gone to the sea or to the mountains (10) to roam; whether gone to war to the country of the enemy—

now let the sweet and soothing cedar essence lure thee! Come home into thy temple! Here I am entreating thee with sacrificial loaves and libations, (15) allow thyself to be lured forth! Let me speak to thee alone and whatever I say unto thee —lend me thine ear, O god, and hearken to it!

Thou, Telepinus, art a noble god; thy godhead and the gods' temples are firmly established in the Hatti land.[1] But (20) in no other land anywhere are they so. Festivals (and) sacrifices pure (and) holy they present to thee in the Hatti land. [But in no other country anywhere do they present them so.

(25) Lofty temples adorned with silver and gold thou hast in the Hatti land. But in no other country anywhere hast thou their like. (ii) Cups (and) rhyta,[2] silver, gold and (precious) stones thou hast in the Hatti land. But in no other country hast thou their like.

Festivals too—the festival of the month, the festivals of the *new year*, the ceremonies of winter and spring, (5) and of the summer, the festivals of entreaty— men celebrate for thee in the Hatti land. But in no other country anywhere do they celebrate their like. Thy divinity, O Telepinus, (10) is honored in the Hatti land, and Mursilis, the king, thy servant, and the queen, thy handmaid, and also the princes, thy servants, are reverent toward thee in the Hatti land. They undertake the celebration of communion feasts, sacrifices and festivals for thee, Telepinus. (15) Everything they present to thee is holy (and) pure. Moreover, reverence is paid to thy temple, thy rhyta,[thy cups] (and) thy utensils and they are cared for scrupulously. To the utensils [of thy worship] no one draws near.

From *Ancient Near Eastern Texts Relating to the Old Testament*, ed. James B. Pritchard, 3d ed. (Princeton, N.J.: Princeton University Press, 1969), 396–97.

[1]The Hittite kingdom. [— Ed.]

[2]Drinking horns. [— Ed.]

Hymn

Thou, Telepinus, art a noble god; (30) thy name is noble among names. Thy godhead is noble among the gods; among the gods art thou noble, O Telepinus. Great art thou, O Telepinus; there is no other deity more noble and mighty than thou. Of sure (35) judgment thou art lord; thou watchest over kingship in heaven and on earth. Thou settest the bounds of the lands; thou hearkenest to entreaties. Thou, Telepinus, art a merciful god; (40) thou art forever showing thy mercy. The godly man is dear to thee, O Telepinus, and thou, Telepinus, dost exalt him. In the orbit of heaven and earth thou, Telepinus, art the (source of) light; (45) throughout the lands art thou a god who is celebrated. Of every land thou art father (and) mother; the inspired lord of judgment art thou. In the place of judgment thou art untiring; among the Olden Gods thou art (50) the one who is celebrated. For the gods thou, Telepinus, assignest the rites; to the Olden Gods thou assignest their portions. For thee they open the door of heaven; thou, the celebrated Telepinus, (35) art allowed to pass through the gate of heaven. The gods of heaven are obedient to thee, O Telepinus; the gods of the earth are obedient to thee, O Telepinus. Whatever thou sayest, O Telepinus, the gods bow down to thee. Of the oppressed, the orphan and the window thou art father (and) mother; the cause of the orphan, the oppressed thou, Telepinus, dost take to heart.

Blessings and Curses

... Turn with favor [toward the king and the queen], and toward the princes [and the Hatti land!] Take thy stand, O Telepinus, strong god, [beside the king (and) the queen and the] princes! Grant them enduring life, health, long years [(and) strength]! Into their souls place [ligh]t and joy!

Grant them sons (and) daughters, grandsons (and) great-grandsons! (10) Grant them ...! Grant them fertility of grain (and) vine, of sheep, cattle (and) people! Grant them a man's valiant (and) victorious weapon! Set the countries of the enemy (15) beneath their feet and let [them die by the sword]!

From the Hatti land drive forth the evil fever, plague, famine and *misery*!

And (as for) the enemy countries that are in revolt and turmoil— some refuse the due respect to thee, Telepinus, (20) and to the Hattian gods; others are out to burn your temples; (iv) others seek to obtain the rhyta, the cups (and) the utensils of silver (and) gold; others seek to lay waste your plowland and pasture, vineyards, gardens (and) groves; (5) others seek to capture your plowmen, vine-dressers, gardeners (and) millwomen— give evil fever, plague, famine (and) *misery* to these enemy countries.

But to the king (and) the queen, to the princes and to the Hatti land (10) grant life, health, strength, long and enduring years and joy! Grant everlasting fertility to their crops, vines, fruit-bearing *trees,* cattle, sheep, goats, pigs, mules (and) asses together with the beasts of the fields, and to (their) people! Let them flourish! Let the rains [come]! Let the winds of prosperity pass over! Let all thrive (and) prosper in the Hatti land!

And the congregation shouts: "Let it be so!"

DISCUSSION QUESTIONS
1. In what ways did the Hittites honor Telepinus, and why?
2. How would you describe the Hittites' attitudes toward war?
3. What does the prayer reveal about the nature of the Hittite economy?

COMPARATIVE QUESTIONS
1. What evidence do Documents 1 and 2 provide on cultural interaction between the Mesopotamian and Hebrew peoples?
2. Despite their common ground, how do the laws delineated in the first two documents differ, and why?
3. In what ways do the Hebrew God, Yahweh (Document 2), and the Hittite god, Telepinus (Document 4), assume similar roles in their respective cultures?
4. Based on your analysis of all four documents, what similarities do you see among Egyptian, Mesopotamian, and Hittite civilizations?

2

New Paths for Western Civilization
c. 1000–500 B.C.

S U M M A R Y   Although dire economic conditions and foreign invasions wreaked havoc across the Near East and the Mediterranean from 1200 to 1000 B.C., by the eighth century B.C., local economies and societies were well on their way to recovery, yielding remarkable and enduring results. The documents in this chapter allow us to chart the course of renewal in both regions, beginning with the Persian Empire. Between the sixth and fifth centuries, Persian rulers enhanced the traditional Near Eastern model of monarchical government, with its emphasis on the king's divine right to rule, by conquering new territories and enriching their treasury. The last three documents illuminate Greek society at the time, which soon became a target of Persia's imperial ambitions. As they reveal, Greece did not rely on the past alone to forge its future. Instead, it created innovative social, political, and cultural forms—ranging from the city-state to lyric poetry—that left permanent imprints on Western civilization.

1
Inscription Honoring Cyrus,
King of Persia
r.c. 557–530 B.C.

The Persian king, Cyrus, founded the third in a series of powerful kingdoms that emerged from the shadows of the Dark Age in the Near East. Following the example of his Babylonian and Assyrian counterparts, Cyrus embraced imperial monarchy as a model of government while striving to expand his wealth and territorial holdings. This inscription, etched originally on a clay barrel, recounts a pivotal event in

Cyrus's reign, his conquest of Babylon in 539 B.C. The inscription also exposes the foundations of Cyrus's success: military might, cultural tolerance, and the belief in his divine right to rule. Following his lead, his successors built an even more formidable empire that threatened everything in its path, including the Greek city-states.

(one line destroyed)

... [r]ims (of the world) ... a weakling has been installed as the *enû*[1] of his country; [the correct images of the gods he removed from their thrones, imi]tations he ordered to place upon them. A replica of the temple Esagila he has ... for Ur and the other sacred cities inappropriate rituals ... daily he did blabber [incorrect prayers]. He (furthermore) interrupted in a fiendish way the regular offerings, he did ... he established within the sacred cities. The worship of Marduk, the king of the gods, he [chang]ed into abomination, daily he used to do evil against his (i.e. Marduk's) city. ... He [tormented] its [inhabitant]s with corvé-work (lit.: a yoke) without relief, he ruined them all.

Upon their complaints the lord of the gods became terribly angry and [he departed from] their region, (also) the (other) gods living among them left their mansions, wroth that he had brought (them) into Babylon. (But) Marduk [who does care for] ... on account of (the fact that) the sanctuaries of all their settlements were in ruins and the inhabitants of Sumer and Akkad had become like (living) dead, turned back (his countenance) [his] an[ger] [abated] and he had mercy (upon them). He scanned and looked (through) all the countries, searching for a righteous ruler willing to lead him (i.e. Marduk) (in the annual procession). (Then) he pronounced the name of Cyrus, king of Anshan,[2] declared him (lit.: pronounced [his] name) to be(come) the ruler of all the world. He made the Guti country and all the Manda-hordes bow in submission to his (i.e. Cyrus') feet. And he (Cyrus) did always endeavour to treat according to justice the black-headed whom he (Marduk) has made him conquer. Marduk, the great lord, a protector of his people/worshipers, beheld with pleasure his (i.e. Cyrus') good deeds and his upright mind (lit.: heart) (and therefore) ordered him to march against his city Babylon. He made him set out on the road to Babylon going at his side like a real friend. His widespread troops—their number, like that of the

---

From *Ancient Near Eastern Texts Relating to the Old Testament*, ed. James B. Pritchard, 3d ed. (Princeton, N.J.: Princeton University Press, 1969), 315–16.

[1]The old Sumerian title appears here in a context which seems to indicate that the primitive concept concerning the intimate connection between the physical vitality of the ruler and the prosperity of the country was still valid in the political speculations of the Babylonian clergy.

[2]Persia.

water of a river, could not be established — strolled along, their weapons packed away. Without any battle, he made him enter his town Babylon, sparing Babylon any calamity. He delivered into his (i.e. Cyrus') hands Nabonidus, the king who did not worship him (i.e. Marduk). All the inhabitants of Babylon as well as of the entire country of Sumer and Akkad, princes and governors (included), bowed to him (Cyrus) and kissed his feet, jubilant that he (had received) the kingship, and with shining faces. Happily they greeted him as a master through whose help they had come (again) to life from death (and) had all been spared damage and disaster, and they worshiped his (very) name.

I am Cyrus, king of the world, great king, legitimate king, king of Babylon, king of Sumer and Akkad, king of the four rims (of the earth), son of Cambyses, great king, king of Anshan, grandson of Cyrus, great king, king of Anshan, descendant of Teispes, great king, king of Anshan, of a family (which) always (exercised) kingship; whose rule Bel and Nebo love, whom they want as king to please their hearts.

When I entered Babylon as a friend and (when) I established the seat of the government in the palace of the ruler under jubilation and rejoicing, Marduk, the great lord, [induced] the magnanimous inhabitants of Babylon [to love me], and I was daily endeavouring to worship him. My numerous troops walked around in Babylon in peace, I did not allow anybody to terrorize (any place) of the [country of Sumer] and Akkad. I strove for peace in Babylon and in all his (other) sacred cities. As to the inhabitants of Babylon, [who] against the will of the gods [had/were . . . , I abolished] the corvé (lit.: yoke) which was against their (social) standing. I brought relief to their dilapidated housing, putting (thus) an end to their (main) complaints. Marduk, the great lord, was well pleased with my deeds and sent friendly blessings to myself, Cyrus, the king who worships him, to Cambyses, my son, the offspring of [my] loins, as well as to all my troops, and we all [praised] his great [godhead] joyously, standing before him in peace.

All the kings of the entire world from the Upper to the Lower Sea, those who are seated in throne rooms, (those who) live in other [types of buildings as well as] all the kings of the West land living in tents, brought their heavy tributes and kissed my feet in Babylon. (As to the region) from. . . as far as Ashur and Susa, Agade, Eshnunna, the towns Zamban, Me-Turnu, Der as well as the region of the Gutians, I returned to (these) sacred cities on the other side of the Tigris, the sanctuaries of which have been ruins for a long time, the images which (used) to live therein and established for them permanent sanctuaries. I (also) gathered all their (former) inhabitants and returned (to them) their habitations. Furthermore, I resettled upon the command of Marduk, the great lord, all the gods of Sumer and Akkad whom Nabonidus has brought into Babylon to the anger of the lord of the gods, unharmed, in their (former) chapels, the places which make them happy.

May all the gods whom I have resettled in their sacred cities ask daily Bel and Nebo for a long life for me and may they recommend me (to him); to Marduk, my lord, they may say this: "Cyrus, the king who worships you, and Cambyses, his son, . . ." . . . all of them I settled in a peaceful place . . . ducks and doves, . . . I endeavoured to fortify/repair their dwelling places.

DISCUSSION QUESTIONS

1. According to the inscription, why did Cyrus conquer Babylon? What does this reveal about the relationship between political and religious beliefs at the time?
2. How did the residents of the city and the neighboring regions respond to the Persian conquest, and why?
3. What specific examples does the inscription provide of Cyrus's religious tolerance?
4. What do you think the purpose of this inscription was, and who was its intended audience?

2
Tyrtaeus of Sparta and Solon of Athens
Poems
Seventh–Sixth Centuries B.C.

Among the most remarkable products of Greece's recovery from its Dark Age was the creation of a new social and political entity, the city-state. These poems elucidate the values shaping two of these communities, Sparta and Athens. The author of the first, Tyrtaeus of Sparta (originally from Athens, according to some ancient sources), was active when Sparta launched the Second Messenian War in the mid-sixth century B.C. His poem reveals the preeminent importance of military glory to the Spartans' communal identity. The author of the second work, the Athenian statesman Solon, emphasizes shared justice as the ideal basis of society. Democratic reforms instituted in the late sixth century B.C. transformed his vision into reality. Both poems are written in the elegiac meter, a style often used at the time to instruct the public.

Tyrtaeus

Beautiful-and-honorable [*kalon*] it is for a brave [*agathos*] warrior to die, fallen among the foremost fighters, in battle for his native land; but to leave his polis and rich fields and beg—that is most painful of all, as he wanders with his dear mother and aged father, his small children and wedded wife. Detested he will be in the eyes of all those to whom he comes, constrained by need and hateful

From *The Greek Polis*, ed. Arthur W. H. Adkins and Peter White, vol. 1, University of Chicago Readings in Western Civilization (Chicago: University of Chicago Press, 1986), 23–26.

poverty. He shames his birth and belies his glorious appearance; dishonor and misery are his companions. If no account is taken of a warrior who is a wanderer, if there is no respect for him or his family in the future, then let us fight with all our hearts for this land and die for our children, no longer hesitating to risk our lives. Young men, stand firm beside each other and fight. Do not begin shameful flight or fear. Rather create a mighty, valorous spirit in your breasts, and do not show love for your lives when you are fighting with warriors. Do not flee, abandoning the older men, whose knees are no longer nimble. For shameful-and-ugly [*aischron*] it is for an older warrior to fall among the foremost fighters and lie out ahead of the young men—a man whose hair is already white and his beard gray—as he breathes out his valorous spirit in the dust, holding his bloody genitals in his own hands, his body laid bare. Shameful-and-ugly [*aischra*] is this to the eyes, and a cause of resentment to look upon. But to the young men all is seemly, while the glorious flower of lovely youth is theirs. To men the young man is admirable to look upon, and to women lovable while he lives, and beautiful-and-honorable when he lies among the foremost fighters. So let a man take a firm stance and stand fast, with both feet planted upon the ground, biting his lip with his teeth.

Solon

Our polis will never perish as a result of the apportionment of Zeus and the intentions of the blessed immortal gods; for such a great-hearted guardian, daughter of a mighty father, Pallas Athena, holds her hands in protection over it. But the citizens themselves, persuaded by wealth, are willing to destroy a mighty polis by their follies, and the mind of the leaders of the people is unjust. For the leaders it is prepared that they should suffer many griefs as a result of their great hubris. For they do not know how to restrain the excesses sprung from satiety or how to discipline in peaceful quiet the present merriments of the feast. . . . They grow wealthy, relying on unjust deeds. . . . Sparing neither sacred nor public property, they steal by snatching, one from one source, one from another, nor do they reverence the august abode where justice is set, she who in silence knows what is happening, and what has occurred in the past, and in time at all events comes to exact requital.

This is now coming upon the whole polis as an inescapable wound, and it comes swiftly to grievous slavery, which stirs up civic strife among the people and sleeping [civil?] war, which destroys the lovely prime of many. For by the action of enemies a much-beloved polis is swiftly brought to hardship in meetings by those who wrong their friends. These woes go to and fro in the land; and, of the poor, many arrive at another land, sold and bound in unseemly fetters. . . . Thus a woe of the people comes home to each individual, and the courtyard gates are no longer willing to shut it out, but it leaps over the high fence and finds a man nonetheless, even if he is in flight in a corner of his chamber.

These things my heart bids me tell the Athenians: that *dusnomia*[1] causes very many woes to a polis. *Eunomia* shows forth everything orderly and appropriate and often puts shackles on the unjust; she makes the rough smooth, ends the insolence of satiety, dims hubris, and dries up the growing blossoms of infatuation, straightens crooked judgments, and tames proud deeds; she ends the deeds of civil conflict, ends the wrath of grievous strife, and all things among mankind are appropriate and prudent under her rule.

DISCUSSION QUESTIONS

1. What does Tyrtaeus reveal about the values and comportment that Spartan hoplites were expected to uphold?
2. How does Tyrtaeus describe warriors who do not live up to these expectations? What do his criticisms reveal about Spartan culture?
3. Why does Solon think Athenian citizens pose a threat to the polis?
4. What message does he seek to convey to them in this poem?

3

The Foundation of Cyrene
Late Seventh Century B.C.

Greece's recovery from its Dark Age extended far beyond the boundaries of its new city-states. Beginning around 775 B.C., many Greeks ventured from their homes to live in settlements scattered across the Mediterranean, opening up new channels for cultural and economic interaction. Although most Greek colonies appear to have stemmed from private initiative, this inscription provides an example of direct state involvement. Dating from the fourth century B.C., it recounts the establishment of the colony of Cyrene in northern Africa by the city-state Thera, allegedly including the original decree promulgated by the Therans three centuries earlier. The inscription thus illuminates the growth of state power at the time, as well as the motivations driving the settlement process.

---

[1]*Eunomia* and *dusnomia* cannot be neatly rendered. *Nomos*, at least in somewhat later Greek, can mean "law," and the words have been supposed to characterize states of affairs in which the laws are good and bad, respectively, or states of affairs in which the laws are obeyed or disobeyed. But *eunomia* and *dusnomia* are derived from the root *nem*, "to apportion," and can readily mean, respectively, states of affairs in which everything is shared out well or badly—a sense that is not irrelevant to Solon's political program. None of the possible senses needs be excluded: The words were as imprecise in Solon's day as they appear to us. They are political slogans and, like many political slogans since, combine a high emotive charge with a vague denotation.

God. Good Fortune. | Damis son of Bathykles made the motion. As to what is said by the Therans, | Kleudamas son of Euthykles, in order that the city may prosper and the Pe|ople of Cyrene enjoy good fortune, the Therans shall be given t||he citizenship according to that ancestral custom which our forefathers establish|ed, both those who *founded* Cyrene from Thera and those at Thera who re|mained — just as Apollo granted Battos and the Thera|ns who founded Cyrene good fortune if they abided by *the* | sworn agreement which our ancestors concluded with them when || they sent out the colony according to the command of Apo|llo *Archagetes*. With good fortune. It has been resolved by the People | that the Therans shall continue to enjoy equal citizenship in Cyrene in the sa|me way (as of old). There shall be sworn by all Therans who are domicil||led in Cyrene the same oath which the others onc||e swore, and they shall be assigned to a tribe and a phratry and n|ine Hetaireiai. This decree shall be written on a stele | of marble and placed in the ancestral shrine of | Apollo Pythios; and that sworn agreement also shall be written down on the stele | which was made by the colonists when they sailed to Libya wit||h Battos from Thera to Cyrene. As to the expenditure necessary for *the s|tone* or for the engraving, let the Superintendents of the Accounts pr|ovide it from Apollo's revenues. | The sworn agreement of the settlers. | Resolved by the Assembly. Since Apollo spontaneously told B[at]||tos and the Therans *to colonize* Cyrene, it has been decided by the Ther|ans to send Battos off to *Libya*, as Archagetes | *and* as King, with the Therans to sail *as his Companions.* On equal a|nd fair terms shall they sail *according to family* (?), with one son to be consc|ripted adults and from the [ot||her] Therans those who are free-born shall sail. If they (the colonists) establi|sh the settlement, *kinsmen* who sail | later to *Libya* shall be entitled to *citizenship* and offices | and *shall be allotted portions of the land which has no owner.* But if they do not successfully estab||lish the settlement and *the Therans* are incapable of giving it assistan||ce, and they are pressed by hardship for five years, from that land *shall* they depart, | without fear, to Thera, to their own property, and they shall be citiz|ens. Any man who, if the city sends him, refuses to sail, will be liable to the death-|penalty and his property shall be confiscated. The man ha|rboring him or concealing him, whether he be a father (aiding his) son or a brother his brot||her, is to suffer the same penalty as the man who refuses to sail. On these conditions a sworn agreement was ma|de by those who stayed there and by those who sailed to foun|d the colony, and they invoked curses against those transgressors who would not ab|ide by it—whether they were those settling in Libya or those who rem|ained. They made waxen images and burnt them, calling down (the following) c||urse, everyone having assembled together, men, wom|en, boys, girls: "The person who does not abide by this | sworn agreement but transgresses it shall melt away and di|ssolve like the images—himself, his descendants and his prope|rty; but those who abide by the sworn agreement—those || sailing to Libya *and* [those] *staying* in Thera—shall have an abundan|ce of good things, both *themselves* [and] *their descendants.*

From *Archaic Times to the End of the Peloponnesian War,* ed. Charles W. Fornara (Baltimore: Johns Hopkins University Press, 1977), 22–23.

DISCUSSION QUESTIONS

1. Why did Thera decide to establish a colony in Cyrene?

2. According to the sworn agreement of the settlers included in the inscription, how were the first settlers selected? Did they have a choice?

3. What were the penalties incurred by transgressors of the agreement? What do the penalties reveal about the fundamental beliefs of Greek religion?

4

Sappho of Lesbos
Poems
Sixth Century B.C.

The poetry of Sappho of Lesbos allows us the opportunity to hear a woman's voice emanating from Greece during the Archaic Age. Although little is known about her life, her legacy endures in her lyric poems, almost all of which have survived only in fragments. In both their rhythmic form and emphasis on inner, personal emotions, her poems reflect the cultural innovation characteristic of the period. As these selections reveal, Sappho used her poetry to express her innermost feelings of love and longing as a woman living in a male-dominated society. Her poems were revered throughout the ancient world, and they established an influential precedent for later lyric poets.

To Aphrodite (Fr. 1. G)

Aphrodite on your intricate throne, immortal, daughter of Zeus, weaver of plots, I beg you, do not tame me with pain or my heart with anguish

but come here, as once before when I asked you, you heard my words from afar and listened, and left your father's golden house and came

you yoked your chariot, and lovely swift sparrows brought you, fast whirling over the dark earth from heaven through the midst of the bright air

and soon they arrived. And you, O blessed goddess, smiled with your immortal face and asked what was wrong with me, and why did I call now,

and what did I most want in my maddened heart to have for myself. "Whom now am I to persuade to your love, who, Sappho, has done you wrong? For if she flees, soon she'll pursue you, and if she won't take gifts, soon she'll give them, and if she won't love, soon she will love you, even if she doesn't want to."

Come to me now again, release me from my cruel anxiety, accomplish all that my heart wants accomplished. You yourself join my battle.

From *Women's Life in Greece and Rome,* ed. Mary R. Lefkowitz and Maureen B. Fant, 2d ed. (Baltimore: Johns Hopkins University Press, 1992), 2–4.

When I look at you (Fr. 31. G)

The man seems to me strong as a god, the man who sits across from you and listens to your sweet talk nearby

and your lovely laughter—which, when I hear it, strikes fear in the heart in my breast. For whenever I glance at you, it seems that I can say nothing at all

but my tongue is broken in silence, and that instant a light fire rushes beneath my skin, I can no longer see anything in my eyes and my ears are thundering,

and cold sweat pours down me, and shuddering grasps me all over, and I am greener than grass, and I seem to myself to be little short of death

But all is endurable, since even a poor man . . .

Anactoria (Fr. 16. G)

Some would say an army of cavalry, others of infantry, others of ships, is the fairest thing on the dark earth, but I say it's whatever you're in love with

It's completely easy to make this clear to everyone, for Helen, who far surpassed other people in beauty, left behind the most aristocratic

of husbands and went to Troy. She sailed away, and did not remember at all her daughter or her beloved parents, but [Aphrodite] took her aside

(3 lines missing) which makes me remember Anactoria who is no longer near,

her lovely step and the brilliant glancing of her face I would rather see than the Lydians' chariots or their infantry fighting in all their armour.

Parting (Fr. 94. G)

"The truth is, I wish I were dead." She left me, weeping often, and she said this, "Oh what a cruel fate is ours, Sappho, yes, I leave you against my will."

And I answered her: "Farewell, go and remember me, for you know how we cared for you.

"If you do remember, I want to remind you . . . and were happy. . . of violets . . . you set beside me and with woven garlands made of flowers around your soft neck

"and with perfume, royal, rich . . . you anointed yourself and on soft beds you would drive out your passion

"and then . . . sanctuary . . . was . . . from which we were away. . ."

Remembering the girl Atthis (Fr. 96. G)

. . . you, like a goddess renowned, in your song she took most joy. Now she is unique among Lydian women, as the moon once the sun sets

stands out among all the stars, and her light grasps both the salt sea and the flowering meadows

and fair dew flows forth, and soft roses and chervil and fragrant melilot bloom.

Often as she goes out, she remembers gentle Atthis, and her tender heart is eaten by grief . . .

The wedding of Hector and Andromache (Fr. 44. G)

". . . Hector and his comrades are bringing a girl with dark eyes from holy Thebes and . . . Plakia, soft Andromache in their ships across the salt sea; many curved bands of gold and purple robes and intricate playthings, countless silver cups and ivory." So he spoke. And [Hector's] beloved father quickly got up, and the story went out to his friends throughout the city [of Troy] with its wide dancing places. Then the Trojan women led mules to wheeled carts and a crowd of women came out, and also of . . . -ankled maidens, and separately the daughters of Priam and men brought horses with chariots (*unknown number of lines missing*) . . . and the sweet-sounding *aulos* was mixed with the noise of castanets, and the maidens sang a sacred song and the holy sound reached heaven . . . bowls and goblets . . . perfume and cassia and incense were mixed and all the older women shouted out, and all the men cried out a fair loud song, calling on Paean, the far-shooter, the lyre player, to sing of Hector and Andromache, who were like gods . . .

DISCUSSION QUESTIONS

1. Do you think that Sappho's status as a woman shaped the content of her poetry? Who seem to be the principal objects of her affections?
2. What do Sappho's poems suggest about Greek notions of love at the time?
3. Aside from aspects of love, what else do the images and themes used by Sappho reveal about Greek society?

COMPARATIVE QUESTIONS

1. Based on Cyrus's inscription and Solon's poem, how did Near Eastern and Greek social and political organization differ at the time?
2. Do you see any similarities between Spartan and Persian culture as revealed in Cyrus's inscription and Tyrtaeus's poem?
3. How would you compare the content and function of the poems by Tyrtaeus, Solon, and Sappho? What does this suggest about the differences between the status of men and women in Greek society?

CHAPTER

3

The Greek Golden Age
c. 500–400 B.C.

S U M M A R Y   In the fifth century, Athens entered a period of extraordinary prosperity and achievement. Its economy was booming and its culture flourishing while at the same time its male citizens developed the first democracy in history. Under their guidance, Athens became the leader of the Greek world. The first three documents elucidate the dynamism of the times in a variety of related arenas, all of which attest to Athens's enduring legacy to Western civilization. They also reveal that even as innovation fueled the city-state's rise to glory, the pull of traditional beliefs remained strong. Such beliefs were especially influential in demarcating the boundaries of the lives of Athenian women. As the fourth document demonstrates, a woman's status was inextricably linked to her roles as wife and mother. To put either in jeopardy threatened the very foundations of Athenian society.

1
Thucydides
The Funeral Oration of Pericles
429 B.C.

The most renowned Athenian politician in his day, Pericles (c. 495–429 B.C.) contributed greatly to the brilliance of Athens's Golden Age. Not only did he help to build the city-state's empire abroad, but he also devoted much of his career to strengthening democracy at home. In his History of the Peloponnesian War, *Thucydides brings Pericles to life in a description of a speech he delivered to honor those who had died in the first year of fighting. The Peloponnesian War pitted Athens against its authoritarian rival, Sparta, from 431 to 404 B.C., ending ultimately with Athens's defeat. Pericles's words reveal, however, that at the time of his speech, Athens was still brimming with confidence in the greatness of its people and government.*

During the same winter, in accordance with traditional custom, the funeral of those who first fell in this war was celebrated by the Athenians at the public charge. . . .

Over the first who were buried, Pericles was chosen to speak. At the fitting moment he advanced from the sepulcher to a lofty stage, which had been erected in order that he might be heard as far away as possible by the crowd, and spoke somewhat as follows: . . .

"I will speak of our ancestors first, for it is right and seemly that on such an occasion as this we should also render this honor to their memory. Men of the same stock, ever dwelling in this land, in successive generations to this very day, by their valor handed it down as a free land. They are worthy of praise, and still more are our fathers, who added to their inheritance, and after many a struggle bequeathed to us, their sons, the great empire we possess. . . . But before I praise the dead, I shall first proceed to show by what kind of practices we attained to our position, and under what kind of institutions and manner of life our empire became great. For I conceive that it would not be unsuited to the occasion that this should be told, and that this whole assembly of citizens and foreigners may profitably listen to it.

"Our institutions do not emulate the laws of others. We do not copy our neighbors: rather, we are an example to them. Our system is called a democracy, for it respects the majority and not the few; but while the law secures equality to all alike in their private disputes, the claim of excellence is also recognized; and when a citizen is in any way distinguished, he is generally preferred to the public service, not in rotation, but for merit. Nor again is there any bar in poverty and obscurity of rank to a man who can do the state some service. It is as free men that we conduct our public life, and in our daily occupations we avoid mutual suspicions; we are not angry with our neighbor if he does what he likes; we do not put on sour looks at him which, though harmless, are not pleasant. While we give no offense in our private intercourse, in our public acts we are prevented from doing wrong by fear; we respect the authorities and the laws, especially those which are ordained for the protection of the injured as well as those unwritten laws which bring upon the transgressor admitted dishonor.

"Furthermore, none have provided more relaxations for the spirit from toil; we have regular games and sacrifices throughout the year; our homes are furnished with elegance; and the delight which we daily feel in all these things banishes melancholy. Because of the greatness of our city, the fruits of the whole earth flow in upon us so that we enjoy the goods of other countries as freely as our own.

"Then, again, in military training we are superior to our adversaries, as I shall show. Our city is thrown open to the world, and we never expel a foreigner or

From Thucydides, *The Peloponnesian Wars*, trans. Benjamin Jowett (New York: Twayne Publishers, 1963), 65–72.

prevent him from seeing or learning anything which, if not concealed, it might profit an enemy to see. We rely not so much upon preparations or stratagems, as upon our own courage in action. And in the matter of education, whereas from early youth they are always undergoing laborious exercises which are to make them brave, we live at ease and yet are equally ready to face perils to which our strength is equal. And here is the evidence. The Lacedaemonians march against our land not by themselves, but with all their allies: we invade a neighbor's country alone; and although our opponents are fighting for their homes and we are on a foreign soil, we seldom have any difficulty in overcoming them. . . .

"Nor is this the only cause for marveling at our city. We are lovers of beauty without extravagance and of learning without loss of vigor. Wealth we employ less for talk and ostentation than when there is a real use for it. To avow poverty with us is no disgrace: the true disgrace is in doing nothing to avoid it. The same persons attend at once to the concerns of their households and of the city, and men of diverse employments have a very fair idea of politics. If a man takes no interest in public affairs, we alone do not commend him as quiet but condemn him as useless; and if few of us are originators, we are all sound judges of a policy. In our opinion action does not suffer from discussion but, rather, from the want of that instruction which is gained by discussion preparatory to the action required. For we have an exceptional gift of acting with audacity after calculating the prospects of our enterprises, whereas other men are bold from ignorance but hesitate upon reflection. But it would be right to esteem those men bravest in spirit who have the clearest understanding of the pains and pleasures of life and do not on that account shrink from danger. . . .

"This is why I have dwelt upon the greatness of Athens, showing you that we are contending for a higher prize than those who enjoy no like advantages, and establishing by manifest proof the merit of these men whom I am now commemorating. Their loftiest praise has been already spoken; for in descanting on the city, I have honored the qualities which earned renown for them and for men such as they. And of how few Hellenes can it be said as of them, that their deeds matched their fame! In my belief an end such as theirs proves a man's worth; it is at once its first revelation and final seal. For even those who come short in other ways may justly plead the valor with which they have fought for their country; they have blotted out evil with good, and their public services have outweighed the harm they have done in their private actions. . . . And when the moment for fighting came, they held it nobler to suffer death than to yield and save their lives; it was the report of dishonor from which they fled, but on the battlefield their feet stood fast; and while for a moment they were in the hands of fortune, at the height, less of terror than of glory, they departed.

"Such was the conduct of these men; they were worthy of Athens. The rest of us must pray for a safer issue to our courage and yet disdain to show any less daring towards our enemies. We must not consider only what words can be uttered on the utility of such a spirit. Anyone might discourse to you at length on all the advantages of resisting the enemy bravely, but you know them just as well yourselves. It is better that you should actually gaze day by day on the power of the city until you are filled with the love of her; and when you are convinced of her greatness, reflect that it was acquired by men of daring who knew their duty and feared dishonor in the hour of action, men who if they ever failed in an enterprise, even then disdained to deprive the city of their prowess but offered themselves up as the finest contribution to the common cause. . . .

"To you who are the sons and brothers of the departed, I see that the struggle to emulate them will be arduous. For all men praise the dead; and, however preeminent your virtue may be, you would hardly be thought their equals, but somewhat inferior. The living have their rivals and detractors; but when a man is out of the way, the honor and good will which he receives is uncontested. And, if I am also to speak of womanly virtues to those of you who will now be widows, let me sum them up in one short admonition: 'Your glory will be great if you show no more than the infirmities of your nature, a glory that consists in being least the subjects of report among men, for good or evil.'

"I have spoken in obedience to the law, making use of such fitting words as I had. The tribute of deeds has been paid in part, for the dead have been honorably interred; it remains only that their children shall be maintained at the public charge until they are grown up: this is the solid prize with which, as with a garland, Athens crowns these men and those left behind after such contests. For where the rewards of virtue are greatest, there men do the greatest services to their cities. And now, when you have duly lamented, everyone his own dead, you may depart."

DISCUSSION QUESTIONS

1. According to Pericles, what sets Athens apart from its neighbors and adversaries?
2. As described here, what are the guiding principles of Athenian democracy?
3. How does Pericles characterize his fellow Athenians and their contributions to the city's glory?
4. What obligations does Pericles believe Athenian citizens have to the state?

2

Plato

The Apology of Socrates
399 B.C.

Political innovation was not the only distinctive feature of fifth-century Athens. Socrates (469–399 B.C.) was a famous philosopher of the day, and his views on ethics and morality challenged conventional values while steering Greek philosophy in new directions. Unlike the sophists, Socrates offered no classes and did not write his ideas down. He relied instead on conversation and critical questioning to draw people into his way of thinking. In this document we hear Socrates speaking for himself before a jury as described by his pupil, Plato. At the time, Socrates was on trial for impiety, and he spoke these words to convince his fellow citizens of his innocence. Sadly, his efforts were in vain; he was convicted and sentenced to death.

How you, O Athenians, have been affected by my accusers, I cannot tell; but I know that they almost made me forget who I was — so persuasively did they speak; and yet they have hardly uttered a word of truth. But of the many false-hoods told by them, there was one which quite amazed me;—I mean when they said that you should be upon your guard and not allow yourselves to be deceived by the force of my eloquence. To say this, when they were certain to be detected as soon as I opened my lips and proved myself to be anything but a great speaker, did indeed appear to me most shameless—unless by the force of eloquence they mean the force of truth; for if such is their meaning, I admit that I am eloquent. But in how different a way from theirs! Well, as I was saying, they have scarcely spoken the truth at all; but from me you shall hear the whole truth: not, however, delivered after their manner in a set oration duly ornamented with words and phrases. No, by heaven! but I shall use the words and arguments which occur to me at the moment; for I am confident in the justice of my cause. . . .

I will begin at the beginning, and ask what is the accusation which has given rise to the slander of me, and in fact has encouraged Meletus to prefer this charge against me. Well, what do the slanderers say? They shall be my prosecutors, and I will sum up their words in an affidavit: "Socrates is an evildoer, and a curious person, who searches into things under the earth and in heaven, and he makes the worse appear the better cause; and he teaches the aforesaid doctrines to others." Such is the nature of the accusation: it is just what you have yourselves seen in the comedy of Aristophanes, who has introduced a man whom he calls Socrates, going about and saying that he walks in air, and talking a deal of non-sense concerning matters of which I do not pretend to know either much or little —not that I mean to speak disparagingly of any one who is a student of natural philosophy. I should be very sorry if Meletus could bring so grave a charge against me. But the simple truth is, O Athenians, that I have nothing to do with physical speculations. Very many of those here present are witnesses to the truth of this, and to them I appeal. . . .

Men of Athens, this reputation of mine has come of a certain sort of wisdom which I possess. If you ask me what kind of wisdom, I reply, wisdom such as may perhaps be attained by man, for to that extent I am inclined to believe that I am wise; whereas the persons of whom I was speaking have a superhuman wisdom, which I may fail to describe, because I have it not myself; and he who says that I have, speaks falsely, and is taking away my character. And here, O men of Athens, I must beg you not to interrupt me, even if I seem to say something extravagant. For the word which I will speak is not mine. I will refer you to a witness who is worthy of credit; that witness shall be the God of Delphi—he will tell you about my wisdom, if I have any, and of what sort it is. You must have known Chaerephon; he was early a friend of mine, and also a friend of yours, for he shared in the recent exile of the people, and returned with you. Well, Chaerephon, as you know, was very impetuous in all his doings, and he went to Delphi and

From *Dialogues of Plato,* trans. Benjamin Jowett, ed. J. D. Kaplan (New York: Pocket Books, 1950), 5–14, 21–24, 39–40.

boldly asked the oracle to tell him whether—as I was saying, I must beg you not to interrupt—he asked the oracle to tell him whether any one was wiser than I was, and the Pythian prophetess answered, that there was no man wiser. Chaerephon is dead himself; but his brother, who is in court, will confirm the truth of what I am saying.

Why do I mention this? Because I am going to explain to you why I have such an evil name. When I heard the answer, I said to myself, What can the God mean? and what is the interpretation of his riddle? for I know that I have no wisdom, small or great. What then can he mean when he says that I am the wisest of men? And yet he is a god, and cannot lie; that would be against his nature. After long consideration, I thought of a method of trying the question. I reflected that if I could only find a man wiser than myself, then I might go to the god with a refutation in my hand. I should say to him, "Here is a man who is wiser than I am; but you said that I was the wisest." Accordingly I went to one who had the reputation of wisdom, and observed him—his name I need not mention; he was a politician whom I selected for examination—and the result was as follows: When I began to talk with him, I could not help thinking that he was not really wise, although he was thought wise by many, and still wiser by himself; and thereupon I tried to explain to him that he thought himself wise, but was not really wise; and the consequence was that he hated me, and his enmity was shared by several who were present and heard me. So I left him, saying to myself, as I went away: Well, although I do not suppose that either of us knows anything really beautiful and good, I am better off than he is,—for he knows nothing, and thinks that he knows; I neither know nor think that I know. In this latter particular, then, I seem to have slightly the advantage of him. Then I went to another who had still higher pretensions to wisdom, and my conclusion was exactly the same. Whereupon I made another enemy of him, and of many others besides him.

Then I went to one man after another, being not unconscious of the enmity which I provoked, and I lamented and feared this: but necessity was laid upon me,—the word of God, I thought, ought to be considered first. And I said to myself, Go I must to all who appear to know, and find out the meaning of the oracle. And I swear to you, Athenians, by the dog I swear!—for I must tell you the truth—the result of my mission was just this: I found that the men most in repute were all but the most foolish; and that others less esteemed were really wiser and better. I will tell you the tale of my wanderings and of the "Herculean" labours, as I may call them, which I endured only to find at last the oracle irrefutable. After the politicians, I went to the poets; tragic, dithyrambic, and all sorts. And there, I said to myself, you will be instantly detected; now you will find out that you are more ignorant than they are. Accordingly I took them some of the most elaborate passages in their own writings, and asked what was the meaning of them—thinking that they would teach me something. Will you believe me? I am almost ashamed to confess the truth, but I must say that there is hardly a person present who would not have talked better about their poetry than they did themselves. Then I knew that not by wisdom do poets write poetry, but by a sort of genius and inspiration; they are like diviners or soothsayers who also say many fine things, but do not understand the meaning of them. The poets appeared to me to be much in the same case; and I further observed that upon the strength of their poetry they believed themselves to be the wisest of men in other things in which they were not wise. So I departed, conceiving myself to be superior to them for the same reason that I was superior to the politicians.

At last I went to the artisans, I was conscious that I knew nothing at all, as I may say, and I was sure that they knew many fine things; and here I was not mistaken, for they did know many things of which I was ignorant, and in this they certainly were wiser than I was. But I observed that even the good artisans fell into the same error as the poets;—because they were good workmen they thought that they also knew all sorts of high matters, and this defect in them overshadowed their wisdom; and therefore I asked myself on behalf of the oracle, whether I would like to be as I was, neither having their knowledge nor their ignorance, or like them in both; and I made answer to myself and to the oracle that I was better off as I was.

This inquisition has led to my having many enemies of the worst and most dangerous kind, and has given occasion also to many calumnies. And I am called wise, for my hearers always imagine that I myself possess the wisdom which I find wanting in others: but the truth is, O men of Athens, that God only is wise; and by his answer he intends to show that the wisdom of men is worth little or nothing; he is not speaking of Socrates, he is only using my name by way of illustration, as if he said, He, O men, is the wisest, who, like Socrates, knows that his wisdom is in truth worth nothing. And so I go about the world obedient to the god, and search and make enquiry into the wisdom of any one, whether citizen or stranger, who appears to be wise; and if he is not wise, then in vindication of the oracle I show him that he is not wise; and my occupation quite absorbs me, and I have no time to give either to any public matter of interest or to any concern of my own, but I am in utter poverty by reason of my devotion to the god.

There is another thing:—young men of the richer classes, who have not much to do, come about me of their own accord; they like to hear the pretenders examined, and they often imitate me, and proceed to examine others; there are plenty of persons, as they quickly discover, who think that they know something, but really know little or nothing; and then those who are examined by them instead of being angry with themselves are angry with me: This confounded Socrates, they say; this villainous misleader of youth!—and then if somebody asks them, Why, what evil does he practise or teach? they do not know, and cannot tell; but in order that they may not appear to be at a loss, they repeat the ready-made charges which are used against all philosophers about teaching things up in the clouds and under the earth, and having no gods, and making the worse appear the better cause; for they do not like to confess that their pretence of knowledge has been detected—which is the truth; and as they are numerous and ambitious and energetic, and are drawn up in battle array and have persuasive tongues, they have filled your ears with their loud and inveterate calumnies. And this is the reason why my three accusers, Meletus and Anytus and Lycon, have set upon me; Meletus, who has a quarrel with me on behalf of the poets; Anytus, on behalf of the craftsmen and politicians; Lycon, on behalf of the rhetoricians: and, as I said at the beginning, I cannot expect to get rid of such a mass of calumny all in a moment. And this, O men of Athens, is the truth and the whole truth; I have concealed nothing, I have dissembled nothing. And yet, I know that my plainness of speech makes them hate me, and what is their hatred but a proof that I am speaking the truth? Hence has arisen the prejudice against me; and this is the reason of it. . . .

Some one will say: And are you not ashamed, Socrates, of a course of life which is likely to bring you to an untimely end? To him I may fairly answer: There you are mistaken: a man who is good for anything ought not to calculate the chance of living or dying; he ought only to consider whether in doing anything he is doing right or wrong—acting the part of a good man or of a bad. . . .

For the fear of death is indeed the pretence of wisdom, and not real wisdom, being a pretence of knowing the unknown; and no one knows whether death, which men in their fear apprehend to be the greatest evil, may not be the greatest good. Is not this ignorance of a disgraceful sort, the ignorance which is the conceit that a man knows what he does not know? And in this respect only I believe myself to differ from men in general, and may perhaps claim to be wiser than they are:—that whereas I know but little of the world below, I do not suppose that I know: but I do know that injustice and disobedience to a better, whether God or man, is evil and dishonourable, and I will never fear or avoid a possible good rather than a certain evil. And therefore if you let me go now, and are not convinced by Anytus, who said that since I had been prosecuted I must be put to death; (or if not that I ought never to have been prosecuted at all); and that if I escape now, your sons will all be utterly ruined by listening to my words—if you say to me, Socrates, this time we will not mind Anytus, and you shall be let off, but upon one condition, that you are not to enquire and speculate in this way any more, and that if you are caught doing so again you shall die;—if this was the condition on which you let me go, I should reply: Men of Athens, I honour and love you; but I shall obey God rather than you, and while I have life and strength I shall never cease from the practice and teaching of philosophy, exhorting any one whom I meet and saying to him after my manner: You, my friend,—a citizen of the great and mighty and wise city of Athens,—are you not ashamed of heaping up the greatest amount of money and honour and reputation, and caring so little about wisdom and truth and the greatest improvement of the soul, which you never regard or heed at all? And if the person with whom I am arguing, says: Yes, but I do care; then I do not leave him or let him go at once; but I proceed to interrogate and examine and cross-examine him, and if I think that he has no virtue in him, but only says that he has, I reproach him with undervaluing the greater, and overvaluing the less. And I shall repeat the same words to every one whom I meet, young and old, citizen and alien, but especially to the citizens, inasmuch as they are my brethren. For know that this is the command of God; and I believe that no greater good has ever happened in the State than my service to the God. For I do nothing but go about persuading you all, old and young alike, not to take thought for your persons or your properties, but first and chiefly to care about the greatest improvement of the soul. I tell you that virtue is not given by money, but that from virtue comes money and every other good of man, public as well as private. This is my teaching, and if this is the doctrine which corrupts the youth, I am a mischievous person. But if any one says that this is not my teaching, he is speaking an untruth. Wherefore, O men of Athens, I say to you, do as Anytus bids or not as Anytus bids, and either acquit me or not; but whichever you do, understand that I shall never alter my ways, not even if I have to die many times. . . .

Wherefore, O judges, be of good cheer about death, and know of a certainty, that no evil can happen to a good man, either in life or after death. He and his are not neglected by the gods; nor has my own approaching end happened by mere chance. But I see clearly that the time had arrived when it was better for me to die and be released from trouble; wherefore the oracle gave no sign. For which reason, also, I am not angry with my condemners, or with my accusers; they have done me no harm, although they did not mean to do me any good; and for this I may gently blame them.

Still, I have a favour to ask of them. When my sons are grown up, I would ask you, O my friends, to punish them; and I would have you trouble them, as I have troubled you, if they seem to care about riches, or anything, more than about virtue; or if they pretend to be something when they are really nothing,—then reprove them, as I have reproved you, for not caring about that for which they ought to care, and thinking that they are something when they are really nothing. And if you do this, both I and my sons will have received justice at your hands.

The hour of departure has arrived, and we go our ways—I to die, and you to live. Which is better God only knows.

DISCUSSION QUESTIONS

1. According to Socrates, what accusations have been levied against him, and why?
2. In refuting these accusations, what does Socrates reveal about his fundamental intellectual beliefs and methods?
3. Why do you think many of Socrates's contemporaries found his views so threatening?
4. What impressions do Socrates's words give you of him as a man?

3

Building Accounts of the Parthenon
434–433 B.C.

and *Inventory of Its Treasures*
422–421 B.C.

Golden Age Athens provided a visual feast for its residents and visitors. New public buildings and gathering places sprang up around the city—monumental symbols of its power and wealth. Greece's most well-known building, the Parthenon, was built at this time. Dedicated to the patron goddess of Athens, Athena, it combined the tra-

ditional function and design of temples with a sculptural frieze intended to convey a bold and innovative message: Athenians enjoyed the special favor of the gods. These documents allow us to witness this architectural masterpiece in the making and the riches it contained. They also offer insight into contemporary religious beliefs and practices.

Building Accounts of the Parthenon. Marble stele, developed Attic letters, irregular stoichedon, Athens. 434/3 b.c.

For the Commissioners, for whom | Antikles was Secretary, | in the (year of the) fourteenth Boule, in which Metallgenes was first Secretary, in Krates' archlonship over the Athenians (434/3), | the receipts for this year | (are) as follows:‖

1,470 (dr.)[1]	Balance from the previous year.
7[4]	Gold staters [of Lamps] acus
27 and 1/6	[Gold] staters of C[yzic] us
25,000(dr.) (i.e., 4 T. 1,000 dr.)	*From the Treasurers* [of the] Goddess' *Treasury* for whom Krates was secretary, of Lamptrai:
1,372 (dr.)	From gold sold *off;* in weight, 9[8 dr.]: payment for it:
1,305 (dr.) 4 (ob.)	From ivory *sold off,* in weight, [3] T. 60 dr.: Payment [for it]:
	Expenditures
[. . .]200	for purchases
[	]2 (dr.) 1 (ob.)	

From *Archaic Times to the End of the Peloponnesian War,* ed. Charles W. Fornara (Baltimore: Johns Hopkins University Press, 1977), 132–34, 159–60.

[1]The Attic system of coinage was based on the drachma: 6 obols (ob.) equaled 1 drachma (dr.); 100 drachmae equaled 1 mna; and 6,000 drachmae equaled 1 talent (T.). The average worker earned approximately 1 drachma per day.

1,[9] 26 (dr.) 2 (ob.)	For contracting for the workmen [at Pentelicus who also have the marble loaded on to the wagons]:
16, 392 (dr.) (i.e., 2 T. 4,392 dr.)	*For sculptors of the pediment-sculptures: the pay:*
[1,]800	*For monthly wages.*
[..] 11 (dr.) 2 (ob.) [--] [--] [74] [27] [1/6]	*Balance* (at the end) *of this* [year]: [Gold staters] [of Lampsacus.] [Gold staters] [of Cyzicus]

Inventory of the Treasures in the Parthenon. Marble slab (now lost), developed Attic writing, Athens. 422/1 B.C.

Gods. [Ath]e[na. Fortune.] I The following was paid over by the four boards, which rendered *their* [account from (Great) Panathenaia] to (Great) P[ana-thenaia, to the] Tlreasurers for whom Presbias son of Semi[os of Phe] <g>aia was Secretary. [The Treasurers, for whom Pres] bias son of Se[mios of Phegaia] I was Secretary, paid over to the Treasurers for whom Nikeas son of Eu[thykles of Halimous] *was Secretary,* [to Euphemos] II of Kollytos and (his) colleagues, in the Parthenon: Crown *of gold,* [weight] *of this,* 60 dr. Saucers [of gold, 5], welight of these, 782 dr. Uncoined gold, weight of this, [1 dr. 4 ob. Drinking cup] of gold, its *bottom gilt silvler,* consecrated to Herakles of *Elaious,* weight *of this,* 138 dr. Pair of nails, underneath silver, gillt, weight of these, 1 [8] 4 dr. Mask with silver underneath, *gilt, weight* of this, 116 dr. *Saucers of sillver,* 138 dr. Silver drinking horn. Weight of these: 2 T. 3,30[7 dr. By number], the following: Short (Persian) swords *set in gold,* [6]. II standing crop set in gold, ears of corn, 1[2]. Breadbas-kets, wooden underneath, gilt, [2. Censer], wooden underneath, *gilt,* I 1. Maiden on a stele, gilt, [1]. Bed, wooden underneath, gilt, [1]. *Gorgon* mask, with skull gilt. [Horlse], griffin, front part of a griffin, griffin, lion's head, *necklace of flowers,* [snake]: these gilt. [Helmet] *gillt.* Shields gilt with wood underneath, 15. [Chian-made beds, 8]. Milesian-made [beds], 10. *Saberls,* 9. Swords, 5. Breastplates, 1[6]. Shields with devices, 6. Shields [covered with bronze, 3] 1. *Chairs,* 6. Stools, [4]. *Camplstools,* 9. Lyre gilt, 1. Lyres of ivory, 4. Lyres, 4. [Table] inlaid with ivory. Helmets [of bronze, 3]. Bledposts covered with silver, [13]. (Small leather) *shield.*

Saucers of silver, 4. [Small cup covered with silver, 2]. Horse of *silver.* [Weigh|t] of these, 900 dr. Shields, gilt, with wood underneath, [2]. Short (Persian) sword, *gilt, unweighed.* Saucers [of silver, 8]. *Wel|ight* of these, 807 dr. Chalcidian drinking cups of silver, 4, weight [of these], 124 dr. *Flute case* [from Methy]|mna of ivory, gilt. Shield from Lesbos with device. Helmet from [L]esbos, of Illryian [bronze. Saucer||s] of silver, 2. Drinking cups of silver, [2]. Weight of these, 580 dr. L[e]s[b]ian [cups] of *silver,* 3, *weight* [of these, 3]|70 dr. Crown of gold, weight of this, 18 dr. 3 ob. Crown of gold, *weight* of this, 2[9 dr. Athena N]like's golden crown, weight of this, 29 dr. Crown of *gold, weight* of this, 3[3 dr. Athena N]like's crown of gold, weight of this, 33 dr. Tetradrachm [of gold], weight of this, [7 dr. 2 $^1/_2$ ob. Onyx stone]| on a golden ring, *unweighed.*

DISCUSSION QUESTIONS

1. Based on the building accounts, how did the city finance this phase of the Parthenon's construction?

2. Only priests and priestesses were regularly allowed to enter the Parthenon. Using the inventory as a guide, what do you think they may have done once inside?

3. What do the temple's contents reveal about the distinctive way in which it honored Athena?

4

Euphiletus
A Husband Speaks in His Own Defense
c. 400 B.C.

In contrast to the trial of Socrates, that of an ordinary Athenian recounted below illuminates the more mundane aspects of life in fifth-century Athens. It also indicates that despite the momentous changes of the age, ancient traditions retained their grip on much of society, especially women. The testimony is that of a man named Euphiletus who was put on trial for murdering his wife's lover. He presented the following arguments in his own defense, as prepared for him by the speechwriter Lysias (c. 440–380 B.C.). The outcome of the trial is unknown. Nevertheless, Euphiletus's testimony opens a window onto domestic routines at the time and the ways in which they were expected to serve as the anchor of a woman's identity and her husband's honor.

I would give a great deal, members of the jury, to find you, as judges of this case, taking the same attitude towards me as you would adopt towards your own behaviour in similar circumstances. I am sure that if you felt about others in the same way as you did about yourselves, not one of you would fail to be angered by

From *The Murder of Herodes and Other Trials from the Athenian Law Courts,* ed. Kathleen Freeman (London: MacDonald & Co., 1946), 43–52.

these deeds, and all of you would consider the punishment a small one for those guilty of such conduct.

Moreover, the same opinion would be found prevailing not only among you, but everywhere throughout Greece. This is the one crime for which, under any government, democratic or exclusive, equal satisfaction is granted to the meanest against the mightiest, so that the least of them receives the same justice as the most exalted. Such is the detestation, members of the jury, in which this outrage is held by all mankind.

Concerning the severity of the penalty, therefore, you are, I imagine, all of the same opinion: not one of you is so easy-going as to believe that those guilty of such great offences should obtain pardon, or are deserving of a light penalty. What I have to prove, I take it, is just this: that Eratosthenes seduced my wife, and that in corrupting her he brought shame upon my children and outrage upon me, by entering my home; that there was no other enmity between him and me except this; and that I did not commit this act for the sake of money, in order to rise from poverty to wealth, nor for any other advantage except the satisfaction allowed by law.

I shall expound my case to you in full from the beginning, omitting nothing and telling the truth. In this alone lies my salvation, I imagine—if I can explain to you everything that happened.

Members of the jury: when I decided to marry and had brought a wife home, at first my attitude towards her was this: I did not wish to annoy her, but neither was she to have too much of her own way. I watched her as well as I could, and kept an eye on her as was proper. But later, after my child had been born, I came to trust her, and I handed all my possessions over to her, believing that this was the greatest possible proof of affection.

Well, members of the jury, in the beginning she was the best of women. She was a clever housewife, economical and exact in her management of everything. But then, my mother died; and her death has proved to be the source of all my troubles, because it was when my wife went to the funeral that this man Eratosthenes saw her; and as time went on, he was able to seduce her. He kept a look out for our maid who goes to market; and approaching her with his suggestions, he succeeded in corrupting her mistress.

Now first of all, gentlemen, I must explain that I have a small house which is divided into two—the men's quarters and the women's—each having the same space, the women upstairs and the men downstairs.

After the birth of my child, his mother nursed him; but I did not want her to run the risk of going downstairs every time she had to give him a bath, so I myself took over the upper storey, and let the women have the ground floor. And so it came about that by this time it was quite customary for my wife often to go downstairs and sleep with the child, so that she could give him the breast and stop him from crying.

This went on for a long while, and I had not the slightest suspicion. On the contrary, I was in such a fool's paradise that I believed my wife to be the chastest woman in all the city.

Time passed, gentlemen. One day, when I had come home unexpectedly from the country, after dinner, the child began crying and complaining. Actually it was the maid who was pinching him on purpose to make him behave so, because—as I found out later—this man was in the house.

Well, I told my wife to go and feed the child, to stop his crying. But at first she refused, pretending that she was so glad to see me back after my long absence. At last I began to get annoyed, and I insisted on her going.

"Oh, yes!" she said. "To leave *you* alone with the maid up here! You mauled her about before, when you were drunk!"

I laughed. She got up, went out, closed the door—pretending that it was a joke—and locked it. As for me, I thought no harm of all this, and I had not the slightest suspicion. I went to sleep, glad to do so after my journey from the country.

Towards morning, she returned and unlocked the door.

I asked her why the doors had been creaking during the night. She explained that the lamp beside the baby had gone out, and that she had then gone to get a light from the neighbours.

I said no more. I thought it really was so. But it did seem to me, members of the jury, that she had done up her face with cosmetics, in spite of the fact that her brother had died only a month before. Still, even so, I said nothing about it. I just went off, without a word.

After this, members of the jury, an interval elapsed, during which my injuries had progressed, leaving me far behind. Then, one day, I was approached by an old hag. She had been sent by a woman—Eratosthenes' previous mistress, as I found out later. This woman, furious because he no longer came to see her as before, had been on the look-out until she had discovered the reason. The old crone, therefore, had come and was lying in wait for me near my house.

"Euphiletus," she said, "please don't think that my approaching you is in any way due to a wish to interfere. The fact is, the man who is wronging you and your wife is an enemy of ours. Now if you catch the woman who does your shopping and works for you, and put her through an examination, you will discover all. The culprit," she added, "is Eratosthenes from Oea. Your wife is not the only one he has seduced—there are plenty of others. It's his profession."

With these words, members of the jury, she went off.

At once I was overwhelmed. Everything rushed into my mind, and I was filled with suspicion. I reflected how I had been locked into the bedroom. I remembered how on that night the middle and outer doors had creaked, a thing that had never happened before; and how I had had the idea that my wife's face was rouged. All these things rushed into my mind, and I was filled with suspicion.

I went back home, and told the servant to come with me to market. I took her instead to the house of one of my friends; and there I informed her that I had discovered all that was going on in my house.

"As for you," I said, "two courses are open to you: either to be flogged and sent to the tread-mill, and never be released from a life of utter misery; or to confess the whole truth and suffer no punishment, but win pardon from me for your wrong-doing. Tell me no lies. Speak the whole truth."

At first she tried denial, and told me that I could do as I pleased—she knew nothing. But when I named Eratosthenes to her face, and said that he was the man who had been visiting my wife, she was dumbfounded, thinking that I had found out everything exactly. And then at last, falling at my feet and exacting a promise from me that no harm should be done to her, she denounced the villain. She described how he had first approached her after the funeral, and then how in the end she had passed the message on, and in course of time my wife had been over-persuaded. She explained the way in which he had contrived to get into the house, and how when I was in the country my wife had gone to a religious service with this man's mother, and everything else that had happened. She recounted it all exactly.

When she had told all, I said:

"See to it that nobody gets to know of this; otherwise the promise I made you will not hold good. And furthermore, I expect you to show me this actually happening. I have no use for words. I want the *fact* to be exhibited, if it really is so."

She agreed to do this.

Four or five days then elapsed, as I shall prove to you by important evidence. But before I do so, I wish to narrate the events of the last day.

I had a friend and relative named Sôstratus. He was coming home from the country after sunset when I met him. I knew that as he had got back so late, he would not find any of his own people at home; so I asked him to dine with me. We went home to my place, and going upstairs to the upper storey, we had dinner there. When he felt restored, he went off; and I went to bed.

Then, members of the jury, Eratosthenes made his entry; and the maid wakened me and told me that he was in the house.

I told her to watch the door; and going downstairs, I slipped out noiselessly.

I went to the houses of one man after another. Some I found at home; others, I was told, were out of town. So collecting as many as I could of those who were there, I went back. We procured torches from the shop near by, and entered my house. The door had been left open by arrangement with the maid.

We forced the bedroom door. The first of us to enter saw him still lying beside my wife. Those who followed saw him standing naked on the bed.

I knocked him down, members of the jury, with one blow. I then twisted his hands behind his back and tied them. And then I asked him why he was committing this crime against me, of breaking into my house.

He answered that he admitted his guilt; but he begged and besought me not to kill him—to accept a money-payment instead.

But I replied:

"It is not I who shall be killing you, but the law of the State, which you, in transgressing, have valued less highly than your own pleasures. You have preferred to commit this great crime against my wife and my children, rather than to obey the law and be of decent behaviour."

Thus, members of the jury, this man met the fate which the laws prescribe for wrong-doers of his kind.

Eratosthenes was not seized in the street and carried off, nor had he taken refuge at the altar, as the prosecution alleges. The facts do not admit of it: he was struck in the bedroom, he fell at once, and I bound his hands behind his back. There were so many present that he could not possibly escape through their midst, since he had neither steel nor wood nor any other weapon with which he could have defended himself against all those who had entered the room.

No, members of the jury: you know as well as I do how wrong-doers will not admit that their adversaries are speaking the truth, and attempt by lies and trickery of other kinds to excite the anger of the hearers against those whose acts are in accordance with Justice.

(*To the Clerk of the Court*):

Read the Law.

(*The Law of Solon is read, that an adulterer may be put to death by the man who catches him.*)

He made no denial, members of the jury. He admitted his guilt, and begged and implored that he should not be put to death, offering to pay compensation. But I would not accept his estimate. I preferred to accord a higher authority to the law of the State, and I took that satisfaction which you, because you thought it the most just, have decreed for those who commit such offences.

Witnesses to the preceding, kindly step up.

(*The witnesses come to the front of the Court, and the Clerk reads their depositions. When the Clerk has finished reading, and the witnesses have agreed that the depositions are correct, the defendant again addresses the Clerk*):

Now please read this further law from the pillar of the Court of the Areopagus:

(*The Clerk reads another version of Solon's law, as recorded on the pillar of the Areopagus Court.*)

You hear, members of the jury, how it is expressly decreed by the Court of the Areopagus itself, which both traditionally and in your own day has been granted the right to try cases of murder, that no person shall be found guilty of murder who catches an adulterer with his wife and inflicts this punishment. The Lawgiver was so strongly convinced of the justice of these provisions in the case of married women, that he applied them also to concubines, who are of less importance. Yet obviously, if he had known of any greater punishment than this for cases where married women are concerned, he would have provided it. But in fact, as it was impossible for him to invent any more severe penalty for corrup-

tion of wives, he decided to provide the same punishment as in the case of concubines.

(*To the Clerk of the Court*):

Please read me this Law also.

(*The Clerk reads out further clauses from Solon's laws on rape.*)

You hear, members of the jury, how the Lawgiver ordains that if anyone debauch by force a free man or boy, the fine shall be double that decreed in the case
of a slave. If anyone debauch a woman—in which case it is *permitted* to kill him
—he shall be liable to the same fine. Thus, members of the jury, the Lawgiver
considered violators deserving of a lesser penalty than seducers: for the latter he
provided the death-penalty; for the former, the doubled fine. His idea was that
those who use force are loathed by the persons violated, whereas those who have
got their way by persuasion corrupt women's minds, in such a way as to make
other men's wives more attached to themselves than to their husbands, so that
the whole house is in their power, and it is uncertain who is the children's father,
the husband or the lover. These considerations caused the Lawgiver to affix death
as the penalty for seduction.

And so, members of the jury, in my case the laws not only hold me innocent,
but actually order me to take this satisfaction; but it depends on you whether
they are to be effective or of no moment. The reason, in my opinion, why all
States lay down laws is in order that, whenever we are in doubt on any point, we
can refer to these laws and find out our duty. And therefore it is the laws which in
such cases enjoin upon the injured party to exact this penalty. I exhort you to
show yourselves in agreement with them; otherwise you will be granting such
impunity to adulterers that you will encourage even burglars to declare themselves adulterers, in the knowledge that if they allege this reason for their action
and plead that this was their purpose in entering other men's houses, no one will
lay a finger on them. They will all realize that they need not bother about the law
on adultery, but need only fear your verdict, since this is the supreme authority
in the State.

Consider, members of the jury, their accusation that it was I who on that day
told the maid to fetch the young man. In my opinion, gentlemen, I should have
been justified in using any means to catch the seducer of my wife. If there had
been only words spoken and no actual offence, I should have been doing wrong;
but when by that time they had gone to all lengths and he had often gained entry
into my house, I consider that I should have been within my rights whatever
means I employ to catch him. But observe that this allegation of the prosecution
is also false. You can easily convince yourselves by considering the following:

I have already told you how Sôstratus, an intimate friend of mine, met me
coming in from the country around sunset, and dined with me, and when he felt
refreshed, went off. Now in the first place, gentlemen, ask yourselves whether, if
on that night I had had designs on Eratosthenes, it would have been better for
me that Sôstratus should dine elsewhere, or that I should take a guest home with

me to dinner. Surely in the latter circumstances Eratosthenes would have been less inclined to venture into the house. Further, does it seem to you probable that I would have let my guest go, and been left alone, without company? Would I not rather have urged him to stay, so that he could help me to punish the adulterer?

Again, gentlemen, does it not seem to you probable that I would have passed the word round among my friends during the daytime, and told them to assemble at the house of one of my friends who lived nearest, rather than have started to run round at night, as soon as I found out, without knowing whom I should find at home and whom away? Actually, I called for Harmodius and certain others who were out of town—I did not know it—and others, I found, were not at home, so I went along taking with me whomever I could. But if I had known beforehand, does it not seem to you probable that I would have arranged for servants and passed the word round to my friends, so that I myself could go in with the maximum of safety—for how did I know whether he too might not have had a dagger or something?—and also in order that I might exact the penalty in the presence of the greatest number of witnesses? But in fact, since I knew nothing of what was going to happen on that night, I took with me whomever I could get.

Witnesses to the preceding, please step up.

(*Further witnesses come forward, and confirm their evidence as read out by the Clerk.*)

You have heard the witnesses, members of the jury. Now consider the case further in your own minds, inquiring whether there had ever existed between Eratosthenes and myself any other enmity but this. You will find none. He never brought any malicious charge against me, nor tried to secure my banishment, nor prosecuted me in any private suit. Neither had he knowledge of any crime of which I feared the revelation, so that I desired to kill him; nor by carrying out this act did I hope to gain money. So far from ever having had any dispute with him, or drunken brawl, or any other quarrel, I had never even set eyes on the man before that night. What possible object could I have had, therefore, in running so great a risk, except that I had suffered the greatest of all injuries at his hands? Again, would I myself have called in witnesses to my crime, when it was possible for me, if I desired to murder him without justification, to have had no confidants?

It is my belief, members of the jury, that this punishment was inflicted not in my own interests, but in those of the whole community. Such villains, seeing the rewards which await their crimes, will be less ready to commit offences against others if they see that you too hold the same opinion of them. Otherwise it would be far better to wipe out the existing laws and make different ones, which will penalise those who keep guard over their own wives, and grant full immunity to those who criminally pursue them. This would be a far more just procedure than to set a trap for citizens by means of the laws, which urge the man who catches an adulterer to do with him whatever he will, and yet allow the injured party to undergo a trial far more perilous than that which faces the law-breaker who seduces other men's wives. Of this, I am an example—I, who now stand in danger of losing life, property, everything, because I have obeyed the laws of the State.

DISCUSSION QUESTIONS

1. What does Euphiletus's testimony reveal about the role women were expected to play in Athenian society?
2. How does the husband justify his actions?
3. Why does he think adultery is especially worthy of severe punishment?

COMPARATIVE QUESTIONS

1. What do you think Socrates's reaction would have been to Pericles's description of the role of wealth in Athenian society?
2. In what ways did the construction of the Parthenon embody this passage in Pericles's oration?
3. Do you see any similarities between Pericles's and Euphiletus's understanding of the relationship between the individual and the state?
4. How did Socrates challenge this relationship?

4

From the Classical to the Hellenistic World
c. 400–30 B.C.

S U M M A R Y   Just as war against Persia helped propel Greece to greatness, so, too, did war against itself initiate its decline. Following the end of
the Peloponnesian War in 404 B.C., the Greek city-states fell victim to internal squabbling and disunity as each vied to dominate Greece. The first document elucidates how Macedonian kings seized this opportunity to become
masters of the region and beyond. Their successors capitalized on their legacy,
carving out individual kingdoms from the Macedonian empire. In the second
document, we see the Hellenistic world through the eyes of an official working in
one of its hubs, Egypt. Against this backdrop, the once mighty Greek city-states
became second-rate powers, prompting many Greek thinkers, such as Polybius
(Document 3), to reexamine the role of fate and chance in human life. The final
document allows us to understand better where women fit into this new landscape, which was colored by both change and tradition.

1

Arrian
The Campaigns of Alexander
Second Century A.D.

*During his reign from 336 to 323 B.C., the Macedonian king Alexander the Great
forever changed the eastern Mediterranean world. Following his father's lead,
Alexander not only secured Macedonia's position as the leading power in Greece, but
he also conquered the mighty Persian Empire. This excerpt from the most reliable
known account of Alexander's Asian campaign,* The Campaigns of Alexander *by
Arrian of Nicomedia, written in the second century A.D., paints a vivid picture of
Alexander as a warrior and king. In this passage, he has just returned to Persia in*

324 b.c. from his expedition to India, where his exhausted soldiers had forced him to turn back because they wanted to return home. His decision to discharge disabled veterans sparked anger among his Macedonian troops, who feared they were to be replaced by foreigners. Alexander delivered the following speech to chastise them, while glorifying his father's and his own accomplishments.

"My countrymen, you are sick for home—so be it! I shall make no attempt to check your longing to return. Go whither you will; I shall not hinder you. But, if go you must, there is one thing I would have you understand—what I have done for you, and in what coin you will have repaid me.

"First I will speak of my father Philip, as it is my duty to do. Philip found you a tribe of impoverished vagabonds, most of you dressed in skins, feeding a few sheep on the hills and fighting, feebly enough, to keep them from your neighbours—Thracians and Triballians and Illyrians. He gave you cloaks to wear instead of skins; he brought you down from the hills into the plains; he taught you to fight on equal terms with the enemy on your borders, till you knew that your safety lay not, as once, in your mountain strongholds, but in your own valour. He made you city-dwellers; he brought you law; he civilized you. He rescued you from subjection and slavery, and made you masters of the wild tribes who harried and plundered you; he annexed the greater part of Thrace, and by seizing the best places on the coast opened your country to trade, and enabled you to work your mines without fear of attack.[1] Thessaly, so long your bugbear and your dread, he subjected to your rule, and by humbling the Phocians he made the narrow and difficult path into Greece a broad and easy road.[2] The men of Athens and Thebes, who for years had kept watching for their moment to strike us down, he brought so low—and by this time I myself was working at my father's side[3] that they who once exacted from us either our money or our obedience, now, in their turn, looked to us as the means of their salvation. Passing into the Peloponnese, he settled everything there to his satisfaction, and when he was made supreme commander of all the rest of Greece for the war against Persia, he claimed the glory of it not for himself alone, but for the Macedonian people.

"These services which my father rendered you are, indeed, intrinsically great; yet they are small compared with my own. I inherited from him a handful of gold and silver cups, coin in the treasury worth less than sixty talents and over eight times that amount of debts incurred by him; yet to add to this burden I borrowed a further sum of eight hundred talents, and, marching out from a coun-

---

From Arrian, *The Campaigns of Alexander*, trans. Aubrey de Sélincourt (London: Penguin Books, 1971), 360–66.

[1]The gold and silver mines at Mount Pangaeum near Philippi are said to have brought Philip more than 1,000 talents a year.

[2]In 346 b.c.

[3]He refers principally, no doubt, to his part in the battle of Chaeroneia in 338 b.c.

try too poor to maintain you decently, laid open for you at a blow, and in spite of Persia's naval supremacy, the gates of the Hellespont. My cavalry crushed the *satraps* [governors] of Darius, and I added all Ionia and Aeolia, the two Phrygias and Lydia to your empire. Miletus I reduced by siege; the other towns all yielded of their own free will—I took them and gave them you for your profit and enjoyment. The wealth of Egypt and Cyrene, which I shed no blood to win, now flows into your hands; Palestine and the plains of Syria and the Land between the Rivers are now your property; Babylon and Bactria and Susa are yours; you are masters of the gold of Lydia, the treasures of Persia, the wealth of India—yes, and of the sea beyond India, too. You are my captains, my generals, my governors of provinces.

"From all this which I have laboured to win for you, what is left for myself except the purple and this crown? I keep nothing for my own; no one can point to treasure of mine apart from all this which you yourselves either possess, or have in safe keeping for your future use. Indeed, what reason have I to keep anything, as I eat the same food and take the same sleep as you do? Ah, but there are epicures among you who, I fancy, eat more luxuriously than I; and this I know, that I wake earlier than you—and watch, that you may sleep.

"Perhaps you will say that, in my position as your commander, I had none of the labours and distress which you had to endure to win for me what I have won. But does any man among you honestly feel that he has suffered more for me than I have suffered for him? Come now—if you are wounded, strip and show your wounds, and I will show mine. There is no part of my body but my back which has not a scar; not a weapon a man may grasp or fling the mark of which I do not carry upon me. I have sword-cuts from close fight; arrows have pierced me, missiles from catapults bruised my flesh; again and again I have been struck by stones or clubs—and all for your sakes: for your glory and your gain. Over every land and sea, across river, mountain, and plain I led you to the world's end, a victorious army. I married as you married, and many of you will have children related by blood to my own. Some of you have owed money—I have paid your debts, never troubling to inquire how they were incurred, and in spite of the fact that you earn good pay and grow rich from the sack of cities. To most of you I have given a circlet of gold as a memorial for ever and ever of your courage and of my regard.[4] And what of those who have died in battle? Their death was noble, their burial illustrious; almost all are commemorated at home by statues of bronze; their parents are held in honour, with all dues of money or service remitted, for under my leadership not a man among you has ever fallen with his back to the enemy.

"And now it was in my mind to dismiss any man no longer fit for active service—all such should return home to be envied and admired. But you all wish to leave me. Go then! And when you reach home, tell them that Alexander your King, who vanquished Persians and Medes and Bactrians and Sacae; who crushed

---

[4]Surely an exaggeration.

the Uxii, the Arachotians, and the Drangae, and added to his empire Parthia, the Chorasmian waste, and Hyrcania to the Caspian Sea; who crossed the Caucasus beyond the Caspian Gates, and Oxus and Tanais and the Indus, which none but Dionysus had crossed before him, and Hydaspes and Acesines and Hydraotes—yes, and Hyphasis too, had you not feared to follow; who by both mouths of the Indus burst into the Great Sea beyond, and traversed the desert of Gedrosia, untrodden before by any army; who made Carmania his own, as his troops swept by, and the country of the Oreitans; who was brought back by you to Susa, when his ships had sailed the ocean from India to Persia—tell them, I say, that you deserted him and left him to the mercy of barbarian men, whom you yourselves had conquered. Such news will indeed assure you praise upon earth and reward in heaven. Out of my sight!"

As he ended, Alexander sprang from the rostrum and hurried into the palace. All that day he neither ate nor washed nor permitted any of his friends to see him. On the following day too he remained closely confined. On the third day he sent for the Persian officers who were in the highest favour and divided among them the command of the various units of the army. Only those whom he designated his kinsmen were now permitted to give him the customary kiss.[5]

On the Macedonians the immediate effect of Alexander's speech was profound. They stood in silence in front of the rostrum. Nobody made a move to follow the King except his closest attendants and the members of his personal guard; the rest, helpless to speak or act, yet unwilling to go away, remained rooted to the spot. But when they were told about the Persians and Medes—how command was being given to Persian officers, foreign troops drafted into Macedonian units, a Persian Corps of Guards called by a Macedonian name, Persian infantry units given the coveted title of Companions, Persian Silver Shields[6] and Persian mounted Companions, including even a new Royal Squadron, in process of formation—they could contain themselves no longer. Every man of them hurried to the palace; in sign of supplication they flung their arms on the ground before the doors and stood there calling and begging for admission. They offered to give up the ringleaders of the mutiny and those who had led the cry against the King, and swore they would not stir from the spot day or night unless Alexander took pity on them.

Alexander, the moment he heard of this change of heart, hastened out to meet them, and he was so touched by their grovelling repentance and their bitter lamentations that the tears came into his eyes. While they continued to beg for his pity, he stepped forward as if to speak, but was anticipated by one Callines, an officer of the Companions, distinguished both by age and rank. "My lord," he cried, "what hurts us is that you have made Persians your kinsmen—Persians are called Alexander's kinsmen—Persians kiss you. But no Macedonian has yet had a taste of this honour."

---

[5] *Kinsman* was an honorific title bestowed by the Persian king on leading Persians.

[6] This is a later name for the Guards (*Hypaspists*).

"Every man of you," Alexander replied, "I regard as my kinsman, and from now on that is what I shall call you."

Thereupon Callines came up to him and kissed him, and all the others who wished to do so kissed him too. Then they picked up their weapons and returned to their quarters singing the song of victory at the top of their voices.

To mark the restoration of harmony, Alexander offered sacrifice to the gods he was accustomed to honour, and gave a public banquet which he himself attended, sitting among the Macedonians, all of whom were present.[7] Next them the Persians had their places, and next to the Persians distinguished foreigners of other nations; Alexander and his friends dipped their wine from the same bowl and poured the same libations, following the lead of the Greek seers and the Magi (Persian priests). The chief object of his prayers was that Persians and Macedonians might rule together in harmony as an imperial power. It is said that 9,000 people attended the banquet; they unanimously drank the same toast, and followed it by the paean of victory.[8]

DISCUSSION QUESTIONS

1. According to Alexander, how did Philip II transform Macedonia from a backward, minor kingdom to a great power?

2. What does Alexander reveal about the impact Macedonia's rise to power had on the Greek city-states?

3. Why does Alexander consider his achievements to be even greater than those of his father?

4. Based on Alexander's speech, how would you characterize his method of rule?

2

Zenon, Egyptian Official
Records
259–250 B.C.

Alexander the Great's imperial glory was short-lived. Upon his death in 323 B.C., his army commanders divided his empire among themselves into separate kingdoms over which they assumed control. To rule effectively, these new kings and their successors relied on a hierarchical bureaucracy staffed by Greeks and local administrators to oversee their affairs. These extracts illuminate the busy life of one such official, a Greek named Zenon, who was an agent for Apollonius, the financial minister to King Ptolemy Philadelphus of Egypt (r. 285–246 B.C.). At the time, Egypt was full of both Greeks and indigenous peoples who contributed to a vibrant urban culture and

---

[7]An evident exaggeration, unless only officers are meant.

[8]This banquet was held to celebrate the reconciliation between Alexander and his Macedonians and (it was hoped) between them and the Persians.

economy. *These extracts include instructions from Apollonius, requests for help, a desk diary, and other records from Zeno's daily affairs.*

Letter from Hierocles (257 b.c.)

Hierocles to Zenon greeting. If you are well, it would be excellent. I too am in good health. You wrote to me about Pyrrhus, telling me to train[1] him if I am quite certain of his success, but if not, to avoid incurring useless expense and distracting him from his studies. Now as for my being certain, the gods should know best, but it seems to Ptolemaeus, as far as a man can tell, that Pyrrhus is much better than those now being trained, though they started long before him, and that in a very short time he will be far ahead of them; moreover he is pursuing his other studies as well; and to speak with the gods' leave, I hope to see you crowned. Make haste to send him a bathing-apron, and if possible let it be of goatskin or, if not, of thin sheepskin, and a tunic and cloak, and the mattress, coverlet and pillows, and the honey. You wrote to me that you were surprised at my not understanding that all these things are subject to toll. I know it, but you are well able to arrange for them to be sent in perfect security.[2] (Addressed) To Zenon. (Docketed) Hierocles about Pyrrhus. Year 29, Xandicus 3, at Memphis.

Letter from Promethion (256 b.c.)

Promethion[3] to Zenon greeting. I suffered anxiety when I heard of your long protracted illness, but now I am delighted to hear that you are convalescent and already on the point of recovery. I myself am well. I previously gave your agent Heraclides 150 drachmae in silver from your account, as you wrote to me to do, and he is bringing you now 10 *hins* of perfume in 21 vases which have been sealed with my finger-ring. For though Apollonius wrote to me to buy and give him also 300 wild pomegranate wreaths, I did not manage to give him these at the same time, as they were not ready, but Pa . . . will bring them to him at Naucratis; for they will be finished before the 30th. I have paid the price both of these and of the perfume from your account, as Apollonius wrote. I have also paid a charge of 10 drachmae in copper for the boat in which he is sailing up. And 400 drachmae in silver have been paid to Iatrocles for the papyrus rolls which are being manufactured in Tanis for Apollonius. Take note then that these affairs have been settled thus. And please write yourself if ever you need anything here. Goodbye. Year 29, Choiach 28. (Addressed) To Zenon. (Docketed) Year 29, Peritius 3. Promethion about what he has paid.

From *Select Papyri*, trans. A. S. Hunt and C. C. Edgar, vol. 1 (London and New York: William Heinemann Ltd., 1932), 269–77, 397–99, 409–15.

[1]For competition in the public games.

[2]That is, by using his influence as an agent of the financial minister.

[3]A banker in Mendes.

Letter From Apollonius the Dioecetes (256 B.C.)

Apollonius to Zenon greeting. From the dry wood put on board a boat as many of the thickest logs as possible and send them immediately to Alexandria that we may be able to use them for the festival of Isis. Goodbye. Year 30, Dius 3, Phaophi 23. (Addressed) To Zenon. At once.[4] (Docketed by Zenon) Year 30, Dius 18, Hathur 18. Apollonius about wood for the Isis festival. (Docketed by sender) Wood for the Isis festival.

Letter from Platon (255 B.C.)

Platon to Zenon greeting. The father of Demetrius the bearer of this letter happens, it seems, to be residing in the Arsinoite nome,[5] and the lad therefore wishes to find employment there himself. On hearing of your kindly disposition some of his friends asked me to write to you about him, begging you to give him a post in your service. Please then do me a favour and provide some employment for him, whatever you may think suitable, and otherwise look after him, if you find him useful. As a token (of goodwill) I have sent you, from Sosus, 2 artabae[6] of chick-peas bought at 5 drachmae each, and if there are any at Naucratis, I will try to buy you about 20 artabae more and bring them up to you myself. Goodbye. Year 31, Dius 12. (Addressed) To Zenon.

Letter from Artemidorus (252 B.C.)

Artemidorus[7] to Zenon greeting. If you are well, it would be excellent. I too am well and Apollonius is in good health and other things are satisfactory. As I write this, we have just arrived in Sidon after escorting the princess[8] to the frontier, and I expect that we shall soon be with you. Now you will do me a favour by taking care of your own health and writing to me if you want anything done that I can do for you. And kindly buy me, so that I may get them when I arrive, 3 metretae[9] of the best honey and 600 artabae of barley for the animals, and pay the cost of them out of the produce of the sesame and croton,[10] and also see to the house in Philadelphia in order that I may find it roofed when I arrive. Try also as best you can to keep watch on the oxen and the pigs and the geese and the rest of the stock

---

[4]An admonition to the persons concerned to send the letter immediately.

[5]**Nome** means region. [— Ed.]

[6]**Artabae** means baskets. [— Ed.]

[7]A physician in the service of the dioecetes.

[8]The princess Berenice, who was escorted to Syria by Apollonius on the occasion of her marriage to Antiochus II.

[9]**Metretae** means jars. [— Ed.]

[10]The two oils chiefly used in Egypt at this period were made from sesame and croton (the castor-oil plant), the former for food and the latter for lamps.

there; I shall have a better supply of provisions if you do. Also see to it that the crops are harvested somehow, and if any outlay is required, do not hesitate to pay what is necessary. Goodbye. Year 33, intercalary Peritius 6. (Addressed) To Zenon. To Philadelphia. (Docketed) Year 33, Phamenoth 6. Artemidorus.

Letter from an Invalid (259–257 B.C.)

Memorandum to Zenon from Cydippus. If in accordance with the doctors' orders I could have purchased any of the following things in the market, I should not have troubled you; but as it is I have written you a note of what I require, as Apollonius thought I ought to do. So if you have them in store, send me a jar of wine, either Lesbian or Chian, of the very sweetest, and if possible a chous[11] of honey or, if not, as much as you can; and order them to fill me the vessel with salt fish. For both these things they consider to be most needful. And if my health improves and I go abroad to Byzantium, I will bring you back some excellent salt fish. (On the back) Memorandum from Cydippus.

Letter from a House-Painter (c. 255 B.C.)

Memorandum to Zenon from Theophilus the . . . About the work in the house of Diotimus: for the portico, [I undertake] to have the cornice painted with a purple border, the upper part of the wall variegated, the lower course like vetch-seed,[12] and the pediment with circular veining, providing myself with all materials, for 30 drachmae. For the dining-room with seven couches, I will do the vault according to the pattern which you saw, and give the lower course an agreeable tint and paint the Lesbian cornice, providing myself with all materials, for 20 drachmae. And for the dining-rooms with five couches, I will paint the cornices, providing myself with all materials, for 3 drachmae. The sum total is 53 drachmae. But if you provide everything, it will come to 30 drachmae. Goodbye.

Zenon's Agenda (c. 250 B.C.)

To ask Herodotus about the goat hair. To ask Aminias at how much the mina he sold it. The letter to Dioscurides about the boat. To make an agreement with Timaeus about the pigs. To draft the contract with Apollodorus and write to him to hand over. To load the boat with wood. To write to Jason to let Dionysius put the wool on board and take it down the river when cleaned; the fourth part of the Arabian wool; to let him take down the sour wine. To write to Meliton to plant shoots of the *bumastus* vine belonging to Neoptolemus, and to Alcimus to do likewise if he approves. To Theogenes about twelve yokes of bulls. To give

---

[11]**Chous** means container. [— Ed.]

[12]Vetch-seed is pea-colored. [— Ed.]

Apollodorus and Callippus ... From Metrodorus to Athenagoras about the same year's produce. To Theophilus granting a favour and about the state of the work. To write about corn to Iatrokles and Theodorus before the water from the canal ...

Zenon's Agenda (c. 250 B.C.)

To get the olive kernels. The oil from Heragoras. To buy for the horses 4 strigils, 4 rubbing cloths, 4 scrapers, and for Phatres 1 strigil. To get shoots of the walnut trees. To ascertain the registration of the wine carried down, for which nome it has been registered. To receive Hermon's boy.

List of Foreign Goods (257 B.C.)

Year 29, Xandicus 11, at Hermopolis.[13] We have left behind these articles which Charmus has handed over to Apollodotus: in a basket 5 small bags of nard sealed and 1 small wallet sealed, 1 small wallet, sealed, containing dice of gazelle bone; purple dye in one pillow-case; 1 strip of variegated cloth; 3 half-strips of variegated cloth; 2 strips of white cloth; 4 strips of purple cloth; 3 bags and 1 small bag of frankincense sealed; 3 small bags of myrrh sealed; 1 wallet containing dice of gazelle bone; 1 small wallet of purple dye sealed; 1 small wallet of saffron sealed.

List of Zenon's Clothes (c. 257 B.C.)

Zenon's trunk in which are contained: 1 linen wrap, washed; 1 clay-coloured cloak, for winter, washed, and 1 worn, 1 for summer, half-worn, 1 natural-coloured, for winter, washed, and 1 worn, 1 vetch-coloured, for summer, new; 1 white tunic for winter, with sleeves, washed, 1 natural-coloured, for winter, with sleeves, worn, 1 natural-coloured, for winter, worn, 2 white, for winter, washed, and 1 half-worn, 3 for summer, white, new, 1 unbleached, 1 half-worn; 1 outer garment, white, for winter, washed; 1 coarse mantle; 1 summer garment, white, washed, and 1 half-worn; 1 pair of Sardian pillow-cases; 2 pairs of socks, clay-coloured, new, 2 pairs of white, new; 2 girdles, white, new. (Endorsed) From Pisicles, a list of Zenon's clothes.

DISCUSSION QUESTIONS
1. If you had to write a job description for Zenon based on these records, what responsibilities would it include?
2. What do Zenon's records reveal about the nature of the local economy?
3. What evidence do you find here of cross-cultural influences within the Hellenistic world?

---

[13]Hermopolis Parva in the Delta.

3

Polybius
The Histories
Second Century B.C.

The rise of the Macedonian and Hellenistic kings forever crippled the Greek city-states' political independence. At the same time, a new power, Rome, was vying for supremacy. Polybius (203? B.C.–c. 120 B.C.) was a Greek statesman and historian who witnessed these changes firsthand while working at home and abroad, including in Rome, where he spent many years as a private tutor. Here he observed the city's institutions and people with a keen eye for detail, laying the groundwork for his forty-volume Histories. *This excerpt is a fragmentary part of this work. It is remarkable for its discussion of a prominent concern among contemporary thinkers striving to explain the tumultuous and seemingly random course of recent Greek history: the relationship between human affairs and the power of luck and chance. In arguing that inexplicable phenomena are the result of fate, not human action, Polybius also reveals the influence on his views of Stoicism, one of the leading new philosophical schools of his day.*

For my part, says Polybius, in finding fault with those who ascribe public events and incidents in private life to Fate and Chance, I now wish to state my opinion on this subject as far as it is admissible to do so in a strictly historical work. Now indeed as regards things the causes of which it is impossible or difficult for a mere man to understand, we may perhaps be justified in getting out of the difficulty by setting them down to the action of a god or of chance, I mean such things as exceptionally heavy and continuous rain or snow, or on the other hand the destruction of crops by severe drought or frost, or a persistent outbreak of plague or other similar things of which it is not easy to detect the cause. So in regard to such matters we naturally bow to popular opinion, as we cannot make out why they happen, and attempting by prayer and sacrifice to appease the heavenly powers, we send to ask the gods what we must do and say, to set things right and cause the evil that afflicts us to cease. But as for matters the efficient and final cause of which it is possible to discover we should not, I think, put them down to divine action. For instance, take the following case. In our own time the whole of Greece has been subject to a low birth-rate and a general decrease of the population, owing to which cities have become deserted and the land has ceased to yield fruit, although there have neither been continuous wars nor epidemics. If, then, any one had advised us to send and ask the gods about this, and find out what we ought to say or do, to increase in number and make our cities more populous, would it not seem absurd, the cause of the evil being evident and the remedy being in our own hands? For as men had fallen into such a state

---

From Polybius, *The Histories,* trans. W. R. Paton, vol. 6 (Cambridge, Mass.: Harvard University Press, 1960), 383–87.

of pretentiousness, avarice, and indolence that they did not wish to marry, or if they married to rear the children born to them, or at most as a rule but one or two of them, so as to leave these in affluence and bring them up to waste their substance, the evil rapidly and insensibly grew. For in cases where of one or two children the one was carried off by war and the other by sickness, it is evident that the houses must have been left unoccupied, and as in the case of swarms of bees, so by small degrees cities became resourceless and feeble. About this it was of no use at all to ask the gods to suggest a means of deliverance from such an evil. For any ordinary man will tell you that the most effectual cure had to be men's own action, in either striving after other objects, or if not, in passing laws making it compulsory to rear children. Neither prophets nor magic were here of any service, and the same holds good for all particulars. But in cases where it is either impossible or difficult to detect the cause the question is open to doubt. One such case is that of Macedonia. For the Macedonians had met with many signal favours from Rome; the country as a whole had been delivered from the arbitrary rule and taxation of autocrats, and, as all confessed, now enjoyed freedom in place of servitude, and the several cities had, owing to the beneficent action of Rome, been freed from serious civil discord and internecine massacres. . . . But now they witnessed in quite a short time more of their citizens exiled, tortured and murdered by this false Philip than by any of their previous real kings. . . . But while they were defeated by the Romans in fighting for Demetrius and Perseus, yet now fighting for a hateful man and displaying great valour in defence of his throne, they worsted the Romans. How can anyone fail to be nonplused by such an event? for here it is most difficult to detect the cause. So that in pronouncing on this and similar phenomena we may well say that the thing was a heaven-sent infatuation, and that all the Macedonians were visited by the wrath of God, as will be evident from what follows.

DISCUSSION QUESTIONS

1. Does Polybius believe that humans have control over their lives?
2. How does he distinguish between the power of divine action and human action to dictate the course of events on earth?
3. What does Polybius reveal about Hellenistic religious beliefs and practices? For example, as described here, how did people typically seek to solve the evils and troubles of human existence?

4

Funerary Inscriptions and Epitaphs
Fifth–First Centuries B.C.

These inscriptions and epitaphs provide a glimpse of women's place in the Classical and Hellenistic worlds as described by family members and admirers after their deaths. The words preserved in this form do not simply mark each woman's passing from this world to the next, but they hold her up as an exemplar of female behavior. As in the past, a woman's identity revolved principally around her roles as daughter, wife, and mother. Yet not all women's lives were confined to domestic duties. Some were royal attendants, priestesses, and even physicians, whose daily activities extended into the public sphere.

Archedice, Athens, Fifth Century B.C.

This dust hides Archedice, daughter of Hippias, the most important man in Greece in his day. But though her father husband, brothers, and children were tyrants, her mind was never carried away into arrogance.

Aspasia, Chios, c. 400 B.C.

Of a worthy wife this is the tomb—here, by the road that throngs with people— of Aspasia, who is dead; in response to her noble disposition Euopides set up this monument for her; she was his consort.

Dionysia, Athens, Fourth Century B.C.

It was not clothes, it was not gold that this woman admired during her lifetime; it was her husband and the good sense that she showed in her behaviour. But in return for the youth you shared with him, Dionysia, your tomb is adorned by your husband Antiphilus.

Claudia, Rome, Second Century B.C.

Friend, I have not much to say; stop and read it. This tomb, which is not fair, is for a fair woman. Her parents gave her the name Claudia. She loved her husband in her heart. She bore two sons, one of whom she left on earth, the other beneath it. She was pleasant to talk with, and she walked with grace. She kept the house and worked in wool. That is all. You may go.

An Accomplished Woman, Sardis, First Century B.C.

[An inscription set up by the municipality of Sardis in honour of Menophila, daughter of Hermagenes.] This stone marks a woman of accomplishment and beauty. Who she is the Muses' inscriptions reveal: Menophila. Why she is honoured is shown by a carved lily and an alpha, a book and a basket, and with these a wreath. The book shows that you were wise, the wreath that you wore on your head shows that you were a leader; the letter alpha that you were an only child;

From *Women's Life in Greece and Rome*, ed. Mary R. Lefkowitz and Maureen B. Fant, 2d ed. (Baltimore: Johns Hopkins University Press, 1992), 16–17, 190, 206, 219, 221–22, 263, 266–67, 274.

the basket is a sign of your orderly excellence; the flower shows the prime of your life, which Fate stole away. May the dust lie light on you in death. Alas; your parents are childless; to them you have left tears.

Posilla Senenia, Monteleone Sabino, First Century B.C.

Posilla Senenia, daughter of Quartus and Quarta Senenia, freedwoman of Gaius.

Stranger, stop and, while you are here, read what is written: that a mother was not permitted to enjoy her only daughter, whose life, I believe, was envied by some god.

Since her mother was not allowed to adorn her while she was alive, she does so just the same after death; at the end of her time, [her mother] with this monument honours her whom she loved.

Xenoclea, Piraeus, 360? B.C.

Leaving two young girls, Xenoclea, daughter of Nicarchus, lies here dead; she mourned the sad end of her son, Phoenix, who died out at sea when he was eight years old.

There is no one so ignorant of grief, Xenoclea, that he doesn't pity your fate. You left behind two young girls and died of grief for your son, who has a pitiless tomb where he lies in the dark sea.

Handiwork, Athens, after 350 B.C.

I worked with my hands; I was a thrifty woman, I, Nicarete who lie here.

A Storeroom Attendant, Cape Zoster, near Athens, 56–55 B.C.

[An epitaph by a mother for a daughter who worked for Cleopatra at the royal court of Alexandria.] Her mother, an Athenian woman, raised her to be an attendant of foreign storerooms. She too rushed for her child's sake to come to the palace of the king who had set her over his rich possessions. Yet still she could not bring her daughter back alive. But the daughter has a tomb in Athens instead of on Libyan sand.

Epitaph for a Woman Who Died while Pregnant, Egypt, Second–First Centuries B.C.

Dosithea, daughter of—. Look at these letters on the polished rock. Thallo's son Chaeremon married me in his great house. I die in pain, escaping the pangs of childbirth, leaving the breath of life when I was 25 years old; from a disease which he died of before, I succumbed after. I lie here in Schedia. Wayfarers, as you go by, all of you, say: "Beloved Dosithea, stay well, also among the dead."

A Midwife and Physician, Athens, Fourth Century b.c.

[The memorial tablet represents two women, one seated, one standing, surrounded by infants of both sexes.] Phanostrate, a midwife and physician, lies here. She caused pain to none, and all lamented her death.

A Nurse, Athens, after 350 b.c.

[Epitaph for] Apollodorus the immigrant's daughter, Melitta, a nurse. Here the earth covers Hippostrate's good nurse; and Hippostrate still misses you. "I loved you while you were alive, nurse, I love you still now even beneath the earth and now I shall honour you as long as I live. I know that for you beneath the earth also, if there is reward for the good, honours will come first to you, in the realm of Persephone and of Pluto."

Epitaph for a Priestess, Miletus, Third Century b.c.

Bacchae[1] of the City, say, "Farewell you holy priestess." This is what a good woman deserves. She led you to the mountain and carried all the sacred objects and implements, marching in procession before the whole city. Should some stranger ask for her name: Alcmeonis, daughter of Rhodius, who knew her share of the blessings.

Discussion Questions

1. Judging from these texts, what particular qualities did people admire in women, and why?
2. Scholars have described Greek society at the time as patriarchal. Do the epitaphs and inscriptions support this view? What do they reveal about the social and economic standing of the women they describe?
3. What do these sources suggest about contemporary attitudes toward death?

Comparative Questions

1. Do you see any similarities or difference between Polybius's views on fate and those expressed in the inscriptions and epitaphs?
2. How could Polybius's views be seen as a reaction to the changes glorified by Alexander the Great in his speech?
3. Among the most significant legacies of Alexander the Great was that he brought the Greek and Near Eastern worlds closer together than ever before. After his death, the interaction between Greek and indigenous traditions fueled the political, cultural, and economic development of the eastern Mediterranean region. What evidence of this interaction can you find in the documents?

---

[1]Women worshipers of Dionysus. [— Ed.]

5

The Rise of Rome
c. 753–44 B.C.

S U M M A R Y   When the Roman republic was founded in 509 B.C., few could have foreseen its future as a mighty imperialist state. At the time, Greece was on the threshold of its Golden Age, which was soon followed by Macedonia's meteoric rise to power. Yet throughout this period, the Romans gradually expanded their territories and wealth, so that by the end of the second century B.C., they controlled most of southern Europe, North Africa, and beyond. Victory came at a price, however, as Roman politicians and military leaders came to value their individual successes more than that of the republic. The documents in this chapter help us chart the republic's development from several different angles. Together, they reveal the pillars of the republic—law, tradition, and communal values—while providing a glimpse of their ultimate demise.

1
The Twelve Tables
451–449 B.C.

Although Rome's elite successfully overthrew the Roman monarchy and established the republic in 509 B.C., more challenges lay ahead. For the next two centuries, the city's patricians and the rest of its citizens battled over the course the new government should take and their respective roles in it. Promulgated between 451 and 449 B.C., the Twelve Tables were a turning point in this struggle, marking the republic's first step toward establishing a fair system of justice. Surviving in fragments only, this code, the earliest in Roman law, was based largely on existing customs. The following excerpts illuminate not only the social and economic landscape of early Rome, but also the foundation of Roman jurisprudence.

67

Table I. Proceedings Preliminary to Trial

If the plaintiff summons the defendant to court the defendant shall go. If the defendant does not go the plaintiff shall call a witness thereto. Only then the plaintiff shall seize the defendant.

If the defendant attempts evasion or takes flight the plaintiff shall lay hand on him.

If sickness or age is an impediment he who summons the defendant to court shall grant him a vehicle. If he does not wish he shall not spread a carriage with cushions.

For a freeholder[1] a freeholder shall be surety;[2] for a proletary[3] anyone who wishes shall be surety.

There shall be the same right of bond and of conveyance with the Roman people for a steadfast person and for a person restored to allegiance.[4]

When the parties agree on the matter the magistrate shall announce it.

If they agree not on terms the parties shall state their case before the assembly in the meeting place or before the magistrate in the market place before noon. Both parties being present shall plead the case throughout together.

If one of the parties does not appear the magistrate shall adjudge the case, after noon, in favor of the one present.

If both parties are present sunset shall be the time limit of the proceedings. . . .

Table II. Trial

The penal sum[5] in an action by solemn deposit shall be either 500 asses or 50 asses[6] . . . It shall be argued by solemn deposit with 500 asses, when the property is valued at 1,000 asses or more, but with 50 asses, when the property is valued at less than 1,000 asses. But if the controversy is about the freedom of a person, although the person may be very valuable, yet the case shall be argued by a solemn deposit of 50 asses. . . .

From *Ancient Rome Statutes,* trans. Allan Chester Johnson et al. (Austin: Uniersity of Texas Press, 1961), 9–17.

[1] A taxpayer whose fortune is valued at not less than 1,500 asses.

[2] That is, for his appearance at trial.

[3] A proletary is a nontaxpayer whose fortune is rated at less than a freeholder's.

[4] Apparently this allows the Latin allies who had revolted and afterward returned into allegiance to enjoy the same rights and to use the same legal formulas in contractual matters and in transferring property as those who had remained loyal.

[5] Each litigant deposited a sum with the court as a kind of "wager on oath" that his cause was right. The defeated party forfeited his deposit to the state. On account of the desire to show special favor to persons illegally held as slaves and claiming their freedom, the law made the deposit for them very low, only fifty asses in such cases.

[6] Bronze coin. [— Ed.]

Table III. Execution of Judgment

Thirty days shall be allowed by law for payment of confessed debt and for settlement of matters adjudged in court.

After this time the creditor shall have the right of laying hand on the debtor. The creditor shall hale the debtor into court.

Unless the debtor discharges the debt adjudged or unless someone offers surety for him in court the creditor shall take the debtor with him. He shall bind him either with a thong or with fetters of not less than fifteen pounds in weight, or if he wishes he shall bind him with fetters of more than this weight.

If the debtor wishes he shall live on his own means. If he does not live on his own means the creditor who holds him in bonds shall give him a pound of grits daily. If he wishes he shall give him more.

. . . . Meanwhile they shall have the right to compromise, and unless they make a compromise the debtors shall be held in bonds for sixty days. During these days they shall be brought to the praetor[7] into the meeting place on three successive market days, and the amount for which they have been judged liable shall be declared publicly. Moreover, on the third market day they shall suffer capital punishment or shall be delivered for sale abroad across the Tiber River.

On the third market day the creditors shall cut shares. If they have cut more or less than their shares it shall be without prejudice.

Table IV. Paternal Power

A notably deformed child shall be killed immediately.

To a father . . . shall be given over a son the power of life and death.

If a father thrice surrenders a son for sale the son shall be free from the father.[8]

To repudiate his wife her husband shall order her. . . to have her own property for herself, shall take the keys, shall expel her.[9]

A child born within ten months of the father's death shall enter into the inheritance. . . .

---

[7] A *praetor* is a high elected official. [— Ed.] This statute comes from Gellius, who gives *praetorem* for (the expected) *consulem*. Because the praetorship was not instituted till 367 B.C., Gellius is guilty of anachronism, unless he was enough of an antiquarian to remember that *praetor* was an early equivalent for *consul* or unless *consules* were still called *praetores* in the time of the Twelve Tables.

[8] In the early days of Rome a Roman father could sell his son into slavery. If the buyer freed the son the son reentered his father's control (*patria potestas*).

[9] The formula for a valid repudiation (*repudium*) of the other by either the husband or the wife is said to have contained the words *tuas res tibi habeto* or *agito* (have [or manage] your own property for yourself). Dissolution of marriage by mutual consent is divorce (*divortium*). In either event an essential feature is the husband's return of the wife's dowry, if any, whose investment he had controlled during marriage.

Table V. Inheritance and Guardianship

... Women, even though they are of full age,[10] because of their levity of mind shall be under guardianship ... except vestal virgins, who ... shall be free from guardianship. ...

The conveyable possessions of a woman who is under guardianship of male agnates[11] shall not be acquired by prescriptive right unless they are transferred by the woman herself with the authorization of her guardian. ...

According as a person has made bequest regarding his personal property or the guardianship of his estate so shall be the law.

If anyone who has no direct heir dies intestate the nearest male agnate shall have the estate.

If there is not a male agnate the male clansmen shall have the estate.

Persons for whom by will ... a guardian is not given, for them ... their male agnates shall be guardians.

If a person is insane authority over him and his personal property shall belong to his male agnates and in default of these to his male clansmen. ...

If a Roman citizen freedman dies intestate without a direct heir, to his patron shall fall the inheritance ... from said household ... into said household. ...

Table VI. Ownership and Possession

... If any woman is unwilling to be subjected in this manner[12] to her husband's marital control she shall absent herself for three successive nights in every year and by this means shall interrupt his prescriptive right of each year.[13] ...

One shall not take from framework timber fixed in buildings or in vineyard. ... One shall be permitted neither to remove nor to claim stolen timber fixed in buildings or in vineyards, ... but against the person who is convicted of having fixed such timber there an action for double damages shall be given. ...

---

[10]For females "full age" is twenty-five years. According to the law of this period, a woman never has legal independence: if she is not in her father's power (*potestas*), she is dependent on her husband's control (*manus*) or, if unmarried and fatherless, she is subject to her guardian's governance (*tutela*).

[11]**Agnates** are relatives from the father's family. [— Ed.]

[12]That is, by prescriptive right (*usus*).

[13]This method, the so-called *ius trinoctii* (right of three nights; that is, the right acquired by an absence of three successive nights), enabled a wife to remain married to her husband and yet neither to come into nor to remain in his marital control (*manus*). If the prescriptive right (*usus*) has been interrupted for three consecutive nights annually, the time of *usus* must commence afresh, because the husband's previous possession is considered to be canceled.

Table VII. Real Property

If a watercourse conducted through a public place does damage to a private person the said person shall have the right to bring an action . . . that security against damage may be given to the owner.

. . . . Branches of a tree shall be pruned all around to a height of fifteen feet.

If a tree from a neighbor's farm has been felled by the wind over one's farm, . . . one rightfully can take legal action for that tree to be removed.

. . . It shall be lawful to gather fruit falling upon another's farm. . . .

A slave is ordered in a will to be a free man under this condition: "if he has given 10,000 asses to the heir"; although the slave has been alienated by the heir, yet the slave by giving the said money to the buyer shall enter into his freedom. . . .

Table VIII. Torts or Delicts

. . . If anyone sings or composes an incantation that can cause dishonor or disgrace to another . . . he shall suffer a capital penalty.[14]

If anyone has broken another's limb there shall be retaliation in kind unless he compounds for compensation with him.

. . . If a person breaks a bone of a freeman with hand or by club, he shall undergo a penalty of 300 asses; or of 150 asses, if of a slave.

If one commits an outrage against another the penalty shall be twenty-five asses.

. . . One has broken. . . . One shall make amends.

If a quadruped is said to have caused damage an action shall lie therefor . . . either for surrendering that which did the damage to the aggrieved person . . . or for offering an assessment of the damage.

If fruit from your tree falls onto my farm and if I feed my flock off it by letting the flock onto it . . . no action can lie against me either on the statute concerning pasturage of a flock, because it is not being pastured on your land, or on the statute concerning damage caused by an animal. . . .

If anyone pastures on or cuts by night another's crops obtained by cultivation the penalty for an adult shall be capital punishment and after having been hung up, death as a sacrifice to Ceres. . . . A person below the age of puberty at the praetor's decision shall be scourged and shall be judged as a person either to be surrendered to the plaintiff for damage done or to pay double damages.

Whoever destroys by burning a building or a stack of grain placed beside a house . . . shall be bound, scourged, burned to death, provided that knowingly and consciously he has committed this crime; but if this deed is by accident, that is, by negligence, either he shall repair the damage or if he is unable he shall be corporally punished more lightly.

---

[14]The infliction of this penalty perhaps may have included clubbing (to death), according to one ancient account.

Whoever fells unjustly another's trees shall pay twenty-five asses for each tree.

If a thief commits a theft by night, if the owner kills the thief, the thief shall be killed lawfully.

By daylight . . . if a thief defends himself with a weapon . . . and the owner shall shout.

In the case of all other . . . thieves caught in the act freemen shall be scourged and shall be adjudged as bondsmen to the person against whom the theft has been committed provided that they have done this by daylight and have not defended themselves with a weapon; slaves caught in the act of theft . . . shall be whipped with scourges and shall be thrown from the rock;[15] but children below the age of puberty shall be scourged at the praetor's decision and the damage done by them shall be repaired. . . .

If a patron defrauds a client he shall be accursed.[16]

Unless he speaks his testimony whoever allows himself to be called as a witness or is a scales-bearer shall be dishonored and incompetent to give or obtain testimony. . . .

If anyone pastures on or cuts stealthily by night. . . . another's crops . . . the penalty shall be capital punishment, and, after having been hung up, death as a sacrifice to Ceres, a punishment more severe than in homicide. . . .

Table IX. Public Law

Laws of personal exception shall not be proposed. Laws concerning capital punishment of a citizen shall not be passed . . . except by the Greatest Assembly. . . .

. . .Whoever incites a public enemy or whoever betrays a citizen to a public enemy shall be punished capitally.

For anyone whomsoever to be put to death without a trial and unconvicted . . . is forbidden.

Table X. Sacred Law

A dead person shall not be buried or burned in the city.[17]. . .

. . .Expenses of a funeral shall be limited to three mourners wearing veils and one mourner wearing an inexpensive purple tunic and ten flutists. . . .

---

[15]A southern spur of the Capitoline Hill, which overlooks the Forum.

[16]That is, declared forfeited to the nether gods and liable to be slain by anyone with impunity.

[17]If not derived from a primitive tribal taboo (for certainly vestals, whether chaste or unchaste, were buried in Rome), inhumation on a large scale and in a crowded community not only was insanitary but also took too much space. Cremation could involve hazards from fire (see Cicero, Leg. 2, 23, 58).

Women shall not tear their cheeks or shall not make a sorrowful outcry on account of a funeral.

A dead person's bones shall not be collected that one may make a second funeral.

An exception is for death in battle and on foreign soil. . . .

Table XI. Supplementary Laws

. . . There shall not be intermarriage between plebeians and patricians.

Table XII. Supplementary Laws

It is forbidden to dedicate for consecrated use a thing concerning whose ownership there is a controversy; otherwise a penalty of double the value involved shall be suffered . . .

DISCUSSION QUESTIONS

1. What are the tables' principal concerns?
2. What do these concerns suggest about Roman society at the time?
3. In what ways did these laws represent a triumph for the plebeian class?

2

Roman Women Demonstrate against the Oppian Law
195 B.C.

Women in ancient Rome were most valued as wives and mothers, yet sometimes they stepped outside the boundaries of family life to make their voices heard. In his History of Rome, *the Roman historian Livy (59 B.C.–A.D. 17) reconstructs a heated debate that erupted on one such occasion. In 195 B.C., upper-class women from the city and its environs joined together to demonstrate publicly against the Oppian law, which had been passed during wartime and restricted the amount of finery women could wear and their use of carriages in an effort to reduce friction between rich and poor. Their demand for the law's repeal so that they could once again display their elite status sparked both disdain and sympathy among various leaders, to whom they appealed for support. Each camp, represented here by the consul, Cato, and the tribune, Valerius, claimed to have tradition on its side.*

Amid the anxieties of great wars, either scarce finished or soon to come, an incident occurred, trivial to relate, but which, by reason of the passions it aroused,

From Livy, *History of Rome,* trans. Evan T. Sage, vol. 9 (Cambridge, Mass.: Harvard University Press, 1961), 413–21, 425–39.

developed into a violent contention. Marcus Fundanius and Lucius Valerius, tribunes of the people, proposed to the assembly the abrogation of the Oppian law. The tribune Gaius Oppius had carried this law in the heat of the Punic War, in the consulship of Quintus Fabius and Tiberius Sempronius, that no woman should possess more than half an ounce of gold or wear a parti-coloured garment or ride in a carriage in the City or in a town within a mile thereof, except on the occasion of a religious festival. The tribunes Marcus and Publius Iunius Brutus were supporting the Oppian law, and averred that they would not permit its repeal; many distinguished men came forward to speak for and against it; the Capitoline was filled with crowds of supporters and opponents of the bill. The matrons could not be kept at home by advice or modesty or their husbands' orders, but blocked all the streets and approaches to the Forum, begging the men as they came down to the Forum that, in the prosperous condition of the state, when the private fortunes of all men were daily increasing, they should allow the women too to have their former distinctions restored. The crowd of women grew larger day by day; for they were now coming in from the towns and rural districts. Soon they dared even to approach and appeal to the consuls, the praetors, and the other officials, but one consul, at least, they found adamant, Marcus Porcius Cato, who spoke thus in favour of the law whose repeal was being urged.

"If each of us, citizens, had determined to assert his rights and dignity as a husband with respect to his own spouse, we should have less trouble with the sex as a whole; as it is, our liberty, destroyed at home by female violence, even here in the Forum is crushed and trodden underfoot, and because we have not kept them individually under control, we dread them collectively. . . .

For myself, I could not conceal my blushes a while ago, when I had to make my way to the Forum through a crowd of women. Had not respect for the dignity and modesty of some individuals among them rather than of the sex as a whole kept me silent, lest they should seem to have been rebuked by a consul, I should have said, 'What sort of practice is this, of running out into the streets and blocking the roads and speaking to other women's husbands? Could you not have made the same requests, each of your own husband, at home? Or are you more attractive outside and to other women's husbands than to your own? And yet, not even at home, if modesty would keep matrons within the limits of their proper rights, did it become you to concern yourselves with the question of what laws should be adopted in this place or repealed.' Our ancestors permitted no woman to conduct even personal business without a guardian to intervene in her behalf;[1] they wished them to be under the control of fathers, brothers, husbands; we (Heaven help us!) allow them now even to interfere in public affairs, yes, and to visit the Forum and our informal and formal sessions. What else are they doing now on the streets and at the corners except urging the bill of the tribunes

---

[1] A woman was never *sui iuris* and was not a person in the legal sense. If she was not under the *potestas* of a father or the *manus* of a husband, a *tutor* was appointed to act for her in legal matters.

and voting for the repeal of the law? Give loose rein to their uncontrollable nature and to this untamed creature and expect that they will themselves set bounds to their licence; unless you act, this is the least of the things enjoined upon women by custom or law and to which they submit with a feeling of injustice. It is complete liberty or, rather, if we wish to speak the truth, complete licence that they desire.

"If they win in this, what will they not attempt? Review all the laws with which your forefathers restrained their licence and made them subject to their husbands; even with all these bonds you can scarcely control them. What of this? If you suffer them to seize these bonds one by one and wrench themselves free and finally to be placed on a parity with their husbands, do you think that you will be able to endure them? The moment they begin to be your equals, they will be your superiors. . . . No law is entirely convenient for everyone; this alone is asked, whether it is good for the majority and on the whole. If every law which harms anyone in his private affairs is to be repealed and discarded, what good will it do for all the citizens to pass laws which those at whom they are aimed will at once annul? . . . What pretext, respectable even to mention, is now given for this insurrection of the women? 'That we may glitter with gold and purple,' says one, 'that we may ride in carriages on holidays and ordinary days, that we may be borne through the city as if in triumph over the conquered and vanquished law and over the votes which we have captured and wrested from you; that there may be no limits to our spending and our luxury.' . . .

"She who can buy from her own purse will buy; she who cannot will beg her husband. Poor wretch that husband, both he who yields and he who yields not, since what he will not himself give he will see given by another man. Now they publicly address other women's husbands, and, what is more serious, they beg for a law and votes, and from sundry men they get what they ask. In matters affecting yourself, your property, your children, you, Sir, can be importuned; once the law has ceased to set a limit to your wife's expenditures you will never set it yourself. Do not think, citizens, that the situation which existed before the law was passed will ever return. It is safer for a criminal to go unaccused than to be acquitted; and luxury, left undisturbed, would have been more endurable then than it will be now, when it has been, like a wild beast, first rendered angry by its very fetters and then let loose. My opinion is that the Oppian law should on no account be repealed; whatever is your decision, I pray that all the gods may prosper it."

After this the tribunes of the people who had declared that they would veto the bill spoke briefly to the same effect, and then Lucius Valerius argued thus for the measure which he had proposed: . . . "Now, since that most influential man, the consul Marcus Porcius, has attacked our proposal not only with his authority, which unexpressed would have had enough of weight, but also in a long and carefully-prepared speech, it is necessary to make a brief reply. And yet he used up more words in reproving the matrons than he did in opposing our bill, and, in fact, left it in doubt whether the conduct for which he rebuked the matrons was spontaneous or inspired by us. I propose to defend the measure rather than ourselves, at whom the consul directed his insinuations, more to have something to say than to make a serious charge. This gathering of women he called a sedition and sometimes 'a female secession,' because the matrons, in the streets, had requested you to repeal, in a time of peace and in a rich and prosperous commonwealth, a law that was passed against them in the trying days of a war. . . .

"What new thing, pray, have the matrons done in coming out into the streets in crowds in a case that concerned them? Have they never before this moment appeared in public? Let me unroll your own *Origines* against you.[2] Hear how often they have done it and always, indeed, for the general good. . . . These cases, you say, are different. It is not my purpose to prove them similar; it suffices if I prove that this is nothing new. But what no one wonders that all, men and women alike, have done in matters that concern them, do we wonder that the women have done in a case peculiarly their own? What now have they done? We have proud ears, upon my word, if, although masters do not scorn to hear the petitions of slaves, we complain that we are appealed to by respectable women. . . .

"Laws passed in time of peace, war frequently annuls, and peace those passed in times of war, just as in handling a ship some means are useful in fair weather and others in a storm. Since they are so distinguished by nature, to which class, I ask, does the law which we are trying to repeal seem to belong? Well? Is it an ancient regal law, born with the City itself, or, what is next to that, one inscribed on the twelve tables by the decemvirs appointed to codify the law? Is it a law without which our ancestors held that a matron's virtue could not be preserved, and which we too must fear to repeal lest along with it we repeal the modesty and purity of our women? Who is there, then, who does not know that this is a new law, passed twenty years ago, in the consulship of Quintus Fabius and Tiberius Sempronius? Since for so many years our matrons lived virtuous lives without it, what danger is there that when it is repealed they will rush into riotous luxury? . . .

"Who fails to see that the poverty and distress of the state wrote that law, since all private property had to be diverted to public use, and that the law was to remain in force so long as the cause of its enactment lasted?[3]

"All other orders, all men, will feel the change for the better in the state; shall our wives alone get no enjoyment from national peace and tranquillity? . . . By Hercules, there is mourning and anger among all when they see the wives of allies of the Latin confederacy permitted the ornaments which are refused to them, when they see them decked out in gold and purple, when they see them riding through the city, and themselves following on foot, as if dominion resided in the Latin towns and not in Rome. A thing like this would hurt the feelings even of

---

[2]Valerius quotes or pretends to quote from Cato's own historical work, which treated of early Roman history. The *Origines* had not actually been written at the time of the feminist agitation. The scroll form of the ancient book explains the choice of the verb *revolvam*.

[3]Valerius argues that the Oppian law was merely one of a series of emergency measures by which all elements in the state were affected. To leave this one law in force would mean continued discrimination against one element, the women, after the other methods had been abandoned.

men: what do you think is its effect upon weak women, whom even little things disturb? No offices, no priesthoods, no triumphs, no decorations, no gifts, no spoils of war can come to them; elegance of appearance, adornment, apparel — these are the woman's badges of honour; in these they rejoice and take delight; these our ancestors called the woman's world. What else do they lay aside in times of mourning than purple and jewellery? What do they put on when they have finished their time of mourning? What do they add save more splendid jewels in times of congratulations and thanksgiving? Of course, if you repeal the Oppian law, you will have no authority if you wish to forbid any of these things which now the law forbids; daughters, wives, even sisters of some will be less under control — never while their males survive is feminine slavery shaken off; and even they abhor the freedom which loss of husbands and fathers gives.[4] They prefer to have their finery under your control and not the law's; you too should keep them in control and guardianship and not in slavery, and should prefer the name of father or husband to that of master." . . .

When these speeches against and for the bill had been delivered, the next day an even greater crowd of women appeared in public, and all of them in a body beset the doors of the Bruti, who were vetoing their colleagues' proposal, and they did not desist until the threat of veto was withdrawn by the tribunes. After that there was no question that all the tribes would vote to repeal the law. The law was repealed twenty years after it was passed.

DISCUSSION QUESTIONS

1. Why did Cato object to repealing the Oppian law? What was the basis of his objections?
2. How did Valerius counter Cato's assertions? What evidence did he use?
3. What do both men reveal about contemporary attitudes toward women and their place in the republic?
4. What does this excerpt show about the republic's government?

3

Cicero

On the Commonwealth

54 B.C.

During his illustrious public career in Rome, Marcus Tullius Cicero (106–43 B.C.) was a lawyer, statesman, author, and orator. In each role, he displayed his keen intelligence, fierce patriotism, and high moral standards. This excerpt is from the last chapter of his treatise On the Commonwealth *(54-51 B.C.), written at a time when*

---

[4]Under the stricter Roman law, a woman was throughout life under the *potestas* of her father or his representative or the *manus* of her husband. Valerius makes the point that this domestic authority will be resumed in full with the repeal of the law, and that the same restrictions that the law provided can be enforced if desired.

Rome was rife with political and social conflicts. Here Cicero uses an imaginary conversation between two military heroes from the Punic Wars—Publius Cornelius Scipio Africanus (236–183 b.c.) and his adopted grandson, Publius Cornelius Scipio Aemilianus Africanus the Younger (185–129 b.c.)—to highlight the moral values and sense of destiny that he considered to be at the heart of the republic's greatness. Set in 129 b.c., the story begins with Scipio Africanus speaking to Publius Scipio the Younger in a dream.

Take courage, my Scipio, be not afraid, and carefully remember what I shall say to you.

XI. Do you see that city Carthage, which, though brought under the Roman yoke by me, is now renewing former wars, and cannot live in peace? (and he pointed to Carthage from a lofty spot, full of stars, and brilliant, and glittering;) to attack which city you are this day arrived in a station not much superior to that of a private soldier. Before two years, however, are elapsed, you shall be consul, and complete its overthrow; and you shall obtain, by your own merit, the surname of Africanus, which, as yet, belongs to you no otherwise than as derived from me. And when you have destroyed Carthage, and received the honour of a triumph, and been made censor, and, in quality of ambassador, visited Egypt, Syria, Asia, and Greece, you shall be elected a second time consul in your absence, and, by utterly destroying Numantia, put an end to a most dangerous war.

But when you have entered the Capitol in your triumphal car, you shall find the Roman commonwealth all in a ferment, through the intrigues of my grandson Tiberius Gracchus.

XII. It is on this occasion, my dear Africanus, that you show your country the greatness of your understanding, capacity, and prudence. But I see that the destiny, however, of that time is, as it were, uncertain; for when your age shall have accomplished seven times eight revolutions of the sun, and your fatal hours shall be marked out by the natural product of these two numbers, each of which is esteemed a perfect one, but for different reasons,—then shall the whole city have recourse to you alone, and place its hopes in your auspicious name. On you the senate, all good citizens, the allies, the people of Latium, shall cast their eyes; on you the preservation of the state shall entirely depend. In a word, *if you escape the impious machinations of your relatives*, you will, in quality of dictator, establish order and tranquillity in the commonwealth. . . .

XIII. Now, in order to encourage you, my dear Africanus, continued the shade of my ancestor, to defend the state with the greater cheerfulness, be assured that for all those who have in any way conduced to the preservation, defence, and enlargement of their native country, there is a certain place in heaven, where they shall enjoy an eternity of happiness. For nothing on earth is more

From *The Treatises of M. T. Cicero,* trans. C. D. Yonge (London: Henry G. Bohn, 1853), 381–88.

agreeable to God, the Supreme Governor of the universe, than the assemblies and societies of men united together by laws, which are called States. It is from heaven their rulers and preservers came, and thither they return.

XIV. Though at these words I was extremely troubled, not so much at the fear of death, as at the perfidy of my own relations; yet I recollected myself enough to inquire, whether he himself, my father Paulus, and others whom we look upon as dead, were really living.

Yes, truly, replied he, they all enjoy life who have escaped from the chains of the body as from a prison. But as to what you call life on earth, that is no more than one form of death. But see, here comes your father Paulus towards you! And as soon as I observed him, my eyes burst out into a flood of tears; but he took me in his arms, embraced me, and bade me not weep.

XV. When my first transports subsided, and I regained the liberty of speech, I addressed my father thus:—Thou best and most venerable of parents, since this, as I am informed by Africanus, is the only substantial life, why do I linger on earth, and not rather haste to come hither where you are?

That, replied he, is impossible; unless that God, whose temple is all that vast expanse you behold, shall free you from the fetters of the body, you can have no admission into this place. Mankind have received their being on this very condition, that they should labour for the preservation of that globe, which is situated, as you see, in the midst of this temple, and is called earth.

Men are likewise endowed with a soul, which is a portion of the eternal fires, which you call stars and constellations; and which, being round spherical bodies, animated by divine intelligences, perform their cycles and revolutions with amazing rapidity. It is your duty, therefore, my Publius, and that of all who have any veneration for the Gods, to preserve this wonderful union of soul and body; nor without the express command of him who gave you a soul, should the least thought be entertained of quitting human life, lest you seem to desert the post assigned you by God himself.

But rather follow the examples of your grandfather here, and of me, your father, in paying a strict regard to justice and piety; which is due in a great degree to parents and relations, but most of all to our country. Such a life as this is the true way to heaven, and to the company of those, who, after having lived on earth and escaped from the body, inhabit the place which you now behold.

XVI. This was the shining circle, or zone, whose remarkable brightness distinguishes it among the constellations, and which, after the Greeks, you call the Milky Way.

From thence, as I took a view of the universe, everything appeared beautiful and admirable; for there, those stars are to be seen that are never visible from our globe, and everything appears of such magnitude as we could not have imagined. The least of all the stars, was that removed furthest from heaven, and situated next to the earth; I mean our moon, which shines with a borrowed light. Now the globes of the stars far surpass the magnitude of our earth, which at that distance appeared so exceedingly small, that I could not but be sensibly affected on seeing our whole empire no larger than if we touched the earth as it were at a single point....

While I was busied in admiring the scene of wonders, I could not help casting my eyes every now and then on the earth.

XIX. On which Africanus said—I perceive that you are still employed in contemplating the seat and residence of mankind. But if it appears to you so small, as in fact it really is, despise its vanities, and fix your attention for ever on these heavenly objects. Is it possible that you should attain any human applause or glory that is worth the contending for? The earth, you see, is peopled but in a very few places, and those too of small extent; and they appear like so many little spots of green scattered through vast uncultivated deserts. And those who inhabit the earth are not only so remote from each other as to be cut off from all mutual correspondence, but their situation being in oblique or contrary parts of the globe, or perhaps in those diametrically opposite to yours, all expectation of universal fame must fall to the ground. . . .

If, then, you wish to elevate your views to the contemplation of this eternal seat of splendour, you will not be satisfied with the praises of your fellow-mortals, nor with any human rewards that your exploits can obtain; but Virtue herself must point out to you the true and only object worthy of your pursuit. Leave to others to speak of you as they may, for speak they will. Their discourses will be confined to the narrow limits of the countries you see, nor will their duration be very extensive, for they will perish like those who utter them, and will be no more remembered by their posterity.

XXIV. When he had ceased to speak in this manner, I said—Oh, Africanus, if indeed the door of heaven is open to those who have deserved well of their country, although, indeed, from my childhood, I have always followed yours and my father's steps, and have not neglected to imitate your glory, still I will from henceforth strive to follow them more closely.

Follow them, then, said he, and consider your body only, not yourself, as mortal. For it is not your outward form which constitutes your being, but your mind; not that substance which is palpable to the senses, but your spiritual nature. *Know, then, that you are a god*—for a god it must be which flourishes, and feels, and recollects, and foresees, and governs, regulates and moves the body over which it is set, as the Supreme Ruler does the world which is subject to him. For as that Eternal Being moves whatever is mortal in this world, so the immortal mind of man moves the frail body with which it is connected.

XXV. For whatever is always moving must be eternal, but that which derives its motion from a power which is foreign to itself, when that motion ceases must itself lose its animation.

That alone, then, which moves itself can never cease to be moved, because it can never desert itself. Moreover, it must be the source, and origin, and principle of motion in all the rest. There can be nothing prior to a principle, for all things must originate from it, and it cannot itself derive its existence from any other source, for if it did it would no longer be a principle. And if it had no beginning it can have no end, for a beginning that is put an end to will neither be renewed by any other cause, nor will it produce anything else of itself. All things, therefore, must originate from one source. Thus it follows, that motion must have its source in something which is moved by itself, and which can neither have a beginning nor an end. Otherwise all the heavens and all nature must perish, for it is impossible that they can of themselves acquire any power of producing motion in themselves.

XXVI. As, therefore, it is plain that what is moved by itself must be eternal, who will deny that this is the general condition and nature of minds? For, as everything is inanimate which is moved by an impulse exterior to itself, so what is animated is moved by an interior impulse of its own; for this is the peculiar nature and power of mind. And if that alone has the power of self-motion, it can neither have had a beginning, nor can it have an end.

Do you, therefore, exercise this mind of yours in the best pursuits. And the best pursuits are those which consist in promoting the good of your country. Such employments will speed the flight of your mind to this its proper abode; and its flight will be still more rapid, if, even while it is enclosed in the body, it will look abroad, and disengage itself as much as possible from its bodily dwelling, by the contemplation of things which are external to itself.

This it should do to the utmost of its power. For the minds of those who have given themselves up to the pleasures of the body, paying as it were a servile obedience to their lustful impulses, have violated the laws of God and man; and therefore, when they are separated from their bodies, flutter continually round the earth on which they lived, and are not allowed to return to this celestial region, till they have been purified by the revolution of many ages.

Thus saying he vanished, and I awoke from my dream.

DISCUSSION QUESTIONS

1. Based on this excerpt, what social and political values did Cicero consider essential to leading a good life on earth and gaining eternal life in the hereafter?

2. According to Cicero, how were these values being undermined, and with what consequences?

3. What does this story suggest about the Romans' view of the world and their place in it?

4

The Gracchan Reforms
133 B.C.

By the second century B.C., decades of war had exacted an economic toll on the Roman republic. Despite the vast territories and riches of the elite, many Roman citizens struggled to survive, especially veterans who had been displaced from their farms. In 133 B.C., the newly elected tribune (an official elected by the plebs to protect their rights), Tiberius Gracchus (d. 133 B.C.), initiated a reform program to relieve the people's plight, described here by his biographer, Plutarch (c. A.D. 50–120). As Plutarch vividly recounts, Tiberius's senatorial colleagues vehemently opposed him and viewed his efforts as a threat to their elite status and wealth. Tiberius paid for his reform initiative with his life, and thereby opened a new and violent chapter in Roman politics. Henceforth, Roman citizens became increasingly more divisive and polarized, which set the stage for civil war.

But his brother Gaius has left it us in writing, that when Tiberius went through Tuscany to Numantia, and found the country almost depopulated, there being hardly any free peasants or shepherds, but for the most part only barbarian, imported slaves, he then first conceived the course of policy which in the sequel proved so fatal to his family. Though it is also most certain that the people themselves chiefly excited his zeal and determination in the prosecution of it, by setting up writings upon the porches, walls, and monuments, calling upon him to reinstate the poor citizens in their former possessions.

However, he did not draw up his law without the advice and assistance of those citizens that were then most eminent for their virtue and authority; amongst whom were Crassus, the high-priest, Mucius Scaevola, the lawyer, who at that time was consul, and Claudius Appius, his father-in-law. Never did any law appear more moderate and gentle, especially being enacted against such great oppression and avarice. For they who ought to have been severely punished for transgressing the former laws, and should at least have lost all their titles to such lands which they had unjustly usurped, were notwithstanding to receive a price for quitting their unlawful claims, and giving up their lands to those fit owners who stood in need of help. But though this reformation was managed with so much tenderness, that, all the former transactions being passed over, the people were only thankful to prevent abuses of the like nature for the future, yet, on the other hand, the moneyed men, and those of great estates, were exasperated, through their covetous feelings against the law itself, and against the law giver, through anger and party spirit. They therefore endeavored to seduce the people, declaring that Tiberius was designing a general redivision of lands, to overthrow the government, and put all things into confusion.

But they had no success. For Tiberius, maintaining an honorable and just cause, and possessed of eloquence sufficient to have made a less creditable action appear plausible, was no safe or easy antagonist, when, with the people crowding around the hustings, he took his place, and spoke in behalf of the poor. "The savage beasts," said he, "in Italy, have their particular dens, they have their places of repose and refuge; but the men who bear arms, and expose their lives for the safety of their country, enjoy in the mean time nothing more in it but the air and light; and having no houses or settlements of their own, are constrained to wander from place to place with their wives and children." He told them that the commanders were guilty of a ridiculous error, when, at the head of their armies, they exhorted the common soldiers to fight for their sepulchres and altars; when not any amongst so many Romans is possessed of either altar or monument, neither have they any houses of their own, or hearths of their ancestors to defend. They fought indeed, and were slain, but it was to maintain the luxury and the wealth of other men. They were styled the masters of the world, but in the mean time had not one foot of ground which they could call their own. An harangue of this nature, spoken to an enthusiastic and sympathizing audience, by a person of commanding spirit and genuine feeling, no adversaries at that time were competent to oppose. Forbearing, therefore, all discussion and debate, they addressed themselves to Marcus Octavius, his fellow-tribune, who, being a young man of a steady, orderly character, and an intimate friend of Tiberius, upon this account declined at first the task of opposing him; but at length, over persuaded with the repeated importunities of numerous considerable persons, he was prevailed upon to do so, and hindered the passing of the law; it being the rule that any tribune has a power to hinder an act, and that all the rest can effect nothing, if only one of them dissents. . . .

When the day appointed was come, and the people summoned to give their votes, the rich men seized upon the voting urns, and carried them away by force; thus all things were in confusion. . . .

But when the senate assembled, and could not bring the business to any result, through the prevalence of the rich faction, he [Tiberius] then was driven to a course neither legal nor fair, and proposed to deprive Octavius of his tribuneship, it being impossible for him in any other way to get the law brought to the vote. . . .

He referred the whole matter to the people, calling on them to vote at once, whether Octavius should be deposed or not; and when seventeen of the thirty-five tribes had already voted against him, and there wanted only the votes of one tribe more for his final deprivation, Tiberius put a short stop to the proceedings, and once more renewed his importunities; he embraced and kissed him before all the assembly, begging, with all the earnestness imaginable, that he would neither suffer himself to incur the dishonor, nor him to be reputed the author and promoter of so odious a measure. Octavius, we are told, did seem a little softened and moved with these entreaties; his eyes filled with tears, and he continued silent for a considerable time. But presently looking towards the rich men and proprietors of estates, who stood gathered in a body together, partly for shame, and partly for fear of disgracing himself with them, he boldly bade Tiberius use any severity he pleased. The law for his deprivation being thus voted, Tiberius ordered one of his servants, whom he had made a freeman, to remove Octavius from the rostra, employing his own domestic freed servants in the stead of the public officers. And it made the action seem all the sadder, that Octavius was dragged out in such an ignominious manner. The people immediately assaulted him, whilst the rich men ran in to his assistance. Octavius, with some difficulty, was snatched away, and safely conveyed out of the crowd; though a trusty servant of his, who had placed himself in front of his master that he might assist his escape, in keeping off the multitude, had his eyes struck out, much to the displeasure of Tiberius, who ran with all haste, when he perceived the disturbance, to appease the rioters.

This being done, the law concerning the lands was ratified and confirmed, and three commissioners were appointed, to make a survey of the grounds and see the same equally divided. These were Tiberius himself, Claudius Appius, his father-in-law, and his brother, Caius Gracchus, who at this time was not at Rome, but in the army under the command of Scipio Africanus before Numantia. These things were transacted by Tiberius without any disturbance, none daring to offer any resistance to him. . . .

About this time, king Attalus, surnamed Philometor, died, and Eudemus, a Pergamenian, brought his last will to Rome, by which he had made the Roman people his heirs. Tiberius, to please the people, immediately proposed making a law, that all the money which Attalus left, should be distributed amongst such poor citizens as were to be sharers of the public lands, for the better enabling them to proceed in stocking and cultivating their ground; and as for the cities that were in the territories of Attalus, he declared that the disposal of them did not at all belong to the senate, but to the people, and that he himself would ask their pleasure herein. By this he offended the senate more than ever he had done before.

DISCUSSION QUESTIONS

1. According to Plutarch, what specific factors prompted Tiberius to take action in the people's favor?
2. In his address to the crowd, how does Tiberius characterize his opponents, and why?
3. As portrayed by Plutarch, what fundamental Roman values did Tiberius embody?

COMPARATIVE QUESTIONS

1. Although the Roman republic was not a democracy, its nonelite citizens were an important political force. What evidence can you find in *Roman Women Demonstrate against the Oppian Law* and *The Gracchan Reforms* to support this claim?
2. Do you think Cicero would have agreed with Plutarch's admiring portrait of Tiberius?
3. How do all four documents lend support to the argument that the importance of law was a basic Roman value?
4. What do both Cicero and Plutarch reveal about war's impact on Roman society and politics?

The Roman Empire
C. 44 B.C.–A.D. 284

S U M M A R Y   The civil wars sparked by the assassination of Julius Caesar in 44 B.C. may have marked the death of the Roman republic, but they
also signaled the birth of the Roman Empire. Through masterful political
and military maneuvering, Caesar's heir Octavian (63 B.C.–A.D. 14) emerged from
the wars as Rome's undisputed leader. In recognition of this fact, in A.D. 27, the
Senate granted him special powers and a new title, Augustus ("divinely favored").
He thereupon forged a new system of government that laid the foundations for
two hundred years of peace and prosperity. The documents in this chapter bring
the empire to life in both the words of its emperor and those of the people living
under imperial rule, from an official carrying out imperial orders to a prostitute
advertising her services. In the final document, these words provide a hint of
troubles to come with the emergence of a new religion, Christianity, which threatened traditional beliefs and practices.

1
Augustus
The Accomplishments of Augustus
A.D. 14

*When Augustus assumed power in A.D. 27, he did not cast himself as an innovator
but rather as a guardian of tradition. In fact, over the next four decades, he used republican customs to cloak his true intent: the creation of a monarchical government
in which he reigned supreme. In this document, Augustus describes how he achieved
this goal and thereby transformed the republic into an empire. He composed the text
to describe the course of his rule, and ordered it to be engraved on bronze tablets
upon his death and erected outside his mausoleum in Rome. This copy did not survive, but an almost complete one did, inscribed on the walls of a temple in modern-*

day Ankara, Turkey. Here Augustus commemorates the offices and honors bestowed upon him, his expenditures, and his triumphs in war and peace.

At the age of nineteen, on my own initiative and at my own expense, I raised an army by means of which I liberated the Republic, which was oppressed by the tyranny of a faction.[1] For which reason the senate, with honorific decrees, made me a member of its order in the consulship of Gaius Pansa and Aulus Hirtius [43 B.C.], giving me at the same time consular rank in voting, and granted me the *imperium*.[2] It ordered me as propraetor, together with the consuls, to see to it that the state suffered no harm.[3] Moreover, in the same year, when both consuls had fallen in the war, the people elected me consul and a triumvir for the settlement of the commonwealth.

Those who assassinated my father[4] I drove into exile, avenging their crime by due process of law; and afterwards when they waged war against the state, I conquered them twice on the battlefield [the two battles of Phillippi (42 B.C.)].

I waged many wars throughout the whole world by land and by sea, both civil and foreign, and when victorious I spared all citizens who sought pardon. Foreign peoples who could safely be pardoned I preferred to spare rather than to extirpate. About 500,000 Roman citizens were under military oath to me. Of these, when their terms of service were ended, I settled in colonies or sent back to their own municipalities a little more than 300,000, and to all of these I allotted lands or granted money as rewards for military service. I captured 600 ships, exclusive of those which were of smaller class than triremes.[5] . . .

The dictatorship offered to me in the consulship of Marcus Marcellus and Lucius Arruntius [22 B.C.] by the people and by the senate, both in my absence and in my presence, I refused to accept. In the midst of a critical scarcity of grain I did not decline the supervision of the grain supply, which I so administered that within a few days I freed the whole people from imminent panic and danger

---

From *Roman Civilization: Selected Readings,* ed. Naphtali Lewis and Meyer Reinhold, 3d ed., vol. 1 (New York: Columbia University Press, 1990), 561–72.

[1]Antony and his adherents are meant. The period referred to is late 44 to early 43 B.C., when Octavian (as Augustus was then known) was in coalition with the Senate against Antony.

[2]**Imperium** was the supreme administrative right or power to command (in military, religious, and judicial matters), held first by Roman kings and in the republic by chief officials. [— Ed.]

[3]The formula for the "ultimate decree of the Senate." Augustus refers here to the war against Antony, which culminated in the two battles at Mutina in April of 43 B.C.

[4]Julius Caesar, his adoptive father. Yet in general Augustus sought to distance himself from the image and policies of Julius Caesar.

[5]The naval victories over Sextus Pompey (at Mylae and Naulochus) and over Antony and Cleopatra (at Actium) are meant. *Trirems* were the standard Greek war galley used until the Hellenistic period.

by my expenditures and efforts.[6] The consulship, too, which was offered to me at that time as an annual office for life, I refused to accept.

In the consulship of Marcus Vinicius and Quintus Lucretius, and again in that of Publius Lentulus and Gnaeus Lentulus, and a third time in that of Paullus Fabius Maximus and Quintus Tubero [in 19, 18, and 11 B.C.], though the Roman senate and people unitedly agreed that I should be elected sole guardian of the laws and morals with supreme authority, I refused to accept any office offered me which was contrary to the traditions of our ancestors.[7] The measures which the senate desired at that time to be taken by me I carried out by virtue of the tribunician power.[8] In this power I five times voluntarily requested and was given a colleague by the senate.[9] . . .

I built the following structures:[10] the senate house and the Chalcidicum adjoining it; the temple of Apollo on the Palatine with its porticoes; the temple of the deified Julius; the Lupercal; the portico at the Circus Flaminius, which I allowed to be called Octavia after the name of the man who had built an earlier portico on the same site; the state box at the Circus Maximus; the temples of Jupiter the Smiter and Jupiter the Thunderer on the Capitoline; the temple of Quirinus; the temples of Minerva and Queen Juno and of Jupiter Freedom on the Aventine; the temple of the Lares at the head of the Sacred Way; the temple of the Penates on the Velia; the temple of Youth and the temple of the Great Mother on the Palatine.

I repaired the Capitol and the theater of Pompey with enormous expenditures on both works, without having my name inscribed on them. I repaired the conduits of the aqueducts which were falling into ruin in many places because of age, and I doubled the capacity of the aqueduct called Marcia by admitting a new spring into its conduit. I completed the Julian Forum and the basilica which was between the temple of Castor and the temple of Saturn, works begun and far advanced by my father, and when the same basilica was destroyed by fire, I enlarged its site and began rebuilding the structure, which is to be inscribed with the names of my sons; and in case it should not be completed while I am still alive, I left instructions that the work be completed by my heirs. In my sixth consulship [28 B.C.] I repaired eighty-two temples of the gods in the city, in accordance with a resolution of the senate, neglecting none which at that time required repair. In my seventh consulship [27 B.C.] I reconstructed the Flaminian Way from the city

---

[6]This marks the beginning of the assumption by the Roman emperors of the *cura annonae* ("administration of the grain supply") of Rome as a permanent function of the imperial administration.

[7]In effect, Augustus was thus offered permanent dictatorship in a new guise.

[8]Augustus here refers to his moral and social legislation, the first installments of which were issued in 18 B.C.

[9]Marcus Agrippa, twice; Tiberius, three times.

[10]To identify for the reader each of the public works listed in this and the two following paragraphs would require a series of footnotes longer than the text.

as far as Ariminum, and also all the bridges except the Mulvian and the Minucian.

On my own private land I built the temple of Mars Ultor and the Augustan Forum from spoils of war. On ground bought for the most part from private owners I built the theater adjoining the temple of Apollo which was to be inscribed with the name of my son-in-law Marcus Marcellus. In the Capitol, in the temple of the deified Julius, in the temple of Apollo, in the temple of Vesta, and in the temple of Mars Ultor I consecrated gifts from spoils of war which cost me about 100,000,000 sesterces.[11] In my fifth consulship [29 b.c.] I remitted to the municipalities and colonies of Italy 35,000 pounds of crown gold which they were collecting in honor of my triumphs; and afterwards, whenever I was acclaimed *imperator,* I did not accept the crown gold, though the municipalities and colonies decreed it with the same enthusiasm as before.

I gave a gladiatorial show three times in my own name, and five times in the names of my sons or grandsons; at these shows about 10,000 fought. Twice I presented to the people in my own name an exhibition of athletes invited from all parts of the world, and a third time in the name of my grandson. I presented games in my own name four times, and in addition twenty-three times in the place of other magistrates.[12] On behalf of the college of fifteen, as master of that college, with Marcus Agrippa as my colleague, I celebrated the Secular Games in the consulship of Gaius Furnius and Gaius Silanus. In my thirteenth consulship [2 b.c.] I was the first to celebrate the Games of Mars, which subsequently the consuls, in accordance with a decree of the senate and a law, have regularly celebrated in the succeeding years. Twenty-six times I provided for the people, in my own name or in the names of my sons or grandsons, hunting spectacles of African wild beasts in the circus or in the Forum or in the amphitheaters; in these exhibitions about 3,500 animals were killed. . . .

I brought peace to the sea by suppressing the pirates.[13] In that war I turned over to their masters for punishment nearly 30,000 slaves who had run away from their owners and taken up arms against the state. The whole of Italy voluntarily took an oath of allegiance to me and demanded me as its leader in the war in which I was victorious at Actium.[14] The same oath was taken by the provinces of the Gauls, the Spains, Africa, Sicily, and Sardinia. More than 700 senators served at that time under my standards; of that number eighty-three attained the consulship and about 170 obtained priesthoods, either before that date or subsequently, up to the day on which this document was written.

---

[11]A **sesterce** is a Roman silver coin. [— Ed.]

[12]These were games in the theatrical and circus shows.

[13]The naval war with Sextus Pompey that ended in 36 b.c.

[14]The war against Antony and Cleopatra, who were defeated at Actium in 31 b.c.

I extended the frontiers of all the provinces of the Roman people on whose boundaries were peoples not subject to our empire.[15] I restored peace to the Gallic and Spanish provinces and likewise to Germany, that is to the entire region bounded by the Ocean from Gades to the mouth of the Elbe river. I caused peace to be restored in the Alps, from the region nearest to the Adriatic Sea as far as the Tuscan Sea, without undeservedly making war against any people. My fleet sailed the Ocean from the mouth of the Rhine eastward as far as the territory of the Cimbrians, to which no Roman previously had penetrated either by land or by sea. The Cimbrians, the Charydes, the Semnones, and other German peoples of the same region through their envoys sought my friendship and that of the Roman people.[16] At my command and under my auspices two armies were led almost at the same time into Ethiopia and into Arabia which is called Felix; and very large forces of the enemy belonging to both peoples were killed in battle, and many towns were captured. In Ethiopia a penetration was made as far as the town of Napata, which is next to Meroe; in Arabia the army advanced into the territory of the Sabaeans to the town of Mariba.[17]

I added Egypt to the empire of the Roman people.[18] . . .

I established colonies of soldiers in Africa, Sicily, Macedonia, in both Spanish provinces, in Achaea, Asia, Syria, Narbonese Gaul, and Pisidia. Italy, moreover, has twenty-eight colonies established by me, which in my lifetime have grown to be famous and populous.

A number of military standards lost by other generals I recovered, after conquering the enemy, from Spain, Gaul, and the Dalmatians. The Parthians I compelled to restore to me the spoils and standards of three Roman armies and to seek the friendship of the Roman people as suppliants.[19] The standards, moreover, I deposited in the inner shrine of the temple of Mars Ultor.

Through Tiberius Nero, who was then my stepson and legate, I conquered and subjected to the empire of the Roman people the Pannonian tribes, to which before my principate no army of the Roman people had ever penetrated; and I extended the frontier of Illyricum to the bank of the Danube River. An army of the Dacians which had crossed to our side of the river was conquered and de-

---

[15]The emphasis is on the frontier policy in the west. The eastern provinces were hardly as well stabilized under Augustus.

[16]The reference is to the campaign of A.D. 5, when Tiberius penetrated Germany as far as the Elbe River.

[17]This is the disastrous expedition of Aelius Gallus in 25–24 B.C. against Arabia Felix (Yemen); the punitive Ethiopian expedition under Gaius Petronius in 24–22 B.C. achieved greater success.

[18]On the death of Cleopatra in 30 B.C.

[19]These were the standards lost by Crassus at the battle of Carrhae in 53 B.C. and in Mark Antony's disastrous operations against the Parthians in 36 B.C. They were restored as the result of diplomatic negotiations; Augustus's version is calculated to salve Roman pride.

stroyed under my auspices, and later on, my army crossed the Danube and compelled the Dacian tribes to submit to the orders of the Roman people. . . .

In my sixth and seventh consulships,[20] after I had put an end to the civil wars, having attained supreme power by universal consent, I transferred the state from my own power to the control of the Roman senate and the people. For this service of mine I received the title of Augustus by decree of the senate, and the doorposts of my house were publicly decked with laurels, the civic crown was affixed over my doorway, and a golden shield was set up in the Julian senate house, which, as the inscription on this shield testifies, the Roman senate and people gave me in recognition of my valor, clemency, justice, and devotion. After that time I excelled all in authority, but I possessed no more power than the others who were my colleagues in each magistracy.

When I held my thirteenth consulship, the senate, the equestrian order, and the entire Roman people gave me the title of "father of the country" and decreed that this title should be inscribed in the vestibule of my house, in the Julian senate house, and in the Augustan Forum on the pedestal of the chariot which was set up in my honor by decree of the senate. At the time I wrote this document I was in my seventy-sixth year.

DISCUSSION QUESTIONS

1. What does this document reveal about the ways in which Augustus used tradition to effect political change?
2. Upon what foundation does Augustus's power and success as a ruler seem to rest?
3. What do you think Augustus's primary goal was in composing this account of his political career?

2

Pliny the Younger
Letters
A.D. 111–113

Although Augustus describes his rise to power and ensuing glories in vivid detail, he provides little insight into the mechanics of running a vast and diverse empire. These letters help fill this gap. Pliny the Younger (A.D. 61/62–c. 114) wrote them while serving as governor of Bithynia, a Roman province in modern-day Turkey. A lawyer by training, Pliny had enjoyed a distinguished public career in Rome. Emperor Trajan (r. A.D. 98–117) appointed him to the provincial governorship in A.D. 111 to combat local fiscal mismanagement. Such internal disorder undermined not only the stabil-

---

[20]28 and 27 B.C. The reorganization of 28–27 B.C. put an end to the unlimited powers exercised by Augustus without legal title from the expiration of the triumvirate in 33 B.C. to that date. Augustus justifies his extralegal position by affirming that he held it "by universal consent."

ity of the empire but also the glory of the emperor. More than one hundred pieces of Pliny's official correspondence regarding Bithynia are extant, including his letters to the emperor and the emperor's replies.

Gaius Pliny to the Emperor Trajan: . . . I entered Bithynia some days later than I had hoped, on the 17th of September. Still, I can't complain about the delay, since I did have the auspicious opportunity of celebrating your birthday in the province. Now I am examining the disbursements, revenues, and debtor lists of the municipality of Prusa. The closer my involvement becomes, the more I realize how necessary it is. In a number of cases, funds are being detained by private individuals for various reasons, and besides that, money is being paid out for expenses that are by no means legitimate. That is what I have to tell you, Sir, fresh upon my arrival. (10.17a)

Gaius Pliny to the Emperor Trajan: Sir, the citizens of Prusa have a public bath. It is dingy and old. Naturally they set a high priority on building a new one, and I think you can acquiesce in their aim. There will be the money to do it—first of all, those sums in private hands which I have begun to call in and collect. And second, the townspeople are prepared to apply toward construction the money which has always gone to subsidize the dole of olive oil. But money aside, the prestige of the town and the magnificence of your reign are tied up in this project. (10.23)

Trajan to Pliny: If the construction of a new bath will not overtax the resources of Prusa, then we can acquiesce in their aim—provided that no assessment is levied for it, and that it does not force them to curtail basic operations later on. (10.24)

Gaius Pliny to the Emperor Trajan: While I was touring the other end of the province, a tremendous fire at Nicomedia destroyed many private homes and two public buildings on opposite sides of the same street, the temple of Isis and the civic boosters' center. The fire spread as far as it did thanks both to a high wind and to the shiftlessness of bystanders who chose to stand stock-still contemplating the disaster. But apart from that, the town had no pumps or buckets, or any kind of fire-fighting apparatus at all. Well, the equipment will be procured: I have already given instructions on that score. But please consider, Sir, whether you think a corps of professionals should be formed, limited to 150 persons. (10.33)

From *Rome: Late Republic and Principate*, ed. Walter Emile Kaegi Jr. and Peter White, vol. 2, University of Chicago Readings in Western Civilization (Chicago: University of Chicago Press, 1986), 178–82.

Trajan to Pliny: Your idea that a corps of firemen could be formed at Nicomedia has many precedents in its favor. But we need to keep in mind that your province and particularly the cities in that area have had trouble with just such outfits. Whatever name, for whatever purpose, we give to people who band together, they will turn into political groups in no time at all. Therefore it is better to provide equipment which will be of use in fighting fires, and to put property owners on notice that they should take action themselves, and call on the services of bystanders if circumstances require. (10.34)

Gaius Pliny to the Emperor Trajan: Sir, the citizens of Nicomedia have spent 3,318,000 sesterces on an aqueduct which was halted before it was finished, and finally torn down. They then committed 200,000 sesterces to a second aqueduct, but since this one was also abandoned, they face further expense on top of all the money they have already thrown away, if they are to have any water. I have personally inspected the spring, which is crystal-clear. I think the water should be carried by elevated conduit, according to the original plan, so that the supply will reach more than just the lower levels of the town. A few arches are still in place; some new ones could be built with dressed stone taken from the second project; and I think a fair stretch should be constructed of brick, which is cheaper and more convenient. But it is critically important that you send out a hydraulic engineer or an architect so that past experience here does not repeat itself. I can only assure you that in terms of utility and beauty, this project is fully worthy of your reign. (10.37)

Trajan to Pliny: Arrangements should be made to supply water to the town of Nicomedia. I have every confidence that you will set to work with the diligence that is called for. But, good lord, part of that diligence should be to find out whose fault it was that the Nicomedians wasted so much money up till now. We don't want them just scratching each other's backs with this starting and stopping of aqueducts. Therefore bring to my attention whatever you find out. (10.38)

Gaius Pliny to the Emperor Trajan: Sir, at Nicaea a theater which is well into the construction phase but not finished has already cost more than 10,000,000 sesterces (at any rate, that is what I am told; I have not gone over the books). All wasted, I am afraid. The structure has settled and developed huge cracks, possibly because it was built on soft, wet ground, or because the stone used was weak and porous. The question is to decide whether to continue work, or to stop, or even to demolish the building—the foundations and lower tiers that support the rest look a lot more grandiose than solid to me. With the interruption of work on the main part, some complementary structures which were promised by private citizens (halls outside, and a colonnade around the top of the auditorium) are now in limbo.

Before I arrived here, the citizens of Nicaea also began to restore their gymnasium, which had been destroyed by fire. The plans called for a more spacious complex with more buildings than before. They have already invested a fair amount, but to no practical purpose I fear: the layout is poorly designed and the buildings are too far apart. Furthermore an architect (admittedly a rival of the man who began the job) tells me that though the walls are twenty-two feet thick, they will not take the weight put on them: that is because the core consists of loose stone, and there is no outer girdle of brick.

At Claudiopolis, too, building is underway (if it should not be called excavation) for an enormous public bath sited in a hollow at the foot of a mountain. The funds in this case come from entrance fees which have either been paid already by the new members you graciously added to the town council, or which will be paid when I move to collect.

I am very anxious that good use be made of the public funds at Nicaea, and of your kind involvement (more precious than money) at Claudiopolis. And so I feel obliged to ask that you send out an architect to have a look at the baths as well as the theater. We need to know whether it makes more sense, after all the money that has been spent, to finish the projects as best we can according to plan, or whether to rebuild what needs rebuilding or move what needs moving so that we do not throw good money after bad. (10.39)

Trajan to Pliny: Since you are on the spot, you are in the best position to resolve what should be done about the theater under construction at Nicaea. I will be content to have some note of your decision. Wait till the theater is finished before pressing members of the community to follow through on projects meant to accompany it. These Greeks are in love with gymnasiums, which is probably why the Nicaeans were too ambitious when they started building. They should be content with something that meets their needs. Decide for yourself what to tell the citizens of Claudiopolis about their ill-located bath. It is not possible that you have no architects; there are men with experience and talent in every province. At least you shouldn't imagine that it saves time to have them sent from Rome, as we usually get them from Greece ourselves. (10.40)

Gaius Pliny to the Emperor Trajan: That day on which you saved the realm by taking it under your care, Sir, we commemorated with all the joy the thought inspires in us. We prayed that the gods would bless and protect you for the good of all mankind, because our security is linked to your well-being. I administered the oath of allegiance to the soldiers at the traditional ceremony, and the people of the province manifested their devotion by chiming in. (10.52)

Trajan to Pliny: My dear Pliny, I am grateful for your letter about the fealty and joy which soldiers and civilians alike showed during the ceremonies you organized on the anniversary of my accession. (10.53)

DISCUSSION QUESTIONS

1. What aspects of the local administration within Bithynia do both Pliny and Trajan regard as problematic, and why?
2. What challenges did Pliny face in his efforts to correct these problems?
3. What do these letters reveal about the relationship between central and local authority in the Roman Empire?

3

Notices and Graffiti Describe Life in Pompeii
First Century A.D.

Among the remarkable features of the Roman Empire was not simply its immense expanse, but the many many cities, both new and old, that dotted its landscape. The following messages, graffiti, and election notices from the Roman municipality of Pompeii illuminate the hustle and bustle of urban life in the first century of the empire. Located at the foot of Mount Vesuvius in southern Italy, Pompeii at the time was a thriving commercial city, with a fashionable resort nearby. In A.D. 79, Mount Vesuvius erupted, burying the city in cinders and ash. Although the local population was destroyed or fled, remarkably, the city's buildings were preserved, as were hundreds of announcements painted in red on white-washed walls, along with the scribbles of passersby. Here we see many facets of people's daily lives within the empire, from political appeals to lovesick lamentations.

In the Arrius Pollio block owned by Gnaeus Alleius Nigidius Maius, to let from the fifteenth of next July, shops with their stalls, high-class second-story apartments, and a house. Prospective lessees may apply to Primus, slave of Gnaeus Alleius Nigidus Maius.

On the property owned by Julia Felix, daughter of Spurius, to let from the thirteenth of next August to the thirteenth of the sixth August hence, or five consecutive years, the élite Venus Baths, shops, stalls, and second-story apartments. Interested parties may apply to the lessor in the matter.

The fruit dealers together with Helvius Vestalis unanimously urge the election of Marcus Holconius Priscus as duovir[1] with judicial power.

The goldsmiths unanimously urge the election of Gaius Cuspius Pansa as aedile.[2]

I ask you to elect Gaius Julius Polybius aedile. He gets good bread [for us].

The muleteers urge the election of Gaius Julius Polybius as duovir.

The worshippers of Isis unaminously urge the election of Gnaeus Helvius Sabinus as aedile.

From *Roman Civilization: Selected Readings*, ed. Naphtali Lewis and Meyer Reinhold, 3d ed., vol. 2 (New York: Columbia University Press, 1990), 126–27, 237–38, 276–78.

[1]A **duovir** was one of two chief magistrates of Roman municipalities. [— Ed.]

[2]An **aedile** was a municipal administrator. [— Ed.]

Proculus, make Sabinus aedile and he will do as much for you.

His neighbors urge you to elect Lucius Statius Receptus duovir with judicial power; he is worthy. Aemilius Celer, a neighbor, wrote this. May you take sick if you maliciously erase this!

Satia and Petronia support and ask you to elect Marcus Casellius and Lucius Albucius aediles. May we always have such citizens in our colony!

I ask you to elect Epidius Sabinus duovir with judicial power. He is worthy, a defender of the colony, and in the opinion of the respected judge Suedius Clemens and by agreement of the council, because of his services and uprightness, worthy of the municipality. Elect him!

If upright living is considered any recommendation, Lucretius Fronto is well worthy of the office.

Genialis urges the election of Bruttius Balbus as duovir. He will protect the treasury.

I ask you to elect Marcus Cerrinius Vatia to the aedileship. All the late drinkers support him. Florus and Fructus wrote this.

The petty thieves support Vatia for the aedileship.

I ask you to elect Aulus Vettius Firmus aedile. He is worthy of the municipality. I ask you to elect him, ballplayers. Elect him!

I wonder, O wall, that you have not fallen in ruins from supporting the stupidities of so many scribblers.[3]

Twenty pairs of gladiators of Decimus Lucretius Satrius Valens, life-time flamen[4] of Nero son of Caesar Augustus, and ten pairs of gladiators of Decimus Lucretius Valens, his son, will fight at Pompeii on April 8, 9, 10, 11, 12. There will be a full card of wild beast combats, and awnings [for the spectators]. Aemilius Celer [painted this sign], all alone in the moonlight.

Market days: Saturday in Pompeii, Sunday in Nuceria, Monday in Atella, Tuesday in Nola, Wednesday in Cumae, Thursday in Puteoli, Friday in Rome.

---

[3]Unlike the others, this inscription is a *graffito,* scratched on the wall.

[4]A **flamen** was a priest.[— Ed.]

6th: cheese 1, bread 8, oil 3, wine 3[5]

7th: bread 8, oil 5, onions 5, bowl 1, bread for the slave[?] 2, wine 2

8th: bread 8, bread for the slave[?] 4, grits 3

9th: wine for the winner 1 *denarius,* bread 8, wine 2, cheese 2

10th: . . . 1 *denarius,* bread 2, for women 8, wheat 1 *denarius,* cucumber 1, dates 1, incense 1, cheese 2, sausage 1, soft cheese 4, oil 7

Pleasure says: "You can get a drink here for an *as,* a better drink for two, Falernian[6] for four.

A copper pot is missing from this shop. 65 sesterces reward if anybody brings it back, 20 sesterces if he reveals the thief so we can get our property back.

The weaver Successus loves the innkeeper's slave girl, Iris by name. She doesn't care for him, but he begs her to take pity on him. Written by his rival. So long.

[Answer by the rival:] Just because you're bursting with envy, don't pick on a handsomer man, a lady-killer and a gallant.

[Answer by the first writer:] There's nothing more to say or write. You love Iris, who doesn't care for you.

Take your lewd looks and flirting eyes off another man's wife, and show some decency on your face!

Anybody in love, come here. I want to break Venus' ribs with a club and cripple the goddess' loins. If she can pierce my tender breast, why can't I break her head with a club?

I write at Love's dictation and Cupid's instruction;
But damn it! I don't want to be a god without you.

[A prostitute's sign:] I am yours for 2 *asses* cash.

DISCUSSION QUESTIONS

1. Based on these messages and notices, how would you describe life in Pompeii? What did people do for a living? What did the city look like?

2. What do the election announcements reveal about the residents' political expectations and their role in local politics?

3. Did any of these messages surprise you? Where might you find similar messages today?

---

[5]The initial number is the day of the months, the numbers following the items of food indicate expenditures in *asses,* except where *denarii* are specified. A *denarius* was a Roman silver coin originally valued at ten, and later sixteen, asses. It was the equivalent of the Greek drachma. [— Ed.]

[6]One of the prized wines of the Italian countryside (named after a district in Campania), best known from the poems of Horace that sing its praises.

4

Interrogation of Christians
A.D. 180

Despite their immense power and wealth, Roman emperors in the second century faced many threats, from political infighting to attacks on the empire's frontiers. Another, more novel menace to tradition also gained ground at this time, Christianity, as it gradually spread from Palestine to other regions in the empire. Although Christians were a minority, many people, including Roman authorities, perceived their renunciation of traditional religious beliefs as a danger to peace and social order. This account of the interrogation of six Christians in the province of Africa by an imperial official, Vigellius Saturninus, brings this clash of faith and politics to life. The document also reveals the crucial role persecution played in shaping Christians' sense of identity and mission. Despite all efforts to crush them, Christians and their church would ultimately survive and prosper.

On July 17, Speratus, Nartzalus, Cittinus, Donata, Secunda, and Vestia were put on trial in the [governor's] council chamber at Carthage. The proconsul[1] Saturninus said, "You can secure the indulgence of our lord the emperor if you return to your senses."

Speratus said, "We have never done any wrong; we have lent ourselves to no injustice; we have never spoken ill of anyone; but when we have been ill-treated, we have given thanks, because we honor our emperor."

The proconsul Saturninus said, "We, also, are religious, and our religion is simple; and we swear by the *genius* [spirit] of our lord the emperor, and pray for his welfare, as you too ought to do."

Speratus said, "If you grant me your undivided attention, I will tell you the mystery of simplicity."

Saturninus said, "I shall not grant you a hearing, if you begin to speak evil about our sacred rites; but swear rather by the *genius* of our lord the emperor."

Speratus said, "The empire of this world I do not recognize; but rather I serve that God whom no man has seen nor can see with human eyes. I have not committed theft; if I buy anything, I pay the tax, because I recognize my Lord, the King of kings and Emperor of all peoples."

The proconsul Saturninus said to the others, "Cease to be of this persuasion."

Speratus said, "It is an evil persuasion to commit murder, or to bear false witness."

The proconsul Saturninus said, "Do not participate in this madness."

Cittinus said, "We have none other to fear except only our Lord God who is in heaven."

From *Roman Civilization: Selected Readings*, ed. Naphtali Lewis and Meyer Reinhold, 3d ed., vol. 1 (New York: Columbia University Press, 1990), 564–66.

[1]A **proconsul** was a provincial governor. [— Ed.]

Donata said, "Honor to Caesar as to Caesar, but fear to God."

Vestia said, "I am a Christian."

Secunda said, "What I am, that I wish to be."

The proconsul Saturninus said to Speratus, "Do you persist in being a Christian?"

Speratus said, "I am a Christian." And they all concurred with him.

The proconsul Saturninus said, "Do you desire some time to reconsider?"

Speratus said, "In a matter so just there is no reconsidering."

The proconsul Saturninus said, "What are the things in your box?"

Speratus said, "The Books, and the letters of Paul, a just man."

The proconsul Saturninus said, "Take a postponement of thirty days and reconsider."

Speratus said again, "I am a Christian." And they all concurred with him.

The proconsul Saturninus read out the decree from the tablet: "Since Speratus, Nartzalus, Cittinus, Donata, Vestia, Secunda, and the rest who have confessed that they live according to the rite of the Christians have obstinately persevered when an opportunity was offered them to return to the practice of the Romans, it is my decision that they be punished with the sword."

Speratus said, "We give thanks to God."

Nartzalus said, "Today we are martyrs in heaven; thanks to God!"

The proconsul Saturninus ordered the herald to proclaim: "I have ordered the execution of Speratus, Nartzalus, Cittinus, Veturius, Felix, Aquilinus, Laetantius, Januaria, Generosa, Vestia, Donata, and Secunda."

They all said, "Thanks be to God!"

And so they were crowned with martyrdom all together: and they reign with the Father and the Son and the Holy Ghost forever and ever. Amen.

DISCUSSION QUESTIONS

1. Based on this document, what were some of the basic tenets of the Christian faith at this time?

2. In what ways were these tenets at odds with traditional Roman beliefs and rites?

3. What does this document suggest about the means by which Christianity spread and gained adherents?

COMPARATIVE QUESTIONS

1. Based on his *Accomplishments,* how would you describe Augustus's pattern for effective rule? In what ways did Emperor Trajan conform to this pattern as revealed in his exchange of letters with Pliny?

2. What do Pliny's letters and the messages, graffiti, and election notices from Pompeii reveal about municipal affairs in cities under Roman rule?

3. In what ways do all four documents convey a similar image of the Roman emperor? How did Christians, as described in Document 4, challenge this image?

7

The Transformation of the Roman Empire
C. A.D. 284–600

S U M M A R Y   The Roman Empire had faced many challenges since its formation at the end of the first century B.C., but by the fourth century A.D., the forces of change proved too powerful to resist, as the documents in this chapter attest. Christianity was spreading far and wide, even gaining the allegiance of the emperor, Constantine, in 312. Although polytheism persisted, over the course of the fourth century Christianity gained the upper hand, and this permanently transformed Roman culture and society. At the same time, waves of Germanic peoples penetrated the empire's borders and migrated westward. Here they eventually established their own kingdoms that replaced imperial government. These new regimes became the heirs of Roman civilization in the West, setting the stage for the development of medieval Europe, whereas in the East the imperial legacy lived on in the Byzantine Empire.

1
Symmachus and St. Ambrose
The Altar of Victory Sparks a Religious Debate
A.D. 384

Although Christianity spread rapidly after Constantine's conversion and the promulgation of his edict of religious toleration in 313, the transformation from polytheist empire to Christian state did not come easily. Polytheism persisted, especially within elite social circles. The subject of this document and the next illuminates the conflict between paganism and Christianity with particular clarity. The emperor's removal of the Altar of Victory in 382 from the Senate house generated a heated response from a prominent Roman politician, Aurelius Symmachus, who demanded its restoration in his memorial to Emperor Valentinian, excerpted here. When the

*prominent church leader St. Ambrose (A.D. 339–397) caught wind of the memorial,
he voiced his opposing views to Valentinian in the following letter. Ambrose's words
foreshadowed the future. In 391, Christianity became the official religion of the
empire.*

Ambrose, Bishop, to the most blessed Prince and most Christian Emperor Valentinian.

As all men who live under the Roman sway engage in military service under
you, the Emperors and Princes of the world, so too do you yourselves owe service
to Almighty God and our holy faith. For salvation is not sure unless everyone
worship in truth the true God, that is the God of the Christians, under Whose
sway are all things; for He alone is the true God, Who is to be worshipped from
the bottom of the heart; for "the gods of the heathen," as Scripture says, "are devils."

Now everyone is a soldier of this true God, and he who receives and worships Him in his inmost spirit, does not bring to His service dissimulation, or
pretence, but earnest faith and devotion. And if, in fine, he does not attain to this,
at least he ought not to give any countenance to the worship of idols and to profane ceremonies. For no one deceives God, to whom all things, even the hidden
things of the heart, are manifest.

Since, then, most Christian Emperor, there is due from you to the true God
both faith and zeal, care and devotion for the faith, I wonder how the hope has
risen up to some, that you would feel it a duty to restore by your command altars
to the gods of the heathen [polytheists], and furnish the funds requisite for profane sacrifices; for whatsoever has long been claimed by either the imperial or
the city treasury you will seem to give rather from your own funds, than to be
restoring what is theirs. . . .

If to-day any heathen Emperor should build an altar, which God forbid, to
idols, and should compel Christians to come together thither, in order to be
amongst those who were sacrificing, so that the smoke and ashes from the altar,
the sparks from the sacrilege, the smoke from the burning might choke the breath
and throats of the faithful; and should give judgment in that court where members were compelled to vote after swearing at the altar of an idol (for they explain
that an altar is so placed for this purpose, that every assembly should deliberate
under its sanction, as they suppose, though the Senate is now made up with a
majority of Christians), a Christian who was compelled with a choice such as
this to come to the Senate, would consider it to be persecution, which often happens, for they are compelled to come together even by violence. Are these Christians, when you are Emperor, compelled to swear at a heathen altar? What is an
oath, but a confession of the divine power of Him Whom you invoke as watcher

From *A Select Library of Nicene and Post-Nicene Fathers of the Christian Church*, 2d ser.,
vol. 10 (New York: Christian Literature Co., 1896), 411–15.

over your good faith? When you are Emperor, this is sought and demanded that you should command an altar to be built, and the cost of profane sacrifices to be granted.

But this cannot be decreed without sacrilege, wherefore I implore you not to decree or order it, nor to subscribe to any decrees of that sort. I, as a priest of Christ, call upon your faith, all of us bishops would have joined in calling upon you, were not the report so sudden and incredible, that any such thing had been either suggested in your council, or petitioned for by the Senate. But far be it from the Senate to have petitioned this, a few heathen are making use of the common name. . . .

I call upon your own feelings not to determine to answer according to this petition of the heathen, nor to attach to an answer of such a sort the sacrilege of your subscription. Refer to the father of your Piety, the Emperor Theodosius, whom you have been wont to consult in almost all matters of greater importance. Nothing is greater than religion, nothing more exalted than faith. . . .

The Memorial of Symmachus, Prefect of the City.

As soon as the most honourable Senate, always devoted to you, knew that crimes were made amenable to law, and that the reputation of late times was being purified by pious princes, it, following the example of a more favourable time, gave utterance to its long suppressed grief, and bade me be once again the delegate to utter its complaints. . . .

In the exercise, therefore, of a twofold office, as your Prefect I attend to public business, and as delegate I recommend to your notice the charge laid on me by the citizens. . . .

For to what is it more suitable that we defend the institutions of our ancestors, and the rights and destiny of our country, than to the glory of these times, which is all the greater when you understand that you may not do anything contrary to the custom of your ancestors? We demand then the restoration of that condition of religious affairs which was so long advantageous to the state. . . .

Who is so friendly with the barbarians as not to require an Altar of Victory? We will be careful henceforth, and avoid a show of such things. But at least let that honour be paid to the name which is refused to the goddess — your fame, which will last for ever, owes much and will owe still more to victory. Let those be averse to this power, whom it has never benefited. Do you refuse to desert a patronage which is friendly to your triumphs? That power is wished for by all, let no one deny that what he acknowledges is to be desired should also be venerated.

But even if the avoidance of such an omen were not sufficient, it would at least have been seemly to abstain from injuring the ornaments of the Senate House. Allow us, we beseech you, as old men to leave to posterity what we received as boys. . . .

Where shall we swear to obey your laws and commands? by what religious sanction shall the false mind be terrified, so as not to lie in bearing witness? All things are indeed filled with God, and no place is safe for the perjured, but to be urged in the very presence of religious forms has great power in producing a fear of sinning. That altar preserves the concord of all, that altar appeals to the good faith of each, and nothing gives more authority to our decrees than that the whole of our order issues every decree as it were under the sanction of an oath. . . .

Let us now suppose that Rome is present and addresses you in these words: "Excellent princes, fathers of your country, respect my years to which pious rites have brought me. Let me use the ancestral ceremonies, for I do not repent of them. Let me live after my own fashion, for I am free. This worship subdued the world to my laws, these sacred rites repelled Hannibal from the walls, and the Senones from the capitol. Have I been reserved for this, that in my old age I should be blamed? I will consider what it is thought should be set in order, but tardy and discreditable is the reformation of old age."

We ask, then, for peace for the gods of our fathers and of our country. It is just that all worship should be considered as one. We look on the same stars, the sky is common, the same world surrounds us. What difference does it make by what pains each seeks the truth? We cannot attain to so great a secret by one road.

Discussion Questions

1. Why does Symmachus think that the restoration of the Altar of Victory is so important? What does the altar represent for him and his non-Christian colleagues?

2. Why is Ambrose opposed to Symmachus's petition? What does the Altar of Victory symbolize to him?

3. Based on Symmachus's and Ambrose's views, why do you think Christians and polytheists were increasingly at odds in this period?

2

St. Jerome
Letter 107
A.D. 403

The Christianization of the Roman Empire extended beyond public debates into family life, as this letter elucidates. Biblical scholar and monk St. Jerome (A.D. c. 345–420) wrote the letter in A.D. 403 to Laeta, a Christian woman in Rome, regarding how best to educate her daughter, Paula. For Jerome, the answer was simple: send her to a monastery. There she would be trained to be a temple of God, shielded from the world's evils. Jerome's advice reveals the growing appeal of monasticism and its underlying ascetic ideals, which elevated virginity and sexual renunciation as the highest of Christian virtues. Monasticism thus offered women an identity outside the confines of their traditional roles as wives and mothers. Laeta heeded Jerome's advice, and Paula eventually became the head of a female monastery in Bethlehem, where Jerome himself lived and worked.

Letter CVII
To Laeta[1]
A Girl's Education
Written A.D. 403

The blessed apostle Paul, writing to the Corinthians and instructing Christ's novice church in the ways of sacred discipline, among his other precepts laid down also the following rule: "The woman that hath an husband that believeth not, and if he be pleased to dwell with her, let her not leave him. For the unbelieving husband is sanctified by the believing wife, and the unbelieving wife is sanctified by the believing husband; else were your children unclean, but now they are holy."[2] . . . You yourself are the child of a mixed marriage; but now you and my dear Toxotius are Paula's parents. Who would ever have believed that the granddaughter of the Roman pontiff Albinus would be born in answer to a mother's vows; that the grandfather would stand by and rejoice while the baby's yet stammering tongue cried "Alleluia"; and that even the old man would nurse in his arms one of Christ's own virgins? . . . Christians are not born but made. The gilded Capitol to-day looks dingy, all the temples in Rome are covered with soot and cobwebs, the city is shaken to its foundations, and the people hurry past the ruined shrines and pour out to visit the martyrs' graves. . . .

Even in Rome now heathenism [polytheism] languishes in solitude. Those who once were the gods of the Gentiles are left beneath their deserted pinnacles to the company of owls and night-birds. The army standards bear the emblem of the cross. The purple robes of kings and the jewels that sparkle on their diadems are adorned with the gibbet sign that has brought to us salvation. To-day even the Egyptian Serapis[3] has become a Christian: Marnas[4] mourns in his prison at Gaza, and fears continually that his temple will be overthrown. From India, from Persia and from Ethiopia we welcome crowds of monks every hour. The Armenians have laid aside their quivers, the Huns are learning the psalter, the frosts of Scythia are warmed by the fire of faith. The ruddy, flaxen-haired Getae carry tent-

From *Select Letters of St. Jerome,* trans. F. A. Wright (Cambridge, Mass.: Harvard University Press, 1963), 338–47, 351, 359, 363–67.

[1]Laeta, to whom this letter was sent in A.D. 403, married Toxotius, son of Paula and Toxotius, "in whose veins ran the noble blood of Aeneas" (Letter CVIII, 4). She herself was the daughter of a pagan, the pontiff Albinus, and had written to Jerome concerning the education of her child, Paula. The advice given in this letter — that the little girl should be sent to Bethlehem to be educated by her grandmother Paula and her aunt Eustochium — was accepted, and she eventually succeeded Eustochium as head of the nunnery there.

[2]1 Corinthians, vii. 13.

[3]In A.D. 389, the temple of Serapis at Alexandria was pulled down, and a Christian church was built on the site.

[4]The chief Syrian god in Gaza.

churches about with their armies; and perhaps the reason why they fight with us on equal terms is that they believe in the same religion. . . .

It was my intention, in answer to your prayers and those of the saintly Marcella, to direct my discourse to a mother, that is, to you, and to show you how to bring up our little Paula, who was consecrated to Christ before she was born, the child of prayers before the hour of conception. In our own days we have seen something such as we read of in the prophets: Hannah exchanged her barrenness for fruitful motherhood, you have exchanged a fertility bound up with sorrow for children who will live for ever. I tell you confidently that you who have given your first-born to the Lord will receive sons at His hand. The first-born are the offerings due under the Law. . . .

Thus must a soul be trained which is to be a temple of God. It must learn to hear nothing and to say nothing save what pertains to the fear of the Lord. It must have no comprehension of foul words, no knowledge of worldly songs, and its childish tongue must be imbued with the sweet music of the psalms. Let boys with their wanton frolics be kept far from Paula: let even her maids and attendants hold aloof from association with the worldly, lest they render their evil knowledge worse by teaching it to her. Have a set of letters made for her, of boxwood or of ivory, and tell her their names. Let her play with them, making play a road to learning, and let her not only grasp the right order of the letters and remember their names in a simple song, but also frequently upset their order and mix the last letters with the middle ones, the middle with the first. Thus she will know them all by sight as well as by sound. When she begins with uncertain hand to use the pen, either let another hand be put over hers to guide her baby fingers, or else have the letters marked on the tablet so that her writing may follow their outlines and keep to their limits without straying away. Offer her prizes for spelling, tempting her with such trifling gifts as please young children. Let her have companions too in her lessons, so that she may seek to rival them and be stimulated by any praise they win. You must not scold her if she is somewhat slow; praise is the best sharpener of wits. . . .

Her very dress and outward appearance should remind her of Him to whom she is promised. Do not pierce her ears, or paint with white lead and rouge the cheeks that are consecrated to Christ. Do not load her neck with pearls and gold, do not weigh down her head with jewels, do not dye her hair red and thereby presage for her the fires of hell. . . .

Let her every day repeat to you a portion of the Scriptures as her fixed task. A good number of lines she should learn by heart in the Greek, but knowledge of the Latin should follow close after. If the tender lips are not trained from the beginning, the language is spoiled by a foreign accent and our native tongue debased by alien faults. You must be her teacher, to you her childish ignorance must look for a model. Let her never see anything in you or her father which she would do wrong to imitate. Remember that you are a virgin's parents and that you can teach her better by example than by words. Flowers quickly fade; violets, lilies, and saffron are soon withered by a baleful breeze. Let her never appear in public without you, let her never visit the churches and the martyrs' shrines except in your company. Let no youth or curled dandy ogle her. Let our little virgin never stir a finger's breadth from her mother when she attends a vigil or an all-night service. I would not let her have a favourite maid into whose ear she might frequently whisper: what she says to one, all ought to know. . . .

If ever you visit the country, do not leave your daughter behind at Rome. She should have neither the knowledge nor the power to live without you, and should tremble to be alone. Let her not converse with worldlings [worldly people], nor associate with virgins who neglect their vows. Let her not be present at slaves' weddings, nor take part in noisy household games. I know that some people have laid down the rule that a Christian virgin should not bathe along with eunuchs or with married women, inasmuch as eunuchs are still men at heart, and women big with child are a revolting sight. For myself I disapprove altogether of baths in the case of a full-grown virgin. She ought to blush at herself and be unable to look at her own nakedness. If she mortifies and enslaves her body by vigils and fasting, if she desires to quench the flame of lust and to check the hot desires of youth by a cold chastity, if she hastens to spoil her natural beauty by a deliberate squalor, why should she rouse a sleeping fire by the incentive of baths?[5] . . .

You will answer: "How shall I, a woman of the world living in crowded Rome, be able to keep all these injunctions?" Do not then take up a burden which you cannot bear. . . . Let her be reared in a monastery amid bands of virgins, where she will learn never to take an oath, and to regard a lie as sacrilege. Let her know nothing of the world, but live like the angels; let her be in the flesh and without the flesh, thinking all mankind to be like herself.

DISCUSSION QUESTIONS

1. At the time Jerome wrote this letter, Christianity had been the official religion of the empire for more than a decade. What explicit signs of Christianity's triumph does Jerome describe?

2. How does Jerome think Paula should be raised, and why?

3. What do Jerome's views on Paula's education suggest about Christianity's attitudes toward women in general and female sexuality in particular?

3

The Burgundian Code
c. 475–525

The migration of Germanic tribes into the West changed imperial politics and society just as profoundly as Christianity did. These newcomers gradually formed independent kingdoms based on a mixture of their own and Roman traditions, which soon superseded Roman provincial government. Law codes that were established by Germanic leaders from the fifth century on were a crucial component of their state-building efforts. Rome provided a powerful precedent in this regard, with its empha-

---

[5]That is, the Roman, or as we call them "Turkish," baths.

sis on written law as both the basis of social order and a manifestation of state authority. These excerpts are drawn from one of the most comprehensive early Germanic law codes, the Burgundian Code, compiled by the kings of the Burgundians, an East Germanic tribe, in the late fifth and early sixth centuries. At this time, they ruled over a large kingdom encompassing much of the Roman province of Gaul.

First Constitution

In the name of God in the second year of the reign of our lord the most glorious king Gundobad, this book concerning laws past and present, and to be preserved throughout all future time, has been issued on the fourth day before the Kalends of April (March 29) at Lyons. . . .

For the love of justice, through which God is pleased and the power of earthly kingdoms acquired, we have obtained the consent of our counts (*comites*) and leaders (*proceres*), and have desired to establish such laws that the integrity and equity of those judging may exclude all rewards and corruptions from themselves.

Therefore all administrators (*administrantes*) and judges must judge from the present time on between Burgundians and Romans according to our laws which have been set forth and corrected by a common method, to the end that no one may hope or presume to receive anything by way of reward or emolument from any party as the result of the suits or decisions; but let him whose case is deserving obtain justice and let the integrity of the judge alone suffice to accomplish this. . . .

Therefore let all nobles (*obtimates*), counsellors (*consiliarii*), bailiffs (*domestici*), mayors of our palace (*maiores domus nostrae*), chancellors (*cancellarii*), counts (*comites*) of the cities or villages, Burgundian as well as Roman, and all appointed judges and military judges (*judices militantes*) know that nothing can be accepted in connection with those suits which have been acted upon or decided, and that nothing can be sought in the name of promise or reward from those litigating; nor can the parties (to the suit) be compelled by the judge to make a payment in order that they may receive anything (from their suit). . . .

Indeed if any judge, barbarian as well as Roman, shall not render decisions according to those provisions which the laws contain because he has been prevented by ignorance or negligence, and he has been diverted from justice for this reason, let him know that he must pay thirty solidi[1] and that the case must be judged again on behalf of the aggrieved parties. . . .

From *The Burgundian Code*, trans. Katherine Fischer Drew (Philadelphia: University of Pennsylvania Press, 1972), 17–24, 30–33, 40–47.

[1]A **solidi** was a gold coin. [— Ed.]

Of Murders.

If anyone presumes with boldness or rashness bent on injury to kill a native freeman of our people of any nation or a servant of the king, in any case a man of barbarian tribe, let him make restitution for the committed crime not otherwise than by the shedding of his own blood.

We decree that this rule be added to the law by a reasonable provision, that if violence shall have been done by anyone to any person, so that he is injured by blows of lashes or by wounds, and if he pursues his persecutor and overcome by grief and indignation kills him, proof of the deed shall be afforded by the act itself or by suitable witnesses who can be believed. Then the guilty party shall be compelled to pay to the relatives of the person killed half his wergeld according to the status of the person: that is, if he shall have killed a noble of the highest class (*optimas nobilis*), we decree that the payment be set at one hundred fifty solidi, i.e., half his wergeld; if a person of middle class (*mediocris*), one hundred solidi; if a person of the lowest class (*minor persona*), seventy-five solidi.

If a slave unknown to his master presumes to kill a native freeman, let the slave be handed over to death, and let the master not be made liable for damages.

If the master knows of the deed, let both be handed over to death.

If the slave himself flees (*defuerit*) after the deed, let his master be compelled to pay thirty solidi to the relatives of the man killed for the value (wergeld) of the slave.

Similarly in the case of royal slaves, in accordance with the status of such persons, let the same condition about murderers be observed.

In such cases let all know this must be observed carefully, that the relatives of the man killed must recognize that no one can be pursued except the killer; because just as we have ordered the criminals to be destroyed, so we will suffer the innocent to sustain no injury. . . .

Let Burgundians and Romans Be Held Under the Same Condition in the Matter of Killing Slaves.

If anyone kills a slave, barbarian by birth, a trained (select) house servant or messenger, let him compound sixty solidi; moreover, let the amount of the fine be twelve solidi. If anyone kills another's slave, Roman or barbarian, either ploughman or swineherd, let him pay thirty solidi.

Whoever kills a skilled goldsmith, let him pay two hundred solidi.

Whoever kills a silversmith, let him pay one hundred solidi.

Whoever kills a blacksmith, let him pay fifty solidi.

Whoever kills a carpenter, let him pay forty solidi. . . .

Of the Stealing of Girls.

If anyone shall steal a girl, let him be compelled to pay the price set for such a girl ninefold, and let him pay a fine to the amount of twelve solidi.

If a girl who has been seized returns uncorrupted to her parents, let the abductor compound six times the wergeld of the girl; moreover, let the fine be set at twelve solidi.

But if the abductor does not have the means to make the above-mentioned payment, let him be given over to the parents of the girl that they may have the power of doing to him whatever they choose.

If indeed, the girl seeks the man of her own will and comes to his house, and he has intercourse with her, let him pay her marriage price threefold; if moreover, she returns uncorrupted to her home, let her return with all blame removed from him.

If indeed a Roman girl, without the consent or knowledge of her parents, unites in marriage with a Burgundian, let her know she will have none of the property of her parents. . . .

Of Succession.

Among Burgundians we wish it to be observed that if anyone does not leave a son, let a daughter succeed to the inheritance of the father and mother in place of the son.

If by chance the dead leave neither son nor daughter, let the inheritance go to the sisters or nearest relatives.

It is pleasing that it be contained in the present law that if a woman having a husband dies without children, the husband of the dead wife may not demand back the marriage price (*pretium*) which had been given for her.

Likewise, let neither the woman nor the relatives of the woman seek back that which a woman pays when she comes to her husband if the husband dies without children.

Concerning those women who are vowed to God and remain in chastity, we order that if they have two brothers they receive a third portion of the inheritance of the father, that is, of that land which the father, possessing by the right of *sors* (allotment), left at the time of his death. Likewise, if she has four or five brothers, let her receive the portion due to her.

If moreover she has but one brother, let not a half, but a third part go to her on the condition that, after the death of her who is a woman and a nun, whatever she possesses in usufruct from her father's property shall go to the nearest relatives, and she will have no power of transferring anything therefrom, unless perhaps from her mother's goods, that is, from her clothing or things of the cell (*rescellulae*), or what she has acquired by her own labor.

We decree that this should be observed only by those whose fathers have not given them portions; but if they shall have received from their father a place where they can live, let them have full freedom of disposing of it at their will. . . .

Of Burgundian Women Entering a Second or Third Marriage.

If any Burgundian woman, as is the custom, enters a second or third marriage after the death of her husband, and she has children by each husband, let her possess the marriage gift (*donatio nuptialis*) in usufruct while she lives; after her death, let what his father gave her be given to each son, with the further provision that the mother has the power neither of giving, selling, or transferring any of the things which she received in the marriage gift.

If by chance the woman has no children, after her death let her relatives receive half of whatever has come to her by way of marriage gift, and let the relatives of the dead husband who was the donor receive half.

But if perchance children shall have been born and they shall have died after the death of their father, we command that the inheritance of the husband or children belong wholly to the mother. Moreover, after the death of the mother, we decree that what she holds in usufruct by inheritance from her children shall belong to the legal heirs of her children. Also we command that she protect the property of her children dying intestate.

If any son has given his mother something by will or by gift, let the mother have the power of doing whatever she wishes therewith; if she dies intestate, let the relatives of the woman claim the inheritance as their possession.

If any Burgundian has sons (children?) to whom he has given their portions, let him have the power of giving or selling that which he has reserved for himself to whomever he wishes. . . .

Of Knocking Out Teeth.

If anyone by chance strikes out the teeth of a Burgundian of the highest class, or of a Roman noble, let him be compelled to pay fifteen solidi.

For middle-class freeborn people, either Burgundian or Roman, if a tooth is knocked out, let composition be made in the sum of ten solidi.

For persons of the lowest class, five solidi.

If a slave voluntarily strikes out the tooth of a native freeman, let him be condemned to have a hand cut off; if the loss which has been set forth above has been committed by accident, let him pay the price for the tooth according to the status of the person.

If any native freeman strikes out the tooth of a freedman, let him pay him three solidi. If he strikes out the tooth of another's slave, let him pay two solidi to him to whom the slave belongs. . . .

Of Injuries Which Are Suffered by Women.

If any native freewoman has her hair cut off and is humiliated without cause (when innocent) by any native freeman in her home or on the road, and this can be proved with witnesses, let the doer of the deed pay her twelve solidi, and let the amount of the fine be twelve solidi.

If this was done to a freedwoman, let him pay her six solidi.

If this was done to a maidservant, let him pay her three solidi, and let the amount of the fine be three solidi.

If this injury (shame, disgrace) is inflicted by a slave on a native freewoman, let him receive two hundred blows; if a freedwoman, let him receive a hundred blows; if a maidservant, let him receive seventy-five blows.

If indeed the woman whose injury we have ordered to be punished in this manner commits fornication voluntarily (i.e., if she yields), let nothing be sought for the injury suffered.

Of Divorces.

If any woman leaves (puts aside) her husband to whom she is legally married, let her be smothered in mire.

If anyone wishes to put away his wife without cause, let him give her another payment such as he gave for her marriage price, and let the amount of the fine be twelve solidi.

If by chance a man wishes to put away his wife, and is able to prove one of these three crimes against her, that is, adultery, witchcraft, or violation of graves, let him have full right to put her away: and let the judge pronounce the sentence of the law against her, just as should be done against criminals.

But if she admits none of these three crimes, let no man be permitted to put away his wife for any other crime. But if he chooses, he may go away from the home, leaving all household property behind, and his wife with their children may possess the property of her husband.

Of the Punishment of Slaves Who Commit a Criminal Assault on Freeborn Women.

If any slave does violence to a native freewoman, and if she complains and is clearly able to prove this, let the slave be killed for the crime committed.

If indeed a native free girl unites voluntarily with a slave, we order both to be killed.

But if the relatives of the girl do not wish to punish their own relative, let the girl be deprived of her free status and delivered into servitude to the king.

DISCUSSION QUESTIONS

1. What do these laws reveal about the social and political structure of the Burgundian kingdom? For example, did the king act alone in establishing the laws? Do the laws place the same value on all social groups?
2. What does the code reveal about Burgundian women and family life?
3. Historians regard the interaction between Germanic and Roman peoples as a key component of the process by which Germanic kingdoms replaced imperial government in western Europe. What evidence of such interaction can you find in this document?

4

Procopius
Buildings
c. 553–554

The emperors of the eastern Roman provinces successfully resisted the tides of change that engulfed the West. In the process, they forged a new empire, Byzantium. Its roots extended back to 293, when Diocletian reorganized imperial territory into four districts—two in the east and two in the west. In 395, the empire was formally divided into eastern and western halves. Emperor Justinian (r. 527–565) played a pivotal role in shaping Byzantium's emerging identity as a bastion of Roman imperial glory and civilization. Here is a contemporary account of one of Justinian's most famous achievements, the reconstruction of the Church of the Holy Wisdom (Hagia Sophia) in the Byzantine capital, Constantinople. A courtier from Palestine, Procopius (d. after 562?), included the description in his book Buildings, *which he wrote to honor Justinian's architectural projects. Procopius sets the rebuilding of Hagia Sophia against the backdrop of the emperor's accomplishments as a whole, portraying the church as the embodiment of his power and divine favor.*

In our own age there has been born the Emperor Justinian, who, taking over the State when it was harrassed by disorder, has not only made it greater in extent, but also much more illustrious, by expelling from it those barbarians who had from of old pressed hard upon it, . . . witness the way he has already added to the Roman domain many states which in his own times had belonged to others, and has created countless cities which did not exist before. And finding that the belief in God was, before his time, straying into errors and being forced to go in many directions, he completely destroyed all the paths leading to such errors, and brought it about that it stood on the firm foundation of a single faith. Moreover, finding the laws obscure because they had become far more numerous than they should be, and in obvious confusion because they disagreed with each other, he preserved them by cleansing them of the mass of their verbal trickery, and by controlling their discrepancies with the greatest firmness; as for those who plotted against him, he of his own volition dismissed the charges against them, and causing those who were in want to have a surfeit of wealth, and crushing the spiteful fortune that oppressed them, he wedded the whole State to a life of prosperity. Furthermore, he strengthened the Roman domain, which everywhere lay exposed to the barbarians, by a multitude of soldiers, and by constructing strongholds he built a wall along all its remote frontiers.

However, most of the Emperor's other achievements have been described by me in my other writings, so that the subject of the present work will be the benefits which he wrought as a builder. They do indeed say that the best king of whom we know by tradition was the Persian Cyrus, and that he was chiefly responsible for the founding of the kingdom of Persia for the people of his race. . . . But in the case of the king of our times, Justinian (whom one would rightly, I think, call a king by nature as well as by inheritance, since he is, as Homer says, "as gentle as a father"), if one should examine his reign with care, he will regard the rule of Cyrus as a sort of child's play. The proof of this will be that the Roman Empire, as I have just said, has become more than doubled both in area and in power generally. . . .

From *Procopius*, trans. H. B. Dewing, vol. 7 (Cambridge, Mass.: Harvard University Press, 1961), 5–17, 27.

But now we must proceed, as I have said, to the subject of the buildings of this Emperor, so that it may not come to pass in the future that those who see them refuse, by reason of their great number and magnitude, to believe that they are in truth the works of one man. For already many works of men of former times which are not vouched for by a written record have aroused incredulity because of their surpassing merit. And with good reason the buildings in Byzantium, beyond all the rest, will serve as a foundation for my narrative. For "o'er a work's beginnings," as the old saying has it, "we needs must set a front that shines afar."

Some men of the common herd, all the rubbish of the city, once rose up against the Emperor Justinian in Byzantium, when they brought about the rising called the Nika Insurrection. . . . And by way of shewing that it was not against the Emperor alone that they had taken up arms, but no less against God himself, unholy wretches that they were, they had the hardihood to fire the Church of the Christians, which the people of Byzantium call "Sophia," an epithet which they have most appropriately invented for God, by which they call His temple; and God permitted them to accomplish this impiety, forseeing into what an object of beauty this shrine was destined to be transformed. So the whole church at that time lay a charred mass of ruins. But the Emperor Justinian built not long afterwards a church so finely shaped, that if anyone had enquired of the Christians before the burning if it would be their wish that the church should be destroyed and one like this should take its place, shewing them some sort of model of the building we now see, it seems to me that they would have prayed that they might see their church destroyed forthwith, in order that the building might be converted into its present form. At any rate the Emperor, disregarding all questions of expense, eagerly pressed on to begin the work of construction, and began to gather all the artisans from the whole world. . . . Indeed this also was an indication of the honour in which God held the Emperor, that He had already provided the men who would be most serviceable to him in the tasks which were waiting to be carried out. And one might with good reason marvel at the discernment of the Emperor himself, in that out of the whole world he was able to select the men who were most suitable for the most important of his enterprises.

So the church has become a spectacle of marvellous beauty, overwhelming to those who see it, but to those who know it by hearsay altogether incredible. For it soars to a height to match the sky, and as if surging up from amongst the other buildings it stands on high and looks down upon the remainder of the city, adorning it, because it is a part of it, but glorying in its own beauty, because, though a part of the city and dominating it, it at the same time towers above it to such a height that the whole city is viewed from there as from a watch-tower. Both its breadth and its length have been so carefully proportioned, that it may not improperly be said to be exceedingly long and at the same time unusually broad. And it exults in an indescribable beauty. For it proudly reveals its mass and the harmony of its proportions, having neither any excess nor deficiency, since it is both more pretentious than the buildings to which we are accustomed, and considerably more noble than those which are merely huge, and it abounds exceedingly in sunlight and in the reflection of the sun's rays from the marble. Indeed one might say that its interior is not illuminated from without by the sun, but that the radiance comes into being within it, such an abundance of light bathes this shrine.... And whenever anyone enters this church to pray, he understands at once that it is not by any human power or skill, but by the influence of God, that this work has been so finely turned. And so his mind is lifted up toward God and exalted, feeling that He cannot be far away, but must especially love to dwell in this place which He has chosen. And this does not happen only to one who sees the church for the first time, but the same experience comes to him on each successive occasion, as though the sight were new each time. Of this spectacle no one has ever had a surfeit, but when present in the church men rejoice in what they see, and when they leave it they take proud delight in conversing about it.

DISCUSSION QUESTIONS

1. As described by Procopius, what were Justinian's most significant accomplishments?
2. What links does Procopius see between these accomplishments and Justinian's relationship with God?
3. What do you think Procopius's goals were in writing this account?

COMPARATIVE QUESTIONS

1. When viewed together, what do these documents reveal about the spread and institutional development of Christianity in the Roman Empire between the fourth and sixth centuries?
2. How does each of these documents illuminate the interplay between politics and religion in this period?
3. Do you see any parallels between Symmachus's and Procopius's expectations regarding the role that the emperor should play as protector of the empire's prosperity? What do these parallels suggest about the ways in which Byzantium preserved and perpetuated its Roman heritage?
4. According to Procopius, Justinian's efforts to codify imperial laws strengthened his authority and the stability of the empire. In what ways does the Burgundian Code reflect a similar attitude toward the function of law in government and society?

CHAPTER

8

The Heirs of the Roman Empire

600–750

S UMMARY   The seventh and eighth centuries marked the beginning of a new era in Western civilization—the Middle Ages. By this period, the Roman Empire had fragmented into three different worlds: Byzantine, Muslim, and western European. Even so, these regions continued to share a common Roman heritage that they adapted to their own interests and circumstances. The documents in this chapter reveal various dimensions of this process, beginning with the eastern empire, Byzantium. Although it inherited much from Rome, Byzantium forged its own political, cultural, and religious identity in response to the distinctive challenges it faced in this period, including the onslaught of foreign invaders. The newly founded Muslim state was extraordinarily successful on this front, and by 730 its warriors had conquered vast expanses of imperial territory. The second set of documents reveals how the Muslim military conquests brought both change and continuity. The third and fourth documents illuminate the development of the western kingdoms, where various barbarian peoples built new societies and cultures on the foundations of the Roman Empire.

1

Theophanes Confessor
Chronicle
Ninth Century

Although Byzantium resisted the effects of the Germanic migrations that changed the West, by 600 it had begun its own process of transformation. For the next 150 years, Byzantium was engaged in almost constant warfare with foreign peoples, especially Muslim Arabs. A historical chronicle written by a Greek monk, Theophanes Confessor (c. 759–818), in the early ninth century elucidates how war shaped two key facets of Byzantium's emerging identity: imperial autocracy and, concomitantly, the interdependency between the spiritual and political realms. In this passage, Theophanes recounts the coincidence of the Arab onslaught with the controversy over the question of icons during the reign of Emperor Leo III (r. 717–741). For Leo, the worship of sacred images was an abomination against God (a view his troops shared) and a threat to his unique status as God's earthly representative. For Theophanes and other Byzantines, however, icons were an essential source of divine intercession.

In the summer season of the same year [726] a vapour as from a fiery furnace boiled up for a few days from the depth of the sea between the islands of Thera and Therasia. As it gradually became thicker and filled with stones because of the heat of the burning fire, all the smoke took on a fiery appearance. Then, on account of the density of the earthy substance, pumice stones as big as hills were thrown up against all of Asia Minor, Lesbos, Abydos, and coastal Macedonia, so that the entire surface of that sea was filled with floating pumice. In the midst of so great a fire an island that had not previously existed was formed and joined to the Sacred Island, as it is called; for, just as the aforementioned islands Thera and Therasia had once been thrown up, so was this one, too, in the present days of God's enemy Leo. Thinking that God's wrath was in his favour instead of being directed against him, he stirred up a more ruthless war on the holy and venerable icons. . . . The populace of the Imperial City were much distressed by the newfangled doctrines and meditated an assault upon him. They also killed a few of the emperor's men who had taken down the Lord's image that was above the great Bronze Gate, with the result that many of them were punished in the cause of the true faith by mutilation, lashes, banishment, and fines, especially those who were prominent by birth and culture. This led to the extinction of schools and of the pious education that had lasted from St. Constantine the Great until our days, but was destroyed, along with many other good things, by this Saracen-minded Leo. . . .

At the summer solstice . . . a multitude of Saracens led by two emirs was drawn up against Nicaea in Bithynia: Amer with 15,000 scouts led the van and surrounded the town which he found unprepared, while Mauias followed with another 85,000 men. After a long siege and a partial destruction of the walls, they did not overpower the town thanks to the acceptable prayers addressed to God by the holy Fathers who are honoured there in a church (wherein their venerable images are set up to this very day and are honoured by those who believe as they did). A certain Constantine, however, who was the *strator* of Artabasdos, on seeing an image of the Theotokos that had been set up, picked up a stone and threw it at her. He broke the image and trampled upon it when it had fallen down. He then saw in a vision the Lady standing beside him and saying to him: "See, what a

From *The Chronicle of Theophanes Confessor*, trans. Cyril Mango and Roger Scott (Oxford: Clarendon Press, 1997), 559–61.

brave thing you have done to me! Verily, upon your head have you done it." The next day, when the Saracens attacked the walls and battle was joined, that wretched man rushed to the wall like the brave soldier he was and was struck by a stone discharged from a siege engine, and it broke his head and face, a just reward for his impiety. After collecting many captives and much booty, the Arabs withdrew. In this manner God showed to the impious one that he had overcome his fellow-countrymen not on account of his piety, as he himself boasted, but for some divine cause and inscrutable judgement, whereby so great an Arab force was driven away from the city of the holy Fathers thanks to their intercession— on account of their most exact likenesses that are honoured therein—and this, too, in reproof and unanswerable condemnation of the tyrant and in vindication of the true believers. Not only was the impious man in error concerning the relative worship of the holy icons, but also concerning the intercession of the all-pure Theotokos and all the saints, and he abominated their relics like his mentors, the Arabs. From this time on he impudently harassed the blessed Germanus, patriarch of Constantinople, blaming all the emperors, bishops, and Christian people who had lived before him for having committed idolatry in worshipping the holy and venerable icons, unable as he was to grasp the argument concerning relative veneration because of his lack of faith and crass ignorance.

Discussion Questions

1. To what does Theophanes attribute the Muslims' withdrawal from Nicaea? What does his explanation reveal about the role of icons in Byzantine religious devotion?

2. According to Theophanes, how did Emperor Leo III threaten this role? Do you think he evaluated Leo's actions objectively?

3. Based on this passage, how would you describe the relationship between the Byzantine church and state?

2

Islamic Terms of Peace
633–643

The remarkable rise of Islam in the seventh century had far-reaching consequences. Muhammad (c. 570–632), a merchant-turned-holy man from the Arabian city of Mecca, founded the new faith, and his teachings soon gained widespread adherence across the Arabian peninsula. Together his converts formed a community united by the worship of God, expressed not only in individual prayer but also in the collective duty to "strive" (jihad) against unbelievers, often in war. War was thus a central component of Islam, and by the eighth century Islamic warriors had conquered all of Persia and much of the Byzantine Empire. These letters dictate the terms of peace to conquered communities and illuminate the Muslims' method of conquest and rule in the decade following Muhammad's death. In exchange for the payment of a special tax (jizya), non-Muslim subjects were allowed to live much as they had before.

Consequently, Islam became not the destroyer of Hellenistic and Roman traditions, but rather their heir.

Bānqiyā and Basmā (633)

In the name of God, the Merciful and the Compassionate.

This is a letter from Khālid ibn al-Walīd to Ṣalūba ibn Nasṭūnā and his people.

I have made a pact with you for *jizya* and defense for every fit man, for both Bānqiyā and Basmā, for 10,000 dinars, excluding coins with holes punched in them, the wealthy according to the measure of his wealth, the poor according to the measure of his poverty, payable annually. You have been made head of your people and your people are content with you. I, therefore, and the Muslims who are with me, accept you, and I [? you] and your people are content. You have protection [*dhimma*] and defense. If we defend you, the *jizya* is due to us; if we do not, it is not, until we do defend you.

Witnessed by Hishām ibn al-Walīd, al-Qa'qā' ibn 'Amr, Jarīr ibn 'Abdallāh al-Ḥimyarī and Ḥanẓala ibn al-Rabī'.

Written in the year 12, in Safar [April–May 633].

Jerusalem (636)

In the name of God the Merciful and the Compassionate.

This is the safe-conduct accorded by the servant of God 'Umar, the Commander of the Faithful, to the people of Aelia [Jerusalem].

He accords them safe-conduct for their persons, their property, their churches, their crosses, their sound and their sick, and the rest of their worship.

Their churches shall neither be used as dwellings nor destroyed. They shall not suffer any impairment, nor shall their dependencies, their crosses, nor any of their property.

No constraint shall be exercised against them in religion nor shall any harm be done to any among them.

No Jew shall live with them in Aelia.

The people of Aelia must pay the *jizya* in the same way as the people of other cities.

They must expel the Romans and the brigands [?] from the city. Those who leave shall have safe-conduct for their persons and property until they reach safety. Those who stay shall have safe-conduct and must pay the *jizya* like the people of Aelia.

Those of the people of Aelia who wish to remove their persons and effects and depart with the Romans and abandon their churches and their crosses shall

From *Islam: From the Prophet Muhammad to the Capture of Constantinople*, ed. Bernard Lewis, vol. 1 (New York: Walker & Co., 1974), 234–36, 238–40.

have safe-conduct for their persons, their churches, and their crosses, until they reach safety.

The country people who were already in the city before the killing of so-and-so may, as they wish, remain and pay the *jizya* the same way as the people of Aelia or leave with the Romans or return to their families. Nothing shall be taken from them until they have gathered their harvest.

This document is placed under the surety of God and the protection [*dhimma*] of the Prophet, the Caliphs and the believers, on condition that the inhabitants of Aelia pay the *jizya* that is due from them.

Witnessed by Khālid ibn al-Walīd, 'Amr ibn al-'Āṣ, 'Abd al-Raḥmān ibn 'Awf, Mu'āwiya ibn Abī Sufyān, the last of whom wrote this document in the year 15 [636].

Jurjān (639)

In the name of God, the Merciful and the Compassionate.

This is a letter from Suwayd ibn Muqarrin to Ruzbān Ṣūl ibn Ruzbān, the inhabitants of Dihistān, and the rest of the inhabitants of Jurjān.

You have protection and we must enforce it on the condition that you pay the *jizya* every year, according to your capacity, for every adult male. If we seek help from any of you, the help counts as his *jizya* in place of the payment. They have safe-conduct for themselves, their property, their religions, and their laws. There will be no change in what is due to them as long as they pay and guide the wayfarer and show good will and lodge the Muslims and do not spy or betray. Whoever stays with them shall have the same terms as they have, and whoever goes forth has safe-conduct until he reaches a place of safety, provided that if anyone insults a Muslim he is severely punished, and if he strikes a Muslim, his blood is lawful.

Witnessed by Sawād ibn Quṭba, Hind ibn 'Amr, Simāk ibn Makhrama, and 'Utayba ibn al-Naḥḥās.

Written in the year 18 [639].

Isfahān (642)

In the name of God, the Merciful and the Compassionate.

A letter from 'Abdallāh to the Fādhūsafān and the inhabitants of Iṣfahān and its surroundings.

You are safe as long as you discharge your obligations, which are: to pay the *jizya*, which you must pay according to your capacity every year, paying it to whoever is the governor of your country, for every adult male; you must also guide the Muslim [traveler], keep his road in repair, lodge him for a day and a night, and provide the walker with a mount for one stage.

Do not assert your authority over any Muslim. What you owe to the Muslims is your goodwill and the payment of your dues; you have safe-conduct (*amān*) as long as you comply. But if you change anything, or if anyone among you changes anything and you do not hand him over, then you have no safe-conduct. If anyone insults a Muslim, he will be severely punished for it. If he strikes a Muslim, we shall kill him.

Written and witnessed by 'Abdallāh ibn Qays, 'Abdallāh ibn Warqā', and 'Iṣma ibn 'Abdallāh.

Rayy (642-643)

In the name of God, the Merciful and the Compassionate.

This is what Nu'aym ibn Muqarrin gave to al-Zaynabī ibn Qūla. He gave him safe-conduct (*amān*) for the inhabitants of Rayy and others who were with them, on condition of the annual payment of the *jizya*, according to capacity, for every adult male and on condition that they show goodwill and guide travelers, that they neither spy nor betray, that they lodge the Muslims for a day and a night, that they show deference to the Muslims. Anyone who insults or belittles a Muslim will receive crushing punishment; anyone who strikes a Muslim will be killed. If anyone changes this and his dead body is not handed over, then he will have changed the status of your whole community.

Written and witnessed.

Tiflīs (642-643)

In the name of God, the Merciful and the Compassionate.

This is a letter from Ḥabīb ibn Maslama for the inhabitants of Tiflīs, in the land of Hurmuz, giving safe-conduct to you, your children, your families, your convents, your churches, your religions, and your prayers, on condition that you accept the humiliation [?] of the *jizya* at the rate of a full dinar for every household. You must not join separate households together in order to reduce the *jizya* which you pay, nor may we separate what is joined in order to increase the *jizya* which we receive.

You owe us your goodwill and your help, as far as you can, against the enemies of God and His Prophet and of those who believe; lodging for the Muslim wayfarer for a night, with food and drink such as are lawful for the people of the book; and guidance on the road, as far as this causes no harm to you. If one of the Muslims is stranded among you, you must deliver him to the nearest group of believers and Muslims, unless some obstacle intervenes. If you repent, perform the prayer, and pay the *zakāt*, then you are our brothers in religion [and our *mawālī*]. But he who turns away from the faith, Islam, and the *jizya* is the enemy of God and His Prophet and of those who believe. We seek help from God against him.

If something happens which distracts the Muslims from helping you and your enemy overcomes you, this is not held against them [? you] and does not invalidate the pact with you after you return to the side of the believers and Muslims. This is what is due from you and what is due to you.

Witnessed by God and His Angels and His Prophets and those who believe, and God is sufficient witness.

DISCUSSION QUESTIONS

1. Aside from the payment of a poll tax (*jizya*), what were some of the obligations Muslims imposed on their non-Muslim subjects?
2. What did conquered peoples receive in exchange for the fulfillment of these obligations?
3. What does this system of quid pro quo suggest about Muslim attitudes toward nonbelievers?

3

The Life of Lady Balthild, Queen of the Franks
Late Seventh Century

With the collapse of imperial government in the West in the fifth and sixth centuries, the kings from the Frankish royal dynasty, the Merovingians, came to dominate Roman Gaul. Their queens also wielded power, as The Life of Lady Balthild *demonstrates. Lady Balthild (d. c. 680) was an Anglo-Saxon captive sold as a slave to the mayor of the palace in the Frankish kingdom of Neustria. He eventually offered her in marriage to King Clovis II (r. 638–657), which suggests she was from an important family with which the king sought political ties. On the king's death in 657, Lady Balthild acted as regent until her eldest son came of age in 663 or 664. She thereupon retired from court to a monastery. The author of her Life is unknown, but his or her intent is clear: to hold her up as a model of Christian piety. Religious motives aside, the book illuminates women's place in court life as well as the growing influence of Christianity in Merovingian culture. This excerpt begins with Lady Balthild's rise in station to queen.*

And in this station divine dispensation decided to honour her so that . . . she might obtain union with the king and, from her, royal progeny might come forth. And this has now come to pass, as it is obvious to everyone that the royal offspring reigning now is hers.

But as she had the grace of prudence conferred upon her by God, with watchful eagerness she obeyed the king as her lord, and to the princes she showed herself a mother, to the priests as a daughter, and to the young and the adolescents as the best possible nurse. And she was friendly to all, loving the priests as fathers, the monks as brothers, the poor as a faithful nurse does, and giving to each generous alms. She preserved the honour of the princes and kept their fitting counsel, always exhorting the young to religious studies and humbly and stead-

From *Late Merovingian France: History and Hagiography, 640–720*, ed. Paul Fouracre and Richard A. Gerberding (Manchester and New York: Manchester University Press, 1996), 121–23, 127, 131–32.

fastly petitioning the king for the churches and the poor. While still in secular dress, she desired to serve Christ; she prayed daily, tearfully commending herself to Christ, the heavenly king. And the pious king [Clovis], taking care of her faith and devotion, gave his faithful servant, Abbot Genesius, to her as support, and through his hands she served the priests and the poor, fed the hungry, clothed the naked with garments, and conscientiously arranged the burial of the dead. Through him she sent most generous alms of gold and silver to the monasteries of men and women. . . .

What more is there to say? At God's command, her husband, King Clovis, went forth from his body, leaving a lineage of sons with their mother. In his place after him, his son, the late King Clothar, took the throne of the Franks and then also with the excellent princes, Chrodbert, bishop of Paris, Lord Audoin, and Ebroin, mayor of the palace, along with the other great magnates and very many of the rest. And, indeed, the kingdom of the Franks was maintained in peace. Then indeed, a little while ago, the Austrasians peacefully received her son Childeric as king in Austrasia by the arrangement of Lady Balthild and, indeed, through the advice of the great magnates. But the Burgundians and the Neustrians were united. And we believe that, with God guiding, and in accordance with the great faith of Lady Balthild, these three kingdoms kept the harmony of peace among themselves.

At that time it happened that the heresy of simony stained the Church of God with its depraved practice in which they received the rank of bishop by paying a price for it. By the will of God [acting] through her, and at the urging of the good priests, the above-mentioned Lady Balthild stopped this impious evil so that no one would set a price on the taking of holy orders. Through her, the Lord also arranged for another very evil and impious practice to cease, one in which many men were more eager to kill their offspring than to provide for them in order to avoid the royal exactions which were inflicted upon them by custom, and from which they incurred a very heavy loss of property. This the lady prohibited for her own salvation so that no one presumed to do it. Because of this deed, truly a great reward awaits her.

Who, then, is able to say how many and how great were the sources of income, the entire farms and the large forests she gave up by donating them to the establishments of religious men in order to construct cells or monasteries? And she also built as God's own and private houses a huge nunnery for women consecrated by God at Chelles, near Paris where she placed the religious handmaiden of God, the girl Bertila, in the position of the first mother. And in this place the venerable Lady Balthild in turn decided to dwell under the pure rule of religion and to rest in peace. And in truth she fulfilled this with a devoted will. . . .

Indeed, with a most pious affection she loved her sisters as her own daughters, she obeyed their holy abbess as her mother, and rendered service to them as the lowest of handmaidens out of holy desire, just as [she had done] when she still ruled the royal palace and often visited her holy monastery. So strongly did she exhibit the example of great humility that she even served her sisters in the kitchen, and the lowest acts of cleaning, even the latrines, she herself did. All this she undertook with joy and a cheerful heart, in such humble service for Christ. For who would believe that the height of such power would serve in such lowly things if her most abundant and great love of Christ had not demanded it of her in every way? . . .

Indeed, we recall that other queens in the kingdom of the Franks have been noble and worshippers of God: Clothild, queen of the late King Clovis of old and niece of King Gundobad, who, by her holy exhortations, led both her very brave and pagan husband and many of the Frankish nobles to Christianity and brought them to the Catholic faith. She also was the first to construct the churches in honour of St Peter at Paris and St George in the little monastery for virgins at Chelles, and she founded many others in honour of the saints in order to store up her reward, and she enriched them with many gifts. The same is said of Ultrogoda, queen of the most Christian King Childebert, because she was a comforter of the poor and a helper of the servants of God and of monks. And [it is said] also of Queen Radegund, truly a most faithful handmaiden of God, queen of the late elder King Clothar, whom the grace of the Holy Spirit had so inflamed that she left her husband while he was still alive and consecrated herself to the Lord Christ under the holy veil, and, with Christ as her spouse, accomplished many good things. These things are read in her Acts.

But it is pleasing, nevertheless, to consider this about her whom it here concerns: the Lady Balthild. Her many good deeds were accomplished in our times, and that these things were done by her herself we have learned in the best manner. Concerning these things, we have here commemorated a few out of the many, and we do not think her to be the inferior in merits of those earlier [queens]; rather we know her to have outdone them in holy striving.

DISCUSSION QUESTIONS

1. Why does the author think that Lady Balthild's life is exemplary?
2. To whom do you think the author directed his or her message, and why?
3. What does this source suggest about women's role in Merovingian politics and the relationship between this role and Christian values?

4

Pope Gregory the Great
Letters
598–601

Although Britain stood on the periphery of the empire, it, too, could not escape the turmoil of the late imperial period. After the Roman army was recalled to Italy, the Anglo-Saxons invaded the island in the 440s and replaced local traditions, including

Christianity, with their own. In due course, however, Christianity was reintroduced from a variety of directions, of which Italy was among the most important. From here Pope Gregory I (r. 590–604) dispatched two groups of missionaries to establish Roman-style Christianity in England. The first group, sent in 595, was led by Augustine and the second, sent in 601, by Mellitus; both were monks from Rome. In these letters, Gregory describes the mission's initial progress and then offers strategies for furthering its success. He points not only to the pope's growing influence in the West but also to the interaction between Roman and non-Roman customs.

To Eulogius, Bishop of Alexandria.

Gregory to Eulogius, &c.

Our common son, the bearer of these presents, when he brought the letters of your Holiness found me sick, and has left me sick; whence it has ensued that the scanty water of my brief epistle has been hardly able to exude to the large fountain of your Blessedness. But it was a heavenly boon that, while in a state of bodily pain, I received the letter of your Holiness to lift me up with joy for the instruction of the heretics of the city of Alexandria, and the concord of the faithful, to such an extent that the very joy of my mind moderated the severity of my suffering. And indeed we rejoice with new exultation to hear of your good doings, though at the same time we by no means suppose that it is a new thing for you to act thus perfectly. For that the people of holy Church increases, that spiritual crops of corn for the heavenly garner are multiplied, we never doubted that this was from the grace of Almighty God which flowed largely to you, most blessed ones. . . .

But, since in the good things you do I know that you also rejoice with others, I make you a return for your favour, and announce things not unlike yours; for while the nation of the Angli, placed in a corner of the world, remained up to this time misbelieving in the worship of stocks and stones, I determined, through the aid of your prayers for me, to send to it, God granting it, a monk of my monastery for the purpose of preaching. And he, having with my leave been made bishop by the bishops of Germany, proceeded, with their aid also, to the end of the world to the aforesaid nation; and already letters have reached us telling us of his safety and his work; to the effect that he and those that have been sent with him are resplendent with such great miracles in the said nation that they seem to imitate the powers of the apostles in the signs which they display. Moreover, at the solemnity of the Lord's Nativity which occurred in this first indiction, more than ten thousand Angli are reported to have been baptized by the same our brother and fellow-bishop. This have I told you, that you may know what you are effecting among the people of Alexandria by speaking, and what in the ends of

From *A Select Library of Nicene and Post-Nicene Fathers of the Christian Church*, 2d ser., vols. 12 and 13 (New York: Christian Literature Co., 1895 and 1898), 12:240, 13:84–85.

the world by praying. For your prayers are in the place where you are not, while your holy operations are shewn in the place where you are.

To Mellitus, Abbot.

Gregory to Mellitus, Abbot in France.[1]

Since the departure of our congregation, which is with thee, we have been in a state of great suspense from having heard nothing of the success of your journey. But when Almighty God shall have brought you to our most reverend brother the bishop Augustine, tell him that I have long been considering with myself about the case of the Angli; to wit, that the temples of idols in that nation should not be destroyed, but that the idols themselves that are in them should be. Let blessed water be prepared, and sprinkled in these temples, and altars constructed, and relics deposited, since, if these same temples are well built, it is needful that they should be transferred from the worship of idols to the service of the true God; that, when the people themselves see that these temples are not destroyed, they may put away error from their heart, and, knowing and adoring the true God, may have recourse with the more familiarity to the places they have been accustomed to. And, since they are wont to kill many oxen in sacrifice to demons, they should have also some solemnity of this kind in a changed form, so that on the day of dedication, or on the anniversaries of the holy martyrs whose relics are deposited there, they may make for themselves tents of the branches of trees around these temples that have been changed into churches, and celebrate the solemnity with religious feasts. Nor let them any longer sacrifice animals to the devil, but slay animals to the praise of God for their own eating, and return thanks to the Giver of all for their fulness, so that, while some joys are reserved to them outwardly, they may be able the more easily to incline their minds to inward joys. For it is undoubtedly impossible to cut away everything at once from hard hearts, since one who strives to ascend to the highest place must needs rise by steps or paces, and not by leaps. Thus to the people of Israel in Egypt the Lord did indeed make Himself known; but still He reserved to them in His own worship the use of the sacrifices which they were accustomed to offer to the devil, enjoining them to immolate animals in sacrifice to Himself; to the end that, their hearts being changed, they should omit some things in the sacrifice and retain others, so that, though the animals were the same as what they had been accustomed to offer, nevertheless, as they immolated them to God and not to idols, they should be no longer the same sacrifices. This then it is necessary for thy Love to say to our aforesaid brother, that he, being now in that country, may consider well how he should arrange all things.

---

[1] This letter was sent after the departure of Mellitus with the band of new missionaries from Rome to Britain, being intended to reach him while still in France.

DISCUSSION QUESTIONS

1. Earlier in his papacy, Gregory had advised the destruction of pagan temples. How does Gregory reverse this decision in his letter to Mellitus, and why?

2. What does Gregory's change of approach suggest about the ways in which Latin Christianity adapted to non-Roman cultures?

3. Historians often refer to Gregory I as the "father of the medieval papacy" because of the role he played in transforming the papacy into the moral and spiritual head of the West. What evidence can you find in these letters to support this view?

COMPARATIVE QUESTIONS

1. Based on these documents, in what ways did the Byzantine, Muslim, and w estern European worlds both perpetuate and diverge from the legacy of Rome?

2. What do the first three documents reveal about the relationship between religious beliefs and politics in this period in both Christian and Islamic culture?

3. In his letter to Mellitus, Gregory I recommends adapting Christian practices to local customs. How did this strategy differ from Muslims' approach to other religions?

9

Unity and Diversity in Three Societies
750–1050

S U M M A R Y   The following documents illuminate the forces of unity and fragmentation driving the development of western Europe, Byzantium, and Islam between 750 and 1050. In this period, the Carolingian king Charlemagne (r. 768–814) forged a vast kingdom, the scope of which had not been seen since Roman times. As the first document reveals, his success was based not simply on military victory but also on his ability to administer effectively the diverse regions under his rule. Although the division of Charlemagne's empire in 843 opened the door to local rule, his legacy endured and, as the second document suggests, enhanced Europe's distinctiveness from Byzantium. At this time, the Byzantine emperors had regained much of their lost luster, and they considered themselves to be the rightful successors of Rome. Against this backdrop, the Islamic world continued to forge a unified sense of identity even as it, like the West, fragmented into smaller political units (Document 4).

1
General Capitulary for the Missi
802

Although the Merovingians forged a powerful political polity on the demise of Roman provincial government, their success paled in comparison to that of the Carolingians, who deposed them in 751. By the 790s, the most famous Carolingian king, Charlemagne (r. 768–814), had created an empire across Europe, using imperial Rome as a model. He was crowned emperor in 800 by Pope Leo III, which further exalted his power. To centralize his rule, Charlemagne dispatched officials, or missi, *annually to every part of the empire to review local affairs and enforce royal legislation. This document, known as a capitulary, provided basic guidelines for these an-*

*nual visits. Comprised of regulatory articles (*capitula *in Latin), capitularies were typically compiled at general assemblies convened by Charlemagne to discuss important issues with his magnates. These excerpts illuminate the forces binding the empire together as well as those that ultimately broke it apart.*

First chapter. Concerning the embassy sent out by the lord emperor. Therefore, the most serene and most Christian lord emperor Charles has chosen from his nobles the wisest and most prudent men, both archbishops and some of the other bishops also, and venerable abbots and pious laymen, and has sent them throughout his whole kingdom, and through them by all the following chapters has allowed men to live in accordance with the correct law. Moreover, where anything which is not right and just has been enacted in the law, he has ordered them to inquire into this most diligently and to inform him of it; he desires, God granting, to reform it. And let no one, through his cleverness or astuteness, dare to oppose or thwart the written law, as many are wont to do, or the judicial sentence passed upon him, or to do injury to the churches of God or the poor or the widows or the wards or any Christian. But all shall live entirely in accordance with God's precept, justly and under a just rule, and each one shall be admonished to live in harmony with his fellows in his business or profession; the canonical clergy ought to observe in every respect a canonical life without heeding base gain, nuns ought to keep diligent watch over their lives, laymen and the secular clergy ought rightly to observe their laws without malicious fraud, and all ought to live in mutual charity and perfect peace. And let the *missi* themselves make a diligent investigation whenever any man claims that an injustice has been done to him by any one, just as they desire to deserve the grace of omnipotent God and to keep their fidelity promised to Him, so that entirely in all cases everywhere, in accordance with the will and fear of God, they shall administer the law fully and justly in the case of the holy churches of God and of the poor, of wards and widows and of the whole people. And if there shall be anything of such a nature that they, together with the provincial counts, are not able of themselves to correct it and to do justice concerning it, they shall, without any ambiguity, refer this, together with their reports, to the judgment of the emperor; and the straight path of justice shall not be impeded by any one on account of flattery or gifts from any one, or on account of any relationship, or from fear of the powerful.

Concerning the fidelity to be promised to the lord emperor. And he commanded that every man in his whole kingdom, whether ecclesiastic or layman, and each one according to his vow and occupation, should now promise to him as emperor the fidelity which he had previously promised to him as king; and all of those who had not yet made that promise should do likewise, down to those who were twelve years old. And that it shall be announced to all in public, so that

From *Translations and Reprints from the Original Sources of European History,* vol. 6, ed. Dana Carleton Munro (Philadelphia: University of Pennsylvania Press, 1898), 16–19, 23–24, 26–27.

each one might know, how great and how many things are comprehended in that oath; not merely, as many have thought hitherto, fidelity to the lord emperor as regards his life, and not introducing any enemy into his kingdom out of enmity, and not consenting to or concealing another's faithlessness to him; but that all may know that this oath contains in itself this meaning:

First, that each one voluntarily shall strive, in accordance with his knowledge and ability, to live wholly in the holy service of God in accordance with the precept of God and in accordance with his own promise, because the lord emperor is unable to give to all individually the necessary care and discipline.

Secondly, that no man, either through perjury or any other wile or fraud, on account of the flattery or gift of any one, shall refuse to give back or dare to abstract or conceal a serf of the lord emperor or a district or land or anything that belongs to him; and that no one shall presume, through perjury or other wile, to conceal or abstract his fugitive fiscaline serfs who unjustly and fraudulently say that they are free.

That no one shall presume to rob or do any injury fraudulently to the churches of God or widows or orphans or pilgrims; for the lord emperor himself, after God and His saints, has constituted himself their protector and defender.

That no one shall dare to lay waste a benefice of the lord emperor, or to make it his own property.

That no one shall presume to neglect a summons to war from the lord emperor; and that no one of the counts shall be so presumptuous as to dare to dismiss thence any one of those who owe military service, either on account of relationship or flattery or gifts from any one.

That no one shall presume to impede at all in any way a ban or command of the lord emperor, or to dally with his work or to impede or to lessen or in any way to act contrary to his will or commands. And that no one shall dare to neglect to pay his dues or tax.

That no one, for any reason, shall make a practice in court of defending another unjustly, either from any desire of gain when the cause is weak, or by impeding a just judgment by his skill in reasoning, or by a desire of oppressing when the cause is weak. But each one shall answer for his own cause or tax or debt unless any one is infirm or ignorant of pleading; for these the *missi* or the chiefs who are in the court or the judge who knows the case in question shall plead before the court; or if it is necessary, such a person may be allowed as is acceptable to all and knows the case well; but this shall be done wholly according to the convenience of the chiefs or *missi* who are present. But in every case it shall be done in accordance with justice and the law; and that no one shall have the power to impede justice by a gift, reward, or any kind of evil flattery or from any hindrance of relationship. And that no one shall unjustly consent to another in anything, but that with all zeal and goodwill all shall be prepared to carry out justice.

For all the above mentioned ought to be observed by the imperial oath.

That bishops and priests shall live according to the canons and shall teach others to do the same.

That bishops, abbots, abbesses, who are in charge of others, with the greatest veneration shall strive to surpass their subjects in this diligence and shall not oppress their subjects with a harsh rule or tyranny, but with sincere love shall carefully guard the flock committed to them with mercy and charity or by the examples of good works.. . .

That bishops, abbots and abbesses, and counts shall be mutually in accord, following the law in order to render a just judgment with all charity and unity of peace, and that they shall live faithfully in accordance with the will of God, so that always everywhere through them and among them a just judgment shall be rendered. The poor, widows, orphans and pilgrims shall have consolation and defence from them; so that we, through their good-will, may deserve the reward of eternal life rather than punishment. . . .

That counts and *centenarii*[1] shall compel all to do justice in every respect, and shall have such assistants in their ministries as they can securely confide in, who will observe law and justice faithfully, who will oppress the poor in no manner, who will not dare under any pretext, on account of flattery or reward, to conceal thieves, robbers, murderers, adulterers, magicians, wizards or witches, and all sacrilegious men, but instead will give them up that they may be punished and chastised in accordance with the law, so that, God granting it, all of these evils may be removed from the Christian people.

That judges shall judge justly in accordance with the written law, and not according to their own will.

And we command that no one in our whole kingdom shall dare to deny hospitality to rich or poor or pilgrims, that is, no one shall deny shelter and fire and water to pilgrims traversing our country in God's name, or to anyone travelling for the love of God or for the safety of his own soul. . . .

Concerning embassies coming from the lord emperor. That the counts and *centenarii* shall provide most carefully, as they desire the grace of the lord emperor, for the *missi* who are sent out, so that they may go through their departments without any delay; and he commands to all everywhere that they ought to see to it that no delay is encountered anywhere, but they shall cause them to go on their way in all haste and shall provide for them in such a manner as our *missi* may direct. . . .

And against those who announce the justice of the lord emperor, let no one presume to plot any injury or damage, or to stir up any enmity. But if any one shall have presumed, let him pay the imperial ban or, if he deserves a heavier punishment, it is commanded that he shall be brought to the emperor's presence. . . .

That all shall be fully and well prepared, whenever our order or proclamation shall come. But if any one shall then say that he was unprepared and shall have neglected our command, he shall be brought to the palace; and not only he, but also all who dare to transgress our ban or command. . . .

---

[1]A *centenarius* is the ruler of a *centena;* the latter is a subdivision of province or county.

And that all shall be entirely of one mind with our *missi* in performing jus-tice in every respect. And that they shall not permit the use of perjury at all, for it is necessary that this most evil crime shall be removed from the Christian peo-ple. But if any one after this shall have been proved a perjurer, let him know that he shall lose his right hand; and they shall be deprived of their property until we shall render our decision. . . .

Lastly, therefore, we desire all our decrees to be known in our whole king-dom through our *missi* now sent out, either among the men of the church, bish-ops, abbots, priests, deacons, canons, all monks or nuns, so that each one in his ministry or profession may keep our ban or decree, or where it may be fitting to thank the citizens for their good will, or to furnish aid, or where there may be need still of correcting anything. Likewise also to the laymen and in all places everywhere, whether they concern the guardianship of the holy churches or of widows and orphans and the weaker; or the robbing of them; or the arrange-ments for the assembling of the army; or any other matters; how they are to be obedient to our precept and will, or how they observe our ban, or how each one strives in all things to keep himself in the holy service of God; so that all these good things may be well done to the praise of omnipotent God, and we may re-turn thanks where it is fitting. But where we believe there is anything unpun-ished, we shall so strive to correct it with all our zeal and will that with God's aid we may bring it to correction, both for our own eternal glory and that of all our faithful. Likewise we desire all the above to be fruitfully known by our counts or *centenarii*, our ministerials.

DISCUSSION QUESTIONS

1. What does this document reveal about Charlemagne's vision of himself and his empire? In what ways were his Christian beliefs central to both?
2. Why do you think Charlemagne considered it necessary for all freemen to swear an oath of fidelity to him as emperor? How was the notion of fidelity crucial to the success of his government?
3. What do the oath and the other articles suggest about the means by which Charle-magne sought to unify his empire?

2
Liutprand of Cremona
Report to Otto I
968

Charlemagne's successors could not sustain his unifying vision. Wracked by family squabbles, the empire was divided into three kingdoms in 843. The imperial title lived on, however, in the Ottonian dynasty that succeeded the Carolingians in Ger-many in the tenth century. Fashioning himself in Charlemagne's image, Otto I (r. 936–973) was the most powerful of these rulers. Crowned emperor in 962, Otto treated his Byzantine counterpart as an equal. To enhance his status, Otto dispatched his ambassador, Liutprand, a northern Italian bishop, to Constantinople in 968 to arrange the marriage of Otto's son to a Byzantine princess. With this goal in mind, Liutprand met with the Byzantine emperor Nicephorus Phocas (r. 963–969). As he describes in a report sent to Otto, excerpted here, his efforts were in vain, and the failed mission elucidates the widening gaps between the emerging territorial kingdoms in the West and Byzantium.

> That the Ottos, the invincible august emperors of the Romans and the most noble Adelaide the august empress, may always flourish, prosper and triumph, is the earnest wish, desire and prayer of Liudprand bishop of the holy church of Cremona.

On the fourth of June we arrived at Constantinople, and after a miserable reception, meant as an insult to yourselves, we were given the most miserable and disgusting quarters. The palace where we were confined was certainly large and open, but it neither kept out the cold nor afforded shelter from the heat. Armed soldiers were set to guard us and prevent my people from going out, and any others from coming in. This dwelling, only accessible to us who were shut inside it, was so far distant from the emperor's residence that we were quite out of breath when we walked there—we did not ride. To add to our troubles, the Greek wine we found undrinkable because of the mixture in it of pitch, resin and plaster. The house itself had no water and we could not even buy any to quench our thirst. All this was a serious "Oh dear me!", but there was another "Oh dear me" even worse, and that was our warden, the man who provided us with our daily wants. If you were to seek another like him, you certainly would not find him on earth; you might perhaps in hell. Like a raging torrent he poured upon us every calamity, every extortion, every expense, every grief and every misery that he could invent. . . .

On the fourth of June, as I said above, we arrived at Constantinople and waited with our horses in heavy rain outside the Carian gate until five o'clock in the afternoon. At five o'clock Nicephorus ordered us to be admitted on foot, for he did not think us worthy to use the horses with which your clemency had provided us, and we were escorted to the aforesaid hateful, waterless, draughty stone house. On the sixth of June, which was the Saturday before Pentecost, I was brought before the emperor's brother Leo, marshal of the court and chancellor; and there we tired ourselves with a fierce argument over your imperial title. He called you not emperor, which is Basileus in his tongue, but insultingly Rex, which is king in ours. I told him that the thing meant was the same though the word was different, and he then said that I had come not to make peace but to stir up strife. Finally he got up in a rage, and really wishing to insult us received your letter not in his own hand but through an interpreter. . . .

From *The Works of Liudprand of Cremona*, trans. F. A. Wright (New York: E. P. Dutton, 1930), 235–43.

On the seventh of June, the sacred day of Pentecost, I was brought before Nicephorus himself in the palace called Stephana, that is, the Crown Palace. He is a monstrosity of a man, a dwarf, fat-headed and with tiny mole's eyes; disfigured by a short, broad, thick beard half going gray; disgraced by a neck scarcely an inch long; piglike by reason of the big close bristles on his head; in colour an Ethiopian and, as the poet [Juvenal] says,;s1 "you would not like to meet him in the dark"; a big belly, a lean posterior, very long in the hip considering his short stature, small legs, fair sized heels and feet; dressed in a robe made of fine linen, but old, foul smelling, and discoloured by age; shod with Sicyonian slippers; bold of tongue, a fox by nature, in perjury and falsehood a Ulysses. My lords and august emperors, you always seemed comely to me; but how much more comely now! Always magnificent; how much more magnificent now! Always mighty; how much more mighty now! Always clement; how much more clement now! Always full of virtues; how much fuller now! At his left, not on a line with him, but much lower down, sat the two child emperors, once his masters, now his subjects. He began his speech as follows:—

It was our duty and our desire to give you a courteous and magnificent reception. That, however, has been rendered impossible by the impiety of your master, who in the guise of an hostile invader has laid claim to Rome; has robbed Berengar and Adalbert of their kingdom contrary to law and right; has slain some of the Romans by the sword, some by hanging, while others he has either blinded or sent into exile; and furthermore has tried to subdue to himself by massacre and conflagration cities belonging to our empire. His wicked attempts have proved unsuccessful, and so he has sent you, the instigator and furtherer of this villainy, under pretence of peace to act *comme un espion,* that is, as a spy upon us.

To him I made this reply: "My master did not invade the city of Rome by force nor as a tyrant; he freed her from a tyrant's yoke, or rather from the yoke of many tyrants. Was she not ruled by effeminate debauchers, and what is even worse and more shameful, by harlots? Your power, methinks, was fast asleep then; and the power of your predecessors, who in name alone are called emperors of the Romans, while the reality is far different. If they were powerful, if they were emperors of the Romans, why did they allow Rome to be in the hands of harlots?" . . .

"Come, let us clear away all trickeries and speak the plain truth. My master has sent me to you to see if you will give the daughter of the emperor Romanos and the empress Theophano to his son, my master the august emperor Otto. If you give me your oath that the marriage shall take place, I am to affirm to you under oath that my master in grateful return will observe to do this and this for you. Moreover he has already given you, his brother ruler, the best pledge of friendship by handing over Apulia, which was subject to his rule. . . .

From *Late Meroringian France: History and Hagiography, 640–720,* ed. Paul Fouracre and Richard A. Gerberding (Manchester and New York: Manchester University Press, 1996), 121–23, 127, 131–32.

"It is past seven o'clock," said Nicephorus "and there is a church procession which I must attend. Let us keep to the business before us. We will give you a reply at some convenient season."

I think that I shall have as much pleasure in describing this procession as my masters will have in reading of it. . . .

As Nicephorus, like some crawling monster, walked along, the singers began to cry out in adulation: "Behold the morning star approaches: the day star rises: in his eyes the sun's rays are reflected: Nicephorus our prince, the pale death of the Saracens." And then they cried again: "Long life, long life to our prince Nicephorus. Adore him, ye nations, worship him, bow the neck to his greatness." How much more truly might they have sung:—"Come, you miserable burnt-out coal; old woman in your walk, wood-devil in your look; clodhopper, haunter of byres, goat-footed, horned, double-limbed; bristly, wild, rough, barbarian, harsh, hairy, a rebel, a Cappadocian!" So, puffed up by these lying ditties, he entered St Sophia, his masters the emperors following at a distance and doing him homage on the ground with the kiss of peace. His armour bearer, with an arrow for pen, recorded in the church the era in progress since the beginning of his reign. So those who did not see the ceremony know what era it is.

On this same day he ordered me to be his guest. But as he did not think me worthy to be placed above any of his nobles, I sat fifteenth from him and without a table cloth. Not only did no one of my suite sit at table with me; they did not even set eyes upon the house where I was entertained. At the dinner, which was fairly foul and disgusting, washed down with oil after the fashion of drunkards and moistened also with an exceedingly bad fish liquor, the emperor asked me many questions concerning your power, your dominions and your army. My answers were sober and truthful; but he shouted out:—"You lie. Your master's soldiers cannot ride and they do not know how to fight on foot. The size of their shields, the weight of their cuirasses, the length of their swords, and the heaviness of their helmets, does not allow them to fight either way." Then with a smile he added: "Their gluttony also prevents them. Their God is their belly, their courage but wind, their bravery drunkenness. Fasting for them means dissolution, sobriety, panic. Nor has your master any force of ships on the sea. I alone have really stout sailors, and I will attack him with my fleets, destroy his maritime cities and reduce to ashes those which have a river near them. Tell me, how with his small forces will he be able to resist me even on land?" . . .

I wanted to answer and make such a speech in our defence as his boasting deserved; but he would not let me and added this final insult: "You are not Romans but Lombards." He even then was anxious to say more and waved his hand to secure my silence, but I was worked up and cried: "History tells us that Romulus, from whom the Romans get their name, was a fratricide born in adultery. He made a place of refuge for himself and received into it insolvent debtors, runaway slaves, murderers and men who deserved death for their crimes. This was the sort of crowd whom he enrolled as citizens and gave them the name of Romans. From this nobility are descended those men whom you style 'rulers of the world.' But we Lombards, Saxons, Franks, Lotharingians, Bavarians, Swabians and Burgundians, so despise these fellows that when we are angry with an enemy we can find nothing more insulting to say than—'You Roman!' For us in the word Roman is comprehended every form of lowness, timidity, avarice, luxury, falsehood and vice. You say that we are unwarlike and know nothing of horsemanship. Well, if the sins of the Christians merit that you keep this stiff neck, the next war will prove what manner of men you are, and how warlike we."

DISCUSSION QUESTIONS

1. Liutprand's report does not convey a favorable impression of the Byzantine court. Do you think that Liutprand was an objective observer? Why or why not?

2. At the time of Liutprand's visit, Byzantium was enjoying renewed power and influence. How do you think this fact may have shaped the Byzantine court's attitudes toward Liutprand and his master, Otto I?

3. Why did the Byzantine emperor's brother refer to Otto I as "Rex"? Why did Liutprand find this so insulting? What does this suggest about the ways in which the West and Byzantium had grown different both politically and culturally?

3

Digenis Akritas
Tenth or Eleventh Century

In contrast to western Europe, Byzantium not only remained a unified state in the ninth and tenth centuries; it also achieved new heights of power. In this period, Byzantine troops stemmed the Muslim advance and regained territory, to the benefit of both the emperor's prestige and coffers. Victory came at a price, however, as the military aristocracy charged with defending the empire increased their control in the countryside. Written in the tenth or eleventh century, the Byzantine epic poem Digenis Akritas ("two-blood border lord") celebrates the legendary exploits of Digenis, a member of the military elite born of an Arab mother and a Greek father (hence his name). According to the legend, Digenis grew to be a fierce warrior who successfully battled against the Arabs on Byzantium's eastern frontier. In this selection, Digenis meets the Byzantine emperor (whose identity is uncertain), for whom he has both praise and advice.

On hearing of these deeds, the Emperor
Who at that time was governing the Romans,
Basil the Blesséd, the great trophy winner,
Whose imperial fame was buried with him,

From *Digenis Akritas: The Two-Blood Border Lord*, trans. Denison B. Hull (Athens: Ohio University Press, 1972), 59–61.

Chanced to be on campaign against the Persians
In those same places where the boy [Digenis] was living,
And when he heard about it was amazed.
So wishing greatly he might see the youth,
He sent a letter to him with these words:
"We've learned the stories of your many exploits,
My son, and we have much rejoiced in them,
And offered thanks to God who works with you.
Our purpose is to see you with our own eyes,
And give requital worthy of your deeds.
Come to us gladly, without hesitation,
And don't suspect you'll suffer hurt from us."
When he received this, he returned an answer:
"I am your majesty's most abject slave;
Indeed, I have no right to your good things.
Master, what deed of mine do you admire,
Who am so humble, base, and quite undaring?
Still, he who trusts in God can do all things.
Therefore, since you desire to see your servant,
Be by the Euphrates after a little while.
You'll see me all you wish, my sacred master.
Don't think that I refuse to come before you,
But you have certain inexperienced soldiers,
And if perhaps they say something they shouldn't,
I certainly would deprive you of such men,
For such things, master, happen to the young."
  The Emperor read his letter word by word,
Admired the humbleness of the boy's statement,
And understood with pleasure his high courage.
  Since he wished strongly to behold the youth,
He took along with him a hundred soldiers,
Some spearmen too, and went to the Euphrates,
Ordering all on no account to utter
A word offensive to the Border Lord.
Those posted to keep watch on his account
Shortly announced the Emperor's arrival
To the marvelous Two-Blood Border Lord.
The Two-Blood came out all alone to meet him,
And bowed his head down to the ground, and said,
"Hail, you who take imperial power from God,
And rule us all because of the heathen's sins.
Why has it happened that the whole world's master
Comes before me, who am of no account?"
The Emperor, astonished when he saw him,

Forgot the burden of his majesty,
Advanced a little from his throne, embraced him,
Joyfully kissed him, and admired his stature,
And the great promise of his well-formed beauty.
"My son," he said, "you've proof of all your deeds;
The way you're put together shows your courage.
Would that Romania [Byzantium] had four such men!
So speak, my son, freely and openly,
And then take anything you wish from us."
"Keep everything, my lord," the boy replied,
"Because your love alone is enough for me.
It's not more blesséd to receive than give;
You have immense expenses in your army.
So I beseech your glorious majesty:
Love him who is obedient, pity the poor,
Deliver the oppressed from malefactors,
Forgive those who unwittingly make blunders,
And heed no slanders, nor accept injustice,
Sweep heretics out, confirm the orthodox.
These, master, are the arms of righteousness
With which you can prevail over all foes.
To rule and reign are not part of that power
Which God and His right hand alone can give.
Vile as I am, I grant your majesty
To take what you once gave Iconium
As tribute, and as much again, from them.
Master, I'll make you carefree about this
Until my soul shakes off this mortal coil."
      The Emperor was delighted at these words.
"O marvelous and excellent young man,"
He said, "we name you a patrician now,
And grant you all your grandfather's estates;
We give to you the power to rule the borders,
And will confirm this with a golden bull,
And furnish you with rich imperial raiment."

DISCUSSION QUESTIONS

1. What does Digenis's conversation with the emperor reveal about the basis of imperial authority and prestige?

2. What advice does Digenis offer the emperor on the proper method of rule? What do his words suggest about the characteristics of an ideal emperor?

3. In this passage, it is the emperor, not Digenis, who arranges their meeting, at which the emperor pays homage to him. What does this imply about the status of warriors like Digenis in Byzantine society and the emperor's relationship to them?

4

Ahmad al-Yaʿqūbī
Kitāb al-buldān
Ninth Century

At the same time Charlemagne was forging his empire, Islamic leaders were strength-
ening their own. In 750, a new dynasty of caliphs, the Abbasids, seized control of the
Islamic state, which they brought to new heights of power and influence. The foun-
dation of a new capital city, Baghdad, in 762 by the Abbasids physically embodied
the revolutionary nature of their rule. In the first fifty years of their reign, they trans-
formed Baghdad into the hub of the Islamic state. An early historian of Islam and
descendant of the Abbasid family, Ahmad al-Yaʿqūbī (d. 897), experienced the dy-
namism of the city firsthand during his travels as a young man, and he later in-
cluded his observations in a geographical work, Kitāb al-buldān, *which he wrote*
near the end of his life. Although composed after economic problems had begun to
tarnish the Abbasids' luster, Kitāb al-buldān *elucidates the cultural and economic*
forces binding the Islamic world together even at a time when the caliphate was frag-
menting into separate political units.

I begin with Iraq only because it is the center of this world, the navel of the earth,
and I mention Baghdad first because it is the center of Iraq, the greatest city,
which has no peer in the east or the west of the world in extent, size, prosperity,
abundance of water, or health of climate, and because it is inhabited by all kinds
of people, town-dwellers and country-dwellers. To it they come from all countries, far and near, and people from every side have preferred Baghdad to their
own homelands. There is no country, the peoples of which have not their own
quarter and their own trading and financial arrangements. In it there is gathered
that which does not exist in any other city in the world. On its flanks flow two
great rivers, the Tigris and the Euphrates, and thus goods and foodstuffs come to
it by land and by water with the greatest ease, so that every kind of merchandise
is completely available, from east and west, from Muslim and non-Muslim lands.
Goods are brought from India, Sind, China, Tibet, the lands of the Turks, the
Daylam, the Khazars, the Ethiopians, and others to such an extent that the products of the countries are more plentiful in Baghdad than in the countries from
which they come. They can be procured so readily and so certainly that it is as if
all the good things of the world are sent there, all the treasures of the earth assembled there, and all the blessings of creation perfected there.

From *Islam: From the Prophet Muhammad to the Capture of Constantinople*, vol. 2, ed.
Bernard Lewis (New York: Walker & Co., 1974), 69–73.

Furthermore, Baghdad is the city of the Hashimites, the home of their reign, the seat of their sovereignty, where no one appeared before them and no kings but they have dwelt. Also, my own forbears have lived there, and one of them was governor of the city.

Its name is famous, and its fame widespread. Iraq is indeed the center of the world, for in accordance with the consensus of the astronomers recorded in the writings of ancient scholars, it is in the fourth climate, which is the middle climate where the temperature is regular at all times and seasons. It is very hot in the summer, very cold in the winter, and temperate in autumn and in spring. The passage from autumn to winter and from spring to summer is gradual and imperceptible, and the succession of the seasons is regular. So, the weather is temperate, the soil is rich, the water is sweet, the trees are thriving, the fruit luscious, the seeds are fertile, good things are abundant, and springs are easily found. Because of the temperate weather and rich soil and sweet water, the character of the inhabitants is good, their faces bright, and their minds untrammeled. The people excel in knowledge, understanding, letters, manners, insight, discernment, skill in commerce and crafts, cleverness in every argument, proficiency in every calling, and mastery of every craft. There is none more learned than their scholars, better informed than their traditionists, more cogent than their theologians, more perspicuous than their grammarians, more accurate than their readers, more skillful than their physicians, more melodious than their singers, more delicate than their craftsmen, more literate than their scribes, more lucid than their logicians, more devoted than their worshippers, more pious than their ascetics, more juridical than their judges, more eloquent than their preachers, more poetic than their poets, and more reckless than their rakes.

In ancient days, that is to say in the time of the Chosroes and the Persians, Baghdad was not a city, but only a village in the district of Bādūrayā. The city in Iraq which the Chosroes had chosen for their capital was al-Madā'in, seven parasangs from Baghdad. The audience chamber of Chosroes Anushirvan is still there. At that time there was nothing in Baghdad but a convent situated at a place called Qarn al-Ṣarāt, at the confluence of the Ṣarāt and the Tigris. This convent is called al-Dayr al-'Atīq [the ancient convent] and is still standing at the present time. It is the residence of the Catholicos, the head of the Nestorian Christians.

Nor does Baghdad figure in the wars of the Arabs at the time of the advent of Islam, since the Arabs founded Basra and Kūfa. Kūfa was founded in the year 17 [638] by Sa'd ibn Abī Waqqās al-Zuhrī, one of 'Umar ibn al-Khaṭṭāb's governors. Basra, too, was founded in the year 17 by 'Utba ibn Ghazwān al-Māzinī of the tribe of Māzin of Qays, also a governor of 'Umar ibn al-Khaṭṭāb at that time. The Arabs settled down in these two places, but the important people, the notables, and the rich merchants moved to Baghdad.

The Umayyads lived in Syria and did not stay in Iraq. Mu'āwiya ibn Abī Sufyān, who had been governor of Syria in the name of 'Umar ibn al-Khaṭṭāb and then of 'Uthmān ibn 'Affān for twenty years, lived in Damascus with his family. When he seized power and sovereignty passed to him, he kept his residence and capital in Damascus, where he had his authority, his supporters, and his faction.

The Umayyad kings after Mu'āwiya stayed in Damascus, since they were born there and knew no other place, and its people were their sole supporters.

Then the Caliphate came to the descendants of the paternal uncle of the Apostle of God, may God bless and save him and also his family, the line of 'Abbās ibn 'Abd al-Muṭṭalib. Thanks to clear discernment, sound intelligence, and perfect judgment, they saw the merits of Iraq, its magnificence, spaciousness, and central situation. They saw that it was not like Syria, with its pestilential air, narrow houses, rugged soil, constant diseases, and uncouth people; nor was it like Egypt, with changeable weather and many plagues, situated between a damp and fetid river, full of unhealthy mists that engender disease and spoil food, and the dry, bare mountains, so dry and salty and bad that no plant can grow nor any spring appear; nor like Ifrīqiya, far from the peninsula of Islam and from the holy house of God, with uncouth people and many foes; nor like Armenia, remote, cold and icy, barren, and surrounded by enemies; nor like the districts of the Jabal, harsh, rough, and snow-covered, the abode of the hard-hearted Kurds; nor like the land of Khurāsān, stretching to the east, surrounded on every side by rabid and war-like enemies; nor like the Ḥijāz where life is hard and means are few and the people's food comes from elsewhere, as Almighty God warned us in His book, through His friend Ibrāhīm, who said, "O Lord, I have given to my descendants as dwelling a valley without tillage" [Qur'an]; nor like Tibet, where, because of the foul air and food, the people are discolored, with stunted bodies and tufty hair.

When they understood that Iraq was the best of countries, the 'Abbasids decided to settle there. In the first instance the Commander of the Faithful, Abu'l-'Abbās, that is 'Abdallāh ibn Muḥammad ibn 'Alī ibn 'Abdallāh ibn 'Abbās ibn 'Abd al-Muṭṭalib, stayed in Kūfa. Then he moved to Anbār and built a city on the banks of the Euphrates which he called Hāshimiyya. Abu'l-'Abbās, may God be pleased with him, died before the building of this city was completed.

Then, when Abū Ja'far al-Manṣūr. succeeded to the Caliphate, he founded a new city between Kūfa and Ḥīra, which he also called Hāshimiyya. He stayed there for a while, until the time when he decided to send his son, Muḥammad al-Mahdī, to fight the Slavs in the year 140 [757–758]. He then came to Baghdad and stopped there, and asked, "What is the name of this place?" They answered, "Baghdad." "By God," said the Caliph, "this is indeed the city which my father Muḥammad ibn 'Alī told me I must build, in which I must live, and in which my descendants after me will live. Kings were unaware of it before and since Islam, until God's plans for me and orders to me are accomplished. Thus, the traditions will be verified and the signs and proofs be manifest. Indeed, this island between the Tigris in the east and the Euphrates in the west is a marketplace for the world. All the ships that come up the Tigris from Wāsiṭ, Basra, Ubulla, Ahwāz, Fārs, 'Umān, Yamāma, Baḥrayn, and beyond will anchor here; wares brought on ships down the Tigris from Mosul, Diyār-Rabī'a, Ādharbayjān, and Armenia, and along the Euphrates from Diyār-Muḍar, Raqqa, Syria, the border marches, Egypt, and North Africa, will be brought and unloaded here. It will be the highway for the people of the Jabal, Iṣfahān, and the districts of Khurāsān. Praise be to God who preserved it for me and caused all those who came before me to neglect it. By God, I shall build it. Then I shall dwell in it as long as I live, and my descendants shall dwell in it after me. It will surely be the most flourishing city in the world.

Discussion Questions

1. Considering his family connections, do you think that we can accept Ahmad al-Ya'qubi's view of Baghdad at face value? Why or why not?

2. His potential biases aside, what does Ahmad al-Ya'qubi reveal about the geographical breadth and ethnic diversity of the Islamic empire?

3. As described here, how did trade help unify the Islamic Empire at a time when it was beginning to fragment politically?

Comparative Questions

1. In what ways does Liutprand point to both the success and failure of Charlemagne's political vision as revealed in the capitulary for the *missi*?

2. Based on *Digenis Akritas* and Liutprand's report, how and why did Otto I's imperial image and claims to power compete with those of the Byzantine emperor?

3. How do Liutprand, Ahmad al-Ya'qubi, and Digenis seek to enhance the image of their respective rulers? What does this suggest about the role of praise in both Eastern and Western culture in the tenth century?

4. When viewed together, what do these documents reveal about the development of Byzantium, Islam, and Western Europe as distinctive societies with their own identities in the ninth and tenth centuries?

10

Renewal and Reform
1050–1150

S U M M A R Y   Western Europe was alive with change in the late eleventh and early twelfth centuries. Trade and agricultural production were on the rise, promoting the development of a new, cash-based economy. A greater prevalence of wealth prompted a range of responses at all levels of medieval society. The first document set elucidates how economic growth transformed Europe as new municipalities were established and old ones enlarged. With the economy booming, many ecclesiastical leaders feared that the church was becoming too entangled in its web. The second document suggests how this fear helped spark a religious reform movement that elevated the papacy to new heights of power. Even so, as the third document demonstrates, secular rulers strove to solidify their authority, buttressed by growing, fiscally minded bureaucracies. The final document unveils the intellectual manifestations of these currents of renewal and reform.

1
Urban Charters of Jaca, Spain
c. 1077
and *Loriss, France*
1155

Although cities were common in the Roman Empire, they featured less prominently in early medieval Europe, where wealth and power were derived largely from land. In the eleventh century, however, agricultural and commercial growth resulted in new cities and towns springing up across Europe as places where people congregated to live and work. These two documents attest to the rise of medieval urbanism and its economic and social implications. The first is a charter of laws and freedoms (fuero) bestowed on the community of Jaca in Christian Spain by Sancho I (r. 1063–1094), king of Aragon, around 1077. The second is another charter, this one granted by King Louis VII of France (r. 1137–1180) in 1155, which regulated the governance of the town of Lorris.

[Emblem of Christ] In the name of our Lord Jesus Christ and of the undivided Trinity, Father and Son and Holy Spirit, amen. This is a charter of authority and confirmation which I Sancho, by the grace of God king of the Aragonese and Pamplonese, make to you.

Notice to all men who are even in the east and west and north and south that I wish to establish a city [*civitatem*] in my village [*villa*]¹ which is called "Jaca."

First, I remit to you all bad *fueros* which you had until this day that I established Jaca to be a city; and so, because I wish it to be well settled, I concede and confirm to you and to all who settle in my city Jaca all the good *fueros* which you have asked of me in order that my city be well settled.

And each one may enclose his part as he can.

And if it happen that anyone of you comes to dispute and will strike anyone before me or in my palace when I am standing there, let him fine for 1000 s. or lose the fight.

And if anyone, whether knight or burgher or peasant, should strike another, and not in my presence nor in my palace although I be in Jaca, let him not pay the fine [*calonia*] except according to the *fuero* you have when I am not in the town.

And if it happen that someone be found killed in a robbery in Jaca or its district, you are not obligated to pay homicide.²

I give and concede to you and your successors with good will that you not go in the army [*hoste*] unless with bread for three days. And this should be in the name of battle in the field [*de lite campale*] or where I or my successors are surrounded by our enemies. And if the lord of the house does not wish to go there, let him substitute one armed footman.

And wherever you can buy anything in Jaca or outside of Jaca, or acquire any man's inheritance, you may have it free and unencumbered without any bad cut [*malo cisso*].³

From *Medieval Iberia*, ed. Olivia Remie Constable (Philadelphia: University of Pennsylvania Press, 1997), 123–25; and *A Source Book of Mediaeval History*, Frederic Austin Ogg (New York: American Book Co., 1907), 328–30.

¹The word *villa* does not always mean "village" in medieval Latin, but it does often refer to unwalled settlements in Mediterranean Europe.

²That is, the murder fine sometimes imposed by lords on communities.

³The "cut," like tallage elsewhere, was an arbitrary tax.

And after you hold it undisturbed for a year and a day, anyone wishing to disturb them or take it away from you shall give me 60 s., and shall confirm your inheritance.

And as far as you can go and return in a day, everywhere, you may have pastures and woods, observing the boundaries of the men living there.

And that you should not have duel-war between you, unless agreeable to both; nor with men from elsewhere, unless with consent of the men of Jaca.

And that none of you should sit captive giving pledges of your foot [de vestro pede].[4]

And if any of you commits fornication with any willing woman, except a married one, you shall not pay calumny. And if it happens that he forces her, let him give her a husband or receive her as his wife. And if the raped woman appeals on the first or second day, let her prove by truthful witnesses of Jaca. If she wishes to appeal after three days, it shall avail her nothing.

And if any of you goes against his neighbor in anger and armed with lance, sword, club, or knife, let him fine for it 1000 s. or lose the fight.

And if anyone kills another let him pay 500 s.

And if one strikes another in conflict or grabs him by the hair, let him pay 25 s. for it.

And if he falls to the ground, let him pay 250 s.

And if anyone enters his neighbor's house in anger, or makes seizures there, let him pay 25 s. to the lord of the house.

And that my agent [*merinus*] not receive calumny[5] from any man of Jaca save with the approval of six better men [*vicinis*] of Jaca.

And none of all the men of Jaca should go to judgment anywhere but in Jaca.

And if anyone has false measure or weight, let him pay 60 s.

And that all men should go to mill in mills where they wish, except Jews and those who make bread for sale.

And you should not give or sell your honors to the church or to *infanzones.*[6]

And if any man is imprisoned for debt, let him who wishes to capture him do so with my agent; and let him put [him] in my palace, and let my jailer guard him; and after three days, he who took him should give him farthing's worth [*obolatam*]; and if he refuse to do [this], my jailer may release him.

And if any man seize as pledge the Saracen man or Saracen woman of his neighbor, let him put him in my palace; and the lord of the male and female Saracen shall give him bread and water, because he is a human being [*homo*] and should not starve like a beast.

---

[4]Meaning unclear.

[5]*Calumny* was a payment exacted for slander.

[6]The *infanzones* were the lesser aristocracy of knights in Aragon.

And whoever wishes to disrupt this charter which I make to the settlers of Jaca, let him be excommunicated and anathematized for his cruelty and wholly separated from all God's faithful, whether he be of my stock or of another. Amen, amen, amen.

Every one who has a house in the parish of Lorris shall pay as *cens* sixpence only for his house, and for each acre of land that he possesses in the parish.[7]

No inhabitant of the parish of Lorris shall be required to pay a toll or any other tax on his provisions; and let him not be made to pay any measurage fee on the grain which he has raised by his own labor.[8]

No burgher shall go on an expedition, on foot or on horseback, from which he cannot return the same day to his home if he desires.[9]

No burgher shall pay toll on the road to Étampes, to Orleans, to Milly (which is in the Gâtinais), or to Melun.[10]

No one who has property in the parish of Lorris shall forfeit it for any offense whatsoever, unless the offense shall have been committed against us or any of our *hôtes*.[11]

No person while on his way to the fairs and markets of Lorris, or returning, shall be arrested or disturbed, unless he shall have committed an offense on the same day. . . .[12]

---

[7]This trifling payment of sixpence a year was made in recognition of the lordship of the king, the grantor of the charter. Aside from it, the burgher had full rights over his land.

[8]The burghers, who were often engaged in agriculture as well as commerce, are to be exempt from tolls on commodities bought for their own sustenance and from the ordinary fees due the lord for each measure of grain harvested.

[9]The object of this provision is to restrict the amount of military service due the king. The burghers of small places like Lorris were farmers and traders who made poor soldiers and who were ordinarily exempted from service by their lords. The provision for Lorris practically amounted to an exemption, for such service as was permissible under Chapter 3 of the charter was not worth much.

[10]The Gâtinais was the region in which Lorris was situated. Étampes, Milly, and Melun all lay to the north of Lorris, in the direction of Paris. Orleans lay to the west. The king's object in granting the burghers the right to carry goods to the towns specified without payment of tolls was to encourage commercial intercourse.

[11]This protects the landed property of the burghers against the crown and crown officials. With two exceptions, fine or imprisonment, not confiscation of land, is to be the penalty for crime. *Hôtes* denotes persons receiving land from the king and under his direct protection.

[12]This provision is intended to attract merchants to Lorris by placing them under the king's protection and assuring them that they would not be molested on account of old offenses.

No one, neither we nor any other, shall exact from the burghers of Lorris any tallage, tax, or subsidy. . . . .[13]

If a man shall have had a quarrel with another, but without breaking into a fortified house, and if the parties shall have reached an agreement without bringing a suit before the provost, no fine shall be due to us or our provost, no fine shall be due to us or our provost on account of the affair. . . . .[14]

No inhabitant of Lorris is to render us the obligation of *corvée*, except twice a year, when our wine is to be carried to Orleans, and not elsewhere.[15]

No one shall be detained in prison if he can furnish surety that he will present himself for judgment.

Any burgher who wishes to sell his property shall have the privilege of doing so; and, having received the price of the sale, he shall have the right to go from the town freely and without molestation, if he so desires, unless he has committed some offense in it.

Any one who shall dwell a year and a day in the parish of Lorris, without any claim having pursued him there, and without having refused to lay his case before us or our provost, shall abide there freely and without molestation. . . .[16]

We ordain that every time there shall be a change of provosts in the town the new provost shall take an oath faithfully to observe these regulations; and the same thing shall be done by new sergeants[17] every time that they are installed.

DISCUSSION QUESTIONS

1. What do these two documents reveal about the role of kings in promoting urban growth in medieval Europe?

---

[13]This chapter safeguards the personal property of the burghers, as Chapter 5 safeguards their land. Arbitrary imposts are forbidden and any of the inhabitants who as serfs had been paying arbitrary tallage are relieved of the burden. The nominal *cens* (Chapter 1) was to be the only regular payment due the king.

[14]An agreement outside of court was allowable in all cases except when there was a serious breach of the public peace. The provost was the chief officer of the town. He was appointed by the crown and was charged chiefly with the administration of justice and the collection of revenues. All suits of the burghers were tried in his court. They had no active part in their own government, as was generally true of the franchise towns.

[15]Another part of the charter specifies that only those burghers who owned horses and carts were expected to render the king even this service.

[16]This clause, which is very common in the town charters of the twelfth century (especially in the case of towns on the royal domain) is intended to attract serfs from other regions and so to build up population. As a rule, the towns were places of refuge from seigniorial oppression, and the present charter undertakes to limit the time within which the lord might recover his serf who had fled to Lorris to a year and a day—except in cases where the serf should refuse to recognize the jurisdiction of the provost's court in the matter of the lord's claim.

[17]The sergeants were deputies of the provost, somewhat on the order of town constables.

2. What did Louis VII and Sancho I seek to gain in granting their respective charters? What similarities and differences do you see in each king's goals?

3. Based on these two charters, why do you think people decided to move to newly established cities and towns? What did city life have to offer?

2

Emperor Henry IV and Pope Gregory VII
Letters of the Investiture Conflict
1076

The commercial revolution helped spark not only economic changes but also religious ones. Pope Gregory VII (r. 1073–1085) became the driving force behind a movement for church reform, which strove to liberate the church from secular influence and wealth. His zeal brought him head to head with Emperor Henry IV (r. 1056–1106) who, claiming to be crowned by God, asserted the traditional right to oversee the church in his realm. These two documents illuminate each side of the debate. The first is a letter that Henry sent to the pope in January 1076 after he had denounced him for not obeying papal mandates prohibiting (among other things) laymen from "investing" (that is, appointing) church leaders. In response, the pope excommunicated and deposed Henry. The lines of the conflict were thus drawn, pitting imperial and papal claims of authority against each other. Although the battle ended in 1122 with a compromise, the papacy emerged as a more powerful force than ever before.

O blessed Peter, prince of the Apostles, mercifully incline thine ear, we [*sic*] pray, and hear me, thy servant, whom thou hast cherished from infancy and hast delivered until now from the hand of the wicked who have hated and still hate me for my loyalty to thee. Thou art my witness, as are also my Lady, the Mother of God, and the blessed Paul, thy brother among all the saints, that thy Holy Roman Church forced me against my will to be its ruler. I had no thought of ascending thy throne as a robber, nay, rather would I have chosen to end my life as a pilgrim than to seize upon thy place for earthly glory and by devices of this world. Therefore, by thy favor, not by any works of mine, I believe that it is and has been thy will, that the Christian people especially committed to thee should render obedience to me, thy especially constituted representative. To me is given by thy grace the power of binding and loosing in Heaven and upon earth.

From *The Correspondence of Pope Gregory VII*, trans. Ephraim Emerton (New York: Columbia University Press, 1932), 90–91; and *Imperial Lives and Letters of the Eleventh Century*, trans. Theodor E. Mommsen and Karl F. Morrison (New York: Columbia University Press, 1962), 150–51.

Wherefore, relying upon this commission, and for the honor and defense of thy Church, in the name of Almighty God, Father, Son and Holy Spirit, through thy power and authority, I deprive King Henry, son of the emperor Henry, who has rebelled against thy Church with unheard of audacity, of the government over the whole kingdom of Germany and Italy, and I release all Christian men from the allegiance which they have sworn or may swear to him, and I forbid anyone to serve him as king. For it is fitting that he who seeks to diminish the glory of thy Church should lose the glory which he seems to have.

And, since he has refused to obey as a Christian should or to return to the God whom he has abandoned by taking part with excommunicated persons, has spurned my warnings which I gave him for his soul's welfare, as thou knowest, and has separated himself from thy Church and tried to rend it asunder, I bind him in the bonds of anathema in thy stead and I bind him thus as commissioned by thee, that the nations may know and be convinced that thou art Peter and that upon thy rock the son of the living God has built his Church and the gates of hell shall not prevail against it.

Henry, King not by usurpation, but by the pious ordination of God, to Hildebrand, now not Pope, but false monk:

You have deserved such a salution as this because of the confusion you have wrought; for you left untouched no order of the Church which you could make a sharer of confusion instead of honor, of malediction instead of benediction.

For to discuss a few outstanding points among many: Not only have you dared to touch the rectors of the holy Church—the archbishops, the bishops, and the priests, anointed of the Lord as they are—but you have trodden them under foot like slaves who know not what their lord may do. In crushing them you have gained for yourself acclaim from the mouth of the rabble. You have judged that all these know nothing, while you alone know everything. In any case, you have sedulously used this knowledge not for edification, but for destruction, so greatly that we may believe Saint Gregory, whose name you have arrogated to yourself, rightly made this prophesy of you when he said: "From the abundance of his subjects, the mind of the prelate is often exalted, and he thinks that he has more knowledge than anyone else, since he sees that he has more power than anyone else."

And we, indeed, bore with all these abuses, since we were eager to preserve the honor of the Apostolic See. But you construed our humility as fear, and so you were emboldened to rise up even against the royal power itself, granted to us by God. You dared to threaten to take the kingship away from us—as though we had received the kingship from you, as though kingship and empire were in your hand and not in the hand of God.

Our Lord, Jesus Christ, has called us to kingship, but has not called you to the priesthood. For you have risen by these steps: namely, by cunning, which the monastic profession abhors, to money; by money to favor; by favor to the sword. By the sword you have come to the throne of peace, and from the throne of peace you have destroyed the peace. You have armed subjects against their prelates; you who have not been called by God have taught that our bishops who have been called by God are to be spurned; you have usurped for laymen the bishops' ministry over priests, with the result that these laymen depose and condemn the very men whom the laymen themselves received as teachers from the hand of God, through the imposition of the hands of bishops.

You have also touched me, one who, though unworthy, has been anointed to kingship among the anointed. This wrong you have done to me, although as the tradition of the holy Fathers has taught, I am to be judged by God alone and am not to be deposed for any crime unless—may it never happen—I should deviate from the Faith. For the prudence of the holy bishops entrusted the judgment and the deposition even of Julian the Apostate not to themselves, but to God alone. The true pope Saint Peter also exclaims, "Fear God, honor the king." You, however, since you do not fear God, dishonor me, ordained of Him.

Wherefore, when Saint Paul gave no quarter to an angel from heaven if the angel should preach heterodoxy, he did not except you who are now teaching heterodoxy throughout the earth. For he says, "If anyone, either I or an angel from heaven, preach any other gospel unto you than that which we have preached unto you, let him be accursed." Descend, therefore, condemned by this anathema and by the common judgment of all our bishops and of ourself. Relinquish the Apostolic See which you have arrogated. Let another mount the throne of Saint Peter, another who will not cloak violence with religion but who will teach the pure doctrine of Saint Peter.

I, Henry, King by the grace of God, together with all our bishops, say to you: Descend! Descend!

Discussion Questions

1. What does Henry IV mean by denouncing the pope as a "false monk"?
2. What do the emperor's denunciations reveal about his conception of the source and scope of his power?
3. How did Henry's self-image conflict with Gregory's understanding of his own authority as reflected in his excommunication and deposition of the emperor?

3

The Anglo-Saxon Chronicle
1085–1086

While the papacy was expanding its authority in the eleventh century, regional rulers were doing much the same. William I, duke of Normandy and king of England (r. 1066–1087), provides a case in point, and his efforts on this front helped to make his twelfth-century successors the mightiest kings in Europe. Upon conquering his rival to the throne in the battle of Hastings in 1066, William consolidated his rule by preserving existing institutions and establishing new ones. Among his achievements was the commission of a comprehensive survey of England's land, livestock, taxes, and population, which was conducted in 1086. Later condensed into two volumes, known as Domesday, the survey paints a detailed picture of England's agricultural and urban landscape. Here is a contemporary description of King William and his survey from the Anglo-Saxon Chronicle, *a year-by-year account of English history from the birth of Christ to 1154, which bears witness to the king's immense resources and power.*

In this year people said and declared for a fact, that Cnut, king of Denmark, son of King Swein, was setting out in this direction and meant to conquer this country with the help of Robert, count of Flanders, because Cnut was married to Robert's daughter. When William, king of England, who was then in Normandy —for he was in possession of both England and Normandy—found out about this, he went to England with a larger force of mounted men and infantry from France and Brittany than had ever come to this country, so that people wondered how this country could maintain all that army. And the king had all the army dispersed all over the country among his vassals, and they provisioned the army each in proportion to his land. And people had much oppression that year, and the king had the land near the sea laid waste, so that if his enemies landed, they should have nothing to seize on so quickly. But when the king found out for a fact that his enemies had been hindered and could not carry out their expedition —then he let some of the army go to their own country, and some he kept in this country over winter.

Then at Christmas, the king was at Gloucester with his council, and held his court there for five days, and then the archbishop and clerics had a synod for three days. There Maurice was elected bishop of London, and William for Norfolk, and Robert for Cheshire—they were all clerics of the king.

After this, the king had much thought and very deep discussion with his council about this country—how it was occupied or with what sort of people. Then he sent his men over all England into every shire and had them find out how many hundred hides there were in the shire, or what land and cattle the king himself had in the country, or what dues he ought to have in twelve months from the shire.[1] Also he had a record made of how much land his archbishops had, and his bishops and his abbots and his earls—and though I relate it at too great length—what or how much everybody had who was occupying land in England, in land or cattle, and how much money it was worth. So very narrowly did he have it investigated, that there was no single hide nor virgate of land, nor indeed (it is a shame to relate but it seemed no shame to him to do) one ox nor one cow nor one pig which was there left out, and not put down in his record; and all these records were brought to him afterwards. . . .

This King William of whom we speak was a very wise man,[2] and very powerful and more worshipful and stronger than any predecessor of his had been. He

---

From *The Anglo-Saxon Chronicle,* trans. Dorothy Whitelock (New Brunswick, N.J.: Rutgers University Press, 1961), 161–65.

[1]This initiative resulted in Domesday. A **hide** was a unit of taxation. [—Ed.]

[2]The remarkable account which follows was clearly written by a man who had attended William's court.

was gentle to the good men who loved God, and stern beyond all measure to those people who resisted his will. In the same place where God permitted him to conquer England, he set up a famous monastery and appointed monks for it,[3] and endowed it well. In his days the famous church at Canterbury was built,[4] and also many another over all England. Also, this country was very full of monks, and they lived their life under the rule of St. Benedict, and Christianity was such in his day that each man who wished followed out whatever concerned his order. Also, he was very dignified: three times every year he wore his crown, as often as he was in England. At Easter he wore it at Winchester, at Whitsuntide at Westminster, and at Christmas at Gloucester, and then there were with him all the powerful men over all England, archbishops and bishops, abbots and earls, thegns and knights. Also, he was a very stern and violent man, so that no one dared do anything contrary to his will. He had earls in his fetters, who acted against his will. He expelled bishops from their sees, and abbots from their abbacies, and put thegns in prison, and finally he did not spare his own brother, who was called Odo; he was a very powerful bishop in Normandy (his cathedral church was at Bayeux) and was the foremost man next the king, and had an earldom in England. And when the king was in Normandy, then he was master in this country; and he [the king] put *him* in prison. Amongst other things the good security he made in this country is not to be forgotten—so that any honest man could travel over his kingdom without injury with his bosom full of gold; and no one dared strike[5] another, however much wrong he had done him. And if any man had intercourse with a woman against her will, he was forthwith castrated.

He ruled over England, and by his cunning it was so investigated that there was not one hide of land in England that he did not know who owned it, and what it was worth, and then set it down in his record.[6] Wales was in his power, and he built castles there, and he entirely controlled that race. In the same way, he also subdued Scotland to himself, because of his great strength. The land of Normandy was his by natural inheritance, and he ruled over the county called Maine; and if he could have lived two years more, he would have conquered Ireland by his prudence and without any weapons. Certainly in his time people had much oppression and very many injuries:

He had castles built
And poor men hard oppressed.
The king was so very stark
And deprived his underlings of many a mark
Of gold and more hundreds of pounds of silver,
That he took by weight and with great injustice

---

[3]Battle Abbey.
[4]Lanfranc's rebuilding of Christ Church, Canterbury.
[5]Or "kill."
[6]Domesday.

From his people with little need for such a deed.
Into avarice did he fall
And loved greediness above all.
He made great protection for the game
And imposed laws for the same,
That who so slew hart or hind
Should be made blind.

He preserved the harts and boars
And loved the stags as much
As if he were their father.
Moreover, for the hares did he decree that they should go free.
Powerful men complained of it and poor men lamented it,
But so fierce was he that he cared not for the rancour of them all,
But they had to follow out the king's will entirely
If they wished to live or hold their land,
Property or estate, or his favour great.
Alas! woe, that any man so proud should go,
And exalt himself and reckon himself above all men!
May Almighty God show mercy to his soul
And grant unto him forgiveness for his sins.

These things we have written about him, both good and bad, that good men may imitate their good points, and entirely avoid the bad, and travel on the road that leads us to the kingdom of heaven.

DISCUSSION QUESTIONS

1. How does the *Anglo-Saxon Chronicle* present the Domesday survey as a reflection of William's method of rule in general?
2. What does the chronicle suggest about the basis of William's authority?
3. Do you think that the author of this excerpt was an objective observer? Why or why not?

4

Hildegard of Bingen
Selected Writings
Twelfth Century

As Europe's political, economic, and physical landscape changed in the twelfth century, so, too, did its intellectual life. Although lacking a formal education, Hildegard of Bingen (1098–1179) was among the most creative scholars of her day. Born to a noble German family, Hildegard entered a Benedictine convent as a young girl. Her life there was unremarkable until 1141, when a divine voice ordered her to "tell and write" about the visions she had had since her childhood. Thus began her remark-

able career as an author, preacher, and mystic. Here are two selections from her many writings. The first is a hymn from her collection of liturgical songs, Symphony of the Harmony of Heavenly Revelations *(c. 1158). The* Symphony *reveals Hildegard's passion for music, which lay at the heart of Benedictine monasticism. This fact helps explain why she found it so difficult to comply with the interdict, imposed on her convent by prelates in Mainz in 1178, that forbade the community to chant their prayers and songs. She responded to the prohibition in the following letter; in it she describes the power of music to reveal God's majesty.*

Antiphon for the Virgin

Because it was a woman
who built a house for death
a shining girl tore it down.
So now
when you ask for blessings
seek the supreme one
in the form of a woman
surpassing all that God made
since in her
(O tender! O blessed!)
he became one of us.

By a vision, which was implanted in my soul by God the Great Artisan before I was born, I have been compelled to write these things because of the interdict by which our superiors have bound us, on account of a certain dead man buried at our monastery, a man buried without any objection, with his own priest officiating. Yet only a few days after his burial, these men ordered us to remove him from our cemetery. Seized by no small terror, as a result, I looked as usual to the True Light, and, with wakeful eyes, I saw in my spirit that if this man were disinterred in accordance with their commands, a terrible and lamentable danger would come upon us like a dark cloud before a threatening thunderstorm.

Therefore, we have not presumed to remove the body of the deceased inasmuch as he had confessed his sins, had received extreme unction and communion, and had been buried without objection. Furthermore, we have not yielded to those who advised or even commanded this course of action. Not, certainly, that we take the counsel of upright men or the orders of our superiors lightly, but we would not have it appear that, out of feminine harshness we did injustice to the sacraments of Christ, with which this man had been fortified while he was

From Hildegard of Bingen, *Symphonia,* trans. Barbara Newan, 2d ed. (Ithaca, N.Y.: Cornell University Press, 1998), 117; and *The Letters of Hildegard of Bingen,* vol. 1, trans. Joseph Baird and Radd Ehrman (New York and Oxford: Oxford University Press, 1994), 76–80.

still alive. But so that we may not be totally disobedient we have, in accordance with their injunction, ceased from singing the divine praises and from participation in Mass, as has been our regular monthly custom.

As a result, my sisters and I have been greatly distressed and saddened. Weighed down by this burden, therefore, I heard these words in a vision: It is improper for you to obey human words ordering you to abandon the sacraments of the Garment of the Word of God, Who, born virginally of the Virgin Mary, is your salvation. Still, it is incumbent upon you to seek permission to participate in the sacraments from those prelates who laid the obligation of obedience upon you. For ever since Adam was driven from the bright region of paradise into the exile of this world on account of his disobedience, the conception of all people is justly tainted by that first transgression. Therefore, in accordance with God's inscrutable plan, it was necessary for a man free from all pollution to be born in human flesh, through whom all who are predestined to life might be cleansed from corruption and might be sanctified by the communion of his body so that he might remain in them and they in him for their fortification. That person, however, who is disobedient to the commands of God, as Adam was, and is completely forgetful of Him must be completely cut off from participation in the sacrament of His body, just as he himself has turned away from Him in disobedience. And he must remain so until, purged through penitence, he is permitted by the authorities to receive the communion of the Lord's body again. In contrast, however, a person who is aware that he has incurred such a restriction not as a result of anything that he has done, either consciously or deliberately, may be present at the service of the lifegiving sacrament, to be cleansed by the Lamb without sin, Who, in obedience to the Father, allowed Himself to be sacrificed on the altar of the cross that he might restore salvation to all.

In that same vision I also heard that I had erred in not going humbly and devoutly to my superiors for permission to participate in the communion, especially since we were not at fault in receiving that dead man into our cemetery. For, after all, he had been fortified by his own priest with proper Christian procedure, and, without objection from anyone, was buried in our cemetery, with all Bingen joining in the funeral procession. And so God has commanded me to report these things to you, our lords and prelates. Further, I saw in my vision also that by obeying you we have been celebrating the divine office incorrectly, for from the time of your restriction up to the present, we have ceased to sing the divine office, merely reading it instead. And I heard a voice coming from the Living Light concerning the various kinds of praises, about which David speaks in the psalm: "Praise Him with sound of trumpet: praise Him with psaltery and harp," and so forth up to this point: "Let every spirit praise the Lord" [Ps 150.3,6]. These words use outward, visible things to teach us about inward things. Thus the material composition and the quality of these instruments instruct us how we ought to give form to the praise of the Creator and turn all the convictions of our inner being to the same. When we consider these things carefully, we recall that man needed the voice of the living Spirit, but Adam lost this divine voice through disobedience. For while he was still innocent, before his transgression, his voice blended fully with the voices of the angels in their praise of God. Angels are called spirits from that Spirit which is God, and thus they have such voices by virtue of their spiritual nature. But Adam lost that angelic voice which he had in paradise, for he fell asleep to that knowledge which he possessed before his sin, just as a person on waking up only dimly remembers what he had seen in his dreams. And so when he was deceived by the trick of the devil and rejected the will of his Creator, he became wrapped up in the darkness of inward ignorance as the just result of his iniquity.

God, however, restores the souls of the elect to that pristine blessedness by infusing them with the light of truth. And in accordance with His eternal plan, He so devised it that whenever He renews the hearts of many with the pouring out of the prophetic spirit, they might, by means of His interior illumination, regain some of the knowledge which Adam had before he was punished for his sin.

And so the holy prophets, inspired by the Spirit which they had received, were called for this purpose: not only to compose psalms and canticles (by which the hearts of listeners would be inflamed) but also to construct various kinds of musical instruments to enhance these songs of praise with melodic strains. Thereby, both through the form and quality of the instruments, as well as through the meaning of the words which accompany them, those who hear might be taught, as we said above, about inward things, since they have been admonished and aroused by outward things. In such a way, these holy prophets get beyond the music of this exile and recall to mind that divine melody of praise which Adam, in company with the angels, enjoyed in God before his fall.

Men of zeal and wisdom have imitated the holy prophets and have themselves, with human skill, invented several kinds of musical instruments, so that they might be able to sing for the delight of their souls, and they accompanied their singing with instruments played with the flexing of the fingers, recalling, in this way, Adam, who was formed by God's finger, which is the Holy Spirit. . . .

But when the devil, man's great deceiver, learned that man had begun to sing through God's inspiration and, therefore, was being transformed to bring back the sweetness of the songs of heaven, mankind's homeland, he was so terrified at seeing his clever machinations go to ruin that he was greatly tormented. Therefore, he devotes himself continually to thinking up and working out all kinds of wicked contrivances. Thus he never ceases from confounding confession and the sweet beauty of both divine praise and spiritual hymns, eradicating them through wicked suggestions, impure thoughts, or various distractions from the heart of man and even from the mouth of the Church itself, wherever he can, through dissension, scandal, or unjust oppression.

Therefore, you and all prelates must exercise the greatest vigilance to clear the air by full and thorough discussion of the justification for such actions before your verdict closes the mouth of any church singing praises to God or suspends it from handling or receiving the divine sacraments. And you must be especially certain that you are drawn to this action out of zeal for God's justice, rather than out of indignation, unjust emotions or a desire for revenge, and you must always be on your guard not to be circumvented in your decisions by Satan, who drove man from celestial harmony and the delights of paradise.

Consider, too, that just as the body of Jesus Christ was born of the purity of the Virgin Mary through the operation of the Holy Spirit so, too, the canticle of praise, reflecting celestial harmony, is rooted in the Church through the Holy Spirit. The body is the vestment of the spirit, which has a living voice, and so it is proper for the body, in harmony with the soul, to use its voice to sing praises to God. Whence, in metaphor, the prophetic spirit commands us to praise God with clashing cymbals and cymbals of jubilation, as well as other musical instruments which men of wisdom and zeal have invented, because all arts pertaining to things useful and necessary for mankind have been created by the breath that God sent into man's body. For this reason it is proper that God be praised in all things. . . .

Therefore, those who, without just cause, impose silence on a church and prohibit the singing of God's praises and those who have on earth unjustly despoiled God of His honor and glory will lose their place among the chorus of angels, unless they have amended their lives through true penitence and humble restitution. Moreover, let those who hold the keys of heaven beware not to open those things which are to be kept closed nor to close those things which are to be kept open, for harsh judgment will fall upon those who rule, unless, as the apostle says, they rule with good judgment.

And I heard a voice saying thus: Who created heaven? God. Who opens heaven to the faithful? God. Who is like Him? No one. And so, O men of faith, let none of you resist Him or oppose Him, lest He fall on you in His might and you have no helper to protect you from His judgment. This time is a womanish time,[1] because the dispensation of God's justice is weak. But the strength of God's justice is exerting itself, a female warrior battling against injustice, so that it might fall defeated.

DISCUSSION QUESTIONS

1. How does Hildegard justify her defiance of the prelates of Mainz? What does her defiance suggest about her self-image?
2. Why does Hildegard consider music to be essential to Christian worship?
3. Based on these two selections, in what ways does Hildegard express the heightened emphasis on the humanity of Christ and Mary that was a distinguishing feature of twelfth-century spirituality? Why do you think Mary in particular may have appealed to her?

COMPARATIVE QUESTIONS

1. Even though the number of cities in Europe was on the rise in the eleventh and twelfth centuries, most people at the time still lived in rural areas and farmed for a living. What evidence can you find of this fact in the urban charters and the *Anglo-Saxon Chronicle?*
2. How do you think Pope Gregory VII would have reacted to William I's relationship with the English church, as described in the *Anglo-Saxon Chronicle,* and why?

---

[1]This is a frequent theme in the letters and the other works: the loss of the "virility" of the earlier Church. Hence a woman, paradoxically, has been called by God to help restore this lost virility.

11

An Age of Confidence
1150–1215

S U M M A R Y   Rowdy students, brave knights, pious women, and powerful kings were just a few of the people who infused medieval government,
culture, and religion with new vitality and confidence in the late twelfth
and early thirteenth centuries. The documents in this chapter illuminate how the
vigor of the period found expression in new institutions (Document Set 1), literary styles (Document 2), and organizations (Document Set 3). Despite the diversity of these sources, they all reflect a heightened concern for regulating an
individual's conduct as part of a larger group. The drive to codify and control behavior and beliefs served a variety of purposes—from enhancing political authority and social prestige to gaining salvation. The final document exposes the
dark side of the period. As the lines delineating who fit into certain groups became sharper, so, too, did those delineating who was to be excluded. People who
appeared to threaten accepted norms thus became targets of violence and intolerance.

1

Medieval University Life
Twelfth–Early Thirteenth Centuries

*The development of permanent centers of learning in the twelfth and thirteenth cen-
turies in cities across Europe attests to the vitality of the age. As these documents
suggest, royal patronage and the formation of a sense of common identity among
students were key to the rise of medieval universities as self-governing institutions.
The first two documents consist of special privileges granted by King Frederick I (r.
1152–1190) of Germany in 1158 to all students within his domains, and by King
Philip II of France (r. 1180-1223) in 1200 to students at Paris. In this way, students
were enveloped within both rulers' growing bureaucracies as each strove to increase
his power. We hear the voices of students themselves in the second pair of documents*

—two anonymous poems written by students in the twelfth century describing the anxieties and pleasures of their way of life.

After a careful consideration of this subject by the bishops, abbots, dukes, counts, judges, and other nobles of our sacred palace, we, from our piety, have granted this privilege to all scholars who travel for the sake of study, and especially, to the professors of divine and sacred laws, namely, that they may go in safety to the places in which the studies are carried on, both they themselves and their messengers, and may dwell there in security. For we think it fitting that, during good behavior, those should enjoy our praise and protection, by whose learning the world is enlightened to the obedience of God and of us, his ministers and the life of the subjects is moulded; and by a certain special love we defend them from all injuries.

For who does not pity those who exile themselves through love for learning, who wear themselves out in poverty in place of riches, who expose their lives to all perils and often suffer bodily injury from the vilest men — this must be endured with vexation. Therefore, we declare by this general and ever to be valid law, that in the future no one shall be so rash as to venture to inflict any injury on scholars, or to occasion any loss to them on account of a debt owed by an inhabitant of their province — a thing which we have learned is sometimes done by an evil custom. And let it be known to the violators of this constitution, and also to those who shall at the time be the rulers of the places, that a four-fold restitution of property shall be exacted from all and that, the mark of infamy being affixed to them by the law itself, they shall lose their office forever. . . .

We also order this law to be inserted among the imperial constitutions under the title, *ne filius pro patre, etc.*

Given at Roncaglia, in the year of our Lord 1158, in the month of November. . . .

In the Name of the sacred and indivisible Trinity, amen. Philip, by the grace of God, King of the French.

Concerning the safety of the students at Paris in the future, by the advice of our subjects we have ordained as follows: we will cause all the citizens of Paris to swear that if any one sees an injury done to any student by any layman, he will testify truthfully to this, nor will any one withdraw in order not to see [the act]. And if it shall happen that any one strikes a student, except in self-defense, especially if he strikes the student with a weapon, a club or a stone, all laymen who see [the act] shall in good faith seize the malefactor or malefactors and deliver them to our judge; nor shall they withdraw in order not to see the act, or seize

From *Translations and Reprints from the Original Sources of European History*, vol. 2, no. 3, ed. Dana Carleton Munro (Philadelphia: University of Pennsylvania Press, 1898), 2–7; and *Wine, Women, and Song: Mediaeval Latin Students' Songs*, trans. John Addington Symonds (London: Chatto & Windus, 1907), 58–64.

the malefactor, or testify to the truth. Also, whether the malefactor is seized in open crime or not, we will make a legal and full examination through clerks or laymen or certain lawful persons; and our count and our judges shall do the same. And if by a full examination we or our judges are able to learn that he who is accused, is guilty of the crime, then we or our judges shall immediately inflict a penalty, according to the quality and nature of the crime; notwithstanding the fact that the criminal may deny the deed and say that he is ready to defend himself in single combat, or to purge himself by the ordeal by water.

Also, neither our provost nor our judges shall lay hands on a student for any offence whatever; nor shall they place him in our prison, unless such a crime has been committed by the student, that he ought to be arrested. And in that case, our judge shall arrest him on the spot, without striking him at all, unless he resists, and shall hand him over to the ecclesiastical judge, who ought to guard him in order to satisfy us and the one suffering the injury. And if a serious crime has been committed, our judge shall go or shall send to see what is done with the student. . . .

In order, moreover, that these [decrees] may be kept more carefully and may be established forever by a fixed law, we have decided that our present provost and the people of Paris shall affirm by an oath, in the presence of the scholars, that they will carry out in good faith all the above-mentioned. And always in the future, whosoever receives from us the office of provost in Paris, among the other initiatory acts of his office, namely, on the first or second Sunday, in one of the churches of Paris, — after he has been summoned for the purpose, — shall affirm by an oath, publicly in the presence of the scholars, that he will keep in good faith all the above-mentioned. And that these decrees may be valid forever, we have ordered this document to be confirmed by the authority of our seal and by the characters of the royal name, signed below.

A Wandering Student's Petition

I, a wandering scholar lad,
  Born for toil and sadness,
Oftentimes am driven by
  Poverty to madness.

Literature and knowledge I
  Fain would still be earning,
Were it not that want of pelf[1]
  Makes me cease from learning.

These torn clothes that cover me
  Are too thin and rotten;
Oft I have to suffer cold,
  By the warmth forgotten.

---

[1]**Pelf** means money. [— Ed.]

Scarce I can attend at church,
   Sing God's praises duly;
Mass and vespers both I miss,
   Though I love them truly.

Oh, thou pride of N——,
   By thy worth I pray thee
Give the suppliant help in need,
   Heaven will sure repay thee.

Take a mind unto thee now
   Like unto St. Martin;
Clothe the pilgrim's nakedness,
   Wish him well at parting.

So may God translate your soul
   Into peace eternal,
And the bliss of saints be yours
   In His realm supernal.

A Song Of The Open Road

We in our wandering,
Blithesome and squandering,
   Tara, tantara, teino![2]

Eat to satiety,
Drink with propriety;
   Tara, tantara, teino!

Laugh till our sides we split,
Rags on our hides we fit;
   Tara, tantara, teino!

Jesting eternally,
Quaffing infernally:
   Tara, tantara, teino!

Craft's in the bone of us,
Fear 'tis unknown of us:
   Tara, tantara, teino!

When we're in neediness,
Thieve we with greediness:
   Tara, tantara, teino!

---

[2]This refrain appears to be intended to imitate a bugle-call.

Brother catholical,
Man apostolical,
    Tara, tantara, teino!

Say what you will have done,
What you ask 'twill be done!
    Tara, tantara, teino!

Folk, fear the toss of the
Horns of philosophy!
    Tara, tantara, teino!

Here comes a quadruple
Spoiler and prodigal!
    Tara, tantara, teino!

License and vanity
Pamper insanity:
    Tara, tantara, teino!

As the Pope bade us do,
Brother to brother's true:
    Tara, tantara, teino!

Brother, best friend, adieu!
Now, I must part from you!
    Tara, tantara, teino!

When will our meeting be?
Glad shall our greeting be!
    Tara, tantara, teino!

Vows valedictory
Now have the victory;
    Tara, tantara, teino!

Clasped on each other's breast,
Brother to brother pressed,
    Tara, tantara, teino!

DISCUSSION QUESTIONS

1. Why do you think both Frederick I and Philip II were concerned for students' welfare? What benefits do you think they gained from guaranteeing students certain privileges?

2. What do both sets of privileges reveal about the process of state building at the time? What role did official records such as these play in the process?

3. What picture of student life do the authors paint in the two poems? Do you see any similarities with your own experiences as a student?

4. Many historians argue that in the twelfth century, people became more aware of themselves as members of larger groups with similar concerns and objectives. Do the student poems support this argument?

2
Chrétien de Troyes
Erec and Enide
c. 1170

Students were not the only group to gain a sense of group solidarity in the twelfth century. Nobles likewise forged a common class identity in this period shaped in part by new forms of vernacular literature that flourished in aristocratic circles. Long poems examining the relationships between knights and their lady loves were especially popular. The following excerpt is from one such poem, Erec and Enide, *written in Old French by Chrétien de Troyes (c. 1150–1190) around 1170. Attached to the court of the count and countess of Champagne in the city of Troyes, located southeast of Paris, Chrétien used his poems to entertain his audience while instructing them in the ways of courtliness and proper knightly behavior. Set against the backdrop of King Arthur's court (the first romance of this kind),* Erec and Enide *recounts the "lovely tale of adventure" of one of Arthur's knights, Erec, and his wife, Enide. The story centers on Erec's struggle to find a balance between the duties of marriage and knighthood, which culminates in his and Enide's coronation, described in the final scene below.*

In the middle of the morning, that Christmas
Day, everyone gathered.
The vast joy that was coming
Flooded Erec's heart.
Yet no one, no matter how skilled
In the art, could tell you, in any
Human tongue, a third,
Or a fourth, or a fifth, of all
That took place at that coronation.
I've taken on a fool's
Task, trying to describe it,
But since the responsibility
Is mine, and I must attempt it,
Let me do the very best
I can with my limited ability.
    Two brand-new chairs, fashioned
Of brilliant white ivory, both made

From Chrétien de Troyes, *Erec and Enide*, trans. Burton Raffel (New Haven, Conn.: Yale University Press, 1997), 211–17.

Precisely the same, had been set
In the hall. Clearly, the craftsman
Who'd carved them had been clever and subtle,
For in height, and length, and breadth,
And in decoration, no matter
How you looked, or where,
You saw them exactly the same:
No one could possibly tell
One from the other. And every
Piece in each of those chairs
Was either ivory or gold,
Chiseled with a delicate touch,
The two front feet sculpted
Like a pair of leopards, and the back ones
Like crocodiles. They were gifts
Of homage and respect for Arthur
And his queen, given by a knight
Whose name was Brian of the Islands.
    Arthur sat in one
And Erec, wearing a robe
Of rich black silk, was seated
In the other. The robe was described
In a book I read, written
By Macrobius, who taught the science
Of attentive vision: I mention
His name to prove I'm telling
The truth. I draw the details
Of the cloth from his pages, exactly
As I found them there. It was woven
By four fairies, working
As great and masterful craftsmen.
And the first had spun an accurate
Portrait of Geometry and how
It measures sky and earth,
Capturing every aspect —
Including depth and height,
And length and width, and how
We follow the sea from shore
To shore, measuring its width
And depth: in short, measuring
The world. That was the first fairy's
Work. The second spun
A picture of Arithmetic,
Carefully tracing the steps
By which we count days,

And the hours they're made of, and count
Every drop in the ocean,
And each tiny grain of sand,
And all the stars on high,
And how many leaves on a tree,
And how we frame these numbers —
All accurately counted,
Employing no tricks and no lies,
For this fairy knows what she weaves.
And her subject was Arithmetic.
The third chose to show Music,
Which blends with every human
Pleasure, in counterpoint
And song, with harps and lutes
And viols — a beautiful picture,
With Music seated and in front
Of her her tools and delights.
But the fourth and final fairy
Drew the noblest portrait,
Having chosen the highest art:
Astronomy, which governs
And regulates marvels, the stars
In the sky, and the moon, and the sun.
And in every respect it rules
Entirely by its own arts,
Independently sure
Of whatever it needs to do,
Knowing whatever has been,
Perceiving whatever is still
To come, its learning precise,
Containing no lies and no fraud.
The fairies embroidered these things
In golden thread, on the cloth
From which Erec's robe was made.
And the lining was sewn from the skins
Of strange and wonderful beasts,
Their heads pale and blond,
Their necks dark as a mullet,
Their spines red, their bellies
Mottled, and their tails blue.
They come from the Indies, they're called
Berbiolettes, and they eat
Aromatic spices,
Fresh cloves and cinnamon.
What can I tell you about

The cloak? It was lush and beautiful,
With four gems for its clasps:
Chrysolite green on one side,
Amethyst purple on the other,
And all mounted in gold.
    And still Enide had not yet
Come to the palace; seeing
She was late, the king instructed
Gawain to go and lead her
There at once.
                    . . .
When they reached
The palace, who hurried out
To greet them but Arthur himself,
And then, in a courteous display,
He seated her next to her husband,
Wanting to do her great honor.
And then he ordered his servants
To take a pair of heavy
Gold crowns from his treasure chests,
And they rushed to obey his commands,
Quickly returning with massive
Crowns of gold, embossed
With great red rubies, each of them
Boasting four rich stones,
And even the smallest burned
With a light many times brighter
And clearer than the moon. And those
In the palace who looked at that light
Were unable, for some considerable
Time, to see at all.
The king himself was dazzled
By the brilliant glow, but rejoiced in it
All the same, delighting
That the gems shone so beautifully
Clear. Two girls presented
The first crown, two barons the other.
Then Arthur ordered his bishops
And priests, and his monastery
Abbots, to come and anoint
The new king, according to Christian
Law. And every man
Of the cloth, whether young or old,
Hurried to obey him — and you know
There were plenty of priests at court,

And abbots, and bishops. And then
The great bishop of Nantes,
A truly holy man,
Beautifully consecrated
The new king, and placed
The crown on his head. King Arthur
Ordered a wonderful scepter
Brought out, which all admired.
Listen and hear how this scepter
Was made: it glowed like a bell glass,
For it was set with a single emerald
As fat around as a fist.
And let me tell you the truth:
No fish that swims in the water,
No wild beast, no manner
Of man or flying bird,
But the artist had cut and worked
Its image into the stone.
They brought the scepter to Arthur,
Who stood a moment, admiring it,
And then with no further delay
Placed it in King Erec's
Right hand, making him a proper
King. Then he crowned Enide.

Discussion Questions

1. Based on this scene from *Erec and Enide,* in what ways do you think Chrétien's concerns reflected those of the nobility to whom he catered?

2. What particular message do you think Chrétien was trying to convey in his description of Erec's coronation robe, especially the images of four of the seven liberal arts (geometry, arithmetic, music, and astronomy)?

3. What does this message suggest about aristocratic values and measures of self-worth in the late twelfth century?

3

Saints Francis and Clare of Assisi
Selected Writings
Thirteenth Century

The church was very much entwined in the world of wealth, power, and splendor celebrated in the vernacular literature of the twelfth and early thirteenth centuries. A variety of new religious movements emerged in reaction against the church's perceived worldliness and neglect of its pastoral mission. St. Francis of Assisi (c. 1182–1226) founded what would become the most popular and largest of these movements in Europe, the Franciscans. These excerpts from his Rule, written in 1223, illuminate the fundamental principles guiding the order. The Franciscans' message of poverty, humility, and penance prompted people from all walks of life to follow their path, including Clare of Assisi (1194–1253). Upon hearing Francis preach in 1212, she established a community of pious women modeled after his ideals, which became the Order of the Sisters of St. Francis. Although the sisters were eventually cloistered, the following passages from Clare's Testament reveal not only how their ideals remained true to those of St. Francis but also how medieval women played an important role in cultivating new forms of piety.

This is the rule and way of living of the minorite brothers: namely to observe the holy Gospel of our Lord Jesus Christ, living in obedience, without personal possessions, and in chastity. Brother Francis promises obedience and reverence to our lord pope Honorius, and to his successors who canonically enter upon their office, and to the Roman Church. And the other brothers shall be bound to obey brother Francis and his successors.

If any persons shall wish to adopt this form of living, and shall come to our brothers, they shall send them to their provincial ministers; to whom alone, and to no others, permission is given to receive brothers. But the ministers shall diligently examine them in the matter of the catholic faith and the ecclesiastical sacraments. And if they believe all these, and are willing to faithfully confess them and observe them steadfastly to the end; and if they have no wives, or if they have them and the wives have already entered a monastery, or if they shall have given them permission to do so . . . the ministers shall say unto them the word of the holy Gospel, to the effect that they shall go and sell all that they have and strive to give it to the poor. But if they shall not be able to do this, their good will is enough. And the brothers and their ministers shall be on their guard and not concern themselves for their temporal goods; so that they may freely do with those goods exactly as God inspires them. . . . Afterwards there shall be granted to them the garments of probation: namely two gowns without cowls and a belt, and hose and a cape down to the belt; unless to these same ministers something else may at some time seem to be preferable in the sight of God. But, when the year of probation is over, they shall be received into obedience; promising always to observe that manner of living, and this Rule. . . .

I firmly command all the brothers by no means to receive coin or money, of themselves or through an intervening person. But for the needs of the sick and for clothing the other brothers, the ministers alone and the guardians shall provide through spiritual friends, as it may seem to them that necessity demands,

From *Select Historical Documents of the Middle Ages,* ed. Ernest Henderson (London: G. Bell & Sons, 1921), 344–49; and *Francis and Clare: The Complete Works,* trans. Regis J. Armstrong and Ignatius C. Brady (New York: Paulist Press, 1982), 226–32.

according to time, place and cold temperature. This one thing being always regarded, that, as has been said, they receive neither coin nor money.

Those brothers to whom God has given the ability to labour, shall labour faithfully and devoutly; in such way that idleness, the enemy of the soul, being excluded, they may not extinguish the spirit of holy prayer and devotion; to which other temporal things should be subservient. As a reward, moreover, for their labour, they may receive for themselves and their brothers the necessaries of life, but not coin or money; and this humbly, as becomes the servants of God and the followers of most holy poverty.

The brothers shall appropriate nothing to themselves, neither a house, nor a place, nor anything; but as pilgrims and strangers in this world, in poverty and humility serving God, they shall confidently go seeking for alms. Nor need they be ashamed, for the Lord made Himself poor for us in this world. This is that height of most lofty poverty, which has constituted you my most beloved brothers heirs and kings of the kingdom of Heaven, has made you poor in possessions, has exalted you in virtues. . . .

All the brothers shall be bound always to have one of the brothers of that order as general minister and servant of the whole fraternity, and shall be firmly bound to obey him. . . .

The brothers may not preach in the bishopric of any bishop if they have been forbidden to by him. And no one of the brothers shall dare to preach at all to the people, unless he have been examined and approved by the general minister of this fraternity, and the office of preacher have been conceded to him. I also exhort those same brothers that, in the preaching which they do, their expressions shall be chaste and chosen, to the utility and edification of the people; announcing to them vices and virtues, punishment and glory, with briefness of discourse; for the words were brief which the Lord spoke upon earth.

The brothers who are the ministers and servants of the other brothers shall visit and admonish their brothers and humbly and lovingly correct them; not teaching them anything which is against their soul and against our Rule. But the brothers who are subjected to them shall remember that, before God, they have discarded their own wills. Wherefore I firmly command them that they obey their ministers in all things which they have promised God to observe, and which are not contrary to their souls and to our Rule. . . .

I firmly command all the brothers not to have suspicious intercourse or to take counsel with women. And, with the exception of those to whom special permission has been given by the Apostolic Chair, let them not enter nunneries. Neither may they become fellow god-parents with men or women, lest from this cause a scandal may arise among the brothers or concerning brothers.

Whoever of the brothers by divine inspiration may wish to go among the Saracens and other infidels, shall seek permission to do so from their provincial ministers. But to none shall the ministers give permission to go, save to those whom they shall see to be fit for the mission.

Furthermore, through their obedience I enjoin on the ministers that they demand from the lord pope one of the cardinals of the holy Roman Church, who shall be the governor, corrector and protector of that fraternity, so that, always subjected and lying at the feet of that same holy Church, steadfast in the catholic faith, we may observe poverty and humility, and the holy Gospel of our Lord Jesus Christ; as we have firmly promised.

In the name of the Lord!

Among all the other gifts which we have received and continue to receive daily from our benefactor, *the Father of mercies* (2 Cor 1:3), and for which we must express the deepest thanks to our glorious God, our vocation is a great gift. Since it is the more perfect and greater, we should be so much more thankful to Him for it. For this reason the Apostle writes: "Acknowledge your calling" (1 Cor 1:26).

The Son of God became for us *the Way* which our Blessed Father Francis, His true lover and imitator, has shown and taught us by word and example.

Therefore, beloved Sisters, we must consider the immense gifts which God has bestowed on us, especially those which He has seen fit to work in us through His beloved servant, our blessed Father Francis, not only after our conversion but also while we were still [living among] the vanities of the world.

For, almost immediately after his conversion, while he had neither brothers nor companions, when he was building the Church of San Damiano in which he was totally filled with divine consolation, he was led to abandon the world completely. This holy man, in the great joy and enlightenment of the Holy Spirit, made a prophecy about us which the Lord fulfilled later. Climbing the wall of that church he shouted in French to some poor people who were standing nearby: "Come and help me build the monastery of San Damiano, because ladies will dwell here who will glorify our heavenly Father throughout His holy Church by their celebrated and holy manner of life."

In this, then, we can consider the abundant kindness of God toward us. Because of His mercy and love, He saw fit to speak these words about our vocation and selection through His saint. And our most blessed Father prophesied not only for us, but also for those who were to come to this [same] holy vocation to which the Lord has called us.

With what solicitude and fervor of mind and body, therefore, must we keep the commandments of our God and Father, so that, with the help of the Lord, we may return to Him an increase of His *talents*. For the Lord Himself not only has set us as an example and mirror for others, but also for our [own] sisters whom the Lord has called to our way of life, so that they in turn will be a mirror and example to those living in the world. . . .

After the most high heavenly Father saw fit in His mercy and grace to enlighten my heart to do penance according to the example and teaching of our most blessed Father Francis, shortly after his own conversion, I, together with the few sisters whom the Lord had given me soon after my conversion, voluntarily promised him obedience, since the Lord had given us the Light of His grace through his holy life and teaching.

But when the Blessed Francis saw that, although we were physically weak and frail, we did not shirk deprivation, poverty, hard work, distress, or the shame or contempt of the world — rather, as he and his brothers often saw for themselves, we considered [all such trials] as great delights after the example of the saints and their brothers — he rejoiced greatly in the Lord. And moved by compassion for us, he promised to have always, both through himself and through his Order, the same loving care and special solicitude for us as for his own brothers.

And thus, by the will of God and our most blessed Father Francis, we went to dwell at the Church of San Damiano. There, in a short time, the Lord increased our number by His mercy and grace so that what He had predicted through His saint might be fulfilled. We had stayed in another place [before this], but only for a little while.

Later on he wrote a form of life for us, [indicating] especially that we should persevere always in holy poverty. And while he was living, he was not content to encourage us by many words and examples to love and observe holy poverty; [in addition] he also gave us many writings so that, after his death, we should in no way turn away from it. [In a similar way] the Son of God never wished to abandon this holy poverty while He lived in the world, and our most blessed Father Francis, following His footprints, never departed, either in example or teaching, from this holy poverty which he had chosen for himself and for his brothers.

Therefore, I, Clare, the handmaid of Christ and of the Poor Sisters of the Monastery of San Damiano — although unworthy — and the little plant of the holy Father, consider together with my sisters our most high profession and the command of so great a father. [We also take note] in some [sisters] of the frailty which we feared in ourselves after the death of our holy Father Francis, [He] who was our pillar of strength and, after God, our one consolation and support. [Thus] time and again, we bound ourselves to our Lady, most holy Poverty, so that, after my death, the Sisters present and to come would never abandon her.

And, as I have always been most zealous and solicitous to observe and to have the other sisters observe the holy poverty which we have promised the Lord and our holy Father Francis, so, too, the others who will succeed me in office should be bound always to observe it and have it observed by the other sisters. . . .

In the Lord Jesus Christ, I admonish and exhort all my sisters, both those present and those to come, to strive always to imitate the way of holy simplicity, humility, and poverty and [to preserve] the integrity of [our] holy manner of life, as we were taught by our blessed Father Francis from the beginning of our conversion to Christ. Thus may they always remain *in the fragrance* of a good name, both among those who are afar off and those who are near. [This will take place] not by our own merits but solely by the mercy and grace of our Benefactor, *the Father of mercies.* . . .

I also beg that sister who will have the office [of caring for] the sisters to strive to exceed others more by her virtues and holy life than by her office so that, encouraged by her example, the Sisters may obey her not so much out of duty but rather out of love. Let her also be prudent and attentive to her sisters just as a good mother is to her daughters; and especially, let her take care to provide for them according to the needs of each one from the things which the Lord shall give. Let her also be so kind and so available that all [of them] may reveal their needs with trust and have recourse to her at any hour with confidence as they see fit, both for her sake and that of her sisters.

But the sisters who are subjects should keep in mind that for the Lord's sake they have given up their own wills. Therefore I ask that they obey their mother as they have promised the Lord of their own free will so that, seeing the charity, humility, and unity they have toward one another, their mother might bear all the burdens of her office more lightly. Thus what is painful and bitter might be turned into sweetness for her because of their holy way of life. . . .

So that it may be observed better, I leave this writing for you, my dearest and most beloved Sisters, those present and those to come, as a sign of the blessing of the Lord and of our most blessed Father Francis and of my blessing — I who am your mother and servant.

Discussion Questions

1. Based on his *Rule*, how would you characterize Francis's spirituality and sense of mission? Why do you think they appealed to so many people at the time?
2. How does Clare echo Francis's ideals in her *Testament*?
3. What goals did Francis and Clare share in composing the *Rule* and *Testament*, respectively?
4. What do both documents reveal about contemporary attitudes toward women?

4

Thomas of Monmouth
The Life and Miracles of St. William of Norwich
c. 1173

Although the new institutions, organizations, and literary styles of the twelfth and thirteenth centuries nurtured many people's sense of belonging to a group, they also fostered a spirit of intolerance. Jews in particular increasingly became objects of aggression in this period, not only because of their religion but also because of their professional activities as moneylenders. The propagation of the belief that Jews sacrificed Christian children attests to the rise of anti-Jewish sentiment. This belief appears in a fully developed form for the first time in The Life and Miracles of St. William of Norwich, *excerpted here. This account was written by Thomas of Monmouth, a monk living in the English city of Norwich at the time when the events he describes allegedly took place. The evidence suggests that in fact the body of a boy named William who had met a violent death was found in 1144. From this point on, however, Thomas of Monmouth's story tells us more about the development of systematic anti-Semitism than it does about actual events.*

How he was wont to resort to the Jews, and having been chid by his own people for so doing, how he withdrew himself from them.

When therefore he was flourishing in this blessed boyhood of his and had attained to his eighth year [c.1140], he was entrusted to the skinners[1] to be taught their craft. Gifted with a teachable disposition and bringing industry to bear upon it, in a short time he far surpassed lads of his own age in the craft aforesaid, and he equalled some who had been his teachers. So leaving the country, by the drawing of a divine attraction he betook himself to the city and lodged with a very famous master of that craft, and some time passed away. He was seldom in the country, but was occupied in the city and sedulously gave himself to the practice of his craft, and thus reached his twelfth year.

Now, while he was staying in Norwich, the Jews who were settled there and required their cloaks or their robes or other garments (whether pledged to them, or their own property) to be repaired, preferred him before all other skinners. For they esteemed him to be especially fit for their work, either because they had learnt that he was guileless and skillful, or because attracted to him by their avarice they thought they could bargain with him for a lower price. Or, as I rather believe, because by the ordering of divine providence he had been predestined to martyrdom from the beginning of time, and gradually step by step was drawn on, and chosen to be made a mock of and to be put to death by the Jews, in scorn of the Lord's passion, as one of little foresight, and so the more fit for them. For I have learnt from certain Jews, who were afterwards converted to the Christian faith, how that at that time they had planned to do this very thing with some Christian, and in order to carry out their malignant purpose, at the beginning of Lent they had made choice of the boy William, being twelve years of age and a boy of unusual innocence. So it came to pass that when the holy boy, ignorant of the treachery that had been planned, had frequent dealings with the Jews, he was taken to task by Godwin the priest, who had the boy's aunt as his wife, and by a certain Wulward with whom he lodged, and he was prohibited from going in and out among them any more. But the Jews, annoyed at the thwarting of their designs, tried with all their might to patch up a new scheme of wickedness, and all the more vehemently as the day for carrying out the crime they had determined upon drew near, and the victim which they had thought they had already secured had slipped out of their wicked hands. Accordingly, collecting all the cunning of their crafty plots, they found — I am not sure whether he was a Christian or a Jew — a man who was a most treacherous fellow and just the fitting person for carrying out their execrable crime, and with all haste — for their Passover was coming on in three days — they sent him to find out and bring back with him the victim which, as I said before, had slipped out of their hands.

From Thomas of Monmouth, *The Life and Miracles of St. William of Norwich*, trans. Augustus Jessopp and Montague Rhodes (Cambridge: Cambridge University Press, 1896), 14–17, 19–23.

[1]Furriers. [—Ed.]

How he was seduced by the Jews' messenger.

At the dawn of day, on the Monday after Palm Sunday, that detestable messenger of the Jews set out to execute the business that was committed to him, and at last the boy William, after being searched for with very great care, was found. When he was found, he got round him with cunning wordy tricks, and so deceived him with his lying promises. . . .

How on his going to the Jews he was taken, mocked and slain.

Then the boy, like an innocent lamb, was led to the slaughter. He was treated kindly by the Jews at first, and, ignorant of what was being prepared for him, he was kept till the morrow. But on the next day, which in that year was the Passover for them,[2] after the singing of the hymns appointed for the day in the synagogue, the chiefs of the Jews . . . suddenly seized hold of the boy William as he was having his dinner and in no fear of any treachery, and illtreated him in various horrible ways. For while some of them held him behind, others opened his mouth and introduced an instrument of torture which is called a teazle,[3] and, fixing it by straps through both jaws to the back of his neck, they fastened it with a knot as tightly as it could be drawn. After that, taking a short piece of rope of about the thickness of one's little finger and tying three knots in it at certain distances marked out, they bound round that innocent head with it from the forehead to the back, forcing the middle knot into his forehead and the two others into his temples, the two ends of the rope being most tightly stretched at the back of his head and fastened in a very tight knot. The ends of the rope were then passed round his neck and carried round his throat under his chin, and there they finished off this dreadful engine of torture in a fifth knot.

But not even yet could the cruelty of the torturers be satisfied without adding even more severe pains. Having shaved his head, they stabbed it with countless thorn-points, and made the blood come horribly from the wounds they made. And cruel were they and so eager to inflict pain that it was difficult to say whether they were more cruel or more ingenious in their tortures. For their skill in torturing kept up the strength of their cruelty and ministered arms thereto. And thus, while these enemies of the Christian name were rioting in the spirit of malignity around the boy, some of those present adjudged him to be fixed to a cross in mockery of the Lord's passion, as though they would say, "Even as we condemned the Christ to a shameful death, so let us also condemn the Christian, so that, uniting the Lord and his servant in a like punishment, we may retort upon themselves the pain of that reproach which they impute to us."

Conspiring, therefore, to accomplish the crime of this great and detestable malice, they next laid their blood-stained hands upon the innocent victim, and

---

[2] In 1144, Easter fell on March 26 and Passover on March 25.

[3] A wooden gag. [—Ed.]

having lifted him from the ground and fastened him upon the cross, they vied with one another in their efforts to make an end of him. And we, after enquiring into the matter very diligently, did both find the house, and discovered some most certain marks in it of what had been done there. For report goes that there was there instead of a cross a post set up between two other posts, and a beam stretched across the midmost post and attached to the other on either side. And as we afterwards discovered, from the marks of the wounds and of the bands, the right hand and foot had been tightly bound and fastened with cords, but the left hand and foot were pierced with two nails: so in fact the deed was done by design that, in case at any time he should be found, when the fastenings of the nails were discovered it might not be supposed that he had been killed by Jews rather than by Christians. But while in doing these things they were adding pang to pang and wound to wound, and yet were not able to satisfy their heartless cruelty and their inborn hatred of the Christian name, lo! after all these many and great tortures, they inflicted a frightful wound in his left side, reaching even to his inmost heart, and as though to make an end of all they extinguished his mortal life so far as it was in their power. And since many streams of blood were running down from all parts of his body, then, to stop the blood and to wash and close the wounds, they poured boiling water over him.

Thus then the glorious boy and martyr of Christ, William, dying the death of time in reproach of the Lord's death, but crowned with the blood of a glorious martyrdom, entered into the kingdom of glory on high to live for ever. Whose soul rejoiceth blissfully in heaven among the bright hosts of the saints, and whose body by the omnipotence of the divine mercy worketh miracles upon earth.

DISCUSSION QUESTIONS

1. What do you think Thomas of Monmouth hoped to achieve in composing this text?
2. According to the text, the way the Jews murdered William was designed to mock the crucifixion of Christ. Why do you think this would have been especially threatening to Christians at the time?
3. By the end of the twelfth century, William's cult was firmly established, and his tomb was the purported site of many miracles and visions. Why do you think people accepted the story of his martyrdom and his status as a true saint?

COMPARATIVE QUESTIONS

1. What do the privileges granted to students by Frederick I and Philip II and the passage from *Erec and Enide* suggest about the relationship between political power and the emerging institutions of higher learning at the time?
2. In what ways did the increase in wealth in twelfth-century Europe shape the ideals of Chrétien de Troyes and St. Francis?
3. Both Saints Francis and Clare pledged obedience to the Roman Catholic church and its doctrines, reflecting an increased emphasis in this period on religious or-

thodoxy and conformity. How does this emphasis help to explain the intolerance for Jews as revealed in *The Life and Miracles of St. William of Norwich*?

4. Although rulers like Frederick I and Philip II relied more and more on written documents to run their governments effectively, what do both Chrétien's poetry and St. Francis's *Rule* suggest about the continued importance of the spoken word in medieval culture?

The Elusive Search
for Harmony
1215–1320

S U M M A R Y   Harmony, order, and unity—these were the ideals sought by kings, emperors, popes, clerics, artists, and poets in the period from 1215 to 1320. It was easier said than done, but the search for these qualities is obvious in almost every document of the period in the medieval West. The first three documents reflect the artistic, religious, and literary search for meaning in a world in search of unity. However elusive, the signs were promising: many monarchies consolidated their power, representative institutions developed, and the church appeared to be at its pinnacle. There was a new and hopeful vision of the world and the future. The fourth document, a chronicle dealing largely with the reign of Alexander Nevsky (1220–1263), although seemingly different, exemplifies this search for order and harmony. Russia, ironically, would achieve a measure of unity through both its opposition to and cooperation with a common enemy—both northern and eastern Europeans and the Mongols.

1
Abbot Suger
The Abbey Church of St.-Denis
1144

The royal abbey of St.-Denis, on the northeast outskirts of Paris, sheltered the relics of the patron saint of France and served as the necropolis of its kings. Abbot Suger, a counselor and "biographer" of both Louis VI and Louis VII and regent for the latter during the Second Crusade, headed the abbey from 1122 until his death in 1151. He is generally credited with creating the "Gothic" style at St.-Denis, although elements of it had been present earlier. The rebuilding of St.-Denis began in 1137, according to Suger because it could not contain the crowds, and its inauguration was marked in 1144 by the attendance of King Louis VII, the greatest prelates of the realm, and ordinary men and women. The style of architecture, based on light and height, was intimately bound to new visions of religion and beauty: it reflected the sacral nature and power of French kingship as well as an increasing consciousness of other parts of Europe and the East.

In the twenty-third year of our administration, on a certain day when we sat in general chapter conferring with our brethren about common and private matters, these same dear brothers and sons began to beg me vigorously and in love that I should not remain silent about the fruit of our past labors but rather with pen and ink should preserve for future memory the additions which the munificence of almighty God bestowed upon this church during the time of our leadership in the acquisition of new things, the recovery of lost ones, the multiplication of refurbished possessions, the construction of buildings, and the accumulation of gold, silver, precious gems and quality textiles. From this one thing they promised us two in return: Through this memorial we should earn the prayers of succeeding brothers for the salvation of our soul; and through this example we should arouse in them a zealous commitment to the proper maintenance of God's church. . . .

We managed to have the chapel of St. Romanus dedicated to the service of God and his holy angels by that venerable man Archbishop Hugh of Rouen and by many other bishops. Those who serve God there as if, even as they sacrifice, they dwell at least partly in heaven, know how secluded, hallowed and convenient for the celebration of divine rites this place is. At the same dedication ceremony, two chapels in the lower nave of the church—one for St. Hippolytus and his companions on one side and one for St. Nicholas on the other—were dedicated by those venerable men Manassas, Bishop of Meaux, and Peter, Bishop of Senlis. The single glorious procession of these three men went out through the door of Saint Eustace; then passed in front of the main doors with a throng of singing clergy and a crowd of rejoicing laymen, the bishops walking in front and carrying out the holy consecration; then, thirdly, they entered through the single door of the cemetery which had been transferred from the old building to the new. And when this festive work had been completed to the honor of almighty God and we, a bit tired, were preparing to officiate in the upper part, they revived us, very graciously encouraging us not to be depressed by consideration of the labor and funding problems that lay before us.

. . . [W]e erected the main doors, on which are represented the passion and resurrection or ascension of Christ, with great expense and heavy outlay for their

---

Abbot Suger. *De administratione,* Translation by David Burr. http://www.fordham.edu/halsall/source/sugar.html.

gilding as befits such a noble portico. We also set up new ones on the right, and old ones on the left beneath the mosaic which, contrary to modern custom, we had placed in the tympanum. We also arranged to have the towers and upper crenelations of the front altered with an eye to beauty and, should circumstances require, to utility. We also ordered that, lest it be forgotten, the year of the consecration should be inscribed in copper-gilt letters in this way:

For the glory of the church which nurtured and raised him,
Suger strove for the glory of the church, Sharing with
you what is yours, oh martyr Denis. He prays that by your
prayers he should become a sharer in Paradise. The year
when it was consecrated was the one thousand, one
hundred and fortieth year of the Word.

Furthermore, the verses on the doors are these:

All you who seek to honor these doors,
Marvel not at the gold and expense but at the
craftsmanship of the work.
The noble work is bright, but, being nobly bright, the work
Should brighten the minds, allowing them to travel through
    the lights
To the true light, where Christ is the true door.
The golden door defines how it is imminent in these things.
The dull mind rises to the truth through material things,
And is resurrected from its former submersion when the
    light is seen.

And on the lintel was written,

Receive, stern Judge, the prayers of your Suger,
Let me be mercifully numbered among your sheep.

. . . . For remembrance of the past is foresight of the future. Moreover, the most generous lord, who among other, greater things has provided the makers of our marvelous windows with opulent sapphire and ready cash of around seven hundred pounds or more, will not allow the project to remain incomplete through lack of funds. . . .

Lest forgetfulness, the rival of truth, should slip in and snatch away a good example for future behavior, we have thought it worthwhile to provide a description of the ornaments with which the hand of God has adorned the church, his chosen bride. We confess our lord the thrice-blessed Denis to be so generous and benevolent that, as we believe, he has intervened for us before God so strongly and so often, obtaining so many and so great benefits, that we could have done a hundred times more than we actually did for his church if human weakness, shifting circumstances and changing customs had not prevented it. Nevertheless, what we, by the gift of God, have collected for him is hereby listed. . . . Into this panel, which stands before his most sacred body, we estimate that we have put around forty-two marks of gold, a rich abundance of precious gems—hyacinths, rubies, sapphires, emeralds and topazes—and a variety of pearls, more than we ever hoped to find. You would see kings, princes and many outstanding men, imitating us, remove the rings from their fingers and order that the gold, gems and precious pearls of the rings be set in the panel. In the same way archbishops and bishops, depositing the rings of their investiture there for safekeeping, devoutly offered them up to God and his saints.

Of course the blessed Denis had lain in that same spot for five hundred years and more, from Dagobert's time to our own.

We do not wish to pass in silence over one humorous yet noble miracle which the Lord displayed to us in this connection. Just when I was in need of gems and unable to purchase enough (for rarity makes them more expensive), monks from three abbeys belonging to two different orders—that is, from Citeaux, from another abbey of the same order, and from Fontevrault—entered our little room adjoining the church and offered for sale a greater supply of gems than we would have hoped to find in ten years. They had obtained them as alms from Count Theobold, who had received them through his brother King Stephen of England from the treasury of his uncle the late King Henry. Theobold had stored them up throughout his life in marvelous vessels. . . .

We hastened to decorate the main altar of the blessed Denis, which had only a beautiful and sumptuous frontal panel from the time of Charles the Bald, the third emperor; for at this very altar we had been dedicated to the monastic life. We had it entirely covered, adding gold panels on each side. And a fourth, even more precious one, so that the whole altar would appear to be gold all the way around. On the sides we placed two candlesticks of King Louis, the son of Philip, so that they would not be stolen on some occasion. We added hyacinths, emeralds, and various other precious gems, ordering a diligent search for others which could be added.

I used to confer with Jerusalemites, and I was eager to learn from those who had seen the treasures of Constantinople and decorations of Hagia Sophia whether these here were worth anything in comparison. When some considered these here to be greater, it seemed to us that, through fear of the Franks, those marvelous objects of which we had once heard had been prudently put away lest by the impetuous greed of a few stupid people the friendship nurtured between Greek and Latin should suddenly change to sedition and warfare; for cunning is a preeminently Greek characteristic. Thus it may be that there is more displayed here, where it is safe, than there, where it is unsafe because of disorders. From many trustworthy men, and from Archbishop Hugh of Laon, we have heard wonderful and nearly incredible reports concerning the superior ornamentation of Hagia Sophia and other churches. If these reports are true—or more precisely, because we believe their testimony is indeed true—then such inestimable and incomparable treasures should be set out for the judgment of many people. "Let every man abound in his own sense" (Rom. 14:5).

To me, I confess, it always has seemed right that the most expensive things should be used above all for the administration of the holy eucharist. If golden vessels, vials and mortars were used to collect "the blood of goats or calves or the red heifer, how much more" should gold vases, precious stones and whatever is most valuable among created things be set out with continual reverence and full devotion "to receive the blood of Jesus Christ" (Heb. 9:1 3f).

. . . The date was that of the martyrdom of our lords the blessed martyrs, the eighth day before the ides of October. Archbishops and bishops of various provinces were there. They had come eagerly to bring devout prayers for this solemn celebration, as if paying their debt to the apostolate of Gaul. The archbishops of Lyons, Reims, Tours and Rouen were there, as were the bishops of Soissons, Beauvais, Senlis, Meaux, Rennes, St. Malo and Vannes. There were also a large number of abbots, monks and clerics as well as an uncountable crowd of laity, male and female. . . .

We also discovered the reason why the relics had been deposited there. The Emperor Charles III, who lies gloriously interred beneath this altar, arranged by imperial edict that they be removed from the imperial repository and placed with him for the protection of his soul and body. We also found there evidence, sealed with his ring, which pleased us very much. . . .

We also erected the cross, admirable for its size, which is placed between the altar and Charles' tomb. According to tradition the most noble necklace of Queen Nanthilda, wife of King Dagobert, founder of the church, was affixed to the middle of this cross, while another (smaller but unequaled according to the testimony of the most experienced artisans) was affixed to the forehead of St. Denis. . . .

We also restored the noble throne of the glorious King Dagobert, on which, as tradition relates, the Frankish kings sat to receive the homage of their nobles after they had assumed power. We did so in recognition of its exalted function and because of the value of the work itself.

We also had the eagle in the middle of the choir regilded, for it had been rubbed bare of gold by the frequent touch of admirers.

We also had painted, by the hands of many masters sought out in various nations, a splendid variety of new windows below and above, from the first in the chevet representing the tree of Jesse to the one over the principal door of the entrance. . . .

Since their marvelous workmanship and the cost of the sapphire and painted glass makes these windows very valuable, we appointed a master craftsman for their protection and maintenance, just as we also appointed a skilled goldsmith for the gold and silver ornaments. These would receive their allowances and whatever was apportioned to them in addition, such as coins from the altar and flour from the common storehouse of the brethren, and they were never to neglect their duties.

We also had seven candlesticks of enameled and excellently gilded metal-work made, since the ones made by the emperor Charles for the blessed Denis seemed to be ruined by age. . . .

Moreover, with the devotion due to the blessed Denis, we acquired vessels of gold and precious stones for the service of the Lord's table, in addition to the ones already donated for this purpose by kings of the Franks and those devoted to the church. To be specific, we ordered a big gold chalice containing one hundred forty ounces of gold and decorated with precious gems (hyacinths and topazes) as a substitute for another which had been pawned during the time of our predecessor.

We also offered to the blessed Denis, along with some flowers from the empress' crown, another very precious vessel of praise, carved in the form of a boat, which King Louis, son of Philip, had left in pawn for nearly ten years. When it was offered for our inspection, we had purchased it with the king's permission for sixty marks of silver. This vessel, marvelous for both the quality and the quantity of its precious stones, it decorated with verroterie cloisonné work by St. Eloi and is considered by all goldsmiths to be very precious.

DISCUSSION QUESTIONS

1. Describe Suger's vision of holiness as exemplified in church architecture. Despite critics, the French or Gothic style epitomized Western architecture for several centuries. How is the Gothic intended to draw the viewer to God?

2. Suger inserts his own name in numerous inscriptions on parts of the abbey church. What does this tell you about changing views of art and architecture in the twelfth century?

3. How does Suger intertwine his architectural vision with ideas of French kingship and its relationship with other European kingdoms and the papacy?

4. Look closely at the comment about Hagia Sophia in Constantinople. How did the European view of the world change in response to increasing connections with the Eastern Empire during the period of the Crusades?

2

Hadewijch of Brabant
Letters and Poems of a Female Mystic
1220–1240

The body of work written or dictated by women during the twelfth and thirteenth centuries is considerable—religious and mystical writings, poems, and courtly love literature, medical treatises, and songs. Often the line between the genres was blurred, especially in religious writing. Hadewijch of Brabant was one of many such women writers, and our knowledge of her comes primarily from her writings in her native Dutch, which include thirty-one letters, fourteen visions, forty-five stanzaic poems, and sixteen to twenty-nine other poems. Criticized by members of her own (probably Beguine) community (a community she may have led), Hadewijch nonetheless typifies many women writers in this period. She uses mystical and seemingly erotic language to describe a relationship with Christ. Although some Beguines bordered on the edge of unorthodoxy and even heresy, most works by female mystics fit harmoniously with the writings of such church leaders as Bernard of Clairvaux and Richard and Hugh of St. Victor.

May God let you know, dear child, who He is and how He uses His servants and His handmaidens in particular, and may He consume you in Him. In the depth of His wisdom he shall teach you what he is and how wondrously sweet the beloved dwells in the other beloved, and how thoroughly one dwells in the other, so that neither one nor the other knows themselves apart. But they possess and rejoice in each other mouth in mouth, heart in heart, body in body, soul in soul, and one sweet divine nature flows through them both, and both are one through themselves, yet remain themselves, and will always remain so. . . . Still, I could never endure, dear child, that someone before me loved God as dearly as I. I believe that many loved Him as fondly and dearly, yet I could hardly bear that someone would know Him with such passion.

From the age of ten I have been overwhelmed with such passionate love that I would have died during the first two years of this experience if God had not granted me a power unknown to common people and made me recover with His own being. For He soon granted me reason, sometimes enlightened with many wonderful revelations, and I received many wonderful gifts from Him, when he let me feel His presence and showed Himself to me. I was aware of many signs that were between Him and me, as with friends who are used to concealing little and revealing much when their feelings for each other have grown most intimate, when they taste, eat, and drink and consume each other wholly. Through these many signs God, my lover, showed to me early in life, He made me gain much confidence in Him, and I often thought that no one loved him as dearly as I. . . . I do no longer believe that my love for Him is the dearest, nor do I believe that there is one alive who loves God as dearly as I. Sometimes I am so enlightened with love that I realize my failure to give my beloved what He deserves; sometimes when I am blinded with love's sweetness, when I am tasting and feeling her,

From "The Brabant Mystic: Hadewijch," in *Medieval Women Writers,* ed. Katherina M. Wilson (Athens: University of Georgia Press, 1984), 193–95, 198–201.

I realize she is enough for me; and sometimes when I am feeling so fulfilled in her presence, I secretly admit to her that she is enough for me. . . .

In the fifth unspeakable hour love seduces the heart and the soul, and the soul is driven out of herself and out of love's nature and back into love's nature. The soul has then ceased to wonder about the power and darkness of love's designs, and has forgotten the pains of love. Then the soul knows love only through love herself, which may seem lower but is not. For where knowledge is most intimate the beloved knows least.

In the sixth unspeakable hour love despises reason and all that lies within reason and above it and below. Whatever belongs to reason stands against the blessed state of love. . . .

Born is the new season as the old one that lasted so long is drawing to a close.

Those prepared to do love's service will receive her rewards: new comfort and new strength.

If they love her with the vigor of love, they will soon be one with love in love.

To be one with love is an awesome calling and those who long for it should spare no effort.

Beyond all reason they will give their all and go through all.

For love dwells so deep in the womb of the Father that her power will unfold only to those who serve her with utter devotion. . . .

Those who long to be one with love achieve great things, and shirk no effort.

They shall be strong and capable of any task that will win them the love of love, to help the sick or the healthy, the blind, the crippled, or the wounded.

For this is what the lover owes to love. . . .

Those who trust in love with all their being shall be given all they need.

For she brings comfort to the sad and guidance to those who cannot read.

Love will be pleased with the lover if he accepts no other comfort and trusts in her alone.

Those who desire to live in love alone with all their might and heart shall so dispose all things that they shall soon possess her all.

Like the noble season born to bring us flowers in the fields, so the noble ones are called to bear the yoke, the bonds of love.

Faith grows forever in their deeds, and noble flowers blossom and their fruits.

The world is fashioned with faith, and the lover dwells in highest love, one with her in everlasting friendship. . . .

And outside love their truth cannot be known: to those who do not dwell in love the burden is not light but heavy, and they suffer fears unknown to love.

For the servants' law is fear but love is the law of sons.

What is this burden light in love, this yoke so sweet?

It is that noble thrust inside, that touch of love in the beloved which makes him one with her, one will, one being, one beyond revoke.

And ever deeper digs desire and all that is dug up is drunk by love, for love's demands on love surpass the mind of man.

These things are beyond the mind of man: how the lover whom love has overwhelmed with love beholds the beloved so full of love.

For he rests not an hour, before he sails with love through all that is and looks upon her splendor with devotion.

For in love's face he reads the designs she has for him, and in truth in love's face he sees clear and undeceived so many pains so sweet.

This he clearly sees: the lover must love in truth alone. . . .

All their secret veins will run into that stream where love gives love away, where love's friends are made drunk with love and filled with wonder at her passion.

And all this remains concealed to strangers, but to the wise it stands revealed. . . .

[T]heir life is free and undisturbed, and well may they say, "I am all of love and love is all of me."

For what will harm them when they claim the sun, the moon, and all the stars?

Love be praised for the birds that rejoice now and were sad in winter, and soon the proud hearts will rejoice that dwelled in pain too long.

And in the fullness of her power she shall give them a reward that will surpass the mind of man. . . .

Burning desire is taught in the school of highest love.

She confounds the experienced, she brings happiness to the wretched, she makes them lords of all over which love holds sway.

Of this I am certain beyond all doubt.

To those who can serve love no more I give this good advice.

Let them still beg for her comfort if they falter and serve her with devotion according to the her highest counsel.

Let them think how great love's power is, for only those near to death cannot be healed.

They have risen high that have received love's power, and in that power they shall read her judgment over them.

DISCUSSION QUESTIONS

1. Examine closely the language in which Hadewijch expresses her feelings. How does she use gender imagery and language? Do you believe men and women envisioned their relationship with God in different terms?

2. How would you describe Hadewijch's relationship with God and God's relationship with her? Does it surprise you?

3. Why might some members of Hadewijch's community and some church authorities have been concerned with her writings, as well as those of other female mystics? How did her approach challenge some accepted ways of thinking?

4. How does Hadewijch reflect the religious and cultural change of her times?

3

Dante Alighieri
Human and Divine Love
Late Thirteenth–Early Fourteenth Centuries

Like many Florentines, Dante Alighieri (1265–1321) was heavily involved in politics, serving in the city government, as envoy to Pope Boniface VIII, and eventually suffering exile from his beloved city. But Dante is most celebrated as one of the world's greatest poets. Some of his writings are political, but it is in his vernacular writings, especially the Divine Comedy *and* La Vita Nuova, *that his great genius lies. Dante, through his artistry, is widely credited as making Tuscan the language of Italy and spreading the use of the vernacular.* La Vita Nuova *(1292) is a celebration of human and divine love, written two years after the death of Beatrice, whom Dante tells us he met in 1274. Beatrice Portinari, married to a member of the rich and famous Bardi banking family, became in Dante's words his great love from the moment he first saw her when he was nine. His platonic/philosophical love for her— and what she represented—was in the purest courtly love tradition. It was love for the unattainable woman who teaches her "lover" about the mysteries of love. The* Divine Comedy, *consisting of the* Inferno, Purgatorio, *and* Paradiso, *was written between 1306 and 1320. Although Virgil is Dante's guide in the nether regions, Beatrice allows him to glimpse the wonders of paradise as he journeys to understand the meaning of life.*

From La Vita Nuova

Nine times the heaven of the light had revolved in its own movement since my birth and had almost returned to the same point when the woman whom my mind beholds in glory first appeared before my eyes. She was called Beatrice by many who did not know what it meant to call her this. . . . When exactly nine years had passed since this gracious being appeared to me, as I have described, it happened that on the last day of this intervening period this marvel appeared before me again, dressed in purest white, walking between two other women of distinguished bearing, both older than herself. As they walked down the street she turned her eyes towards me where I stood in fear and trembling, and with her ineffable courtesy, which is now rewarded in eternal life, she greeted me; and such was the virtue of her greeting that I seemed to experience the height of bliss. It was exactly the ninth hour of day when she gave me her sweet greeting. As this was the first time she had ever spoken to me, I was filled with such joy that, my

---

From Dante Alighieri, *La Vita Nuova,* trans. Barbara Reynolds (New York: Penguin Books, 1980), 29, 31, 41, 46, 57; and Dante Alighieri, *The Comedy of Dante Alighieri the Florentine, Cantica III: Paradise,* trans. Dorothy L. Sayers and Barbara Reynolds (New York: Penguin Books, 1981), 53–56, 64, 73, 76, 84, 85, 90, 92, 93.

senses reeling, I had to withdraw from the sight of others. . . . Whenever and wherever she appeared, in the hope of receiving her miraculous salutation I felt I had not an enemy in the world. Indeed, I glowed with a flame of charity which moved me to forgive all who had ever injured me; and if at that moment some-one had asked me a question, about anything, my only reply would have been: "Love." . . . And when this most gracious being actually bestowed the saving power of her salutation, I do not say that Love as an intermediary could dim for me such unendurable bliss. . . .

I became like a person who does not know which road to take on his jour-ney, who wants to set out but does not know where to start. . . .

One imperfection only Heaven has:
The lack of her; so now for her it pleads
And every saint with clamour intercedes,
Only compassion is our advocate.
God understands to whom their prayers relate
And answers them: "My loved ones, bear in peace
That she, your hope, remain until I please
Where one knows he must lose her, soon or late,
And who will say in Hell, 'Souls unconfessed!
I have beheld the hope of Heaven's blessed.'"
My lady is desired in highest heaven.

From the Divine Comedy, Paradiso

O power divine, grant me in song to show
    The blest realm's image—shadow though it be—
    Stamped on my brain; thus far thyself bestow,
       . . .
When Beatrice, intent upon the sun,
    Turned leftward, and so stood and gazed before;
    No eagle e'er so fixed his eyes thereon.
And, as the second ray doth evermore
    Strike from the just and dart back up again,
    Just as the peregrine will stoop and soar,
So through her eyes, her gesture, pouring in
    On my mind's eye, shaped mine; I stared wide-eyed
    On the sun's face, beyond the wont of men.
       . . .
Beatrice stood, her eyes still riveted
    On the eternal wheels; and, constantly,
    Turning mine thence, I gazed on her instead.
       . . .
Whence she to whom my whole self open was

As to myself, to calm my troubled fit
    Stayed not my question, but without pause
Opened her lips: "Thou dullest thine own wit
    With false imagination, nor perceivest
    That which thou wouldst perceive, being rid of it.
Thou art not still on earth, as thou believest;
    Lightning from its sphere falling never matched
    The speed which thou, returning there, achievest."
But I, my first bewilderment despatched
    By these few smiling words, was more perplexed
    · Now, by a new one which I promptly hatched.
I said: "I rest content, no longer vexed
    By one great doubt; but how come I to fly
    Through these light spheres? This doubt assails me next."
She turned on me, after a pitying sigh,
    A look such as a mother's eyes let fall
    Upon her infant, babbling feverishly.
Then she began: "All beings great and small
    Are linked in order; and this orderliness
    Is form, which stamps God's likeness on the All.
Herein the higher creatures see the trace
    Of the Prime Excellence who is the end
    For which that form was framed in the first place."

      . . .

Beatrice gazed on heav'n and I on her;
    Then, while a quarrel might thud home, and wing,
    And from the mocking-point unloose, as 'twere,
I found I'd come where a most wondrous thing
    Enthralled my sight; whence she, being privy thus
    To my whole thought and secret questioning,
Turning to me, as blithe as beautëous:
    "Lift up to God," said she, "thy grateful sense,
    Who with the first star now uniteth us.
Meseemed a cloud enclosed us, lucid, dense,
    Solid, and smooth, like to the diamond stone
    Smitten upon the sun's radiance.
Into itself eternal union
    Received us both, as water doth receive
    A ray of light and still remains all one,

      . . .

The sun that warmed my bosom first with love
    Had brought the beauteous face of truth to light,
    Unveiling it by proof and counter-proof.
Corrected and convinced I must outright
    Confess me, and, the better to convey

These sentiments, I raised my head upright;
But what I saw so carried me away
    To gaze on it, that ere I could confess,
    I had forgotten what I meant to say.

. . .

Toward Beatrice's self I moved me, turning;
    But on mine eyes her light at first so blazed,
    They could not bear the beauty and the burning;
And I was slow to question, being amazed.

. . .

"O Loved," said I, "of the First Lover! O
    Most heavenly Lady, by whose words I live
    More and yet more, bathed in their quickening glow.
My love's whole store is too diminutive,
    Too poor in thanks to give back grace for grace;
    May he that sees, and has the power, so give!
That nothing save the light of truth allays
    Our intellect's disquiet I now see plain—
    God's truth, which holds all truth within its rays.

. . .

This thought invites and makes me more secure
    To ask you, Lady, with all reverence due,
    About a further truth I find obscure.
This would I know: can one atone to you
    For broken vows with other merchandise,
    Nor weigh too short upon your balance true?"
Beatrice looked at me, and lo! her eyes
    Grew so divine, with sparkling love alight,
    That I was lost in wonder and surprise,
My gaze downcast, my powers all put to flight.

. . .

"If in the fire of love I flame thus hot
    Upon thee, past all wont of mortal mood,
    Forcing thine eyes' surrender, marvel not.
This comes of perfect sight, with power endued
    To apprehend, and foot by foot to move
    Deeper into the apprehended good.
Full well I see thine intellect give off
    Splendours already of the eternal light
    Which once to look upon is aye to love;
And if aught else your wandering loves invite,
    Still it is nothing but some gleams of this
    Which there shine through, though not yet known aright.
Fain wouldst thou learn if any service is
    Enough to offset broken vows, and fend

The soul against pursuit for damages."
Thus did Beatrice to my canto lend
 The prelude; nor paused there, but fluently
 Pursued her sacred theme unto the end.

   . . .

Thus unto me, even in the words I write,
 Beatrice; and, all desire, she turned her glance
 Then to where most the world is quick with light.
Her silence and her altered countenance
 Restrained my busy wits from chattering,
 Primed as they were with questions in advance;
And, as the shaft smites home or e'er the string
 Has ceased vibrating, so we found us there,
 Shot to the second realm, untarrying;
And O! such joy I saw my Lady wear
 When to that shining heav'n she entered in
 The planet's self grew brighter yet with her.

DISCUSSION QUESTIONS

1. Some scholars question Beatrice Portinari's existence or her personal inspiration for *La Vita Nuova* and *Paradiso*. Does it matter? Why or why not?

2. How does Dante's writing fit into the courtly love tradition? How does it fit into that of the medieval cult of the Virgin Mary?

3. What, if anything, does it tell you about the status of women that Dante chose Beatrice as his guide to Heaven? What does it mean when he says "she was called Beatrice by many who did not know what it meant to call her this"? How is this statement important?

4. Dante is often portrayed as a "medieval" rather than a "Renaissance" poet. Why? What connections do you see in his poetry with the intellectual culture of the time?

4

Nikonian Chronicle
Russia: The West and the Golden Horde
1241–1381

The principalities of Kiev, Novgorod, and Pskov had dominated "Russian" political and cultural life for centuries. After the marriage of Vladimir (980–1015) to a Byzantine princess, Russia adopted Orthodox Christianity. Conquered by the Chingiz Khan (1162–1227), "Russia" was controlled by the "Golden Horde," as the Mongols in this area were commonly known, until the late fifteenth century. As long as they received tribute brought by the princes, the Mongols usually allowed a measure of self-government, although occasional fierce raids fortified their position. Russia was also attacked from the west, by peoples described as "Germans" and "Romans" (usually a reference to Swedes, Lithuanians, Finns, or Poles). This excerpt from the Nikonian Chronicle *details events in the life of Alexander Nevsky (1220–1263). His policies of opposition to and, ironically, cooperation with a common enemy in the West and the Golden Horde also signaled the beginning of Muscovy's prominence as the center of Russia and the consolidation of princely power.*

This pious, noble, and praiseworthy Grand Prince Aleksandr Iaroslavich was eighth in the line of autocrat Tsar Grand Prince Vladimir Sviatoslavich, who was equal to the Apostles because he enlightened the Russian land through Holy Baptism. . . . Fear of God settled in his heart and he observed God's commandments and behaved according to them, very much respecting the clergy and monks.

Throughout his whole youth he strictly observed the wisdom of humility;

he abstained and stayed awake [praying at night] and he observed purity of soul and body,

he followed the rules of humility and rejected vainglory,

he controlled the desires of his flesh because he was aware that gluttony may destroy chastity. . . .

On his lips were constantly divine words which were sweeter than honey.

He would read the Scripture carefully

and he was filled with the desire to follow its words and practice them in deed. . . .

His power was like that of Solomon and his voice could be heard by all as a trumpet. His bravery was as that of the Roman Emperor Vespasian. . . . And such was this Grand Prince Aleksandr Iaroslavich, who defeated everyone and was never defeated. He was very merciful, in the same way as was his God-preserved father Iaroslav; but in every respect he followed in his steps, giving as ransom for captives much gold and silver. And he would send it to Khan Batu, to the Horde. . . .

When the people learned that godless Khan Batu, with God's permission, had caused much evil in the great Russian land, this blessed Aleksandr went to Novgorod, with his father, Iaroslav. . . . They stayed there and combatted inimical, hostile Lithuanians and Germans, while the murderous Tatars, by God's help, did no manner of battle against them.

Once, in order to see him powerful people from the Western land calling themselves the servants of God came to Grand Prince Aleksandr. . . . They did so just as the Queen of Sheba went to Solomon to see him and to hear his wisdom. . . . He decided to take advantage of the moment, for he was aware of Batu's conquest of Russia. This king of this land hoped to swallow up the remaining part of

From *The Nikonian Chronicle from the Year 1241 to the Year 1381*, vol. 3, trans. Serge A. and Betty Jean Zenkovsky, ed. Serge A. Zenovsky (Princeton, N.J.: Kingston Press, 1986), 1–8, 10, 12–13, 57, 63.

Russia, and in his pride he said, "I will go and I will capture Great Novgorod and other cities, and I will turn the Slavic people into my slaves, and I will defeat Grand Prince Aleksandr, himself, or I will take him prisoner." . . . The Most Gracious and Most Merciful Manloving God, however, wanted to protect and defend His dominion from the evil cunning of foreigners, and so this madman labored in vain because his intentions were contrary to the will of God.

Soon after their arrival came the tidings that the Swedes were marching toward Lagoda, and they sent their envoys to Aleksandr Iaroslavich, saying, "Resist if you can; but I have already arrived here and I will capture you, and you and your sons will be my slaves." When Aleksandr heard these words his heart burned and he went to the church of Holy Sophia. There, kneeling before the altar, he prayed tearfully. . . . And he mounted his horse and marched against the enemy troops.

Aleksandr's voevoda [military governor] was an elder, a notable . . . by the name Pelagius—Philip, in Holy Baptism—who was charged with guarding the seashore. He greatly respected the Holy Martyrs Boris and Gleb. . . . As the sun began to rise he heard an awesome noise coming from the sea, and he saw a ship approaching. In its midst stood the Holy Martyrs Boris and Gleb in red vestments. . . . And Boris said to Gleb, "Brother Gleb! Order them to row faster. Let us help our kinsman, Grand Prince Aleksandr Iaroslavich." . . .

And so [Aleksandr Iaroslavich] marched against them and toward the sixth hour of the day there was a great battle against the Romans. They slew a great many Romans, and he even left a seal on the king's face with his sharp sword. . . .

All this I heard from my lord, Prince Aleksandr Iaroslavich, and from others who were witnesses of this battle. It was a miracle similar to the one which occurred in olden times during the reign of King Hezekiah, when Jerusalem was attacked by Sennacherib, the king of Assyria, who wanted to capture the Holy City: suddenly an angel of the Lord appeared and slew 185,000 Assyrian warriors, and early the next morning their bodies were found there, all dead. The same happened after Aleksandr Iaroslavich's victory. . . .

The same year Batu's Tatars defeated the Hungarians, captured the king's son, Menush, and brought him and a great multitude of high comanders to Batu. The same year Batu's Tatar's killed Prince Mstislav of Ryl'sk. . . .

The same year the Germans . . . killed voevoda Gavrila Goreslavich, and defeated the people of Pskov, slaying many in pursuit, others they captured. And they chased them to the city, setting fire in the suburbs; and there was much evil. They burned the churches, the holy icons and church property, and devastated many towns around Pskov. They besieged the city for one week but were unable to take it. They captured many children of good men and took them into captivity, then retreated. And so it continued, without peace. . . .

The Germans gathered in their land and defeated the troops of Pskov, then put their administrators in Pskov. Hearing of this, Prince Aleksandr Iaroslavich became very sad about the shedding of Christian blood, and without losing time, seized by fervent divine faith, he marched to Novgorod with his brother Andrei, and with all his troops. Coming to Novgorod, he bowed to the cathedral of Holy Sophia with prayer and tears. . . . Grand Prince Aleksandr returned with great glory. . . . And the name of Grand Prince Aleksandr Iaroslavich began to spread through all the lands, from the Varangian Sea to the Pontic Sea, to the Caspian Sea, to the land of the Tiveretses, to Mt. Ararat, and to the other side of the Varangian Sea, and to the Arabian mountains and even up to Great Rome. And his name spread before ten thousand and ten thousand, and before thousands and thousands. And so he came to Novgorod with great victory.

1272

At that time there was a tradition of going to the Horde [to render tribute and hostages]. . . . When they came to the Khan of the Golden Horde they were received with honor.

1279

The same year Thognost, Bishop of Sarai, came for the third time from the Greek land, from Constantinople. He was sent by His Holiness Cyril, Metropolitan of Kiev and all Russia, and by Khan Mangu Temir of the Golden Horde, to Emperor Michael Paleologue of Byzantium, with a charter from His Holiness Metropolitan Cyril and from Khan Mangu Tempir, and with gifts from them both.

The same year the Tatars campaigned in Lithuania and the Russian princes marched with them. They returned home with many captives and booty.

DISCUSSION QUESTIONS

1. How would you compare the role of the Grand Prince in Russia with that of kings and emperors of the time? What are the desirable attributes of a Russian prince?

2. How did the "Russians" deal with Europeans, Byzantines, and Mongols? Compare the relationships they had with the different peoples, and why it might have been in the best interest of both Alexander Nevsky and the chroniclers to emphasize the western threat.

3. Compare descriptions of the piety of Alexandr Nevsky with that of European leaders of the time. Does his piety appear different or similar?

4. There is little in the *Nikonian Chronicle* about Russian culture of the time, although the cities had been known through the centuries for their beautiful icons. How would you explain the lack of any mention of cultural life? How does the nature and purpose of any historical source influence our reading of it?

COMPARATIVE QUESTIONS

1. How does the culture of a time period reflect its society, politics, and religion? How does the nature and content of a source help us make historical determinations?

2. Compare Abbot Suger and Alexander Nevsky, both of whom, whether they realized it or not, were in the process of state building. How did each go about it? What was the relationship of "state" and church in each case, and how would you compare this relationship to developments in the rest of Europe?

3. Look at how both Hadewijch and Dante express female spirituality. How does a female relationship with God compare with or differ from the male expression of female religious belief?

4. Both Abbot Suger and Alexander Nevsky mention the churches of Hagia Sophia and Holy Sophia. Sophia means "wisdom." Can you connect these allusions with the search for meaning found in both Hadewijch and Dante?

chapter 13

The Crisis of Late Medieval Society 1320–1430

S U M M A R Y   Pestilence, warfare, a church in crisis, rebellions, pogroms, famines, and floods—for people living in the fourteenth century, it must have appeared that the end of the world was at hand. Fourteenth-century men and women came up with explanations, yet with the historian's luxury of retrospect, we can see the interconnectedness of events—what French historians call a conjuncture. Overpopulation, soil depletion, and warfare reduced the average life span even before plague struck. During the Black Death, scapegoats were often sought, even though many saw the plague as divine punishment. In its wake, the nobility sought to keep the people "in their place," adding restrictions and taxes that led to rebellions throughout Europe, including the English Peasants' Revolt of 1381. The horrors of war and a burgeoning nationalism are evident in Christine de Pizan's call for sanity. Finally, the church that at its height had claimed to be the spiritual and temporal head of Christendom, could not help, because it was a house divided, as appears clearly in the letters of Catherine of Siena and the conciliar documents.

1

The Black Death
Fourteenth Century

Few events in history have had such a shattering impact on every aspect of society as the plague, which reached Europe in 1347. The Black Death decimated a society already weakened as early as 1300 by a demographic crisis, famines, and climatic disasters. It is estimated that one-third of Europe's population died in the first wave of plague, which was followed by repeated outbreaks. Some cities may have lost over half their people in 1347–1348 alone. The devastation was social, psychological, eco-

nomic, political, and even artistic, yet many historians believe that in the long term it led to significant changes and even improvements in western life. The documents, all from the time period, describe the arrival of the plague in various places and responses to it, including searches for its cause and people on whom to fix blame. Even if the train of events had been set in motion by earlier natural and man-made disasters, the plague precipitated much of the crisis that characterized the fourteenth century.

From Gabriele de' Mussis (d. 1356), a Lawyer in Piacenza

In 1346, in the countries of the East, countless numbers of Tartars and Saracens were struck down by a mysterious illness which brought sudden death. . . . An eastern settlement under the rule of the Tartars called Tana, which lay to the north of Constantinople and was much frequented by Italian merchants, was totally abandoned after an incident there which led to its being besieged and attacked by hordes of Tartars who gathered in a short space of time. The Christian merchants, who had been driven out by force, were so terrified of the power of the Tartars that, to save themselves and their belongings, they fled in an armed ship to Caffa, a settlement in the same part of the world which had been founded long ago by the Genoese.

Oh God! See how the heathen Tartar races, pouring together from all sides, suddenly invested the city of Caffa and besieged the trapped Christians there for almost three years. There, hemmed in by an immense army, they could hardly draw breath, although food could be shipped in, which offered them some hope. But behold, the whole army was affected by a disease which overran the Tartars and killed thousands upon thousands every day. It was as though arrows were raining down from heaven to strike and crush the Tartars' arrogance. All medical advice and attention was useless; the Tartars died as soon as the signs of disease appeared on their bodies: swellings in the armpit or groin caused by coagulating humours, followed by a putrid fever.

The dying Tartars, stunned and stupefied by the immensity of the disaster brought about by the disease, and realising that they had no hope of escape, lost interest in the siege. But they ordered corpses to be placed in catapults and lobbed into the city in the hope that the intolerable stench would kill everyone inside. What seemed like mountains of dead were thrown into the city, and the Christians could not hide or flee or escape from them, although they dumped as many of the bodies as they could in the sea. And soon the rotting corpses tainted the air and poisoned the water supply, and the stench was so overwhelming that hardly one in several thousand was in a position to flee the remains of the Tartar army. Moreover, one infected man could carry the poison to others, and infect people and places with the disease by look alone. No one knew, or could discover, a means of defence.

From *The Black Death*, ed. and trans. Rosemary Horrox (Manchester: Manchester University Press, 1994), 16–21, 23, 207, 208, 219–22.

Thus almost everyone who had been in the East, or in the regions to the south and north, fell victim to sudden death after contracting this pestilential disease, as if struck by a lethal arrow which raised a tumour on their bodies. The scale of the mortality and the form which it took persuaded those who lived, weeping and lamenting, through the bitter events of 1346 to 1348—the Chinese, Indians, Persians, Medes, Kurds, Armenians, Cilicians, Georgians, Mesopotamians, Nubians, Ethiopians, Turks, Egyptians, Arabs, Saracens and Greeks (for almost all the East has been affected) that the last judgement had come. . . .

As it happened, among those who escaped from Caffa by boat were a few sailors who had been infected with the poisonous disease. Some boats were bound for Genoa, others went to Venice and to other Christian areas. When the sailors reached these places and mixed with the people there, it was as if they had brought evil spirits with them: every city, every settlement, every place was poisoned by the contagious pestilence. . . .

Scarcely one in seven of the Genoese survived. In Venice, where an inquiry was held into the mortality, it was found that more than 70% of the people had died, and that within a short period 20 out of 24 excellent physicians had died. The rest of Italy, Sicily and Apulia and the neighbouring regions maintain that they have been virtually emptied of inhabitants. The people of Florence, Pisa and Lucca, finding themselves bereft of their fellow residents, emphasize their losses. The Roman Curia at Avignon, the provinces on both sides of the Rhône, Spain, France, and the Empire cry up their griefs and disasters—all of which makes it extraordinarily difficult for me to give an accurate picture.

By contrast, what befell the Saracens can be established from trustworthy accounts. In the city of Babylon alone (the heart of the Sultan's power), 480,000 of his subjects are said to have been carried off by the disease in less than three months in 1348—and this is known from the Sultan's register which records the names of the dead, because he receives a gold bezant for each person buried. . . .

I am overwhelmed, I can't go on. Everywhere one turns there is death and bitterness to be described. The hand of the Almighty strikes repeatedly, to greater and greater effect. The terrible judgement gains power as time goes by.

From Herman Gigas, a Franciscan Friar in Germany, Whose Account Goes until 1349

In 1347 there was such a great pestilence and mortality throughout almost the whole world that in the opinion of well-informed men scarcely a tenth of mankind survived. The victims did not linger long, but died on the second or third day. . . . Some say that it was brought about by the corruption of the air; others that the Jews planned to wipe out all the Christians with poison and had poisoned wells and springs everywhere. And many Jews confessed as much under torture: that they had bred spiders and toads in pots and pans, and had obtained poison from overseas; and that not every Jew knew about this, only the more powerful ones, so that it would not be betrayed. . . . [M]en say that bags full of poison were found in many wells and springs.

From Heinrich Truchess, a Former Papal Chaplain
and Canon of Constance

The persecution of the Jews began in November 1348, and the first outbreak in Germany was at Sölden, where all the Jews were burnt on the strength of a rumour that they had poisoned wells and rivers, as was afterwards confirmed by their own confessions and also by the confessions of Christians whom they had corrupted. . . . Within the revolution of one year, that is from All Saints [1 November] 1348 until Michaelmas [29 September] 1349 all the Jews between Cologne and Austria were burnt and killed for this crime, young men and maidens and the old along with the rest. And blessed be God who confounded the ungodly who were plotting the extinction of his church.

From the Councillors of Cologne to Conrad von Winterthur to the
Bürgermeister and Councillors of Strassburg on 12 January 1349

Very dear friends, all sorts of rumours are now flying about against Judaism and the Jews prompted by this unexpected and unparalleled mortality of Christians, which, alas, has raged in various parts of the world and is still woefully active in several places. Throughout our city, as in yours, many-winged Fame clamours that this mortality was initially caused, and is still being spread, by the poisonings of springs and wells, and that the Jews must have dropped poisonous substances into them. When it came to our knowledge that serious charges had been made against the Jews in several small towns and villages on the basis of this mortality, we sent numerous letters to you and to other cities and towns to uncover the truth behind these rumours, and set a thorough investigation in train. . . .

If a massacre of the Jews were to be allowed in the major cities (something which we are determined to prevent in our city, if we can, as long as the Jews are found to be innocent of these or similar actions) it could lead to the sort of outrages and disturbances which would whip up a popular revolt among the common people—and such revolts have in the past brought cities to misery and desolation. In any case we are still of the opinion that this mortality and its attendant circumstances are caused by divine vengeance and nothing else. Accordingly we intend to forbid any harassment of the Jews in our city because of these flying rumours, but to defend them faithfully and keep them safe, as our predecessors did—and we are convinced that you ought to do the same.

Papal Bull Sicut Judeis of Clement VI Issued in July 1348

Recently, however, it has been brought to our attention by public fame—or more accurately, infamy—that numerous Christians are blaming the plague with which God, provoked by their sins, has afflicted the Christian people, on poisonings carried out by the Jews at the instigation of the devil, and that out of their own hot-headedness they have impiously slain many Jews, making no exception for age or sex; and that the Jews have been falsely accused of such outrageous behaviour. . . . [I]t cannot be true that the Jews, by such a heinous crime, are the cause or occasion of the plague, because throughout many parts of the world the same plague, by the hidden judgment of God, has afflicted and afflicts the Jews themselves and many other races who have never lived alongside them.

We order you by apostolic writing that each of you upon whom this charge has been laid, should straitly command those subject to you, both clerical and lay . . . not to dare (on their own authority or out of hot-headedness) to capture, strike, wound or kill any Jews or expel them from their service on these grounds; and you should demand obedience under pain of excommunication.

DISCUSSION QUESTIONS

1. Examine the different documents and try to determine their historical accuracy based on internal evidence alone. What gives you clues about an author's objectivity (or lack thereof)?

2. What are the explanations offered for the onset of plague? What (if any) is the understanding of the disease process?

3. Look at both the account by Mussis and the bull of Pope Clement VI. What do they have in common? How did different groups of people react to the plague?

3. Why would some Christian authorities (the city councillors or the pope mentioned in these documents) attempt to protect the Jews? Why was such protection of no avail in many places? Why did some Jews confess? Discuss the attempt of societies (in some cases) to find scapegoats.

2

Thomas Walsingham
Peasant Rebels in London
1381

Thomas Walsingham (d. 1422) was the Benedictine author of six chronicles, including a portion of the famous "St. Alban's Chronicle." Although little is known of his life, his description of the Peasants' Revolt is a riveting and, by the standards of the time, reliable account of events early in the reign of Richard II. The revolt, one of the largest of its kind, was a response to noble demands on a population experiencing declining incomes as a result of the Black Death, the costs of war with France, and the realm's poor administration. The immediate cause was the poll tax imposed on adult males in 1380, which sparked a rebellion (led by Wat Tyler and John Ball, a preacher) of townsmen and peasants in southeastern England. The larger causes can be found in the final breakdown of serfdom—a breakdown vigorously opposed by a nobility in decline and supported by a peasantry with new opportunities that the scarcity of labor brought about.

On the next day [Corpus Christi] the rebels went in and out of London and talked with the simple commons of the city about the acquiring of liberty and the seizure of the traitors, especially the duke of Lancaster whom they hated most of all; and in a short time easily persuaded all the poorer citizens to support them in their conspiracy. And when, later that day, the sun had climbed higher and grown warm and the rebels had tasted various wines and expensive drinks at will and so had become less drunk than mad (for the great men and common people of London had left all their cellars open to the rebels), they began to debate at length about the traitors with the more simple men of the city. Among other things they assembled and set out for the Savoy, the residence of the duke of Lancaster, unrivalled in splendour and nobility within England, which they then set to the flames. . . . This news so delighted the common people of London that, thinking it particularly shameful for others to harm and injure the duke before themselves, they immediately ran there like madmen, set fire to the place on all sides and so destroyed it. In order that the whole community of the realm should know that they were not motivated by avarice, they made a proclamation that no one should retain for his own use any object found there under penalty of execution. Instead they broke the gold and silver vessels, of which there were many at the Savoy, into pieces with their axes and threw them into the Thames or the sewers. They tore the golden cloths and silk hangings to pieces and crushed them underfoot; they ground up rings and other jewels inlaid with precious stones in small mortars, so that they could never be used again. . . .

After these malicious deeds, the rebels destroyed the place called the "Temple Bar" (in which the more noble apprentices of the law lived) because of their anger . . . and there many muniments which the lawyers were keeping in custody were consumed by fire. Even more insanely they set fire to the noble house of the Hospital of St. John at Clerkenwell so that it burnt continuously for the next seven days. . . .

For who would ever have believed that such rustics, and most inferior ones at that, would dare (not in crowds but individually) to enter the chamber of the king and of his mother with their filthy sticks; and undeterred by any of the soldiers, to stroke and lay their uncouth and sordid hands on the beards of several most noble knights. Moreover, they conversed familiarly with the soldiers asking them to be faithful to the ribalds and friendly in the future. . . . [They] gained access singly and in groups to the rooms in the Tower, they arrogantly lay and sat on the king's bed while joking; and several asked the king's mother to kiss them. . . . The rebels, who had formerly belonged to the most lowly condition of serf, went in and out like lords; and swineherds set themselves above soldiers. . . .

When the archbishop finally heard the rebels coming, he said to his men with great fortitude: "Let us go with confidence, for it is better to die when it can no longer help to live. At no previous time of my life could I have died in such security of conscience." A little later the executioners entered crying, "Where is

From Thomas Walsingham, *Historia Anglicana I,* in R. B. Dobson, *The Peasants' Revolt of 1381,* 2d ed. (London: Macmillan, 1983), 169–76, 178–81.

that traitor to the kingdom? Where the despoiler of the common people?" . . .
[They] dragged the archbishop along the passages by his arms and hood to their
fellows once outside the gates on Tower Hill. . . . Words could not be heard among
their horrible shrieks but rather their throats sounded with the bleating of sheep,
or, to be more accurate, with the devilish voices of peacocks. . . .

Scarcely could the archbishop finish [his] speech before the rebels broke out
with the horrible shout that they feared neither an interdict nor the Pope; all that
remained for him, as a man false to the community and treasonable to the realm
was to submit his neck to the executioners' swords. The archbishop now realised
that his death was imminent and inevitable. . . . He was first struck severely but
not fatally in the neck. He put his hand to the wound and said: "Ah! Ah! this is
the hand of God." As he did not move his hand from the place of sorrow the second blow cut off the top of his fingers as well as severing part of the arteries. But
the archbishop still did not die, and only on the eighth blow, wretchedly wounded
in the neck and on the head, did he complete what we believe is worthy to be
called his martyrdom. . . .

Nor did they show any reverence to any holy places but killed those whom
they hated even if they were within churches and in sanctuary. I have heard from
a trustworthy witness that thirty Flemings were violently dragged out of the
church of the Austin Friars in London and executed in the open street. . . .

On the next day, Saturday 15 June (the feasts of Saints Vitus and Modestus),
behold, the men of Kent showed themselves no less persistent in their wicked actions than on the previous day: they continued to kill men and to burn and destroy houses. The king sent messengers to the Kentishmen telling them that their
fellows had left to live in peace henceforward and promising that he would give
them too a similar form of peace if they would accept it. The rebels' greatest
leader was called "Walter Helier" or "Tylere" (for such names had been given to
him because of his trade), a cunning man endowed with much sense if he had
decided to apply his intelligence to good purposes. . . .

On this the king, although a boy and of tender age, took courage and ordered the mayor of London to arrest Tyler. The mayor, a man of incomparable
spirit and bravery, arrested Tyler without question and struck him a blow on the
head which hurt him badly. Tyler was soon surrounded by the other servants of
the king and pierced by sword thrusts in several parts of his body. His death,
as he fell from his horse to the ground, was the first incident to restore to the
English knighthood their almost extinct hope that they could resist the
commons. . . .

But the king, with marvellous presence of mind and courage for so young a
man, spurred his horse towards the commons and rode around them, saying,
"What is this, my men? What are you doing? Surely you do not wish to fire on
your own king? Do not attack me and do not regret the death of that traitor and
ruffian. For I will be your king, your captain and your leader. Follow me into the
field where you can have all the things you would like to ask for." . . .

The commons were allowed to spend the night under the open sky. However
the king ordered that the written and sealed charter which they had requested

should be handed to them in order to avoid more trouble at that time. He knew that Essex was not yet pacified nor Kent settled; and the commons and rustics of both counties were ready to rebel if he failed to satisfy them quickly. . . .

Once they had this charter, the commons returned to their homes. But still the earlier evils by no means ceased.

DISCUSSION QUESTIONS

1. How does the author's class and position affect his recording of events? Compare how he describes the different classes of society.
2. What does this document tell you about economic and political conditions in late-fourteenth-century England? What were the rebels seeking? Against what were they protesting?
3. How did the rebels choose their targets, both human and material?
4. What was their attitude toward religious authority? Can you think of reasons to explain their actions in this regard?

3

Christine de Pizan
Lament on the Evils of the Civil War
1410

Christine de Pizan (fl. 1400–1430) is considered by some to be the first feminist. Born in Italy, she was raised in Paris after her father, a scholar and physician who gave her a superb education, was called to the court of Charles V. After his death, and then that of her husband in 1389, Christine turned to writing to support her children. In the process, she became the first professional female writer in Europe. Patronized by kings, queens, and dukes, Christine is most famous for The Book of the City of Ladies, *a defense of women that attacked the misogyny of Jean de Meung, continuator of the* Roman de la Rose. *Christine wrote numerous works of prose and poetry, including a* Ditié *about Joan of Arc. The epistle quoted here was written in 1410, when France was at a low point in the Hundred Years' War. In the work that follows, Christine urges the leaders of society to look at what their disunity has done to France and its people and urges them to come together instead of fighting one another. "A plague on all your houses" might be an apt description of French and Burgundian royalty and nobility in the Hundred Years' War.*

Alone, and suppressing with great difficulty the tears which blur my sight and pour down my face like a fountain, so much that I am surprised to have the time to write this weary lament, whose writing the pity for the coming disaster makes me erase with bitter tears, and I say in pain: Oh, how can it be that the human

---

From Christine de Pizan, *The Epistle of the Prison of Human Life with an Epistle to the Queen of France and Lament on the Evils of the Civil War,* ed. and trans. Josette A. Wisman (New York and London: Garland Publishing, 1984), 85, 87, 89, 91, 93, 95.

heart, as strange as Fortune is, can make man revert to the nature of a voracious and cruel beast? Where is the reason that gives him the name of a rational animal? How can Fortune have the power to transform a man so much, that he is changed into a serpent, the enemy of mankind? Oh, alas, here is the reason why, noble French princes. With deference to you, where is now the sweet natural blood among you which has been for a long time the true summit of kindness in the world? . . .

For God's sake! For God's sake! High Princes, let these facts open your eyes and may you see as already accomplished what the preparations for taking arms will do in their end; thus you will see ruined cities, towns and castles destroyed, and fortresses razed to the ground. And where? In the very heart of France! The noble knights and youth of France, all of one nature, one single soul and body, which used to defend the crown and the public good, are now gathered in a shameful battle one against another, father against son, brother against brother, relatives against one another, with deadly swords, covering the pitiful fields with blood, dead bodies, and limbs. Oh, dishonorable victory may be to the one who has it! What glory will Fame give to it? . . .

Oh you, knight who comes from such a battle, tell me, I pray you, what honor did you win there? . . . And what will follow, in God's name? Famine, because of the wasting and ruining of things that will ensue, and the lack of cultivation, from which will spring revolts by the people who have been too often robbed, deprived and oppressed, their food taken away and stolen here and there by soldiers, subversion in the towns because of outrageous taxes. . . . So cry, cry, beat your hands and cry—as once the sad Argia did in such a case, along with the ladies of Argos—you ladies, damsels, and women of the kingdom of France! Because the swords that will make you widows and deprive you of your children and kin have already been sharpened! . . .

Oh, crowned Queen of France, are you still sleeping? Who prevents you from restraining now this side of your kin and putting an end to this deadly enterprise? Do you not see the heritage of your noble children at stake? . . .

Come, all you wise men of this realm, come with your queen! What use are you if not for the royal council? Everyone should offer his hand. You used to concern yourselves even with small matters. How shall France be proud of so many wise men, if now they cannot see to her safety, and the fount of the clergy keep her from perishing? Where then are your plans and wise thoughts? . . . For you resemble Nineveh, which God condemned to perish, and which received his wrath because of the great sins which were many there, and because of this, the situation is very doubtful, unless the sentence is not revoked by the intercession of devout prayers.

People, be firm! And you, pious woman, cry mercy for this grievous storm! Ah, France, France, once a glorious kingdom! . . .

Oh, Duke of Berry, Noble Prince, excellent father and scion of royal children, son of a King of France, brother and uncle, father of all the antiquity of the lily! How is it possible that your tender heart can bear to see you, on a given day, assembled in deadly battle array to bear painful arms against your nephews? . . .

So, come, come, Noble Duke of Berry, Prince of High Excellence, and follow the divine law which orders peace! Take a strong hold of the bridle, and stop this dishonorable army, at least until you have talked to the parties. So come to Paris, to your father's city where you were born and which cries to you with tears and sighs, asking and begging for you to come. Come quickly to comfort this suffering city. . . . [A]lthough it is now discussed in various tongues on each side that hopes for victory in the battle and they all say: "We will win and work for it"— they are bragging foolishly. For it must not be ignored that the outcome of all battles is strange and unknown. For although man proposed it, Fortune disposes it. . . . Was the victory of the King of Athens, mortally wounded in battle, of any worth to him? Is a multitude of men an advantage in such a case? Was Xerxes not defeated, although he had so many men that all vales and hills were covered with them? Are a good reason and a just quarrel of any value? If it were so, the king Saint Louis, who obtained so many beautiful victories, would not have been defeated at Tunis by the infidels. . . . And above all, although war and battles are in all cases very dangerous and difficult to avoid, no doubt that among such close kin, tied by nature in one bond of love, they are perverse. . . . I believe the cost would be less, and that this army, by a common will and true unity, should be directed against those who are our natural enemies, and that the good and faithful French should take care of these people, and not kill one another. . . . Ah, Very Reverend Prince, Noble Duke of Berry, do hear this. . . . May the Blessed Holy Spirit, Author of all peace, give you the heart and the courage to achieve such a thing! Amen. And may he greet me, a poor voice crying in this kingdom, wanting peace and welfare for all, your servant Christine, moved by a very fair mind, the gift to see that day!

DISCUSSION QUESTIONS

1. What, in Christine's view, are the costs of war, in human and dynastic terms?
2. How important is it that Christine refers in several instances to "the French" and "France"? To whom does Christine direct her admonitions? Why?
3. What kind of allusions does she use to convince her readers that they should not continue a civil war that is keeping them from fighting the "common enemy"? What does this tell you about her education?
4. Do you think this "poor voice crying in the kingdom" can be seen as a precursor to Joan of Arc? Why or why not?

4

Catherine of Siena
Letters to the Papacy
1376–1417

Because of political chaos in Italy, the papacy moved to Avignon, an enclave inside France, where it remained from 1305 to 1377. Intended as temporary, this relocation increasingly appeared to be permanent. Bureaucracy grew and taxes increased, inducing Petrarch to refer to the Avignon papacy as the Babylonian Captivity.

Catherine of Siena (1347–1380), a Dominican tertiary, was a mover and shaker in the political world of men, addressing herself to religious and political leaders in an effort to restore the papacy to Rome. Seeing the disorder and upheaval all around her, and expecting the universal church to provide leadership, Catherine eventually succeeded at least in her efforts to return the papacy to Rome. But this would not solve the problems facing the church and society. The four decades that followed, known as the Great Schism, saw two and eventually three popes claiming power—a situation that was finally resolved by decisions taken at the Councils of Pisa and Constance, but which posed new problems for the future.

Letter 54: To Pope Gregory XI, January 1376

Those who are in authority, I say, do evil when holy justice dies in them because of their selfish self-centeredness and their fear of incurring the displeasure of others. They see those under them sinning but it seems they pretend not to see and do not correct them. And if they do correct, they do it so feebly and half-heartedly that it is worthless, only a plaster over the vice. They are forever afraid of offending and making enemies — and all this because of self-love. . . .

A shepherd such as this is really a hireling! Not only does he fail to rescue his little sheep from the clutches of the wolf; he devours them himself! And all because he loves himself apart from God. . . . I hope you will not love yourself selfishly, nor your neighbors selfishly, but will love God. . . . I want you to be the sort of true and good shepherd. . . .

If till now you haven't been very firm in truth, I want you, I beg you, for the little time that is left, to be so—courageously and like a brave man—following Christ, whose vicar you are. And don't be afraid, father, no matter what may happen, of these blustery winds that have descended upon you—I mean those rotten members who have rebelled against you. Don't be afraid, for divine help is near. . . . *Do something about it.* . . . Delay no longer, for your delaying has already been the cause of a lot of trouble. . . .

Up, father! No more irresponsibility! . . .

Forgive me, father, for talking to you like this. Out of the fullness of the heart the mouth speaks, you know. I am sure that if you are the kind of tree I want you to be, nothing will stand in your way.

Letter 63: To Pope Gregory XI, March 1376

If you do as I've told you, you will emerge from war into the greatest peace, from persecution to complete unity. . . . [D]o the other two essential things: I mean your return [to Rome] and the raising of the standard of the most holy cross.

From *The Letters of St. Catherine of Siena*, vol. 1, trans. Suzanne Noffke (Binghamton, NY: Medieval and Renaissance Texts and Studies, 1988), 167, 169, 202, 217–18, 222–23; and *Medieval Europe: A Short Sourcebook*, ed. C. Warren Hollister, Joe. W. Leedom, Marc A. Meyer, and David S. Spear (New York: McGraw-Hill, 1992), 243–45.

Don't let your holy desire falter on account of any dissent or rebellion you might see or hear about on the part of the cities. . . .

Ah, my dear father! I am begging you, I am *telling* you: come, and conquer our enemies.

Letter 69: To Pope Gregory XI, March–April 1376

I Caterina, your unworthy daughter, servant and slave of the servants of Jesus Christ, am writing to you in his precious blood. I long to see you a courageous man, free of slavish fear. . . .

Up, then, father; don't sit still any longer! Fire yourself with tremendous desire, expecting divine help and providence. For it seems to me that divine Goodness is about to turn the great wolves into lambs. This is why I am coming there soon, to lay them in your lap, humbled.

Letter 71: To Pope Gregory XI, June or July 1376

See to it, as you value your life, that you are not guilty of irresponsibility. Don't make light of the works of the Holy Spirit that are being asked of you. You can do them if you *want* to. You *can* see that justice is done; you *can* have peace, if you will put aside the world's perverse pretensions and pleasures. . . .

If I were in your place I would be afraid of incurring divine judgment.

Letter 88: To Pope Gregory XI, en route to Rome, December 1376–January 1377

Your poor unworthy daughter Caterina sends you her greetings in his precious blood. I long to see your heart firm, stable, and strengthened in true holy patience, for I believe that a heart weak and inconstant and unwilling to suffer will never succeed in doing the great deeds of God. . . .

Oh, most holy father, my dearest *babbo,* open your mind's eye and understand! If virtue is so necessary for every one of us, if each one of us individually needs it for the salvation of our own soul, how much more do you need this constancy of strength and patience. . . .

And because your burden is greater you need a bold, courageous heart, fearful of nothing that might happen. For you know well, most holy father, that when you accepted holy Church as your bride you agreed also to work hard for her. You expected all these contrary winds of pain and difficulty to confront you in battle, over her. So confront these dangerous winds like a brave man, with strength and patience and enduring perseverance. Never turn back because of pain or discouragement or slavish fear, but persevere, and rejoice in the storms and struggles. . . .

I beg you, for love of Christ crucified, go as soon as you can to your own place, the place of the glorious apostles Peter and Paul. . . . Forgive my presumptiousness.

The Council of Pisa, 1409

The holy and general council, representing the universal church, decrees and declares that the united college of cardinals was empowered to call the council, and that the power to call such a council belongs of right to the aforesaid holy college of cardinals, especially now when there is a detestable schism. The council further declared that this holy council, representing the universal church, caused both claimants of the papal throne to be cited in the gates and doors of the churches of Pisa to come and hear the final decision.

The Council of Constance, Haec Sancta, 1415

This holy synod of Constance . . . declared that this synod, legally assembled, is a general council, and represents the catholic church militant and has its authority directly from Christ; and everybody, of whatever rank or dignity, including also the pope, is bound to obey this council in those things which pertain to the faith, to the ending of this schism, and to a general reformation of the church in its head and members. Likewise, it declares that if anyone, of whatever rank, condition, or dignity, including also the pope, shall refuse to obey the commands, statutes, ordinances, or orders of this holy council, or of any other holy council properly assembled, in regard to the ending of the schism and to the reformation of the church, he shall be subject to the proper punishment.

The Council of Constance, Frequens, 1417

A good way to till the field of the Lord is to hold general councils frequently, because by them briers, thorns, and thistles of heresies, errors, and schisms are rooted out, abuses reformed, and the way of the Lord made more fruitful. But if general councils are not held, all these evils spread and flourish. We therefore decree by this perpetual edict that general councils shall be held five years after the close of this council, the second one seven years after the close of the first, and forever thereafter one shall be held every ten years.

DISCUSSION QUESTIONS

1. In Catherine's letters to Pope Gregory, she often refers to herself as unworthy, poor, and a humble servant, yet she refers to Gregory as *babbo*, "daddy," and is highly critical of him. What is the nature of their relationship?

2. What are Gregory's fears? Are they well founded?

3. How was the church damaged by the Babylonian Captivity and Great Schism? How might individuals at all levels of society have responded?

4. What are the claims of the conciliarists at Pisa and Constance? How would their plans change the way the church and papacy had operated since its height during the pontificate of Innocent III? While the conciliarist's efforts succeeded in some respects, why do you think their general aims failed?

COMPARATIVE QUESTIONS

1. Compare Christine de Pizan and Catherine of Siena. While the works quoted here do not deal with the status of women in society, what impression do you get from these two women, however atypical they were and different from each other? Joan of Arc lived at the end of this time period and was praised by Christine in print. Does it surprise you that at least some women could play important public roles?

2. What connections would you draw between the plague, the persecutions of Jews, and the peasant rebellions that swept over Europe in the decades after 1347?

3. How might the events of the fourteenth century have actually improved the position of the common man or woman?

4. How was the church changed by the Avignon papacy and Great Schism, and what connections might this have had with social and economic developments? What effects do you suppose this would have on state building?

14

Renaissance Europe
1400–1500

S U M M A R Y   By 1400, in the aftermath of disasters that affected most of Europe, the city-states of the northern Italian peninsula continued to experience political chaos. Ironically, in the view of some historians, this may have led to the great creativity of the period that historians (despite debate) often refer to as the Renaissance, the height of which occurred in the quattrocento (1400s). Primarily men of the upper classes defined themselves self-consciously as living in new times. For such men and a few women, this was a time of rebirth (in Italian, *Rinascimento;* in French, *Renaissance*), distinct from what they viewed as the barbarism of a millennium and closer to the values and styles of antiquity. It was defined by the *studia humanitatis* (roughly, the liberal arts), from which the nineteenth-century term *humanism* was derived. Governments changed often (sometimes violently), and young men played an unusually prominent role in civic life. At the same time, Italy had the largest urban concentration and wealth in Europe, which was used increasingly for patronage and art. The first two documents in this chapter illustrate the application and possibilities of humanism, while the final excerpts demonstrate that the realities of Italian life often did not match the ideals, even among the upper classes.

1

Leonardo Bruni and Giovanni Rucellai
Florence in the Quattrocento
1427 and 1457

The Petrarchan ideal of humanism, which had refocused attention on the classics with special attention to language and letters, was given new expression in the quattrocento. While Petrarch eventually found many of his answers through introspection, civic humanists felt the true life could only be lived within the hustle and bustle of Italian city politics. A civic humanist was one who applied humanism's academic principles to the active, political life. The first document is a funeral oration given for a leading citizen by Leonardo Bruni (1369–1444), a noted scholar of the Greek language who served as Florence's chancellor and official historian. The oration was given in the midst of the wars with Milan. The second document is by Giovanni Rucellai (1403–1481), a merchant connected through marriage and patronage to two of the greatest families of Florence, the Strozzis and Medicis, who made their fortunes in business and banking, respectively. Both Bruni and Rucellai paint portraits of Florence and the ideal Renaissance man.

Bruni's Funeral Oration for Nanni Strozzi, 1427

This is so exceptional a funeral oration because it is appropriate neither to weep or lament. . . . His first claim to fame is conferred on him because of his country's merit. For the homeland is the first and chief basis of human happiness and more worthy of our veneration than even our own parents. If we begin therefore by praising the motherland, we will be starting in the right order.

He was born in the most spacious and greatest of cities, wide-ruling and endowed with the mightiest power, without question the foremost of all the Etruscan cities. Indeed, it is second to none of the cities of Italy either in origin, wealth, or size. . . . The Tuscans had been the chief people of Italy and supreme both in authority and wealth. Before the foundation of the Roman empire their power was so great that they had the seas on both sides of Italy under their control and governed the whole length of the country. . . . Finally, this one people diffused the worship of the immortal gods as well as learning and letters throughout Italy. . . .

What city, therefore, can be more excellent, more noble? What descended from more glorious antecedents? . . . [Our fathers] so established and governed it that they were in no way inferior to their own fathers in virtue. Sustained by the most sacred laws, the state was ruled by them with such wisdom that they served as an example of good moral behavior for other peoples and had no need to take others as their model. . . .

Worthy of praise as well are those who are its present-day citizens. They have augmented the power received from their predecessors even more by adding Pisa and a number of other great cities to their empire through their virtue and valor in arms. . . .

Our form of governing the state aims at achieving liberty and equality for each and every citizen. Because it is equal in all respects it is called a popular gov-

From Major Problems in the History of the Italian Renaissance, ed. Benjamin G. Kohl and Alison Andrews Smith (Lexington, Mass., and Toronto: D.C. Heath, 1995), 279–82; and *Images of Quattrocento Florence: Selected Writings in Literature, History, and Art,* ed. Stefano Ugo Baldassarri and Arielle Saiber (New Haven, Conn., and London: Yale University Press, 2000), 73–75.

ernment. We tremble before no lord nor are we dominated by the power of a few. All enjoy the same liberty, governed only by law and free from fear of individuals. Everyone has the same hope of attaining honors and of improving his condition provided he is industrious, has talent and a good sober way of life. For our city requires virtue and honesty in its citizens. . . .

This is true liberty and equality in a city to fear the power of no one nor dread injury from them; to experience equality of law among the citizens and the same opportunity of ruling the state. These advantages cannot be had where one man rules or a few. . . .

This capacity for a free people to attain honors and this ability to pursue one's goals serve in a marvelous way to excite men's talents. For with the hope of honors extended, men raise themselves and surge upward; excluded they become lifeless. . . . Our citizens excel so greatly in talents and intelligence that few equal them and none surpass them. They have vivacity and industry and alacrity and agility in acting with a greatness of spirit equal to all challenges.

We thrive not only in governing the republic, in domestic arts, and in engaging in business everywhere, but we are also distinguished for military glory. . . .

What now shall I say about literature and scholarship in which all concede that Florence is the chief and most splendid leader? . . . But I am speaking about those more civilized and lofty studies which are considered more excellent and worthy of everlasting immortal glory. For who is able to name a poet in our generation or in the last one who is not Florentine? Who but our citizens recalled this skill at eloquence, already lost, to light, to practical use, and to life? Who but they understood Latin literature, already abject, prostrate and almost dead, and raised it up, restored and reclaimed it from destruction? . . . For the same reason, should not our city be proclaimed the parent of the Latin language . . . ? Now the knowledge of Greek literature, which had decayed in Italy for more than seven hundred years, has been revived and restored by our city. . . . Finally, these humanities most excellent and of highest value, especially relevant for human beings, necessary both for private and public life, adorned with a knowledge of letters worthy of free men, have originated in our city and are now thriving throughout Italy. The city enjoys such resources and wealth that I fear to arouse jealousy by referring to its inexhaustible supply of money. This is demonstrated by the long Milanese war waged at an almost incredible cost. . . . Now at the end of the war men are more prompt in paying their taxes than they were at the beginning of the war.

Rucellai's "A Merchant's Praise of Florence"

Most people believe that our age, from 1400 onward, is the most fortunate period in Florence's history. I shall now explain why this is so. It is commonly believed that since 1400 the Italians have been superior to all other nations in the art of war, whereas before 1400 the northern Europeans were thought to be peerless. Thanks to their intelligence, astuteness, cunning, and strategic ability, the Italians are now the best at seizing cities and winning battles. In this age, moreover, there are more outstanding scholars of Greek, Latin, and Hebrew in Florence than ever before. . . . Our men of letters have revived the elegance of the ancient style that has long been lost and forgotten. Those who have participated in the government of the city since 1400 have surpassed all their predecessors. Likewise, the dominion of Florence has considerably expanded. . . .

There have not been such accomplished masters in joinery and woodcarving since the days of antiquity: they are able to produce such skillfully designed works in perspective that a painter could not do any better. The same can be said of our masters in painting and drawing, whose ability, sense of proportion, and precision are so great that Giotto and Cimabue would not even be accepted as their pupils. Similarly, we cannot forget to mention our excellent tapestry makers and goldsmiths.

Never before have men and women dressed in such expensive and elegant clothing. Women wear brocade and embroidered gowns covered with jewels and saunter through the streets in their French-style hats that cost at least two hundred florins apiece. Neither the city nor the countryside has ever had such an abundance of household goods. . . .

This age has also had four notable citizens who deserve to be remembered. The first one is Palla di Nofri Strozzi, who possessed all seven of the things necessary for a man's happiness: a worthy homeland, noble and distinguished ancestors, a good knowledge of Greek and Latin, refinement, physical beauty, a good household, and honestly earned wealth. . . . Then we have Cosimo de' Medici, probably not only the richest Florentine, but the richest Italian of all time. . . . The third citizen I shall mention is Messer Leonardo di Francesco Bruni. Although he was born in Arezzo, he was an honorary citizen of Florence. He had a unique knowledge of and expertise in Greek, Hebrew, and Latin and was more famous than any rhetorician after Cicero. . . . Finally, Filippo, son of Ser Brunellesco, was a master architect and sculptor. He was an accomplished geometer and . . . is the one who rediscovered ancient Roman building techniques.

The earnings of the Florentine commune are now greater than ever. In this period, both in our city and in its countryside, people have witnessed tremendous wars and political upheaval, the like of which were never seen in the past. Churches and hospitals are richer than ever, better supplied with gold and silks paraments and precious silver. There are numerous friars and priests caring for these places, which the faithful visit constantly. Men and women attend Mass and other religious ceremonies with greater devotion than ever. . . .

The citizens have never had so much wealth, merchandise, and property, nor have the Monte's[1] interests ever been so conspicuous; consequently, the sums spent on weddings, tournaments, and various forms of entertainment are greater than ever before. Between 1418 and 1423 Florence's wealth was probably at its height. At the time, in the Mercato Nuovo and the streets nearby, there were seventy-two exchange banks.

---

[1]**Monte della Doti** (dowry fund) was a credit fund established by Florence 1425 to help well-to-do families finance in advance their daughters' marriages. [—Ed.]

DISCUSSION QUESTIONS

1. Bruni's funeral oration for Nanni Strozzi seems to have little to do with the man. What is its true subject? What are its possible purposes?

2. What do both Bruni and Rucellai see as the desirable attributes of a citizen? Why is the city of Florence exemplary? Do you agree that there is liberty for all?

3. What role does wealth play in both literary/artistic and civic humanism?

4. Do you find a resemblance between these documents and those on ancient Athens (Chapter 3)? If so, how do you account for this?

2

Giovanni Pico della Mirandola
Oration on the Dignity of Man
1496

The work of Giovanni Pico della Mirandola (1463–1494), a Neoplatonic thinker and Dominican friar, epitomizes in many ways the philosophical beliefs of human-ism. The Oration on the Dignity of Man, *part of a series of nine hundred theses written when Pico was twenty-three, is in many ways a manifesto of the Renais-sance. Steeped in both the Aristotelian and Platonic traditions, Pico knew Latin, Greek, Hebrew, and Italian. He was also deeply interested in Hebrew mysticism, pre-Socratic thought, and occult knowledge attributed at the time to Hermes Tris-megistus. The discovery of truth from many different sources is known as syncretism. Not surprisingly, some of Pico's ideas were deemed heretical by Pope Innocent VIII. Although Pico was arrested, he lived under the protection of Lorenzo de' Medici un-til he died at the age of thirty-one. The* Oration, *published in 1496, revolves around the concept of free will—the human ability to choose, for good or ill.*

I have read in the ancient annals of the Arabians, most reverend Fathers, that when asked what on the world's stage could be considered most admirable, Ab-dala the Saracen answered that there is nothing more admirable to be seen than man. In agreement with this opinion is the saying of Hermes Trismegistus: "What a great miracle, O Asclepius, is man!"

When I had thought over the meaning of these maxims, the many reasons for the excellence of man advanced by many men failed to satisfy me. . . .

At last, it seems to me that I have understood why man is the most fortunate living thing worthy of all admiration and precisely what rank is his lot in the universal chain of being, a rank to be envied not only by the brutes but even by the stars and by minds beyond this world. It is a matter past faith and extraordi-nary! . . .

From *The Italian Renaissance Reader*, ed. Julia Conaway Bondanella and Mark Musa (New York: Meridian, 1987), 180–83.

God the Father, the supreme Architect, had already built this cosmic home which we behold, this most majestic temple of divinity, in accordance with the laws of a mysterious wisdom. He had adorned the region above the heavens with intelligences, had quickened the celestial spheres with eternal souls and had filled the vile and filthy parts of the lower world with a multitude of animals of every kind. But when the work was completed, the Maker kept wishing that there were someone who could examine the plan of so great an enterprise, who could love its beauty, who could admire its vastness. On that account, when everything was completed, as Moses and Timaeus both testify, He finally took thought of creating man. However, not a single archetype remained from which he might fashion this new creature, not a single treasure remained which he might bestow upon this new son, and not a single seat remained in the whole world in which the contemplator of the universe might sit. All now was complete; all things had been assigned to the highest, the middle, and the lowest orders. But it was not in the nature of the Father's power to fail in this final creative effort, as though exhausted; nor was it in the nature of His wisdom to waver in such a crucial matter through lack of counsel; and it was not in the nature of His Beneficent Love that he who was destined to praise God's divine generosity in regard to others should be forced to condemn it in regard to himself. At last, the Supreme Artisan ordained that the creature to whom He could give nothing properly his own should share in whatever He had assigned individually to the other creatures. He therefore accepted man as a work of indeterminate nature, and placing him in the center of the world, addressed him thus:

"O Adam, we have given you neither a place nor a form nor any ability exclusively your own, so that according to your wishes and your judgment, you may have and possess whatever place, form, or abilities you desire. The nature of all other beings is limited and constrained in accordance with the laws prescribed by us. Constrained by no limits, in accordance with your own free will, in whose hands we have placed you, you shall independently determine the bounds of your own nature. We have placed you at the world's center, from where you may more easily observe whatever is in the world. We have made you neither celestial nor terrestrial, neither mortal nor immortal, so that with honor and freedom of choice, as though the maker and molder of yourself, you may fashion yourself in whatever form you prefer. You shall have the power to degenerate into the inferior forms of life which are brutish; you shall have the power, through your soul's judgment, to rise to the superior orders which are divine." . . .

In man alone, at the moment of his creation, the Father placed the seeds of all kinds and the germs of every way of life. Whatever seeds each man cultivates will mature and bear their own fruit in him; if vegetative, he will be like a plant; if sensitive, he will become a brute; if rational, he will become a celestial being; if intellectual, he will be an angel and the son of God. . . .

Who would not admire this our chameleon? Or who could admire any other being more greatly than man? Asclepius the Athenian justly says that man was symbolized in the mysteries by the figure of Proteus because of his ability to change his character and transform his nature. This is the origin of those metamorphoses or transformations celebrated among the Hebrews and the Pythagoreans. For the occult theology of the Hebrews sometimes transforms the holy Enoch into an angel of divinity and sometimes transforms other people into other divinities. The Pythagoreans transform impious men into beasts and, if Empedocles is to be believed, even into plants. Echoing this, Mohammed often had this saying on his lips: "He who deviates from divine law becomes a beast," and he was right in saying so. For it is not the bark that makes the beast of burden but its irrational and sensitive soul; neither is it the spherical form which makes the heavens, but their undeviating order; nor is it the freedom from a body which makes the angel but its spiritual intelligence. . . .

Are there any who will not admire man? In the sacred Mosaic and Christian writings, man, not without reason, is sometimes described by the name of "all flesh" and sometimes by that of "every creature," since man molds, fashions, and transforms himself according to the form of all flesh and the character of every creature. For this reason, the Persian Evantes, in describing Chaldean theology, writes that man does not have an inborn and fixed image of himself but many which are external and foreign to him; whence comes the Chaldean saying: "Man is a being of varied, manifold, and inconstant nature."

But why do we reiterate all these things? To the end that from the moment we are born we are born into the condition of being able to become whatever we choose.

DISCUSSION QUESTIONS

1. Examine the words Pico uses to describe God and how God went about the process of creation. Why might these ideas have been considered dangerous?

2. What, according to Pico, are man's abilities? Why were these abilities and possibilities given to him?

3. What kinds of sources does Pico use to support his ideas? What is their importance as part of his philosophy?

4. What makes this document a "statement" of Renaissance thought?

3

Alessandra

Letters from a Widow and Matriarch of a Great Family
1450–1465

Although there were differences by region, women in medieval and Renaissance Europe were usually under legal guardianship—typically that of a father or husband. Although women of the lower classes may have had more freedom in terms of work and marriage early in their lives, their upper-class counterparts gained their greatest prestige and power through widowhood. Alessandra (1407–1471) married Matteo Strozzi, a wealthy merchant whose business had branches throughout Europe. But when Matteo died of the effects of the plague while exiled for being in opposition to

*Cosimo de' Medici (1389–1464), Alessandra's financial situation became more diffi-
cult, as she had sons and daughters to marry and a great household to maintain.
She engaged in lengthy correspondence with her sons about political, marital, and
economic conditions that affected the family. In these excerpts of letters to her son
Filippo, we can glimpse the "other" side of the Renaissance—exile; political danger
if one did not agree with the ruling faction; marriages that were contracted solely for
reasons of politics, honor, and clientage; and slavery.*

To Filippo, 1450

Really, as long as there are young girls in the house, you do nothing but work for
them, so when she leaves I will have no one to attend to but you three. And when
I get the house in a little better shape I would love it if you would think about
coming home. You would have no cause to be ashamed with what there is now,
and you could do honor to any friend who dropped in to see you at home. But
two or three years from now it will all be much better. And I would love to get
you a wife; you're of an age now to know how to manage the help and to give me
some comfort and consolation. I have none. . . .

You know that some time ago I bought Cateruccia, our slave, and for several
years now, though I haven't laid a hand on her, she has behaved so badly toward
me and the children that you wouldn't believe it if you hadn't seen it. Our Lorenzo
could tell you all about it. . . . I've always suffered it because I can't chastise her,
and besides I thought you would come once a month so that we could come to a
decision together or she could be brought to better obedience. For several months
now she has been saying and is still saying that she doesn't want to stay here, and
she is so moody that no one can do a thing with her it. If it weren't for love of
Lesandra, I would have told you to sell her, but because of her malicious tongue,
I want to see Lesandra safely out of the house first. But I don't know if I can hold
out that long: mark my words, I'm going to get her out of my sight because I
don't want this constant battle. She pays no more attention to me than if I were
the slave and she were the mistress, and she threatens us all so that Lesandra and
I are both afraid of her.

To Filippo, 1459

It grieves me, my son, that I'm not near you to take some of these troublesome
things off your hands. You should have told me the first day Matteo fell sick so I
could have jumped on a horse and been there in just a few days. But I know that
you didn't do it for fear I would get sick or would be put to trouble. . . . I have
been told that in the honors you arranged for the burial of my son you did honor

From *University of Chicago Readings in Western Civilization, 5: The Renaissance*, ed. Eric
Cochrane and Julius Kirshner (Chicago and London: University of Chicago Press, 1986),
109, 113–17.

to yourself as well as to him. You did all the better to pay him such honor there, since here they don't usually do anything for those who are in your condition [that is, in exile]. Thus I am pleased that you did so. Here these two girls, who are unconsolable over the death of their brother, and I have gone into mourning, and because I had not yet gotten the woolen cloth to make a mantle for myself, I have gotten it now and I will pay for it.

To Filippo, 1465

I told you in my other [letter] what happened about 60 [the daughter of Francesco Tanagli], and there's nothing new there. And you have been advised that there is no talk of 59 [a woman who belonged to the Adimari family] until we have placed the older girl. 13 [Marco Parenti] believes we should do nothing further until we can see our way clearly concerning these two and see what way they will go. Considering their age, this shouldn't take too long. It's true that my wish would be to see both of you with a companion, as I have told you many times before. That way when I die I would think you ready to take the step all mothers want—seeing their sons married—so your children could enjoy what you have acquired with enormous effort and stress over the long years. To that end, I have done my very best to keep up the little I have had, foregoing the things that I might have done for my soul's sake and for that of our ancestors. But for the hope I have that you will take a wife (in the aim of having children), I am happy to have done so. So what I would like would be what I told you. Since then I have heard what Lorenzo's wants are and how he was willing to take her to keep me happy, but that he would be just as glad to wait two years before binding himself to the lady. I have thought a good deal about the matter, and it seems to me that since nothing really advantageous to us is available, and since we have time to wait these two years, it would be a good idea to leave it at that unless something unexpected turns up. Otherwise, it doesn't seem to me something that requires immediate thought, particularly considering the stormy times we live in these days, when so many young men on this earth are happy to inhabit it without taking a wife. The world is in a sorry state, and never has so much expense been loaded on the backs of women as now. No dowry is so big that when the girl goes out she doesn't have the whole of it on her back, between silks and jewels. . . . If 60 works out well, we could sound out the possibility of the other girl for him. There's good forage there if they were to give her, and at any [other] time it would have been a commendable move. As things are going now, it seems to me better to wait and see a while for him. . . . This way something may come of it, and they will not offer a wife without money, as people are doing now, since it seems superfluous to those who are giving 50 to give her a dowry. 13 wrote you that 60's father touched on the matter with him in the way I wrote you about. He says that you should leave it to us to see to it and work it out. For my part, I've done my diligent best, and I can't think what more I could have done—for your consolation than my own. . . .

Niccolò has gone out of office, and although he did some good things, they weren't the ones I would have wanted. Little honor has been paid to him or to the other outgoing magistrates, either when they were in office, or now that they have stepped down. Our scrutineer was quite upset about it, as were we, but I feel that what was done will collapse, and it is thought they will start fresh. This Signoria has spent days in deliberation, and no one can find out anything about them. They have threatened to denounce whoever reveals anything as a rebel, so things are being done in total secrecy. I have heard that 58 [the Medici] is everything and 54 [the Pitti] doesn't stand a chance. For the moment, it looks to me as if they will get back to 56 [the Pucci] in the runoffs, if things continue to go as now. May God, who can do all, set this city right, for it is in a bad way. Niccolò went in proudly and then lost heart—as 14's [Soderini] brother said, "He went in a lion and he will go out a lamb," and that's just what happened to him. When he saw the votes were going against him, he began to humble himself. Now, since he left office, he goes about accompanied by five or six armed men for fear. . . . It would have been better for him if [he had never been elected], for he would never have made so many enemies. . . .

[T]hink about having Niccolò Strozzi touch on the matter with Giovanfrancesco for 45 [Lorenzo], if you think it appropriate. Although I doubt that she would deign [to marry] so low, still, it sometimes happens that you look in places that in other times you wouldn't have dreamed of, by the force of events—deaths or other misfortunes. So think about it.

DISCUSSION QUESTIONS

1. What is Alessandra's role as matriarch of her family? What else can you tell about women during the Renaissance?
2. What is her view of the politics of the city in her day? Why would Alessandra use numbers to designate people?
3. What is Alessandra's relation to her slave? How does the existence of slavery affect your view of Florence's vaunted "liberty for all"?
4. How were marriages formed among the middle and upper classes? What was required before one could marry?

4

Bernardino of Siena
An Italian Preacher: Sins against Nature
1380–1444

At the same time that the great orators, civic humanists, and artists of the Renaissance were attempting to distance themselves from the perceived "barbarity" of earlier times, religion continued to play an enormous role in everyday life. Petrarch (1304–1374) had said he always carried St. Augustine's works with him; Pico was a Dominican; and, later in the quattrocento, Lorenzo de' Medici (1449–1492), called "the Magnificent," begged absolution from the hellfire-and-brimstone preacher Giro-

lamo Savonarola (1452–1498). Even among artists and architects, religious works continued to be the mainstay of their creation, even if secular themes now received more attention. The famous preacher Bernardino of Siena (1380–1444) exemplifies the continuing great importance of religion during this period. One of the most popular preachers of his day, Bernardino was an itinerant Franciscan, canonized only six years after his death. He preached throughout northern Italy and was active in efforts to unify the Roman and Greek churches at the Council of Florence in 1439. His greatest fame, however, came as a preacher of moral reform. Besides discussing the typical subjects one might find in sermons, Bernardino devotes special attention to "problems" he finds in his day, especially sodomy, sorcery, vanity, and the Jews. These excerpts are from several sermons.

Oooo! Have I heard stories. . . . Aooo! Once I was in a certain place where some man had taken as his wife a beautiful young woman. They lived together for six years, and she was still a virgin. That is, she had been with him in all those years in a state of most grave sin against nature. Oh, what disorder, oh, what grievous shame! Ooo, ooo, ooo! Do you know what this poor little thing was reduced to? She was all wasted, pale, pasty, sallow. She begged me for the love of God to help her if I could in any way. She said she had been to the bishop about this matter and even to the mayor; but they answered her that they needed proof of what she was charging. O what ignorance is this to need proof and witnesses for these kinds of things! I'll tell you what is needed: a bonfire, a bonfire. . . .

O ladies, make sure you don't send your sons [where there are sodomites]; send instead your daughters, because there's no danger for them if you send them among such people. They will not be contaminated by anything; and even if they were seized and violated, at least there wouldn't be as much danger and as much sin as there would be [if your sons were violated]. If there is no other way, I would permit it as the lesser evil. . . .

Don't you see that you are showing yourself to be against God, who said to the man and the woman, our first mother and father: "*Crescite et multiplicamini, et replete terram?* Increase and multiply, and fill the earth?" O sodomite of the Devil, what are you doing? It's as if you're saying to God: "I want to spite you; I don't want anyone to be born." . . .

And what do you say? "Oh, it's completely harmless, no one's going to get hurt, he's just a boy, after all." If he were a girl, perhaps you wouldn't be doing this, because she could get herself pregnant this way. And since he can't get pregnant, you're happy and offer up your "flatcake" to the "queen of heaven." And you just keep on doing such things so much that you are provoking the wrath of God; and God, seeing this and all the other vices, is threatening you and says:

From Franco Mormando, *The Preacher's Demons: Bernardino of Siena and the Social Underworld of Early Renaissance Italy* (Chicago and London: University of Chicago Press, 1999), 119–20, 124, 128, 130, 138, 139, 147–48, 152.

"My wrath will come down over your head." Do you know what he will do? He will send you wars, plagues, and famines in order to punish the sodomites, so much so that you won't be left with either livestock, or farms or gardens or money or even your very population. In all these ways, God will show his wrath. . . .

They aren't even dry behind the ears and they're already contaminated and sodomites! Just look at them, fathers and mothers, it's astounding: At such a tender age and they're already contaminated by sodomy! . . .

I've heard about those [boys] who paint themselves up and go around bragging about their sodomizers and make it into a profession and incite others do do likewise. . . .

[T]hese types are never satisfied. Oh, woman, take note, if he's trapped in this vice, you'll never be able to satisfy him! He always complains about everything you do, always. When he comes home, he comes in turmoil, with a head full of frenzy, and nothing does he care for the judgment of God or honor in this world. He's always cranky and agitated, he's afraid—he's afraid of falling out of favor with his wicked little boy. . . . He obeys the boy like a servant and does everything he can to grant his wishes. . . .

[In Venice] I saw three things happening together. I saw [the sodomite] placed at the stake, and tied all the way up. [I saw] a keg of pitch, brushwood, and fire, and an executor who set him on fire, and a lot of people, all around, watching. The sodomite felt the smoke and the fire, and he burned to death; the executioner felt only the smoke, and whoever was standing around watching saw nothing but smoke and fire. What this stands for is that: in hell the sodomites will burn with smoke and fire [while] their torturers down there will get the smoke. . . . Those who stand watching [represent] the blessed spirits in paradise who see the punishment of the sodomites and rejoice over it because they see the justice of God shining forth from it.

DISCUSSION QUESTIONS

1. Why does Bernardino direct many of his comments to women? How would you compare his views of men and women?
2. Bernardino and some other preachers believed prostitution to be preferable to male sodomy. Why?
3. Bernardino refers to the "population" at a number of points. Why would this be a concern?
4. How does Bernardino exhibit an increasing repression of sexuality that is evident in the fifteenth and sixteenth centuries?

COMPARATIVE QUESTIONS

1. Compare the visions of both the human being and the state described by Bruni, Rucellai, and Pico della Mirandola with that of Alessandra Strozzi and Bernardino of Siena. How do they differ, and how would you account for this difference?
2. The excerpts from Bernardino focus on one subject, but would he agree or disagree with Pico della Mirandola's view of humanity?

3. Compare Bernardino and Alessandra on the subject of marriage. Do Alessandra's letters offer any insights on why (seemingly) few men were marrying?

4. One of historian Jacob Buckhardt's chapters in *The Civilisation of the Renaissance in Italy* is entitled "The Discovery of Man and the World." What is "new" about the Renaissance? Do you consider the many discoveries—the new view of humanity, philosophy, the arts, and the state; the printing press and its potential; and the discovery of New Worlds—positive developments? Justify your response.

15

The Struggle for Reformation Europe
1500–1560

S
UMMARY   If fifteenth-century European history had been dominated
by ideas of rebirth, learning, and discovery (in all its forms), religion remained as important as in earlier centuries, although it often assumed new
forms. Despite the ending of the Great Schism with the Council of Constance,
serious damage had been done to the church. Many within the Church tried their
best to institute reforms, but change was slow in coming. Increasing numbers of
laymen and women turned to individual avenues of devotion, including confra-
ternities, the *devotio moderna,* mysticism, and an evangelicalism/biblicalism that
was given life with the advent of the printing press. The problems in the church,
joined with the spirit and methods of the Renaissance, ushered in a period of
questioning that involved not only the leading reformers but also Christian humanists and the laity.

1
Desiderius Erasmus
The Praise of Folly
1514

*Desiderius Erasmus (c. 1467–1536) of Rotterdam was the most famous exponent of
northern or "Christian" humanism. His work, along with that of such figures as
Thomas More and Jacques Lefèvre d'Étaples, built on the linguistic and philological
studies of the Italian humanists. The northern humanists, however, stressed the need
for moral reform and a return to "apostolic simplicity." Erasmus published numerous works, including his influential Greek and Latin New Testament,* The Hand-
book of the Militant Christian, *and* The Praise of Folly *(1511–1514), dedicated to
his then friend More. Although he had given up the monastic life in 1492 after six*

years, Erasmus remained a Catholic. In the increasingly polarized religious times of the sixteenth century, however, his calls for "toleration" went unheeded, and his lack of zeal for dogma made some question his faith.

Folly speaks:

No matter what people commonly say about me . . . I am still the one who makes both gods and men glad. . . . I have no use for those so-called wise persons. . . .

I am not so foolish as to petition painted stone images; they would only detract from my worship, since only stupid and unimaginative people worship these idols, instead of the saints themselves. And the same thing would happen to me that happens to the saints—they are thrown out of doors by their substitutes. I feel that I have many statues erected in my behalf, as many as there are people who bear my living image on their faces, whether against their will or not. . . .

Those who are called closest to [intellectuals] in happiness are generally called "the religious" or "monks," both of which are deceiving names, since for the most part they stay as far away from religion as possible and frequent every sort of place. . . . Though most people detest these men so much that accidentally meeting one is considered to be bad luck, the monks themselves believe that they are magnificent creatures. . . .

Nevertheless, because of all this detail that they employ they think that they are superior to all other people. And what is more, amid all their pretense of Apostolic charity, the members of one order will denounce the members of another order clamorously because of the way in which the habit has been belted or the slightly darker color of it. You will find some among the monks who are so strictly religious and pious that they will wear no outer clothes other than those made of Cilician goat's hair or inner garments other than the ones made of Milesian wool. . . . Members of other orders shrink from the mere touch of money as if it were poison. They do not, however, retreat from the touch of wine or women. . . .

No one, however, even though isolated from public life, will dare to rebuke one of these monks, because through the confessional these men acquire the secrets of everyone. To be sure, they believe it a crime to publish these secrets, but they may accidentally divulge them when drinking heavily or when wishing to promote amusement by relating funny stories. . . .

Show me any actor or charlatan you would rather watch than these monks as they drone through their sermons, trying to exemplify all the art of rhetoric that has been handed down through the ages. Good Lord! How wonderfully they gesture with their hands; how skillfully they pitch their voice; how cleverly they intone their sermons, throwing themselves about, changing facial expressions,

From *The Essential Erasmus,* ed. and trans. John P. Dolan (New York: Meridian, 1964), 101, 136, 148–49, 150, 153, 155, 156, 157, 159, 169, 172, 173.

and in the end leaving their audience in a complete state of confusion by their contradictory arguments. . . .

One further thing; their performances are such that it might seem that they have been taking lessons from wandering players. . . . Most of these gullible people are, it must be said, either women or merchants. These the preachers especially wish to please; because the merchants, when pleased, will reward the preacher with a small sum of their ill-gotten wealth, and the women, although in many cases having betrayed the clergy, are accustomed to seek the advice of these men when they are at outs with their husbands. . . .

Show me a man such as princes commonly are: a man ignorant of the laws; an enemy of the public; intent upon private gain; taken to pleasure; against knowledge, liberty, and truth; never occupied with the safety of the state; and finally measuring all things in terms of his own desire and profit. . . .

Now what shall I say about the noble courtiers? These men desire to be likened as God's foremost creatures, yet the fact is that no group of men is more sordid, more obsequious, more idiotic, or more contemptible than this set of men. One point in which they are as unaspiring as one could be is that, while they are happy to wear gold, jewels, and scarlet on their bodies, they leave to others the virtues and wisdom that accompany these symbols. . . .

Our popes, cardinals, and bishops have, for a long while now, diligently followed the example of the state and the practice of the princes, and have come near to beating these noblemen at their own game. . . .

As to the Supreme Pontiffs, if they would recall that they take the place of Christ . . . [their] forfeitures would be replaced by vigils, fasts, sorrows, prayers, sermons, education, weariness, and a thousand other bothersome tasks of the sort. We should also mention that a great many copyists, notaries, lobbyists, promoters, secretaries, muleteers, grooms, bankers, and pimps—I was about to add something more tender, though rougher on the ears, I am afraid—would be out of jobs. In other words, that large group of men that burdens—I beg your pardon, I meant to say adorns—the Holy Roman See would be done away with and would have to, as a result, resort to begging as means of making a living. Those who are even worse, those very princes of the Church and guiding lights of the world, would become nothing more than a staff and a wallet. . . .

[J]ust as princes transmit to their ministers the ruling of some part of their realm, and these ministers in turn, to one of their subordinates, so also do priests leave to the people the pursuit of piety. . . .

But lest I pursue what is infinite, let me sum up. The whole of the Christian religion seems to have a certain relationship with some kind of folly but fails to agree at all with wisdom. If you would like proof of this, take a look at children, old people, women, and fools and see how they, more than others, take great pleasure in the things of religion. They seem to have a natural impulse to stand closer to the altar. Take the example of the founders of religion. Embracing simplicity they became the most severe enemies of learning. And, finally, what fool could possibly act more foolishly than those whom the ardor of religion has totally consumed? They throw away their wealth, they neglect injuries, permit themselves to be deceived, fail to discriminate between friend and foe, shrink from pleasure, and cram themselves with hunger, vigil, tears, labors, contumelies. They prefer death to life and, in short, seem to have grown impervious to sensation and live as if their souls no longer dwelt in their bodies. What is this other than insanity?

. . .

I hope you are not so foolish as to suppose that after this mélange I can remember anything I have said. There is an old saying, "I hate a drinking companion with a memory." Here is a new one: "I hate a student with a memory." Therefore, to your health, cheers, live and drink, O most celebrated devotees of Folly.

DISCUSSION QUESTIONS

1. For Erasmus, is folly wisdom or wisdom folly? How do you think he defines these terms?
2. What is Erasmus's view of churchmen? What problems does he see in the church of his day? Why do you suppose he remained a Catholic after the Lutheran and Swiss Reformations? What is his prescription for reform?
3. What is his view of kings and princes, merchants, women, and the common man? Although he derides learning, Erasmus was an intellectual. How do you reconcile these apparent contradictions?
4. In a work that is obviously a satire or parody, how can we glean historical information? What care must be used?

2
Argula von Grumbach and John Hooker
Women's Actions in the Reformation
1520s–1530s

Throughout the Middle Ages, laywomen were actively involved in their religion, through attendance at Mass, sermons, and pilgrimages, and their "greater piety" (than that of men) was remarked on by many churchmen. This trend continued in the early decades of the Reformation but assumed new forms, providing a particular window of opportunity for women to defend their faith when challenged through speech, print, or action. The first document is from the writings of Argula von Grumbach (1492–c. 1554), a Bavarian noblewoman who was by 1522 a follower of Martin Luther (1483–1546), whose challenges and writings initiated the Protestant Reformation. Called a silly bag, a shameless whore, and a female desperado, among other epithets, von Grumbach wrote prose and poetry beginning in 1523 in defense of Luther and Philipp Melanchthon (1497–1560), his coworker and follower, and against the arrest of a Lutheran student at Ingolstadt. She also responded in kind to the sarcasm of another student. Tens of thousands of copies of her writings were in circulation within a few years. The second document is by the Englishman John Hooker who was Exeter's city chamberlain during the dissolution of the monasteries, when the city's Catholic women took matters into their own hands on the arrival of Oliver Cromwell's visitors in 1535 or 1536.

Argula von Grumbach

To the Scholars of Ingolstadt

I find there is a text in Matthew 10 which runs: "Whosoever confesses me before another I too will confess before my heavenly Father." . . . Words like these, coming from the very mouth of God, are always before my eyes. For they exclude neither woman or man.

And this is why I am compelled as a Christian to write to you.

To Bavarian Princes

My heart goes out to our princes, whom you have seduced and betrayed so deplorably. For I realize that they are ill informed about divine Scripture. If they could spare the time from other business, I believe they, too, would discover the truth that no one has a right to exercise sovereignty over the word of God. . . . My heart goes out to them; for they have no one with enough integrity to tell them what is going on. And I realize very well that it is for their wealth, torn from them every day, that they are loved rather than for themselves. I am prepared to write to them in this vein, since, because of other business, they have no leisure to sit down and read for themselves.

To the Ingolstadt Scholars

I beseech you for the sake of God, and exhort you by God's judgment and righteousness, to tell me in writing which of the articles written by Martin or Melanchthon you consider heretical. In German not a single one seem heretical to me. And the fact is that a great deal has been published in German, and I've read it all. . . . I beseech and request a reply from you if you consider I am in error, though I am not aware of it. For Jerome was not ashamed of writing a great deal to women, to Blessilla, for example, to Paula, Eustochium, and so on. Yes, and Christ himself, he who is the only teacher of us all, was not ashamed to preach to Mary Magdalene, and to the young woman at the well.

I do not flinch from appearing before you, from listening to you, from discussing with you. For by the grace of God I, too, can ask questions, hear answers, and read in German. . . . I have no Latin, but you have German, being born and brought up in this tongue. What I have written to you is no woman's chit-chat, but the word of God, and as a member of the Christian Church, against which the gates of Hell cannot prevail.

In Response to a Verse Attack by an Ingolstadt Student

Now Judith when this she heard,
To the priests went straight away,
Gave them instruction manifold

From *http://home.infi.net/`ddisse/grumbach.html*; Argula von Grumbach, ". . . A Hundred Women Would Emerge to Write"; and Joyce Youings, *The Dissolution of the Monasteries* (London: Allen & Unwin; New York: Barnes & Noble, 1971), 164–65.

How God their fathers led of old,
When, as now, in tribulation;
Gave ample scriptural demonstration.
She also took the rulers on:
Boldly said: "What have you done
To leave the people in such pain?"
Soon caused there [sic] hearts to lift again.

. . .

God therefore made her hand so strong
That Holofernes was undone.
She then lopped off his very head.
Who'd ever have believed this deed?
That him they called a mighty god
Should thus become a laughing stock.

. . .

More of the same in Judges is found,
You can read of there [sic], if you care.
There was a seer, Deborah by name,
Who was sent by God, much the same,
To lead the people of Israel
To judge and govern them as well.
Had you been living at that time,
Wise man, no doubt you'd have tried
To stop God carrying out his plan
By acting through a poor woman.
You'd surely could never have endured
God's victory through woman assured.

. . .

If you argue I'm too ignorant
Then share with me your wisdom grand!
But a spindle is all you offer,
In every teaching it's what you proffer.
But this fine Master of the Sentence
Would teach me my domestic duties!
These duties I carry out day by day
How could I ever forget them, pray?
Though Christ tells me—I hear his voice—
To hear his words is the very best choice.

Hooker: Popular Reactions at Exeter

The commissioners came to this city in the summertime to execute their commission, and beginning first with the priory of St. Nicholas, after that they [had] viewed the same they went thence to dinner and commanded [a man] in the time of their absence to pull down the rood loft in the church. In the meanwhile, and before they did return, certain women and wives in the city, namely Joan Reeve, Elizabeth Glandfield, Agnes Collaton, Alice Miller, Joan Reed and others, minding to stop the suppressing of that house, came in all haste to the said church, some with spikes, some with shovels, some with pikes, and some with such tools as they could get and, the church door being fast, they broke it open. And finding there the man pulling down the rood loft they all sought, [by] all the means they could, to take him and hurled stones unto him, in so much that for his safety he was driven to take to the tower for his refuge. And yet they pursued him so eagerly that he was enforced to leap out at a window and so to save himself, and very hardly he escaped the breaking of his neck, but yet he brake one of his ribs. John Blakealler, one of the aldermen of the city, being advertised thereof, he with all speed got him to the said monastery, he thinking what with fair words and what with foul words to have stayed and pacified the women. But how so ever he talked with them they were plain with him and the aforesaid Elizabeth Glandfield gave him a blow and set him packing. The Mayor [William Hurst], having understanding hereof and being very loathe the visitors should be advertised of any such disorders and troubles, he came down with his officers, before whose coming they [the women] had made fast the church doors and had bestowed themselves in places meet as they thought to stand to their defences. Notwithstanding, the Mayor broke in upon them and with much ado he apprehended and took them all and sent them to ward. The visitors being then made acquainted herewith, they gave thanks to the Mayor for his care and diligence . . . and so they proceeded to the suppressing of the house, and before their departure they intreated the Mayor for releasing of the women.

Discussion Questions

1. What can you tell of Argula von Grumbach's background and learning from her writings alone?

2. What are the main points she makes against both the princes and, primarily, the Ingolstadt scholars?

3. Why did the Catholic women of Exeter attack the commissioners sent out to dissolve the monastery? Are you surprised by their behavior?

4. Despite their many differences, do you see anything in common between Argula von Grumbach and the women of Exeter?

3

Iconoclasm and Reparations during the Reign of Francis I
1515–1547

It was during the reign of Francis I (1515–1547) that "Lutheranism" (an all-encompassing term that could comprise the Catholic evangelicalism of the king's sister, Marguerite de Navarre [1492–1549], the work of reforming bishops and that of a small number of actual Lutherans, and more radical Swiss reformers) appeared in France. The following account of events is provided by the "Bourgeois of Paris," about whom we know little. Bourgeois could have many meanings in sixteenth-century France, but a bourgeois was a citizen, usually well-to-do, and accorded numerous privileges. This writing is likely the compilation of more than one author, but these authors were almost certainly contemporary with the events described. Although the account sometimes jumps around chronologically, it is generally in agreement on detail with other memoirs and writings of the time. The incident described took place in June 1528, showing how antagonistic religious feeling had become in France even before the Affair of the Placards in 1534. It also demonstrates that the man called "The Renaissance Prince" (Francis I), known for his interest in reform, could as quickly assume the qualities associated with his title of "Most Christian King."

In the same year 1528 on Monday night, the day after the feast of Pentecost, which was the first of June, an amazing event happened in this city of Paris. In the night between Monday and Tuesday of the holiday, some heretics went to an image of Our Lady in stone, holding her child, which was on the wall of the house of Louis de Harlay. . . . [T]hey stabbed this image many times with their knives, cutting off the head and that of the little baby, Our Lord; but no one has any ideas who the people were who smashed the statue. When the king [Francis I], who was in Paris, was told about this, he was so upset and angry that it is said he wept uncontrollably. And forthwith, in the two days that followed, he had cried at the sound of a trumpet in all the quarters of the city, that if anyone knew who did this, that he should come forward and tell those in charge of justice and him personally. He offered 1000 gold *écus*. . . . Yet nevertheless nothing came to light, however hard the king tried and in spite of the fact that he had commissioners go to all the houses in the area to ask questions.

The next Tuesday and for several days, there were many processions in the parishes and other churches of the city. . . . On Tuesday, June 9, the rector of the university, accompanied by all its clergy and doctors, licensees, bachelors, and masters of arts, pupils with their masters who were younger than twelve, each carrying in their hand a lit candle, all went in great reverence in procession to the church of Saint Gervais and to Sainte Catherine . . . until they reached the placed where the statue was. . . .

And on the day of the Feast of God which was Thursday June 11th, the King being in Paris . . . went very devoutly in a procession to the parish of Saint Paul with all the clergy, from which they went in procession to the statue, and the king himself carried a flaming torch of white wax, his head uncovered, with great reverence. He was accompanied by the playing of oboes, clarinets and trumpets. . . . And with him was the Cardinal of Lorraine and a great many prelates, lords, and gentlemen, each carrying a white candle in their hand. . . .

From *Le Journal d'un Bourgeois de Paris sous le Règne de François Ier (1515–1536)*, ed. V.-L. Bourrilly (Paris: Alphonse Picard, 1910), 290–94. Translation by Larissa Taylor.

On Friday June 12, there were general processions in all the parish churches of Paris. Members of the four mendicant orders with all the clergy of the great church of Notre Dame of Paris and the Sainte-Chappelle of the palace proceeded with banners, the cross, and many holy relics, and went to [the place where the statue had been attacked] . . . and there with the Bishop of Lisieux, grand almoner of the king, wearing his episcopal robes, the king carried a beautiful image in silver that he had had newly made. . . . [T]he bishop who was in front of the king carried the statue and placed it high up . . . then the king and the bishop . . . bowed three times before it, with the bishop saying beautiful prayers and praises to the glorious Virgin Mary and to her image. . . . And in the same procession were members of the court of *parlement*, the city magistrates, with archers, and cross-bowmen. . . .

[Another procession occurred on the next day.] Several days later, the [original wooden] image that was carried into the church of Saint Gervais caused several wonderful miracles to occur, restoring to life two children, and several people took offerings and made vows before it as well as the silver image which had replaced the stone one on the side of the said house. . . .

And since the people of Paris were always very pious, they made vows and brought offerings and candles. And there the glorious Virgin caused many miracles to occur.

DISCUSSION QUESTIONS

1. To a Catholic of the time, why would the desecration of the statue of the Virgin and Child have been so shocking and sacrilegious? Why would the miracles have vindicated their belief?

2. Why did iconoclastic events such as this one happen in the early years of the Reformation? Why would the statue be an affront to a "Protestant"?

3. What was the importance of the procession? Why are all the different people of all levels of society, professions, and parishes involved?

4. How does Francis I respond? How do you interpret his several actions regarding this incident?

4

St. Ignatius of Loyola
A New Kind of Catholicism
1546, 1549, 1553

The interests of Ignatius of Loyola (1491–1556), born of a Spanish noble family, centered more on chivalry than religion before his serious injury at the Battle of Pamplona in 1520. While recovering, he experienced a conversion when he began reading the only books available to him, The Golden Legend *(about saints' lives) and the* Life of Christ. *After begging and spending time at the monastery of Montserrat, he began work on* The Spiritual Exercises, *a manual of discernment for the pilgrim journeying to God. After studying at the University of Paris, Ignatius, Francis Xavier (1506–1552), and other friends made vows of chastity and poverty, determining to* travel to Jerusalem. When this became impossible, they went to Italy. The Society of Jesus (the Jesuits), founded by Ignatius and his early companions, was officially recognized by Pope Paul III in 1540 as a new order directly under the papacy. Its spirituality would be expressed most prominently in teaching and missionary work. The letters of Ignatius evince a new form of Catholic spiritual expression that was active and apostolic in its orientation. It was less a "response" to Protestantism than a model for Catholic life and work. Along with the works of other early Jesuits, it embodied a new spirit that so many had sought but not found in the late medieval church.

Conduct at Trent: On Helping Others, 1546

Our main aim [to God's greater glory] during this undertaking at Trent is to put into practice (as a group that lives together in one appropriate place) preaching, confessions and readings, teaching children, giving good example, visiting the poor in the hospitals, exhorting those around us, each of us according to the different talents he may happen to have, urging on as many as possible to greater piety and prayer. . . .

In their preaching they should not refer to points of conflict between Protestants and Catholics, but simply exhort all to upright conduct and to ecclesiastical practice, urging everyone to full self-knowledge and to greater knowledge and love of their Creator and Lord, with frequent allusions to the Council. At the end of each session, they should (as has been mentioned) lead prayers for the Council.

They should do the same with readings as with sermons, trying their best to influence people with greater love of their Creator and Lord as they explain the meaning of what is read; similarly, they should lead their hearers to pray for the Council. . . .

They should spend some time, as convenient, in the elementary teaching of youngsters, depending on the means and disposition of all involved, and with more or less explanation according to the capacity of the pupils. . . . Let them visit the almshouses once or twice a day, at times that are convenient for the patients' health, hearing confessions and consoling the poor, if possible taking them something, and urging them to the sort of prayers mentioned above for confession. If there are three of ours in Trent, each should visit the poor at least once every four days.

When they are urging people in their dealings with them to go to confession and communion, to say mass frequently, to undertake the Spiritual Exercises and other good works, they should also be urging them to pray for the Council.

It was said that there are advantages in being slow to speak and measured in one's statements when doctrinal definitions are involved. The opposite is true

From *Saint Ignatius of Loyola, Personal Writings: Reminiscences, Spiritual Diary, Select Letters, Including the Text of The Spiritual Exercises,* ed. and trans. Joseph A. Munitiz and Philip Endean (New York: Penguin Books, 1996), 165, 166, 230, 233–34, 257, 259, 262–63.

when one is urging people to look to their spiritual progress. Then one should be eloquent and ready to talk, full of sympathy and affection.

Spreading God's Word in a German University, 1549

The aim that they should have above all before their eyes is that intended by the Supreme Pontiff who has sent them: to help the University of Ingolstadt, and as far as is possible the whole of Germany, in all that concerns purity of faith, obedience to the Church, and firmness and soundness of doctrine and upright living. . . .

They must be very competent in them, and teach solid doctrine without many technical terms (which are unpopular), especially if these are hard to understand. The lectures should be learned yet clear, sustained in argument yet not long-winded, and delivered with attention to style. . . . Besides these academic lectures, it seems opportune on feast days to hold sermons on Bible readings, more calculated to move hearts and form consciences than to produce learned minds. . . . They should make efforts to attract their students into a friendship of spiritual quality, and if possible towards confession and making the Spiritual Exercises, even in the full form, if they seem suitable to join the Society. . . .

On occasion they should give time to works of mercy of a more visible character, such as in hospitals and prisons and helping other kinds of poor; such works arouse a "sweet fragrance" in the Lord. Opportunity may also arise to act as peacemakers in quarrels and to teach basic Christian doctrine to the uneducated. Taking account of local conditions and the persons concerned, prudence will dictate whether they should act themselves or through others.

They should make efforts to make friends with the leaders of their opponents, as also with those who are most influential among the heretics or those who are suspected of it yet seem not absolutely immovable. They must try to bring them back from their error by sensitive skill and signs of love. . . . All must try to have at their finger-tips the main points concerning dogmas of faith that are subjects of controversy with heretics, especially at the time and place when they are present, and with those persons with whom they are dealing. Thus they will be able, whenever opportunity arises, to put forward and defend the Catholic truth, to refute errors and to strengthen the doubtful and wavering, whether by lectures and sermons or in the confessional and in conversations. . . .

It will be helpful to lead people, as far as possible, to open themselves to God's grace, exhorting them to a desire for salvation, to prayer, to alms, and to everything that conduces to receiving grace or increasing it. . . .

Let [the duke] understand also what glory it will mean for him if he is the first to introduce into Germany seminaries in the form of such colleges, to foster sound doctrine and religion.

The Final Word on Obedience, 1553, to the Brothers in Portugal

To form an idea of the exceptional intrinsic value of this obedience in the eyes of God Our Lord, one should weigh both the worth of the noble sacrifice offered, involving the highest human power, and the completeness of the self-offering undertaken, as one strips oneself of self, becoming a "living victim" pleasing to the Divine Majesty. Another indication is the intensity of the difficulty experienced as one conquers self for love of God, opposing the natural human inclination felt by us all to follow our own opinions. . . .

Let us be unpretentious and let us be gentle! God Our Lord will grant the grace to enable you, gently and lovingly, to maintain constantly the offering you have made to Him. . . .

All that has been said does not exclude your bringing before your superiors a contrary opinion that may have occurred to you, once you have prayed about the matter and you feel that it would be proper and in accord with your respect for God to do so. . . . Such is the model on which divine Providence "gently disposes all things," so that the lower via the middle, and the middle via the higher, are led to their final ends. . . . The same can be seen upon the earth with respect to all secular constitutions that are duly established, and with respect to the ecclesiastical hierarchy, which is subordinated to you in virtue of holy obedience to select among the many routes open to you that which will bring you back to Portugal as soon and as safely as possible. So I order you in the name of Christ Our Lord to do this, even if it will be so as to return soon to India. . . . Firstly, you are well aware how important for the upkeep and advancement of Christianity in those lands, as also in Guinea and Brazil, is the good order that the King of Portugal can grant from his kingdom. When a prince of such Christian desires and holy intentions as is the King of Portugal receives information from someone of your experience about the state of affairs in those parts, you can imagine what influence this will have on him to do much more in the service of God Our Lord and for the good of those countries that you will describe to him. . . .

You are also aware how important it is for the good of the Indies that the persons sent there should be suitable for the aim that one is pursuing in those and in other lands. . . . Quite apart from all these reasons, which apply to furthering the good of India, it seems to me that you would fire the King's enthusiasm for the Ethiopian project, which has been planned for so many years without anything effective having been seen. Similarly, with regard to the Congo and Brazil, you could give no small help from Portugal, which you cannot do from India as there are not the same commercial relations. If people in India consider that your presence is important given your post, you can continue to act as superior no less from Portugal than from Japan or China, and probably much better. Just as you have gone away on other occasions for longer periods, do the same now.

DISCUSSION QUESTIONS

1. What does the Catholic life mean to Ignatius? What is new and innovative in his program for Catholic reform?
2. What advice does he give about dealing with the problem of heresy?
3. What role does he envision Jesuits playing throughout Europe and the rest of the world? How would you tie this in with the period of exploration and "discovery" in the fifteenth century?

4. How does Ignatius think political leaders can be enlisted to support the aims of the reform movement?

COMPARATIVE QUESTIONS

1. Would Ignatius of Loyola's program for Catholic reform have appealed to Erasmus? Why or why not? Give specific examples.

2. Why were feelings so strong that ordinary people would resort to violence in defense of their religious beliefs? What forms could this violence take?

3. How was the printing press a factor in the spread of Reformation ideas? Whom would you expect to have been most affected by it during these early years?

4. Imagine a meeting between Argula von Grumbach and a Jesuit at the University of Ingolstadt. How would she have convinced him of the righteousness of Lutheran belief? How would he have countered and tried to convince her of her errors?

16

Wars over Beliefs
1560–1648

S U M M A R Y   For kings, nobles, and ordinary folk alike, the late sixteenth through mid-seventeenth centuries were a time of turmoil and change, as the following documents illustrate. Religious wars galvanized much of Europe in this period, fueled by both ecclesiastical and lay leaders' attempts to maintain the commonly held idea that political and social stability depended on religious conformity. With the escalation of violence, however, some people argued successfully that peace would come only if state interests took precedence over religious ones. Europeans' views of the Earth and the heavens also expanded because of the rise of new scientific methods and overseas exploration. At the same time, the lure of traditional beliefs remained strong within communities struggling to make sense of the upheavals occurring around them.

1
Henry IV
Edict of Nantes
1598

Henry IV's promulgation of the Edict of Nantes in 1598 marked the end of the French Wars of Religion by recognizing French Protestants as a legally protected religious minority. Drawing largely on earlier edicts of pacification, the Edict of Nantes was comprised of ninety-two general articles, fifty-six secret articles, and two royal warrants. The two series of articles represented the edict proper and were registered by the highest courts of law in the realm (parlements). The following excerpts from the general articles reveal the triumph of political concerns over religious conformity on the one hand, and the limitations of religious tolerance in early modern France on the other.

Henry, By the Grace of God, King of *France*, and *Navarre*, To all Present, and to Come, greeteth. Among the infinite Mercies that God hath pleased to bestow upon us, that most Signal and Remarkable is, his having given us Power and Strength not to yield to the dreadful Troubles, Confusions, and Disorders, which were found at our coming to this Kingdom, divided into so many Parties and Factions, that the most Legitimate was almost the least, enabling us with Constancy in such manner to oppose the Storm, as in the end to surmount it, reducing this Estate to Peace and Rest. . . . For the general difference among our good Subjects, and the particular evils of the soundest parts of the State, we judged might be easily cured, after the Principal cause (the continuation of the Civil Wars) was taken away, in which we have, by the blessing of God, well and happily succeeded, all Hostility and Wars through the Kingdom being now ceased, and we hope he will also prosper us in our other affairs, which remain to be composed, and that by this means we shall arrive at the establishment of a good Peace, with tranquility and rest. . . . Amongst our said affairs . . . one of the principal hath been, the many complaints we received from divers of our Provinces and Catholick Cities, for that the exercise of the Catholick Religion was not universally re-established, as is provided by Edicts or Statutes heretofore made for the Pacification of the Troubles arising from Religion; as also the Supplications and Remonstrances which have been made to us by our Subjects of the reformed Religion, as well upon the execution of what hath been granted by the said former Laws, as that they desire to have some addition for the exercise of their Religion, the liberty of their Consciences and the security of their Persons and Fortunes; presuming to have just reasons for desiring some inlargement of Articles, as not being without great apprehensions, because their Ruine hath been the principal pretext and original foundation of the late Wars, Troubles, and Commotions. Now not to burden us with too much business at once, as also that the fury of War was not compatible with the establishment of Laws, how good soever they might be, we have hitherto deferred from time to time giving remedy herein. But now that it hath pleased God to give us a beginning of enjoying some Rest, we think we cannot imploy our self better, than to apply to that which may tend to the glory and service of his holy name, and to provide that he may be adored and prayed unto by all our Subjects: and if it hath not yet pleased him to permit it to be in one and the same form of Religion, that it may at the least be with one and the same intention, and with such rules that may prevent amongst them all troubles and tumults. . . . For this cause, we have upon the whole judged it necessary to give to all our said Subjects one general Law, Clear, Pure, and Absolute, by which they shall be regulated in all differences which have heretofore risen among them, or may hereafter rise, wherewith the one and other may be contented, being framed according as the time requires: and having had no other regard in this deliberation than solely the Zeal we have to the service of God, praying that he would henceforward render to all our subjects a durable and Established peace. . . . We

---

English text of "The Edict" as in Edmund Everard, *The Great Pressures and Grievances of the Protestants in France*, London, 1681. Appendix 4 in Roland Mousnier, *The Assassination of Henry IV*, trans. Joan Spencer (London: Faber and Faber, 1973), 316–47.

have by this Edict or Statute perpetuall and irrevocable said, declared, and ordained, saying, declaring, and ordaining;

That the memory of all things passed on the one part and the other, since the beginning of the month of *March,* 1585. untill our coming to the Crown, and also during the other precedent troubles, and the occasion of the same, shall remain extinguished and suppressed, as things that had never been. . . .

We prohibit to all our Subjects of what State and Condition soever they be, to renew the memory thereof, to attaque, resent, injure, or provoke one the other by reproaches for what is past, under any pretext or cause whatsoever, by disputing, contesting, quarrelling, reviling, or offending by factious words; but to contain themselves, and live peaceably together as Brethren, Friends, and fellow-Citizens, upon penalty for acting to the contrary, to be punished for breakers of Peace, and disturbers of the publick quiet.

We ordain, that the Catholick Religion shall be restored and re-established in all places, and quarters of this Kingdom and Countrey under our obedience, and where the exercise of the same hath been intermitted, to be there again, peaceably and freely exercised without any trouble or impediment. . . .

And not to leave any occasion of trouble and difference among our Subjects, we have permitted and do permit to those of the Reformed Religion, to live and dwell in all the Cities and places of this our Kingdom and Countreys under our obedience, without being inquired after, vexed, molested, or compelled to do any thing in Religion, contrary to their Conscience. . . .

We permit also to those of the said Religion to hold, and continue the Exercise of the same in all the Cities and Places under our obedience, where it hath by them been Established and made publick by many and divers times, in the Year 1586, and in 1597, until the end of the Month of *August.* . . .

In like manner the said Exercise may be Established, and re-established in all the Cities and Places where it hath been established, or ought to be by the Statute of Pacification, made in the Year 1577. . . .

As also not to exercise the said Religion in our Court, nor in our Territories and Countries beyond the Mountains, nor in our City of *Paris,* nor within five Leagues of the said City. . . .

We prohibit all Preachers, Readers, and others who speak in public, to use any words, discourse, or propositions tending to excite the People to Sedition; and we enjoin them to contain and comport themselves modestly, and to say nothing which shall not be for the instruction and edification of the Auditors, and maintaining the peace and tranquillity established by us in our said Kingdom. . . .

They shall also be obliged to keep and observe the Festivals of the Catholick Church, and shall not on the same dayes work, sell, or keep open shop, nor likewise the Artisans shall not work out of their shops, in their chambers or houses privately on the said Festivals, and other dayes forbidden, of any trade, the noise whereof may be heard without by those that pass by, or by the Neighbours. . . .

We ordain, that there shall not be made any difference or distinction upon the account of the said Religion, in receiving Scholars to be instructed in the Universities, Colledges, or Schools, nor of the sick or poor into Hospitals, sick houses or publick Almshouses. . . .

We Will and Ordain, that all those of the Reformed Religion, and others who have followed their party, of what State, Quality or Condition soever they be, shall be obliged and constrained by all due and reasonable wayes, and under the penalties contained in the said Edict or Statute relating thereunto, to pay tythes to the Curates, and other Ecclesiasticks, and to all others to whom they shall appertain. . . .

To the end to re-unite so much the better the minds and good will of our Subjects, as is our intention, and to take away all complaints for the future; We declare all those who make or shall make profession of the said Reformed Religion, to be capable of holding and exercising all Estates, Dignities, Offices, and publick charges whatsoever. . . .

We declare all Sentences, Judgments, Procedures, Seisures, Sales, and Decrees made and given against those of the Reformed Religion, as well living as dead, from the death of the deceased King *Henry* the Second our most honoured Lord and Father in Law, upon the occasion of the said Religion, Tumults and Troubles since happning, as also the execution of the same Judgments and Decrees, from henceforward cancelled, revoked, and annulled. . . .

Those also of the said Religion shall depart and desist henceforward from all Practices, Negotiations, and Intelligences, as well within as without our Kingdom; and the said Assemblies and Councels established within the Provinces, shall readily separate, and also all the Leagues and Associations made or to be made under what pretext soever, to the prejudice of our present Edict, shall be cancelled and annulled, . . . prohibiting most expresly to all our Subjects to make henceforwards any Assesments or Leavy's of Money, Fortifications, Enrolments of men, Congregations and Assemblies of other than such as are permitted by our present Edict, and without Arms. . . .

We give in command to the People of our said Courts of Parliaments, Chambers of our Courts, and Courts of our Aids, Bayliffs, Chief-Justices, Provosts and other our Justices and Officers to whom it appertains, and to their Leivetenants, that they cause to be read, published, and Registred this present Edict and Ordinance in their Courts and Jurisdictions, and the same keep punctually, and the contents of the same to cause to be injoyned and used fully and peaceably to all those to whom it shall belong, ceasing and making to cease all troubles and obstructions to the contrary, for such is our pleasure: and in witness hereof we have signed these presents with our own hand; and to the end to make it a thing firm and stable for ever, we have caused to put and indorse our Seal to the same. Given at *Nantes* in the Month of *April* in the year of Grace 1598. and of our Reign the ninth

Signed

HENRY

DISCUSSION QUESTIONS

1. What are the edict's principal objectives?
2. In what ways does the edict balance the demands of both French Catholics and Protestants?
3. What limits does the edict place on Protestants' religious rights?
4. Did Henry IV regard this edict as a permanent solution to the religious divisions in the realm?

2
Galileo
Letter to the Grand Duchess Christina
1615

Italian-born and educated, Galileo Galilei (1564–1642) was among the most illustrious proponents of the new science in the seventeenth century. Early in his studies, he embraced Copernicus's theory that the sun, not the Earth, was at the center of the universe. Having improved on the newly invented telescope in 1609, he was able to substantiate the heliocentric view through his observations of the moon and other planets. Because Galileo's work challenged traditional scientific views, it sparked considerable controversy. In the letter excerpted here, written in 1615 to the Grand Duchess Christina of Tuscany, an important Catholic patron of learning, Galileo defends the validity of his findings while striving to separate matters of religious faith from the study of natural phenomena.

Galileo Galilei
to
The Most Serene
Grand Duchess Mother:

Some years ago, as Your Serene Highness well knows, I discovered in the heavens many things that had not been seen before our own age. The novelty of these things, as well as some consequences which followed from them in contradiction to the physical notions commonly held among academic philosophers, stirred up against me no small number of professors—as if I had placed these things in the sky with my own hands in order to upset nature and overturn the sciences. . . .

Well, the passage of time has revealed to everyone the truths that I previously set forth. . . . But some, besides allegiance to their original error, possess I know not what fanciful interest in remaining hostile not so much toward the things in question as toward their discoverer. No longer being able to deny them, these men now take refuge in obstinate silence, but being more than ever exasperated by that which has pacified and quieted other men, they divert their thoughts to other fancies and seek new ways to damage me. . . .

Persisting in their original resolve to destroy me and everything mine by any means they can think of, these men are aware of my views in astronomy and philosophy. They know that as to the arrangement of the parts of the universe, I hold the sun to be situated motionless in the center of the revolution of the celestial orbs while the earth rotates on its axis and revolves about the sun. . . .

Now as to the false aspersions which they so unjustly seek to cast upon me, I have thought it necessary to justify myself in the eyes of all men, whose judgment

---

Stillman Drake, trans., *Discoveries and Opinions of Galileo* (New York: Doubleday, 1957), 175–86.

in matters of religion and of reputation I must hold in great esteem. I shall therefore discourse of the particulars which these men produce to make this opinion detested and to have it condemned not merely as false but as heretical. To this end they make a shield of their hypocritical zeal for religion. They go about invoking the Bible, which they would have minister to their deceitful purposes. Contrary to the sense of the Bible and the intention of the holy Fathers, if I am not mistaken, they would extend such authorities until even in purely physical matters—where faith is not involved—they would have us altogether abandon reason and the evidence of our senses in favor of some biblical passage, though under the surface meaning of its words this passage may contain a different sense. . . .

The reason produced for condemning the opinion that the earth moves and the sun stands still is that in many places in the Bible one may read that the sun moves and the earth stands still. Since the Bible cannot err, it follows as a necessary consequence that anyone takes an erroneous and heretical position who maintains that the sun is inherently motionless and the earth movable.

With regard to this argument, I think in the first place that it is very pious to say and prudent to affirm that the holy Bible can never speak untruth—whenever its true meaning is understood. But I believe nobody will deny that it is often very abstruse, and may say things which are quite different from what its bare words signify. Hence in expounding the Bible if one were always to confine oneself to the unadorned grammatical meaning, one might fall into error. Not only contradictions and propositions far from true might thus be made to appear in the Bible, but even grave heresies and follies. Thus it would be necessary to assign to God feet, hands, and eyes, as well as corporeal and human affections, such as anger, repentance, hatred, and sometimes even the forgetting of things past and ignorance of those to come. These propositions uttered by the Holy Ghost were set down in that manner by the sacred scribes in order to accommodate them to the capacities of the common people, who are rude and unlearned. For the sake of those who deserve to be separated from the herd, it is necessary that wise expositors should produce the true senses of such passages, together with the special reasons for which they were set down in these words. This doctrine is so widespread and so definite with all theologians that it would be superfluous to adduce evidence for it.

Hence I think that I may reasonably conclude that whenever the Bible has occasion to speak of any physical conclusion (especially those which are very abstruse and hard to understand), the rule has been observed of avoiding confusion in the minds of the common people which would render them contumacious toward the higher mysteries. Now the Bible, merely to condescend to popular capacity, has not hesitated to obscure some very important pronouncements, attributing to God himself some qualities extremely remote from (and even contrary to) His essence. Who, then, would positively declare that this principle has been set aside, and the Bible has confined itself rigorously to the bare and restricted sense of its words, when speaking but casually of the earth, of water, of the sun, or of any other created thing? Especially in view of the fact that these things in no way concern the primary purpose of the sacred writings, which is the service of God and the salvation of souls—matters infinitely beyond the comprehension of the common people.

This being granted, I think that in discussions of physical problems we ought to begin not from the authority of scriptural passages, but from sense-experiences and necessary demonstrations; for the holy Bible and the phenomena of nature proceed alike from the divine Word, the former as the dictate of the Holy Ghost and the latter as the observant executrix of God's commands. It is necessary for the Bible, in order to be accommodated to the understanding of every man, to speak many things which appear to differ from the absolute truth so far as the bare meaning of the words is concerned. But Nature, on the other hand, is inexorable and immutable; she never transgresses the laws imposed upon her, or cares a whit whether her abstruse reasons and methods of operations are understandable to men. For that reason it appears that nothing physical which sense-experience sets before our eyes, or which necessary demonstrations prove to us, ought to be called in question (much less condemned) upon the testimony of biblical passages which may have some different meaning beneath their words. For the Bible is not chained in every expression to conditions as strict as those which govern all physical effects; nor is God any less excellently revealed in Nature's actions than in the sacred statements of the Bible. . . .

From this I do not mean to infer that we need not have an extraordinary esteem for the passages of holy Scripture. On the contrary, having arrived at any certainties in physics, we ought to utilize these as the most appropriate aids in the true exposition of the Bible and in the investigation of those meanings which are necessarily contained therein, for these must be concordant with demonstrated truths. I should judge that the authority of the Bible was designed to persuade men of those articles and propositions which, surpassing all human reasoning, could not be made credible by science, or by any other means than through the very mouth of the Holy Spirit.

Yet even in those propositions which are not matters of faith, this authority ought to be preferred over that of all human writings which are supported only by bare assertions or probable arguments, and not set forth in a demonstrative way. This I hold to be necessary and proper to the same extent that divine wisdom surpasses all human judgment and conjecture.

But I do not feel obliged to believe that that same God who has endowed us with senses, reason, and intellect has intended to forgo their use and by some other means to give us knowledge which we can attain by them. He would not require us to deny sense and reason in physical matters which are set before our eyes and minds by direct experience or necessary demonstrations. This must be especially true in those sciences of which but the faintest trace (and that consisting of conclusions) is to be found in the Bible. Of astronomy, for instance, so little is found that none of the planets except Venus are so much as mentioned, and this only once or twice under the name of "Lucifer." If the sacred scribes had had any intention of teaching people certain arrangements and motions of the heavenly bodies, or had they wished us to derive such knowledge from the Bible, then in my opinion they would not have spoken of these matters so sparingly in comparison with the infinite number of admirable conclusions which are demonstrated in that science. . . .

From these things it follows as a necessary consequence that, since the Holy Ghost did not intend to teach us whether heaven moves or stands still, whether its shape is spherical or like a discus or extended in a plane, nor whether the earth is located at its center or off to one side, then so much the less was it intended to settle for us any other conclusion of the same kind. And the motion or rest of the earth and the sun is so closely linked with the things just named, that without a determination of the one, neither side can be taken in the other matters. Now if the Holy Spirit has purposely neglected to teach us propositions of this sort as irrelevant to the highest goal (that is, to our salvation), how can anyone affirm that it is obligatory to take sides on them, and that one belief is required by faith, while the other side is erroneous? Can an opinion be heretical and yet have no concern with the salvation of souls? Can the Holy Ghost be asserted not to have intended teaching us something that does concern our salvation? I would say here something that was heard from an ecclesiastic of the most eminent degree: "That the intention of the Holy Ghost is to teach us how one goes to heaven, not how heaven goes." . . .

From this it is seen that the interpretation which we impose upon passages of Scripture would be false whenever it disagreed with demonstrated truths. And therefore we should seek the incontrovertible sense of the Bible with the assistance of demonstrated truth, and not in any way try to force the hand of Nature or deny experiences and rigorous proofs in accordance with the mere sound of words that may appeal to our frailty. . . .

To that end they would forbid him the use of reason, divine gift of Providence, and would abuse the just authority of holy Scripture—which, in the general opinion of theologians, can never oppose manifest experiences and necessary demonstrations when rightly understood and applied. If I am correct, it will stand them in no stead to go running to the Bible to cover up their inability to understand (let alone resolve) their opponents' arguments.

DISCUSSION QUESTIONS

1. What is Galileo's goal in writing this letter to the Grand Duchess?
2. What is the basis of the attacks by Galileo's critics?
3. According to Galileo, what role should the Bible play in scientific inquiry?
4. Historians have credited Galileo for helping to popularize the principles and methods of the new science. How does this document lend support to this view?

3

David Pieterzen DeVries
Voyages from Holland to America
1655

In the seventeenth century, the Dutch Republic entered its golden age as the center of a thriving maritime economy. Like other European states at the time, Holland expanded its commercial markets and established permanent colonies in the newly explored regions of North America. The Dutch thus contributed to Europeans' growing knowledge of the topography, peoples, and cultures of the New World. In this excerpt, a French-born Dutch merchant and colonist, David DeVries (1593–1655), describes a violent conflict in 1643 between Dutch settlers and Native Americans in the area around modern New York City. The conflict was sparked by the Native Americans' refusal to relinquish their land. DeVries's account provides a vivid testimony of the clash between the two societies.

The 24th of February, sitting at the table with the governor, he began to state his intentions, that he had a mind to *wipe the mouths* of the Indians; that he had been dining at the house of Jan Claesz. Damen, where Maryn Adriaensz. and Jan Claesz. Damen, together with Jacob Planck, had presented a petition to him to begin this work. I answered him that there was no sufficient reason to undertake it. . . . But it appeared that my speaking was of no avail. He had, with his co-murderers, determined to commit the murder, deeming it a Roman deed, and to do it without warning the inhabitants in the open lands, that each one might take care of himself against the retaliation of the Indians, for he could not kill all the Indians. When I had expressed all these things in full, sitting at the table, and the meal was over, he told me he wished me to go to the large hall, which he had been lately adding to his house. Coming to it, there stood all his soldiers ready to cross the river to Pavonia to commit the murder. Then spoke I again to Governor William Kieft: "Stop this work; you wish to break the mouths of the Indians, but you will also murder our own nation, for there are none of the farmers who are aware of it. My own dwelling, my people, cattle, corn, and tobacco will be lost." He answered me, assuring me that there would be no danger; that some soldiers should go to my house to protect it. But that was not done. So was this business begun between the 25th and 26th of February in the year 1643. I remained that night at the governor's, sitting up. I went and sat in the kitchen, when, about midnight, I heard a great shrieking, and I ran to the ramparts of the fort, and looked over to Pavonia. Saw nothing but firing, and heard the shrieks of the Indians murdered in their sleep. I returned again to the house by the fire. Having sat there awhile, there came an Indian with his squaw, whom I knew well, and who lived about an hour's walk from my house, and told me that they two had fled in a small skiff; that they had betaken themselves to Pavonia; that the Indians from Fort Orange had surprised them; and that they had come to conceal themselves in the fort. I told them that they must go away immediately; that there was no occasion for them to come to the fort to conceal themselves; that they who had killed their people at Pavonia were not Indians, but the Swannekens, as they call the Dutch, had done it. They then asked me how they should get out of the fort. I took them to the door, and there was no sentry there, and so they betook themselves to the woods. When it was day, the soldiers returned to the fort, having

David Pieterzen DeVries, *Voyages from Holland to America*, A.D. *1632 to 1644*, trans. Henry C. Murphy (New York: Billin and Brothers, 1853), 167–71.

massacred or murdered eighty Indians, and considering they had done a deed of Roman valour, in murdering so many in their sleep; where infants were torn from their mother's breasts, and hacked to pieces in the presence of the parents, and the pieces thrown into the fire and in the water, and other sucklings were bound to small boards, and then cut, stuck, and pierced, and miserably massacred in a manner to move a heart of stone. Some were thrown into the river, and when the fathers and mothers endeavored to save them, the soldiers would not let them come on land, but made both parents and children drown,—children from five to six years of age, and also some old and decrepit persons. Many fled from this scene, and concealed themselves in the neighbouring sedge, and when it was morning, came out to beg a piece of bread, and to be permitted to warm themselves; but they were murdered in cold blood and tossed into the water. Some came by our lands in the country with their hands, some with their legs cut off, and some holding their entrails in their arms, and others had such horrible cuts and gashes, that worse than they were could never happen. . . . This is indeed a disgrace to our nation, who have so generous a governor in our Fatherland as the Prince of Orange, who has always endeavoured in his wars to spill as little blood as possible. As soon as the Indians understood that the Swannekens had so treated them, all the men whom they could surprise on the farm-lands, they killed; but we have never heard that they have ever permitted women or children to be killed. They burned all the houses, farms, barns, grain, haystacks, and destroyed everything they could get hold of. So there was an open destructive war begun. They also burnt my farm, cattle, corn, barn, tobacco-house, and all the tobacco. My people saved themselves in the house where I lived, which was made with embrasures, through which they defended themselves. Whilst my people were in this state of alarm, the Indian whom I had aided to escape from the fort came there, and told the other Indians that I was a good chief, that I had helped him out of the fort, and that the killing of the Indians took place contrary to my wish. Then they all cried out together to my people that they would not shoot them; that if they had not destroyed my cattle they would not do it; that they would not burn my house; that they would let my little brewery stand, though they had melted the copper-kettle, in order to make darts for their arrows; but hearing now that it (the massacre) had been done contrary to my wish, they all went away, and left my house unbesieged. When now the Indians had destroyed so many farms and men in revenge for their people, I went to Governor William Kieft, and asked him if it was not as I had said it would be, that he would only effect the spilling of Christian blood.

Discussion Questions

1. What are DeVries's attitudes toward the Native Americans, and how do they differ from those of the governor and the soldiers who carried out his orders?

2. Why does DeVries describe the massacre as a disgrace to his nation?

3. What does this account reveal about the Dutch settlers' way of life?

4

Trial Record of Johannes Junius
The Witch-Persecution at Bamberg
1628

Even as the new science gained support, most Europeans continued to believe in the supernatural, especially at this time of religious wars, economic decline, and social strife. This belief found violent expression in a wave of witchcraft persecutions across Europe between 1560 and 1640. The following selections from the minutes of the witchcraft trial of Johannes Junius and a letter he wrote to his daughter in 1628 attest to the predominant notion that witches were agents of the devil. The trial took place in Bamberg in the Holy Roman Empire during the Thirty Years' War. In content and form, Junius's trial is representative of others from the region with one striking exception, his gender. Accused witches were far more typically women.

. . . On Wednesday, June 28, 1628, was examined without torture Johannes Junius, Burgomaster at Bamberg, on the charge of witchcraft: how and in what fashion he had fallen into that vice. Is fifty-five years old, and was born at Niederwaysich in the Wetterau. Says he is wholly innocent, knows nothing of the crime, has never in his life renounced God; says that he is wronged before God and the world, would like to hear of a single human being who has seen him at such gatherings [as the witch-sabbaths].

Confrontation of Dr. Georg Adam Haan. Tells him to his face he will stake his life on it [*er wolle daraf leben und sterben*], that he saw him, Junius, a year and a half ago at a witch-gathering in the electoral council-room, where they ate and drank. Accused denies the same wholly.

Confronted with Hopffens Elsse. Tells him likewise that he was on Hauptsmoor at a witch-dance; but first the holy wafer was desecrated. Junius denies. Hereupon he was told that his accomplices had confessed against him and was given time for thought.

On Friday, June 30, 1628, the aforesaid Junius was again without torture exhorted to confess, but again confessed nothing, whereupon, . . . since he would confess nothing, he was put to the torture, and first the

Thumb-screws were applied. Says he has never denied God his Saviour nor suffered himself to be otherwise baptized;[1] will again stake his life on it; feels no pain in the thumb-screws.

---

[1] "Otherwise baptized" is the usual phrase for the rite, a parody of baptism, by which the Devil was believed to initiate his followers. [trans.]

Translations and Reprints from the Original Sources of European History (Philadelphia: University of Pennsylvania, 1912), vol. III, no. 4 pp. 23–28.

Leg-screws. Will confess absolutely nothing; knows nothing about it. He has never renounced God; will never do such a thing; has never been guilty of this vice; feels likewise no pain.

Is stripped and examined; on his right side is found a bluish mark, like a clover leaf, is thrice pricked therein, but feels no pain and no blood flows out.

Strappado. He has never renounced God; God will not forsake him; if he were such a wretch he would not let himself be so tortured; God must show some token of his innocence. He knows nothing about witchcraft. . . .

On July 5, the above named Junius is without torture, but with urgent persuasions, exhorted to confess, and at last begins and confesses:

When in the year 1624 his law-suit at Rothweil cost him some six hundred florins, he had gone out, in the month of August, into his orchard at Friedrichsbronnen; and, as he sat there in thought, there had come to him a woman like a grass-maid, who had asked him why he sat there so sorrowful; he had answered that he was not despondent, but she had led him by seductive speeches to yield him to her will. . . . And thereafter this wench had changed into the form of a goat, which bleated and said, "Now you see with whom you have had to do. You must be mine or I will forthwith break your neck." Thereupon he had been frightened, and trembled all over for fear. Than the transformed spirit had seized him by the throat and demanded that he should renounce God Almighty, whereupon Junius said, "God forbid," and thereupon the spirit vanquished through the power of these words. Yet it came straightway back, brought more people with it, and persistently demanded of him that he renounce God in Heaven and all the heavenly host, by which terrible threatening he was obliged to speak this formula: "I renounce God in Heaven and his host, and will henceforward recognize the Devil as my God."

After the renunciation he was so far persuaded by those present and by the evil spirit that he suffered himself to be otherwise baptized in the evil spirit's name. The Morhauptin had given him a ducat as dower-gold, which afterward became only a potsherd.

He was then named Krix. His paramour he had to call Vixen. Those present had congratulated him in Beelzebub's name and said that they were now all alike. At this baptism of his there were among others the aforesaid Christiana Morhauptin, the young Geiserlin, Paul Glaser, [and others]. After this they had dispersed.

At this time his paramour had promised to provide him with money, and from time to time to take him to other witch-gatherings. . . . Whenever he wished to ride forth [to the witch-sabbath] a black dog had come before his bed, which said to him that he must go with him, whereupon he had seated himself upon the dog and the dog had raised himself in the Devil's name and so had fared forth.

About two years ago he was taken to the electoral council-room, at the left hand as one goes in. Above at a table were seated the Chancellor, the Burgomaster Neydekher, Dr. George Haan, [and many others]. Since his eyes were not good, he could not recognize more persons.

More time for consideration was now given him. On July 7, the aforesaid Junius was again examined, to know what further had occurred to him to confess. He confesses that about two months ago, on the day after an execution was held, he was at a witch-dance at the Black Cross, where Beelzebub had shown himself to them all and said expressly to their faces that they must all be burned together on this spot, and had ridiculed and taunted those present. . . .

Of crimes. His paramour had immediately after his seduction demanded that he should make away with his younger son Hans Georg, and had given him for this purpose a gray powder; this, however, being too hard for him, he had made away with his horse, a brown, instead.

His paramour had also often spurred him on to kill his daughter, . . . and because he would not do this he had been maltreated with blows by the evil spirit.

Once at the suggestion of his paramour he had taken the holy wafer out of his mouth and given it to her. . . .

A week before his arrest as he was going to St. Martin's church the Devil met him on the way, in the form of a goat, and told him that he would soon be imprisoned, but that he should not trouble himself—he would soon set him free. Besides this, by his soul's salvation, he knew nothing further; but what he had spoken was the pure truth; on that he would stake his life. On August 6, 1628, there was read to the aforesaid Junius this his confession, which he then wholly ratified and confirmed, and was willing to stake his life upon it. And afterward he voluntarily confirmed the same before the court.

[So ended the trial of Junius, and he was accordingly burned at the stake. But it so happens that there is also preserved in Bamberg a letter, in quivering hand, secretly written by him to his daughter while in the midst of his trial (July 24, 1628):]

Many hundred thousand good-nights, dearly beloved daughter Veronica. Innocent have I come into prison, innocent have I been tortured, innocent must I die. For whoever comes into the witch prison must become a witch or be tortured until he invents something out of his head and—God pity him—bethinks him of something. I will tell you how it has gone with me. When I was the first time put to the torture, Dr. Braun, Dr. Kötzendörffer, and two strange doctors were there. Then Dr. Braun asks me, "Kinsman, how come you here?" I answer, "Through falsehood, through misfortune." "Hear, you," he says, "you are a witch; will you confess it voluntarily? If not, we'll bring in witnesses and the executioner for you." I said "I am no witch, I have a pure conscience in the matter; if there are a thousand witnesses, I am not anxious, but I'll gladly hear the witnesses." Now the chancellor's son was set before me . . . and afterward Hoppfen Elss. She had seen me dance on Haupts-moor. . . . I answered: "I have never renounced God, and will never do it—God graciously keep me from it. I'll rather bear whatever I must." And then came also—God in highest Heaven have mercy—the executioner, and put the thumb-screws on me, both hands bound together, so that the blood ran out at the nails and everywhere, so that for four weeks I could not use my hands, as you can see from the writing. . . . Thereafter they first stripped me, bound my hands behind me, and drew me up in the torture.[2] Then I thought heaven and earth were at an end; eight times did they draw me up and let me fall again, so that I suffered terrible agony. . . .

And this happened on Friday, June 30, and with God's help I had to bear the torture. . . . When at last the executioner led me back into the prison, he said to me: "Sir, I beg you, for God's sake confess something, whether it be true or not. Invent something, for you cannot endure the torture which you will be put to; and, even if you bear it all, yet you will not escape, not even if you were an earl, but one torture will follow after another until you say you are a witch. Not before that," he said, "will they let you go, as you may see by all their trials, for one is just like another." . . .

And so I begged, since I was in wretched plight, to be given one day for thought and a priest. The priest was refused me, but the time for thought was given. Now, my dear child, see in what hazard I stood and still stand. I must say that I am a witch, though I am not,—must now renounce God, though I have never done it before. Day and night I was deeply troubled, but at last there came to me a new idea. I would not be anxious, but, since I had been given no priest with whom I could take counsel, I would myself think of something and say it. It were surely better that I just say it with mouth and words, even though I had not really done it; and afterwards I would confess it to the priest, and let those answer for it who compel me to do it. . . . And so I made my confession, as follows; but it was all a lie. . . .

Dear child, keep this letter secret so that people do not find it, else I shall be tortured most piteously and the jailers will be beheaded. So strictly is it forbidden. . . . Dear child, pay this man a dollar. . . . I have taken several days to write this; my hands are both lame. I am in a sad plight. . . .

Good night, for your father Johannes Junius will never see you more. July 24, 1628.

DISCUSSION QUESTIONS

1. According to the trial minutes, why was Junius targeted for persecution? What does this reveal about contemporary beliefs in witches and their powers?
2. How does Junius's own account of his trial conflict with that of the trial minutes?
3. What does this document suggest about the religious anxieties of the times?

COMPARATIVE QUESTIONS

1. Scholars argue that amidst the conflicts of this period, many European leaders and thinkers increasingly gave precedence to secular concerns over religious ones. How do the Edict of Nantes and Galileo's letter support this argument?
2. Despite this gradual trend towards secularization, what do Galileo's letter and the witchcraft trial minutes reveal about the continued importance of religion in shaping Europeans' understanding of the everyday world?
3. What do the third and fourth documents suggest about the role of violence in European society and culture?

---

[2] This torture of the strappado, which was that in most common use by the courts, consisted of a rope, attached to the hands of the prisoner (bound behind his back) and carried over a pulley at the ceiling. By this he was drawn up and left hanging. To increase the pain, weights were attached to his feet or he was suddenly jerked up and let drop.

17

State Building and the Search for Order

1648–1690

S U M M A R Y   The wars over religion not only left bitter memories in late-seventeenth-century Europe, but also ruined economies and weakened governments. In response, many people sought to impose order on the turbulent world in a variety of ways. As the first two documents reveal, politically, the quest for order fueled the development of two rival systems of state building: absolutism and constitutionalism, with France and England, respectively, taking the lead. Despite their differences, rulers in both systems centralized their power and expanded their bureaucracies, casting an increasingly wide net over their subjects' lives. The third document indicates that not everyone submitted willingly to the expansion of state power, but such resistance was typically fruitless. Even so, as the final document suggests, the emergence of a new literary genre, the novel, in this period points to other, less overt forces at work, counteracting the search for order.

1

Louis de Rouvroy, Duke of Saint-Simon
Memoirs
1694–1723

A nobleman and godson of Louis XIV, Louis de Rouvroy, Duke of Saint-Simon (1675–1755), was raised at the royal palace of Versailles. He began recording his life and impressions of the court at the age of nineteen and continued for almost three decades. The result was his multivolume Memoirs, *which paint an intimate portrait of the Sun King and the workings of the absolutist state. Saint-Simon was not an entirely objective observer, however. Having never achieved great success within the court, he often viewed it through the lens of his own resentment. This excerpt provides insight into both the reasons behind Louis XIV's move to Versailles and his method of rule there.*

Let me touch now upon some other incidents in his career, and upon some points in his character.

He early showed a disinclination for Paris. The troubles that had taken place there during the minority made him regard the place as dangerous; he wished, too, to render himself venerable by hiding himself from the eyes of the multitude; all these considerations fixed him at St. Germains soon after the death of the Queen, his mother. It was to that place he began to attract the world by fêtes and gallantries, and by making it felt that he wished to be often seen.

His love for Madame de la Vallière, which was at first kept secret, occasioned frequent excursions to Versailles, then a little card castle, which had been built by Louis XIII.—annoyed, and his suite still more so, at being frequently obliged to sleep in a wretched inn there, after he had been out hunting in the forest of Saint Leger. That monarch rarely slept at Versailles more than one night, and then from necessity; the King, his son, slept there, so that he might be more in private with his mistress; pleasures unknown to the hero and just man, worthy son of Saint Louis, who built the little château.

These excursions of Louis XIV. by degrees gave birth to those immense buildings he erected at Versailles; and their convenience for a numerous court, so different from the apartments at St. Germains, led him to take up his abode there entirely shortly after the death of the Queen. He built an infinite number of apartments, which were asked for by those who wished to pay their court to him; whereas at St. Germains nearly everybody was obliged to lodge in the town, and the few who found accommodation at the château were strangely inconvenienced.

The frequent fêtes, the private promenades at Versailles, the journeys, were means on which the King seized in order to distinguish or mortify the courtiers, and thus render them more assiduous in pleasing him. He felt that of real favours he had not enough to bestow; in order to keep up the spirit of devotion, he therefore unceasingly invented all sorts of ideal ones, little preferences and petty distinctions, which answered his purpose as well.

He was exceedingly jealous of the attention paid him. Not only did he notice the presence of the most distinguished courtiers, but those of inferior degree also. He looked to the right and to the left, not only upon rising but upon going to bed, at his meals, in passing through his apartments, or his gardens of Versailles, where alone the courtiers were allowed to follow him; he saw and noticed everybody; not one escaped him, not even those who hoped to remain unnoticed. He marked well all absentees from the court, found out the reason of their absence, and never lost an opportunity of acting towards them as the occasion might seem to justify. With some of the courtiers (the most distinguished), it was a demerit

Bayle St. John, trans., *The Memoirs of the Duke of Saint Simon*, vol. II (Philadelphia: Gebbie and Co., 1890), 363–69.

not to make the court their ordinary abode; with others 'twas a fault to come but rarely; for those who never or scarcely ever came it was certain disgrace. When their names were in any way mentioned, "I do not know them," the King would reply haughtily. Those who presented themselves but seldom were thus characterised: "They are people I never see;" these decrees were irrevocable. He could not bear people who liked Paris.

Louis XIV. took great pains to be well informed of all that passed everywhere; in the public places, in the private houses, in society and familiar intercourse. His spies and tell-tales were infinite. He had them of all species; many who were ignorant that their information reached him; others who knew it; others who wrote to him direct, sending their letters through channels he indicated; and all these letters were seen by him alone, and always before everything else; others who sometimes spoke to him secretly in his cabinet, entering by the back stairs. These unknown means ruined an infinite number of people of all classes who never could discover the cause; often ruined them very unjustly; for the King, once prejudiced, never altered his opinion, or so rarely, that nothing was more rare. He had, too, another fault, very dangerous for others and often for himself, since it deprived him of good subjects. He had an excellent memory; in this way, that if he saw a man who, twenty years before, perhaps, had in some manner offended him, he did not forget the man, though he might forget the offence. This was enough, however, to exclude the person from all favour. The representations of a minister, of a general, of his confessor even, could not move the King. He would not yield.

The most cruel means by which the King was informed of what was passing—for many years before anybody knew it—was that of opening letters. The promptitude and dexterity with which they were opened passes understanding. He saw extracts from all the letters in which there were passages that the chiefs of the post-office, and then the minister who governed it, thought ought to go before him; entire letters, too, were sent to him, when their contents seemed to justify the sending. Thus the chiefs of the post, nay, the principal clerks were in a position to suppose what they pleased and against whom they pleased. A word of contempt against the King or the government, a joke, a detached phrase, was enough. It is incredible how many people, justly or unjustly, were more or less ruined, always without resource, without trial, and without knowing why. The secret was impenetrable; for nothing ever cost the King less than profound silence and dissimulation. . . .

He liked splendour, magnificence, and profusion in everything: you pleased him if you shone through the brilliancy of your houses, your clothes, your table, your equipages. Thus a taste for extravagance and luxury was disseminated through all classes of society; causing infinite harm, and leading to general confusion of rank and to ruin.

Discussion Questions

1. How did Louis XIV use court etiquette as a form of power?
2. Why did nobles reside at Versailles? What benefits did they gain?
3. What is Saint-Simon's attitude toward Louis XIV's style of governing?
4. In what ways did court life embody the principles of absolutism?

2
British Parliament
The English Bill of Rights
1689

Louis XIV had many admirers in Europe, including King James II of England. Unlike Louis, however, James faced a major challenge to his power: Parliament. The king and Parliament had been at odds for decades concerning the nature of royal authority, and James's absolutist policies proved too much for Parliament to bear. As a result, in 1688 they ousted the king and offered the throne to Prince William of Orange and his wife, Mary, the eldest of James's adult daughters. In exchange, William and Mary agreed to accept the Bill of Rights, which legally defined the role of Parliament as the monarchy's partner in government. The bill not only marked the victory of constitutionalism over absolutism in England, but it also formed the cornerstone of the idea that government should ensure certain rights by law to protect its citizens from the dangers of arbitrary power.

Whereas the said late King James II having abdicated the government, and the throne being thereby vacant, his Highness the prince of Orange (whom it hath pleased Almighty God to make the glorious instrument of delivering this kingdom from popery and arbitrary power) did (by the advice of the lords spiritual and temporal, and diverse principal persons of the Commons) cause letters to be written to the lords spiritual and temporal, being Protestants, and other letters to the several counties, cities, universities, boroughs, and Cinque Ports, for the choosing of such persons to represent them, as were of right to be sent to parliament, to meet and sit at Westminster upon the two and twentieth day of January, in this year 1689, in order to such an establishment as that their religion, laws, and liberties might not again be in danger of being subverted; upon which letters elections have been accordingly made.

And thereupon the said lords spiritual and temporal and Commons, pursuant to their respective letters and elections, being now assembled in a full and free representation of this nation, taking into their most serious consideration the best means for attaining the ends aforesaid, do in the first place (as their ancestors in like case have usually done), for the vindication and assertion of their ancient rights and liberties, declare:

1. That the pretended power of suspending laws, or the execution of laws, by regal authority, without consent of parliament is illegal.

2. That the pretended power of dispensing with the laws, or the execution of law by regal authority, as it hath been assumed and exercises of late, is illegal.

3. That the commission for erecting the late court of commissioners for ecclesiastical causes, and all other commissions and courts of like nature, are illegal and pernicious.

Great Britain, *The Statutes,* rev. ed. (London: Eyre and Spottiswoode, 1871), vol. II, 10–12.

4. That levying money for or to the use of the crown by pretense of prerogative, without grant of parliament, for longer time or in other manner than the same is or shall be granted, is illegal.

5. That it is the right of the subjects to petition the king, and all commitments and prosecutions for such petitioning are illegal.

6. That the raising or keeping a standing army within the kingdom in time of peace, unless it be with consent of parliament, is against law.

7. That the subjects which are Protestants may have arms for their defense suitable to their conditions, and as allowed by law.

8. That election of members of parliament ought to be free.

9. That the freedom of speech, and debates or proceedings in parliament, ought not to be impeached or questioned in any court or place out of parliament.

10. That excessive bail ought not to be required, nor excessive fines imposed, nor cruel and unusual punishments inflicted.

11. That jurors ought to be duly impaneled and returned, and jurors which pass upon men in trials for high treason ought to be freeholders.

12. That all grants and promises of fines and forfeitures of particular persons before conviction are illegal and void.

13. And that for redress of all grievances, and for the amending, strengthening, and preserving of the laws, parliament ought to be held frequently.

And they do claim, demand, and insist upon all and singular the premises, as their undoubted rights and liberties: and that no declarations, judgments, doings, or proceedings, to the prejudice of the people in any of the said premises, ought in any wise to be drawn hereafter into consequence or example.

To which demand of their rights they are particularly encouraged by the declaration of his Highness the prince of Orange, as being the only means for obtaining a full redress and remedy therein.

Having therefore an entire confidence that his said Highness the prince of Orange will perfect the deliverance so far advanced by him, and will still preserve them from the violation of their rights, which they have here asserted, and from all other attempt upon their religion, rights, and liberties:

The said lords spiritual and temporal, and commons, assembled at Westminster, do resolve that William and Mary, prince and princess of Orange, be, and be declared, king and queen of England, France, and Ireland, the dominions thereunto belonging, to hold the crown and royal dignity of the said kingdoms and dominions to them the said prince and princess during their lives. . . .

Upon which their said Majesties did accept the crown and royal dignity of the kingdoms of England, France, and Ireland, and the dominions thereunto belonging, according to the resolution and desire of the said lords and commons contained in the said declaration.

Discussion Questions

1. In what ways does the bill limit the powers of the crown?
2. What role does the bill grant Parliament in government?
3. How does the Bill of Rights give weight to the attitude of some members of Parliament at the time that they had "made" the king and queen, William and Mary?

3

Ludwig Fabritius
The Revolt of Stenka Razin
1670

Despite its geographical and cultural isolation from the rest of Europe, Russia followed France's lead down the path of absolutism. In the process, Czar Alexei (r. 1645–1676) legally combined millions of slaves and free peasants into a single serf class bound to the land and their aristocratic masters. Not everyone passively accepted this fate, however. In 1667, a Cossak named Stenka Razin led a revolt against serfdom that gained considerable support among people whose social and economic status was threatened by the czar's policies, including soldiers from peasant stock. Razin's ultimate defeat at the hands of the czar elucidates the close ties between the Russian government's enhanced power and the enforcement of serfdom. A Dutch soldier, Ludwig Fabritius, who lived in Russia from 1660 to 1677 while employed as a military expert in the Russian army, wrote the following account of one stage of the revolt.

Then Stenka with his company started off upstream, rowing as far as Tsaritsyn, whence it took him only one day's journey to Panshin, a small town situated on the Don. Here he began straightaway quietly gathering the common people around him, giving them money, and promises of great riches if they would be loyal to him and help to exterminate the treacherous boyars.[1]

This lasted the whole winter, until by about spring he had assembled 4,000 to 5,000 men. With these he came to Tsaritsyn and demanded the immediate surrender of the fortress; the rabble soon achieved their purpose, and although the governor tried to take refuge in a tower, he soon had to give himself up as he was deserted by one and all. Stenka immediately had the wretched governor hanged; and all the goods they found belonging to the Tsar and his officers as well as to the merchants were confiscated and distributed among the rabble.

Stenka now began once more to make preparations. Since the plains are not cultivated, the people have to bring their corn from Nizhniy-Novgorod and Kazan down the Volga in big boats known as *nasady*, and everything destined for Astrakhan has first to pass Tsaritsyn. Stenka Razin duly noted this, and occupied the whole of the Volga, so that nothing could get through to Astrakhan. Here he captured a few hundred merchants with their valuable goods, taking possession of all kinds of fine linen, silks, striped silk material, sables, soft leather, ducats, talers, and many thousands of rubles in Russian money and merchandise of every description. . . .

In the meantime four regiments of *streltsy*[2] were dispatched from Moscow to subdue these brigands. They arrived with their big boats and as they were not used to the water, were easily beaten. Here Stenka Razin gained possession of a

---

[1] **boyars:** Noblemen.
[2] *streltsy:* Sharpshooters.

Anthony Glenn Cross, ed. *Russia under Western Eyes, 1517–1825* (London: Elek Books, 1971), 120–23.

large amount of ammunition and artillery-pieces and everything else he required. While the above-mentioned *streltsy* were sent from Moscow, about 5,000 men were ordered up from Astrakhan by water and by land to capture Stenka Razin. As soon as he had finished with the former, he took up a good position, and, being in possession of reliable information regarding our forces, he left Tsaritsyn and came to meet us half way at Chernyy Yar, confronting us before we had suspected his presence or received any information about him. We stopped at Chernyy Yar for a few days and sent out scouts by water and by land, but were unable to obtain any definite information. On 10 July [*sic*: June] a council of war was held at which it was decided to advance and seek out Stenka. The next morning, at 8 o'clock, our look-outs on the water came hurriedly and raised the alarm as the Cossacks were following at their heels. We got out of our boats and took up battle positions. General Knyaz Semen Ivanovich Lvov went through the ranks and reminded all the men to do their duty and to remember the oath they had taken to His Majesty the Tsar, to fight like honest soldiers against these irresponsible rebels, whereupon they all unanimously shouted: "Yes, we will give our lives for His Majesty the Tsar, and will fight to the last drop of our blood."

In the meantime Stenka prepared for battle and deployed on a wide front; to all those who had no rifle he gave a long pole, burnt a little at one end, and with a rag or small hook attached. They presented a strange sight on the plain from afar, and the common soldiers imagined that, since there were so many flags and standards, there must be a host of people. They [the common soldiers] held a consultation and at once decided that this was the chance for which they had been waiting so long, and with all their flags and drums they ran over to the enemy. They began kissing and embracing one another and swore with life and limb to stand together and to exterminate the treacherous boyars, to throw off the yoke of slavery, and to become free men.

The general looked at the officers and the officers at the general, and no one knew what to do; one said this, and another that, until finally it was decided that they and the general should get into the boats and withdraw to Astrakhan. But the rascally *streltsy* of Chernyy Yar stood on the walls and towers, turning their weapons on us and opened fire; some of them ran out of the fortress and cut us off from the boats, so that we had no means of escape. In the meantime those curs of ours who had gone over to the Cossacks came up from behind. We numbered about eighty men, officers, noblemen, and clerks. Murder at once began. Then, however, Stenka Razin ordered that no more officers were to be killed, saying that there must be a few good men among them who should be pardoned, whilst those others who had not lived in amity with their men should be condemned to well-deserved punishment by the Ataman and his *Krug*. A *Krug* is a meeting convened by the order of the Ataman, at which the Cossacks stand in a circle with the standard in the centre; the Ataman then takes his place beside his best officers, to whom he divulges his wishes, ordering them to make these known to the common brothers and to hear their opinion on the matter]. . . .

A *Krug* was accordingly called and Stenka asked through his chiefs how the general and his officers had treated the soldiers under their command. Thereupon the unscrupulous curs, *streltsy* as well as soldiers, unanimously called out that there was not one of them who deserved to remain alive, and they all asked that their father Stepan Timofeyevich Razin should order them to be cut down. This was granted with the exception of General Knyaz Semen Ivanovich Lvov, whose life was specially spared by Stenka himself. The officers were now brought in order of rank out of the tower, into which they had been thrown bound hand and foot the previous day, their ropes were cut and they were led outside the gate. When all the bloodthirsty curs had lined up, each was eager to deal his former superior the first blow, one with the sword, another with the lance, another with the scimitar, and others again with martels, so that as soon as an officer was pushed into the ring, the curs immediately killed him with their many wounds; indeed, some were cut to pieces and straightaway thrown into the Volga. My stepfather, Paul Rudolf Beem, and Lt. Col. Wundrum and many other officers, senior and junior, were cut down before my eyes.

My own time had not yet come: this I could tell by the wonderful way in which God rescued me, for as I—half-dead—now awaited the final blow, my [former] orderly, a young soldier, came and took me by my bound arms and tried to take me down the hill. As I was already half-dead, I did not move and did not know what to do, but he came back and took me by the arms and led me, bound as I was, through the throng of curs, down the hill into the boat and immediately cut my arms free, saying that I should rest in peace here and that he would be responsible for me and do his best to save my life . . . Then my guardian angel told me not to leave the boat, and left me. He returned in the evening and brought me a piece of bread which I enjoyed since I had had nothing to eat for two days.

The following day all our possessions were looted and gathered together under the main flag, so that both our bloodthirsty curs and the Cossacks got their share.

Discussion Questions

1. What motivated Razin and his followers to take action?
2. Why were Razin and his forces able to defeat the czar's soldiers?
3. What does this account suggest about the role of the military in the growth of the Russian government's authority?
4. With whom do you think Fabritius's sympathies lie, and why?

4

Madame de Lafayette
The Princess of Clèves
1678

Like the Duke of Saint-Simon, French author Marie-Madeline de La Vergne (b. 1634), Countess of Lafayette, was well acquainted with the court of Louis XIV. She also had close ties to intellectual circles in Paris, where she cultivated her formidable writing talents. In 1678, she published anonymously The Princess of Clèves, *which was an overnight literary sensation. The following letters help us to under-*

stand why. *Set during the reign of Henry II, the book centers on the character of Mademoiselle de Chartres, who, upon captivating the court with her wit and beauty, weds the Prince of Clèves. Their union proves an unhappy one, and the princess falls in love with another man, Nemours. She never succumbs to her desire, however, even after her husband's death. The book's portrayal of her emotional struggle scandalized many readers by challenging conventional notions of marriage and proper aristocratic behavior. At the same time, the book abandoned the idealized and lengthy style of the romantic genre, giving birth to a new literary form, the novel.*

Madame de Lafayette to Joseph Marie de Lescheraine

13 April 1678

A little book which appeared fifteen years ago and that people attributed to me makes them want to credit me with *The Princess of Clèves*. But I assure you that I had nothing to do with it and that M. de La Rochefoucauld, to whom the book has also been attributed, had as little to do with it as I did. He declared this under oath so many times that he cannot be doubted, especially about something that could be admitted without shame. As for me, I am flattered that people suspect me of being the author, and I believe that I would acknowledge the book as mine if I could be sure that the author would never show up and ask for it back. I find it a very pleasant work, well written without being perfectly polished, so full of admirably subtle details that it has to be read more than once. And most of all, I find in it a perfect representation of the world of the court and of the way one lives there. The book does not seem like a romance, and there is nothing overdone in it. Assuredly it is not a romance but rather a book of memoirs, and I have been told that such was its title, but they changed it.

So there, Monsieur, is my opinion of *Madame de Clèves*. I would ask yours as well. People are so divided over this book that they could come to blows. Some condemn what others admire in it. So, no matter what you say, don't be afraid of being the only one to say it.

Roger de Bussy-Rabutin to Marie de Sévigné

26 June 1678

But I forgot to tell you that I have finally given *The Princess of Clèves* an impartial reading, not at all prejudiced by the good and bad things people have written. I found the first part admirable; the second didn't seem as good. In the first volume, except a few words that are repeated too often—just a small number— everything is pleasing, everything is natural, nothing is stilted. In the second part, Madame de Clèves's confession is preposterous, and could only be told in a true

---

John D. Lyons, ed. and trans., *Marie-Madeleine de Lafayette*, The Princess of Clèves (New York: Norton, 1994), 121–22.

history; but when one is making a story up it is absurd to depict the heroine as having a sentiment that is so out of the ordinary. The author, by doing so, was thinking of ways to be different from the old romances and was not paying attention to common sense. A wife rarely tells her husband that a man is in love with her and *never* tells her husband that she is in love with another man, and especially not by throwing herself at his feet, a gesture that can make him think she has committed the ultimate offense. Besides, it is implausible that passionate love and virtue should remain for a long time equal in strength. In court society if a woman hasn't completely rejected a suitor in two or three weeks, or at most a month, she is only trying to make herself appear more desirable. And if, against all the odds and in spite of custom, the conflict between love and virtue should last until her husband's death, she would be delighted to harmonize virtue and love by marrying a man of his [Nemours's] quality, the handsomest gallant of his day. The first incident in the gardens at Coulommiers is not plausible and smacks of romance. It is very a calculated arrangement that when the Princess confesses to her husband that she loves another man, M. de Nemours, at just the right moment, is behind the fence listening to them; I don't even see why he had to know her confession, and in any event it should have been arranged so that he learned about [it] in some other way. It's like a romance, as well, when people talk to themselves. Besides the fact that it is not customary for people to talk to themselves, it isn't possible to know what someone says to herself unless she writes her own story: and even then she would say only what she thought. The letter to the Vidame is also like the letters in a romance, obscure, too long, and not at all natural. Just the same, in this second volume everything is just as well narrated, and the turns of phrase are just as beautiful as in the first volume.

Roger de Rabutin, comte de Bussy

DISCUSSION QUESTIONS

1. In seventeenth-century France, it was not deemed proper for noblewomen to publish their writings. In the first letter, how does Madame de Lafayette confront this prejudice and use it to her advantage?
2. Why is Roger de Bussy-Rabutin critical of *The Princess of Clèves*?
3. What do his criticisms suggest about the development of the novel as a new type of literature?

Comparative Questions

1. What do both Saint-Simon and Roger Bussy-Rabutin reveal about court culture during the reign of Louis XIV?
2. Based on the first three documents, how would you describe the relationship between the individual and the state in England, France, and Russia? What similarities and differences do you see?
3. What do these similarities and differences suggest about the basis of authority in constitutional and absolutist governments?

18

The Atlantic System
and Its Consequences
1690–1740

S U M M A R Y   The growth of European domestic economies and overseas colonization in the eighteenth century infused Europe with money,
new products, and a new sense of optimism about the future. Yet, as the
first document illustrates, the good times came at a horrible price for the millions of African slaves who formed the economic backbone of the colonial system. Changes were afoot on the political front, too, with the stabilization of the
European state system. Consequently, states such as Russia shone more brightly
over the political landscape while others lost their luster. The second document
brings Russia's new prominence to life in its leader's own words. The third and
fourth documents reveal that intellectual circles were also ablaze with change as
scholars and writers cast political, social, and religious issues in a new, critical
light. Even women's traditional place in society was for the first time systemati-
cally called into question.

1
Olaudah Equiano
The Interesting Narrative of the Life of Olaudah Equiano
Written by Himself
1789

*The autobiography of Olaudah Equiano (c. 1745–1797) puts a human face on the
eighteenth-century Atlantic slave trade and its tragic consequences. Born in what is
now Nigeria, Equiano was captured by local raiders and sold into slavery in his early
teens. He gained his freedom in 1766 and soon thereafter became a vocal supporter
of the English abolitionist movement. Having learned English as a young man, he
published his autobiography in 1789, a best-seller in its day, with numerous editions*

published in Britain and America. In the following excerpt, Equiano recounts his experience on the slave ship that took him away from his homeland, his freedom, and his very identity. Millions of others shared this same fate.

The first object which saluted my eyes when I arrived on the coast was the sea, and a slave ship which was then riding at anchor and waiting for its cargo. These filled me with astonishment, which was soon converted into terror when I was carried on board. I was immediately handled and tossed up to see if I were sound by some of the crew, and I was now persuaded that I had gotten into a world of bad spirits and that they were going to kill me. Their complexions too differing so much from ours, their long hair and the language they spoke (which was very different from any I had ever heard) united to confirm me in this belief. Indeed such were the horrors of my views and fears at the moment that, if ten thousand worlds had been my own, I would have freely parted with them all to have exchanged my condition with that of the meanest slave in my own country. When I looked round the ship too and saw a large furnace or copper boiling and a multitude of black people of every description chained together, every one of their countenances expressing dejection and sorrow, I no longer doubted of my fate; and quite overpowered with horror and anguish, I fell motionless on the deck and fainted. When I recovered a little I found some black people about me, who I believed were some of those who had brought me on board and had been receiving their pay; they talked to me in order to cheer me, but all in vain. I asked them if we were not to be eaten by those white men with horrible looks, red faces, and loose hair. They told me I was not, and one of the crew brought me a small portion of spirituous liquor in a wine glass, but being afraid of him I would not take it out of his hand. One of the blacks therefore took it from him and gave it to me, and I took a little down my palate, which instead of reviving me, as they thought it would, threw me into the greatest consternation at the strange feeling it produced, having never tasted such any liquor before. Soon after this the blacks who brought me on board went off, and left me abandoned to despair.

I now saw myself deprived of all chance of returning to my native country or even the least glimpse of hope of gaining the shore, which I now considered as friendly; and I even wished for my former slavery in preference to my present situation, which was filled with horrors of every kind, still heightened by my ignorance of what I was to undergo. I was not long suffered to indulge my grief; I was soon put down under the decks, and there I received such a salutation in my nostrils as I had never experienced in my life: so that with the loathsomeness of the stench and crying together, I became so sick and low that I was not able to eat, nor had I the least desire to taste anything. I now wished for the last friend, death, to relieve me; but soon, to my grief, two of the white men offered me eatables, and on my refusing to eat, one of them held me fast by the hands and laid me across I

Abridged and Edited by Paul Edwards, *Equiano's Travels: His Autobiography* (London: Heinemann, 1967), 25–32.

think the windlass, and tied my feet while the other flogged me severely. I had never experienced anything of this kind before, and although, not being used to the water, I naturally feared that element the first time I saw it, yet nevertheless could I have got over the nettings I would have jumped over the side, but I could not; and besides, the crew used to watch us very closely who were not chained down to the decks, lest we should leap into the water: and I have seen some of these poor African prisoners most severely cut for attempting to do so, and hourly whipped for not eating. This indeed was often the case with myself. In a little time after, amongst the poor chained men I found some of my own nation, which in a small degree gave ease to my mind. I inquired of these what was to be done with us; they gave me to understand we were to be carried to these white people's country to work for them. I then was a little revived, and thought if it were no worse than working, my situation was not so desperate: but still I feared I should be put to death, the white people looked and acted, as I thought, in so savage a manner; for I had never seen among my people such instances of brutal cruelty, and this not only shewn towards us blacks but also to some of the whites themselves. One white man in particular I saw, when we were permitted to be on deck, flogged so unmercifully with a large rope near the foremast that he died in consequence of it; and they tossed him over the side as they would have done a brute. This made me fear these people the more, and I expected nothing less than to be treated in the same manner. . . . At last, when the ship we were in had got in all her cargo, they made ready with many fearful noises, and we were all put under deck so that we could not see how they managed the vessel. But this disappointment was the last of my sorrow. The stench of the hold while we were on the coast was so intolerably loathsome that it was dangerous to remain there for any time, and some of us had been permitted to stay on the deck for the fresh air; but now that the whole ship's cargo were confined together it became absolutely pestilential. The closeness of the place and the heat of the climate, added to the number in the ship, which was so crowded that each had scarcely room to turn himself, almost suffocated us. This produced copious perspirations, so that the air soon became unfit for respiration from a variety of loathsome smells, and brought on a sickness among the slaves, of which many died, thus falling victims to the improvident avarice, as I may call it, of their purchasers. This wretched situation was again aggravated by the galling of the chains, now become insupportable, and the filth of the necessary tubs, into which the children often fell and were almost suffocated. The shrieks of the women and the groans of the dying rendered the whole a scene of horror almost inconceivable. Happily perhaps for myself I was soon reduced so low here that it was thought necessary to keep me almost always on deck, and from my extreme youth I was not put in fetters. In this situation I expected every hour to share the fate of my companions, some of whom were almost daily brought upon deck at the point of death, which I began to hope would soon put an end to my miseries. . . . At last we came in sight of the island of Barbados, at which the whites on board gave a great shout and made many signs of joy to us. We did not know what to think of this, but as the vessel drew nearer we plainly saw the harbour and other ships of different kinds and sizes, and we soon anchored amongst them off Bridgetown. Many merchants and planters now came on board, though it was in the evening. They put us in separate parcels and examined us attentively. They also made us jump, and pointed to the land, signifying we were to go there. . . . We were not many days in the merchant's custody before we were sold after their usual manner, which is this: On a signal given, (as the beat of a drum) the buyers rush at once into the yard where the slaves are confined, and make choice of that parcel they like best. The noise and clamour with which this is attended and the eagerness visible in the countenances of the buyers serve not a little to increase the apprehensions of the terrified Africans, who may well be supposed to consider them as the ministers of that destruction to which they think themselves devoted. In this manner, without scruple, are relations and friends separated, most of them never to see each other again. I remember in the vessel in which I was brought over, in the men's apartment there were several brothers who, in the sale, were sold in different lots; and it was very moving on this occasion to see and hear their cries at parting. O, ye nominal Christians! might not an African ask you, Learned you this from your God who says unto you, Do unto all men as you would men should do unto you?

DISCUSSION QUESTIONS

1. What are Equiano's impressions of the white men on the ship and their treatment of the slaves?
2. How does this treatment reflect the slave traders' primary concerns?
3. What message do you think Equiano sought to convey to his readers?
4. Based on this message, to whom do you think his book especially appealed?

2

Tsar Peter I
Letter to his Son, Alexei
October 11, 1715,
and Alexei's Response
October 31, 1715

In the eighteenth century, European states turned much of their attention to the political and military scene burgeoning within Europe, vying to keep one step ahead of their rivals. Tsar Peter I of Russia was especially successful at this game. During his rule from 1689 to 1725, he transformed Russia into a great European power with all the trappings of a Western absolutist state, including a strong army and centralized bureaucracy. Peter wrote the following letter to Alexei, who was then his only son and heir, during the Great Northern War against Sweden, which Peter ultimately won to Russia's great advantage. The letter elucidates the tsar's relentless drive toward greatness on the European stage. Alexei's response reveals not only the striking differences in personality between the two men, but also the tension that marked their tumultuous relationship.

[Peter to Alexis, October 11, 1715:]

Declaration to my son:

Everyone knows how, before the beginning of this war, our people were hemmed in by the Swedes, who not only stole the essential ports of our fatherland . . . but cut us off from communication with the whole world. And also later, in the beginning of this war (which enterprise was and is directed by God alone), oh, what great persecution we had to endure from those eternal enemies of ours because of our incompetence in the art of war, and with what sorrow and endurance we went to this school and, with the help of the above-mentioned guide, achieved a creditable degree [of effectiveness]. We were thus found worthy of looking on this enemy now trembling before us, trembling, perhaps, even more than we did before him. All this has been accomplished with the help of God through my modest labors and through those of other equally zealous and faithful sons of Russia.

However, when, considering this great blessing given by God to our fatherland, I think of my successor, a grief perhaps as strong as my joy gnaws me, when I see you, my heir, unfit for the management of state affairs (for it is not the fault of God, who has not deprived you of mind or health; for although not of a very strong constitution, you are not very weak either). But above all, you have no wish to hear anything about military affairs, which opened to us the way from darkness to light, so that we who were unknown before are now honored. I do not teach you to be inclined to wage war without a just cause, but to love this art and to endow and learn it by all means, for it is one of the two activities necessary for government: order and defense.

I have no wish to give you many examples, but I will mention only the Greeks, who are of the same religion as we. Did they not perish because they laid their arms aside, and were they not vanquished because of their peaceableness? Desirous of tranquil living, they always gave way to their enemy, who changed their tranquillity into endless servitude to tyrants. Perhaps you think that it can all be left to the generals; but this is really not so, for everyone looks up to his chief, to comply with his desires, which is an obvious fact. Thus, in the days of my brother's reign [Theodore, 1676–82], everyone liked clothes and horses above all things, and now they like arms. They may not be really interested in one or the other; but in what the chief is interested all take an interest, and to what he is indifferent, all are indifferent. And if they turn away so lightly from the frivolous pastimes, which are only a pleasure to man, how much more easily will they abandon so burdensome a game as war!

Furthermore, you do not learn anything because you have no desire to learn it, and you have no knowledge of military affairs. Lacking all knowledge, how can you direct these affairs? How can you reward the diligent and punish the negli-

---

A Source Book for Russian History From Early Times to 1917 (New Haven and London: Yale University Press, 1972), vol. II, 338–39.

gent when you yourself do not understand their work? You will be forced to look into people's mouths like a young bird. Do you pretend to be unfit for military work because of weak health? But that is no reason. I ask of you not work, but good will, which no malady can destroy. Ask anyone who remembers my brother whom I spoke of but now, who was, beyond comparison, sicklier than you and could not ride spirited horses, but he had a great liking for them and was always looking at them and kept them before his eyes. . . . So you see, not everything is done by great labor, but also by a strong desire. You say to yourself, perhaps, that many rulers do not themselves go to war, and yet campaigns are still carried on. This is true when, although not going themselves, they have a desire for it, as had the late French king [Louis XIV], who went to war himself but little, and who yet had a great taste for it and showed such magnificent deeds in war that his wars were called the theater and school for the whole world. But he had a taste not only for war, but also for other affairs and for manufactures, through all of which he procured glory for his state more than anybody else.

Now that I have gone into all this, I return again to my original point, thinking of you. I am a man, and subject to death. To whom shall I leave all this sowing, done with God's help, and that harvest which has already grown? To one who, like the idle slave in the Gospel, buried his talent in the ground (which means that he threw away everything that God had given him)? I also keep thinking of your wicked and stubborn disposition; for how many times I used to scold you for that, and not only scold but beat you, and also how many years I have now gone without speaking to you, and all without success! . . .

I have pondered this with much grief, and, seeing that I can in no wise dispose you toward good, I have deemed it appropriate to write to you this last admonition, and to wait a short time for you to mend your ways, and that *not hypocritically* [Peter's emphasis]. If you do not, know that I shall totally disinherit you like a gangrenous member; and do not imagine that, because you are my only son, I write this only to frighten you; I will do it indeed (with God's consent), because I have never spared my own life for my fatherland and people, nor do I now; therefore how can I spare you, unworthy one? Better a good stranger than an unworthy kinsman.

Peter
October 11, 1715
Saint Petersburg

[Alexis to Peter, October 31, 1715:]

Most gracious sovereign and father:

I have read [the letter] that was given me on your behalf on October 27, 1715, after the funeral of my wife. I have nothing to say about it, except that if you wish to disinherit me of the Russian crown because of my worthlessness, let it be as you will. Most humbly I ask you for this very thing, Sire, for I consider myself unqualified and unfit for this task, being most deficient in memory (without which it is impossible to accomplish anything). All my mental and physical capacities are weakened by various illnesses, and I have become unfit to rule such a people, which task requires a man less rotten than I. Therefore, I do not make a claim, nor will I make claim in the future, to the inheritance of the Russian throne after you—God give you health for many years—even if I did not have a brother (but now, thank God, I have one [note: Prince Peter, born to Peter and Catherine on October 29, 1715], God give him health); let God be my witness [in this matter], and to show that I testify truthfully I write this with my own hand.

I entrust my children to your will and ask only for maintenance for myself to the end of my life. This is submitted to your decision and merciful will.

Your most humble slave and son Alexis
Saint Petersburg
October 31, 1715

DISCUSSION QUESTIONS

1. Why does Peter regard the "art of war" as so important to government, and what did he gain by practicing it?
2. Why is Peter so critical of his son?
3. Whom does Peter single out as a political role model, and why is this significant?
4. What do these letters reveal about the tsar's personality?

3

Montesquieu
Persian Letters: Letter 37
1721

As Europe's economy expanded, so did its intellectual horizons with the birth of the Enlightenment in the 1690s. Charles-Louis de Secondat, Baron of Montesquieu (1689–1755), was an especially important literary figure on this front. In 1721 he published Persian Letters, *in which he uses fictional characters to explore an array of topics with the critical, reasoning spirit characteristic of the period. Letter 37 points to one of his and other Enlightenment writers' main targets: Louis XIV and his absolutist state. Along with its criticism of the king's vanity, ostentation, and life at court, the letter implicitly passes even more serious judgment on the aging ruler in noting his esteem for "oriental policies." Montesquieu condemns these same policies elsewhere in the letters as inhumane and unjust.*

Usbek to Ibben, at Smyrna

The King of France is old.[1] We have no examples in our histories of such a long reign as his. It is said that he possesses in a very high degree the faculty of making himself obeyed: he governs with equal ability his family, his court, and his king-

---

[1] Louis XIV. was then seventy-five years old, and had reigned for seventy. [All notes are Davidson's.]

Montesquieu, *Persian Letters*, vol. I, trans. John Davidson (London: Privately printed, 1892), 85–86.

dom: he has often been heard to say, that, of all existing governments, that of the Turks, or that of our august Sultan, pleased him best: such is his high opinion of Oriental statecraft.[2]

I have studied his character, and I have found certain contradictions which I cannot reconcile. For example, he has a minister who is only eighteen years old,[3] and a mistress who is fourscore;[4] he loves his religion, and yet he cannot abide those who assert that it ought to be strictly observed;[5] although he flies from the noise of cities, and is inclined to be reticent, from morning till night he is engaged in getting himself talked about; he is fond of trophies and victories, but he has as great a dread of seeing a good general at the head of his own troops, as at the head of an army of his enemies. It has never I believe happened to anyone but himself, to be burdened with more wealth than even a prince could hope for, and yet at the same time steeped in such poverty as a private person could ill brook.

He delights to reward those who serve him; but he pays as liberally the assiduous indolence of his courtiers, as the labours in the field of his captains; often the man who undresses him, or who hands him his serviette at table, is preferred before him who has taken cities and gained battles; he does not believe that the greatness of a monarch is compatible with restriction in the distribution of favours; and, without examining into the merit of a man, he will heap benefits upon him, believing that his selection makes the recipient worthy; accordingly, he has been known to bestow a small pension upon a man who had run off two leagues from the enemy, and a good government on another who had gone four.

Above all, he is magnificent in his buildings; there are more statues in his palace gardens[6] than there are citizens in a large town. His bodyguard is as strong as that of the prince before whom all the thrones of the earth tremble;[7] his armies are as numerous, his resources as great, and his finances as inexhaustible.

Paris, the 7th of the moon of Maharram, 1713.

Discussion Questions

1. What contradictions does Usbek see in Louis's character, and what do they reveal about his method of rule?

---

[2] When Louis XIV. was in his sixteenth year, some courtiers discussed in his presence the absolute power of the Sultans, who dispose as they like of the goods and the lives of their subjects. "That is something like being a king," said the young monarch. Marshal d'Estrées, alarmed at the tendency revealed in that remark, rejoined, "But, sire, several of these emperors have been strangled even in my time."

[3] Barbezieux, son of Louvois, Louis's youngest minister, held office at twenty-three, not eighteen; and he was dead in 1713.

[4] Madame de Maintenon.

[5] The Jansenists.

[6] At Versailles.

[7] The Shah of Persia.

2. In what ways does this letter reflect Montesquieu's general interest in the foundation of good government?

3. Based on this letter, why do you think that scholars regard Montesquieu as a herald of the Enlightenment?

4

Mary Astell
Reflections upon Marriage
1706

Like Montesquieu, English author Mary Astell (1666–1731) helped to usher in the Enlightenment by surveying society with a critical eye. First published anonymously in 1700, Reflections upon Marriage *is one of her best-known books; it shows her keen interest in the institution of marriage, education, and relations between the sexes. Only the third edition (1706) divulged her gender, but still not her name. As the following excerpt reveals, Astell held a dim view of women's inequality in general and of their submissive role in marriage in particular. She argues that one should abhor the use of arbitrary power within the state, and so, too, within the family. Among the book's principal goals was to present spinsterhood as a viable alternative to marriage. Perhaps not surprisingly, Astell herself never married.*

These Reflections being made in the Country, where the Book that occasion'd them came but late to Hand, the *Reader* is desir'd to excuse their Unseasonableness as well as other Faults; and to believe that they have no other Design than to Correct some Abuses, which are not the less because Power and Prescription seem to Authorize them. If any are so needlessly curious as to enquire from what Hand they come, they may please to know, that it is not good Manners to ask, since the Title-Page does not tell them: We are all of us sufficiently Vain, and without doubt the Celebrated Name of *Author*, which most are so fond of, had not been avoided but for very good Reasons: To name but one; *Who will care to pull upon themselves an Hornet's nest?* 'Tis a very great Fault to regard rather who it is that Speaks, than what is Spoken; and either to submit to Authority, when we should only yield to Reason; or if Reason press too hard, to think to ward it off by Personal Objections and Reflections. Bold Truths may pass while the Speaker is Incognito, but are not endur'd when he is known; few Minds being strong enough to bear what Contradicts their Principles and Practices without Recriminating when they can. And tho' to tell the Truth be the most Friendly Office, yet whosoever is so hardy as to venture at it, shall be counted an Enemy for so doing.

Bridget Hill, ed., *The First English Feminist:* Reflections upon Marriage *and Other Writings by Mary Astell* (New York: St. Martin's Press, 1986), 69–76.

Thus far the old Advertisement, when the Reflections first appear'd, A.D.1700.

But the *Reflector*, who hopes *Reflector* is not bad English, now Governor is happily of the feminine Gender, had as good or better have said nothing; For People by being forbid, are only excited to a more curious Enquiry. A certain Ingenuous Gentleman (as she is inform'd) had the Good-Nature to own these Reflections, so far as to affirm that he had the Original M.S. in his Closet, a Proof she is not able to produce;[1] and so to make himself responsible for all their Faults, for which she returns him all due Acknowledgment. However, the Generality being of Opinion, that a Man would have had more Prudence and Manners than to have Publish'd such unseasonable Truths, or to have betray'd the *Arcana Imperii* of his Sex, she humbly confesses, that the Contrivance and Execution of this Design, which is unfortunately accus'd of being so destructive to the government, of the Men I mean, is entirely her own. She neither advis'd with Friends, nor turn'd over Antient or Modern Authors, nor prudently submitted to the Correction of such as are, or such as *think* they are good Judges, but with an *English* Spirit and Genius, set out upon the Forlorn Hope, meaning no hurt to any body, nor designing any thing but the Publick Good, and to retrieve, if possible, the Native Liberty, the Rights and Privileges of the Subject.

Far be it from her to stir up Sedition of any sort, none can abhor it more; and she heartily wishes that our Masters wou'd pay their Civil and Ecclesiastical Governors the same Submission, which they themselves extract from their Domestic Subjects. Nor can she imagine how she any way undermines the Masculine Empire, or blows the Trumpet of Rebellion to the Moiety of Mankind. Is it by exhorting Women, not to expect to have their own Will in any thing, but to be entirely Submissive, when once they have made choice of a Lord and Master, tho' he happen not to be so Wise, so Kind, or even so Just a Governor as was expected? She did not indeed advise them to think his Folly Wisdom, nor his Brutality that Love and Worship he promised in his Matrimonial Oath, for this required a Flight of Wit and Sense much above her poor Ability, and proper only to Masculine Understandings. However she did not in any manner prompt them to Resist, or to Abdicate the Perjur'd Spouse, tho' the Laws of GOD and the Land make special Provision for it, in a case wherein, as is to be fear'd, few Men can truly plead Not Guilty.

Tis true, thro' Want of Learning, and of that Superior Genius which Men as Men lay claim to, she was ignorant of the *Natural Inferiority* of our Sex, which our Masters lay down as a Self-Evident and Fundamental Truth.[2] She saw nothing in the Reason of Things, to make this either a Principle or a Conclusion, but much to the contrary; it being Sedition at least, if not Treason to assert it in this Reign. For if by the Natural Superiority of their Sex, they mean that every Man is

---

[1] Alas, Mary Astell never revealed the identity of this 'Ingenuous Gentleman'. [All notes are Hill's.]

[2] Possibly a reference to William Nichols, D.D., *The Duty of Inferiours Towards their Superiours in Five Practical Discourses*, 1701, in which he argued that man possesses "a higher state of natural perfection and dignity, and thereupon puts in a just claim of superiority, which everything which is of more worth has a right to, over that which has less" (pp. 87–88).

by Nature superior to every Woman, which is the obvious meaning, and that which must be stuck to if they would speak Sense, it wou'd be a Sin in *any* Woman to have Dominion over *any* Man, and the greatest Queen ought not to command but to obey her Footman, because no Municipal Laws can supersede or change the Law of Nature; so that if the dominion of the Men be such, the *Salique Law*, as unjust as *English Men* have ever thought it, ought to take place over all the Earth, and the most glorious Reigns in the *English, Danish, Castilian*, and other Annals, were wicked Violations of the Law of Nature!

If they mean that *some* Men are superior to *some* Women, this is no great Discovery; had they turn'd the Tables they might have seen that *some* Women are Superior to *some* Men. Or had they been pleased to remember their Oaths of Allegiance and Supremacy, they might have known that *One* Woman is superior to *All* the Men in these Nations, or else they have sworn to very little purpose. And it must not be suppos'd, that their Reason and Religion wou'd suffer them to take Oaths, contrary to the Law of Nature and Reason of things.

By all which it appears, that our Reflector's Ignorance is very pitiable, it may be her Misfortune but not her Crime, especially since she is willing to be better inform'd, and hopes she shall never be so obstinate as to shut her Eyes against the Light of Truth, which is not to be charg'd with Novelty, how late soever we may be bless'd with the Discovery. Nor can Error, be it as Antient as it may, ever plead Prescription against Truth. And since the only way to remove all Doubts, to answer all Objections, and to give the Mind entire Satisfaction, is not by *Affirming*, but by *Proving*, so that every one may see with their *own* Eyes, and Judge according to the best of their *own* Understandings, She hopes it is no Presumption to insist on this Natural Right of Judging for her self, and the rather, because by quitting it, we give up all the Means of Rational Conviction. Allow us then as many Glasses as you please to help our Sight, and as many good Arguments as you can afford to Convince our Understandings: But don't exact of us we beseech you, to affirm that we see such things as are only the Discovery of Men who have quicker Senses; or that we understand and Know what we have by Hearsay only, for to be so excessively Complaisant, is neither to see nor to understand.

That the Custom of the World has put Women, generally speaking, into a State of Subjection, is not deny'd; but the Right can no more be prov'd from the Fact, than the Predominancy of Vice can justifie it. A certain great Man has endeavour'd to prove by Reasons not contemptible, that in the Original State of things the Woman was the Superior, and that her Subjection to the Man is an Effect of the Fall, and the Punishment of her Sin. And that Ingenious Theorist Mr. *Whiston*[3] asserts, That before the Fall there was a greater equality between the two Sexes. However this be 'tis certainly no Arrogance in a Woman to conclude, that she was made for the Service of GOD, and that this is her End. Because GOD

---

[3] William Whiston (1667–1752), divine, mathematician and Newtonian. Author of many works including *A New Theory of the Earth* (1696). He succeeded Newton as the Lucasian Professor and did much to popularise Newton's ideas. In 1710 he was deprived of his chair for casting doubt on the doctrine of the Trinity.

made all Things for Himself, and a Rational Mind is too noble a Being to be Made for the Sake and Service of any Creature. The Service she at any time becomes oblig'd to pay to a Man, is only a Business by the Bye. Just as it may be any Man's Business and Duty to keep Hogs; he was not Made for this, but if he hires himself out to such an Employment, he ought conscientiously to perform it. Nor can anything be concluded to the contrary from St. *Paul's* Argument, *I Cor. II.* For he argues only for Decency and Order, according to the present Custom and State of things. Taking his Words strictly and literally, they prove too much, in that *Praying and Prophecying in the Church* are allow'd the Women, provided they do it with their Head Cover'd, as well as the Men; and no inequality can be inferr'd from hence, their Reverence to the Sacred Oracles who engage them in such Disputes. And therefore the blame be theirs, who have unnecessarily introduc'd them in the present Subject, and who by saying that the *Reflections* were not agreeable to Scripture, oblige the Reflector to shew that those who affirm it must either mistake her Meaning, or the Sense of Holy Scripture, or both, if they think what they say, and do not find fault merely because they resolve to do so. For had she ever writ any thing contrary to those sacred Truths, she wou'd be the first in pronouncing its Condemnation.

But what says the Holy Scripture? It speaks of Women as in a State of Subjection, and so it does of the *Jews* and *Christians* when under the Dominion of the *Chaldeans* and *Romans*, requiring of the one as well as of the other a quiet submission to them under whose Power they liv'd. But will any one say that these had a *Natural Superiority* and Right to Dominion? that they had a superior Understanding, or any Pre-eminence, except what their greater Strength acquir'd? Or that the other were subjected to their Adversaries for any other Reason but the Punishment of their sins, and in order to their Reformation? Or for the Exercise of their Vertue, and because the Order of the World and the Good of Society requir'd it?

If Mankind had never sinn'd, Reason wou'd always have been obey'd, there wou'd have been no struggle for Dominion, and Brutal Power wou'd not have prevail'd. But in the laps'd State of Mankind, and now that Men will not be guided by their Reason but by their Appetites, and do not what they *ought* but what they *can*, the Reason, or that which stands for it, the Will and Pleasure of the Governor is to be the Reason of those who will not be guided by their own, and must take place for Order's sake, altho' it shou'd not be conformable to right Reason. Nor can there be any Society great or little, from Empires down to private Families, with a last Resort, to determine the Affairs of that Society by an irresistible Sentence. Now unless this Supremacy be fix'd somewhere, there will be a perpetual Contention about it, such is the love of Dominion, and let the Reason of things be what it may, those who have least Force, or Cunning to supply it, will have the Disadvantage. So that since Women are acknowledg'd to have least Bodily strength, their being commanded to obey is in pure kindness to them and for their Quiet and Security, as well as for the Exercise of their Vertue. But does it follow that Domestic Governors have more Sense than their Subjects, any more than that other Governors have? We do not find that any Man thinks the worse of his own Understanding because another has superior Power; or concludes himself less capable of a Post of Honour and Authority, because he is not Prefer'd to it. How much time wou'd lie on Men's hands, how empty wou'd the Places of Concourse be, and how silent most Companies, did Men forbear to Censure their Governors, that is in effect to think themselves Wiser. Indeed Government wou'd be much more desirable than it is, did it invest the Possessor with a superior Understanding as well as Power. And if mere Power gives a Right to Rule, there can be no such thing as Usurpation; but a Highway-Man so long as he has strength to force, has also a Right to require our Obedience.

Again, if Absolute Sovereignty be not necessary in a State, how comes it to be so in a family? or if in a Family why not in a State; since no Reason can be alledg'd for the one that will not hold more strongly for the other? If the Authority of the Husband so far as it extends, is sacred and inalienable, why not of the Prince? The Domestic Sovereign is without Dispute Elected, and the Stipulations and Contract are mutual, is it not then partial in Men to the last degree, to contend for, and practise that Arbitrary Dominion in their Families, which they abhor and exclaim against in the State? For if Arbitrary Power is evil in itself, and an improper Method of Governing Rational and Free Agents, it ought not to be Practis'd any where; Nor is it less, but rather more mischievous in Families than in Kingdoms, by how much 100000 Tyrants are worse than one. What tho' a Husband can't deprive a Wife of Life without being responsible to the Law, he may however do what is much more grievous to a generous Mind, render Life miserable, for which she has no Redress, scarce Pity which is afforded to every other Complaintant. It being thought a Wife's Duty to suffer everything without Complaint. *If all Men are born free*, how is it that all Women are born slaves? as they must be if the being subjected to the *inconstant, uncertain, unknown, arbitrary Will* of Men, be the *perfect Condition of Slavery*? and if the Essence of Freedom consists, as our Masters say it does, in having a *standing Rule to live by*? And why is Slavery so much condemn'd and strove against in one Case, and so highly applauded, and held so necessary and so sacred in another?

DISCUSSION QUESTIONS

1. According to Mary Astell, what is women's customary status in society, and why?
2. What evidence does Astell present to challenge this status?
3. What does the language Astell uses reveal about her style of thinking and basic intellectual beliefs?
4. Why do you think scholars characterize *Reflections upon Marriage* as a "feminist" work?

COMPARATIVE QUESTIONS

1. Both Louis XIV and Peter I have been described as "absolute" rulers. Do the documents support this claim? If so, how?
2. In what ways does Astell's discussion of the evils of arbitrary power foreshadow Montesquieu's concerns?
3. Although *Persian Letters* and *Equiano's Travels* belong to different literary genres, how do they adopt similar methods to describe eighteenth-century Europeans and their customs?

Acknowledgments

Chapter 1 King Hammurabi. Excerpts from "The Code of Hammurabi, Early Eighteenth Century B.C." (pp. 164–178) in *Ancient Near Eastern Texts Relating to the Old Testament*, edited by James B. Pritchard. Copyright © 1969 by Princeton University Press. Reprinted with the permission of the publishers.

"The Book of Exodus, Tenth–Sixth Centuries B.C." (Chapters 19–24, pp. 67–72) from *The Holy Bible*, authorized King James Version. Copyright © 1960 by Oxford University Press. Reprinted with the permission of Oxford University Press.

Marion Lichtheim. Excerpts from "Papyrus Lansing: A Schoolbook Twelfth Century B.C." (pp. 168–172) in *Ancient Egyptian Literature, A Book of Readings*, Vol. II: *The New Kingdom*. Copyright © 1973–1980 by the Regents of the University of California. Reprinted with the permission of the University of California Press.

"Daily Prayer of the Hittite King, 1750 B.C." (pp. 396–397) from *Ancient Near Eastern Texts Relating to the Old Testament*, third edition, edited by James B. Pritchard. Copyright © 1969 by Princeton University Press. Reprinted with the permission of the publishers.

Chapter 2 "Inscription Honoring Cyrus, King of Persia, r.c.557–500 B.C." (pp. 315–316) from *Ancient Near Eastern Texts Relating to the Old Testament*, third edition, edited by James B. Pritchard. Copyright © 1969 by Princeton University Press. Reprinted with the permission of the publishers.

Tyrtaeus of Sparta and Solon of Athens. "Exhortation to the Young Hoplite, 7–6th Centuries B.C." (pp. 23–26) from *The Greek Polis*, edited by Arthur W. H. Adkins and Peter White. Copyright © 1986 by The University of Chicago. Reprinted with the permission of The University of Chicago Press.

"The Foundation of Cyrene, late 7th Century B.C." (pp. 22–23) from *Archaic Times to the End of the Peloponnesian War*, edited and translated by Charles W. Fornara. Copyright © 1977. Reprinted with the permission of The Johns Hopkins University Press.

Sappho of Lesbos "To Aphrodite," "When I look at you," "Anactoria," "Parting," "Remembering the girl Atthis," and "The wedding of Hector and Andromache" 6th Century B.C. (pp. 2–4) from *Women's Life in Greece & Rome*, second edition, edited by Mary R. Lefkowitz and Maureen B. Fant. Copyright © 1992. Reprinted with the permission of The Johns Hopkins University Press.

Chapter 3 Thucydides. Excerpt from "The Funeral Speech 429 B.C." (pp. 65–72) from *Thucydides, The Peloponnesian Wars*, translated by Benjamin Jowett, revised and abridged by P. A. Brunt. Copyright © 1963. Reprinted with the permission of Simon & Schuster, Inc.

Plato. "The Apology of Socrates," 399 B.C. (pp. 5–14, 21–24, 39–40) from *Dialogues of Plato*, translated by Benjamin Jowett and edited by J. D. Kaplan. Copyright © 1950. Reprinted with the permission of Pocket Books, a division of Simon & Schuster.

"Building Accounts of the Parthenon 434–433 B.C." & "Inventory of its Treasures 422–421 B.C." (pp. 132–134 & 159–160) from *Archaic Times to the End of the Peloponnesian War*, edited and translated by Charles W. Fornara. Copyright © 1977. Reprinted with the permission of The Johns Hopkins University Press.

Euphiletus. Excerpts from "On the Killing of Eratosthenes the Seducer c. 400 B.C." (pp. 43–52) excerpt from *The Murder of Herodes and Other Trials from the Athenian Law Courts* by Kathleen Freeman. Copyright © 1946. Reprinted with the permission of Hackett Publishing Company. All rights reserved.

Chapter 4 Arrian. Excerpt from "Mutiny at Opis 2nd Century A.D." (pp. 360–366) from *The Campaigns of Alexander*, translated by Aubrey de Selincourt, revised by J.R. Hamilton.

Copyright © 1958 by Aubrey de Selincourt. Reprinted with the permission of Penguin Books, Ltd.

Zenon. "Letters 88, 89, 90, 92, and 93; Memoranda 170, and 171; Agenda 179, and 180; Accounts and Lists 181, and 182, 259–250 B.C." (pp. 269–277, 297–399, 409–415) excerpt from *Select Papyri, Volume I: Private Affairs,* translated by A. S. Hunt and C. C. Edgar. Reprinted with the permission of Routledge.

Polybius. 2nd Century B.C. (pp. 383–387) excerpt from *Polybius: The Histories,* translated by W. R. Paton, vol. VI. Copyright © 1960. Reprinted with the permission of Harvard University Press.

"Funerary Inscriptions and Epitaphs, 5th–1st Centuries B.C." (pp. 16–17, 190, 206, 219, 221–222, 263, 266–267, 274) excerpts from *Women's Life in Greece & Rome: A source book in translation,* 2nd edition, edited by Mary R. Lefkowitz & Maureen B. Fant. Copyright © 1992. Reprinted with the permission of The Johns Hopkins University Press.

Chapter 5 Excerpts from "The Twelve Tables, 451–449 B.C." (pp. 9–17) from *Ancient Roman Statutes,* translated by Allan Chester Johnson, Paul Robinson Coleman-Norton, Frank Card Bourne. Copyright © 1961. Reprinted with the permission of the University of Texas Press.

Livy. "Roman Women Demonstrate against the Oppian Law, 195 B.C." Excerpts from *Livy: Volume IX,* Loeb Classical Library Volume #L295, translated by Evan T. Sage, Cambridge, Mass: Harvard University Press, 1935. The Loeb Classical Library® is a registered trademark of the President and Fellows of Harvard College. Reprinted with the permission of the publishers and The Trustees of the Loeb Classical Library.

Cicero. "On the Commonwealth, 54 B.C." (pp. 381–388) excerpts from *The Treatises of M.T. Cicero or The Nature of the Gods; on Divination; On Fate; On the Republic; On the Laws; and On Standard for the Consulship,* translated and edited by C. D. Yonge. Published by Henry G. Bohn (1853).

"The Gracchan Reforms, 133 B.C." (pp. 514–521) excerpts from *Plutarch's Lives,* vol. IV, revised and translated by A. H. Clough. Published by Little, Brown (1909).

Chapter 6 Augustus. "The Accomplishments of Augustus, A.D. 14" (pp. 561–572) from *Roman Civilization: Selected Readings, Vol. I, The Republic and the Augustan Age Third Edition,* edited by Naphtali Lewis and Meyer Reinhold. Copyright © 1990 by Columbia University Press. Reprinted with the permission of the publishers.

Pliny the Younger. Excerpts from "Letters, A.D. 111–113, 10.17a, 10.33–10.34, 10.37–10.40, and 10.52–10.53" (pp. 178–182) from *Rome: Late Republic and Principate,* Vol. II, translated by Peter White, edited by Walter Emil Kaegi Jr. and Peter White. Copyright © 1986 by The University of Chicago. Reprinted with the permission of the University of Chicago Press.

Pompeiian Notices and Graffiti. Excerpts from "Real Estate Transactions" [i, ii], "Election Notices" [i–xv], and "The Humble Townspeople" [i–x], 1st Century A.D. (pp. 126–127, 237–238, 276–278) from *Roman Civilization: Selected Readings,* Vol. II: *The Empire,* 3rd edition, edited by Naphtali Lewis and Meyer Reinhold. Copyright © 1990 by Columbia University Press. Reprinted with the permission of the publishers.

"Interrogation of Christians, A.D. 180" (pp. 564–566) from *Roman Civilization: Selected Readings,* Vol. I, 3rd edition, edited by Naphtali Lewis and Meyer Reinhold. Copyright © 1990 by Columbia University Press. Reprinted with the permission of the publishers.

Chapter 7 Symmachus and St. Ambrose. "The Altar of Victory Sparks a Religious Debate, A.D. 384" (pp. 411–415) excerpts from *A Select Library of Nicene and Post-Nicene Fa-*

thers of the Christian Church, 2ⁿᵈ series, vol. X, translated and edited by Philip Schaff and Henry Wace. Published by The Christian Literature Company (1896).

St. Jerome. Excerpts from "Letter CVII, A.D. 403" (pp. 338–347, 351, 359, 363–367) from *Select Letters of St. Jerome*, translated by F. A. Wright. Copyright © 1963 by the President and Fellows of Harvard College. Reprinted with the permission of Harvard University Press.

Excerpts from "Book of Constitutions or Law of Gundobad, c. 475–525" (pp. 17–24, 30–33, 40–47) from *The Burgundian Code*, translated by Katherine Fischer Drew. Copyright © 1972 by the University of Pennsylvania Press. Reprinted with the permission of the publishers.

"Buildings, c. 533–554" (pp. 5–17, 27) excerpts from *Procopius*, vol. VII, translated by H. B. Dewing. Copyright © 1961 by the President and Fellows of Harvard College. Reprinted with the permission of Harvard University Press.

Chapter 8   Theophanes. Excerpts from "Chronographia A.D. 621/8, A.D. 725/6, 9ᵗʰ Century" (pp. 559–561) from *The Chronicle of Theophanes Confessor: Byzantine and Near Eastern History, A.D. 284–813*, translated by Cyril Mango and Roger Scott. Reprinted with the permission of Oxford University Press, Ltd.

Excerpts from "Islamic Terms of Peace, c. 633–643" (pp. 234–236, 238–240) from *Islam: From the Prophet Muhammad to the Capture of Constantinople*, vol. I: *Politics and War*, edited and translated by Bernard Lewis. Copyright © 1974. Reprinted with the permission of Walker and Company.

Anonymous. Excerpts from "The Life of Lady Balthild, Queen of the Franks, late 7ᵗʰ Century", (pp. 121–123, 127, 131–132) from *Late Merovingian France: History and Hagiography 640–720*, by Paul Fouracre and Richard A. Gerberding. Copyright © 1996. Reprinted with the permission of Manchester University Press.

Pope Gregory the Great. "Letters, c. 598–601" (pp. 84–85; 240) excerpt from *A Select Library of Nicene and Post-Nicene Fathers of the Christian Church*, 2ⁿᵈ Series, vol. XII: *Leo the Great, Gregory the Great* & vol. XIII, Part II: *Gregory the Great, Ephraim Slaves and Aphrahat*, translated and edited by Philip Schaff and Henry Wace. Published by the Christian Literature Company (1898).

Chapter 9   "General Capitulary for the Missi, c. 802" (pp. 16–19, 23–24, 26–27) excerpts from *Translations and Reprints from the Original Sources of European History*, Vol. VI, edited by Dana Carleton Munro. Published by the University of Pennsylvania Press (1898).

Liutprand of Cremona. Excerpts from "The Embassy to Constantinople, c. 968" (pp. 235–243) excerpts from *The Works of Liudprand of Cremona*, translated by F. A. Wright. Reprinted with the permission of Routledge.

Anonymous. Excerpt from *Digenis Akritas: The Two-Blood Border Lord*, 10ᵗʰ–11ᵗʰ Century (pp. 59–61), translated by Denison B. Hull. Copyright © 1972 by Ohio University Press. Reprinted with the permission of the publishers.

Ahmad al-Ya'qūbī. Excerpt from "Baghdad, 9ᵗʰ Century" (pp. 69–73) from *Islam: From the Prophet Muhammad to the Capture of Constantinople*, vol. II: *Religion and Society*, edited and translated by Bernard Lewis. Copyright © 1974. Reprinted with the permission of Walker and Company.

Chapter 10   "Charter of Jaca, c. 1077", (pp. 123–135) excerpts from *Medieval Iberia: Readings from Christian, Muslim, and Jewish Sources*, translated by Thomas N. Bisson and edited by Olivia Remie Constable. Copyright © 1997 by The University of Pennsylvania Press. Reprinted with the permission of the publishers.

"Loriss, France, c. 1155" (pp. 328–330) excerpts from *A Source Book of Mediaeval History*, edited by Frederic Austin. Published by the American Book Company (1907).

Emperor Henry IV and Pope Gregory VII. "Letters of the Investiture Conflict, 1076" (pp. 90–91) excerpts from *The Correspondence of Pope Gregory VII: Selected Letters from the Registrum* translated by Ephraim Emerton. Published by Columbia University Press (1912). Henry IV. "Letter 12" from *Imperial Lives and Letters of the Eleventh Century* (pp. 150–151), translated by Theodor E. Mommsen and Karl F. Morrison, edited by Robert L. Benson. Copyright © 1962 by Columbia University Press. Reprinted with the permission of the publishers.

Excerpts from *The Anglo-Saxon Chronicle*, 1085–1086 (pp. 161–165), edited by Dorothy Whitelock. Copyright © 1961 by Dorothy Whitelock and David Douglas. Reprinted with the permission of Rutgers Univeristy Press.

Hildegard of Bingen. "Antiphon for the Virgin 12th Century" (p. 117) from *Symphonia: A Critical Edition of the Symphonia armonie celestium revelationum, 2e,* translated by Barbara Newman. Copyright © 1998 by Cornell University Press. "Hildegard to the prelates at Mainz" from *The Letters of Hildegard of Bingen, Vol. I* (pp. 76–80), translated by Joseph Baird and Radd Ehrman. Copyright © 1994 by Oxford University Press. Reprinted with the permission of the publishers.

Chapter 11 "Medieval University Life, 12th–Early 13th Centuries" (pp. 2–7) excerpts from *Translations and Reprints from the Original Sources of European History*, Vol. II, No. 3, edited by Dana Carleton Munro. Published by the University of Pennsylvania Press (1898). Excerpts from *Wine, Women, and Song: Mediaeval Latin Students' Songs* (pp. 58–64), edited by John Addington Symonds. Published by Chatto and Windus (1907).

Chrétien de Troyes. Excerpt (lines 6702–6818 and 6834–6891) from *Erec and Enide*, translated by Burton Raffel. Copyright © 1997 by Yale University. Reprinted with the permission of Yale University Press.

Saints Francis and Clare of Assisi. "Selected Writings" (pp. 344–349) from *Select Historical Documents of the Middle Ages*, edited by Ernest Henderson. Published by Bell and Sons (1921). Excerpts from "The Testament of Saint Clare," from *Francis and Clare: The Complete Works*, translated by Regis J. Armstrong and Ignatius C. Brady. Copyright © 1982 by The Missionary Society of Saint Paul The Apostle in the State of New York. Reprinted with the permission of Paulist Press.

Thomas of Monmouth. Excerpts (pp. 14–17, 19–23) from *The Life and Miracles of St. William of Norwich*, translated by Augustus Jessopp and Montague Rhodes. Published by Cambridge University Press (1896).

Chapter 12 Abbot Suger. *De administratione,* translated by David Burr. http://www.fordham.edu/halsall/source/sugar.html.

Hadewijch of Brabant. Excerpts from Ria Vanderauwera, "The Brabant Mystic: Hadewijch, 1220–1240" (pp. 193–5, 198–201) from *Medieval Women Writers*, edited by Katharina M. Wilson. Copyright © 1984 by The University of Georgia Press. Reprinted with the permission of the publishers.

Dante Alighieri. Excerpts from *La vita nuova*, translated by Barbara Reynolds. Published by Penguin Books (1980). Copyright © 1969 by Barbara Reynolds. Excerpts from *The Comedy of Dante Alighieri the Florentine, Cantica III: Paradise* translated by Dorothy L. Sayers and Barbara Reynolds. Copyright © 1981 by Dorothy L. Sayers and Barbara Reynolds. Both reprinted with the permission of David Higham Associates, Ltd.

Excerpts from *The Nikonian Chronicle: Russia—The West and the Golden Horde 1241–1381*, edited by Serge A. Zenkovsky; *The Nikonian Chronicle: From the Year 1241 to the Year 1381*, vol. 3, translated by Serge A. and Betty Jean Zenkovsky. Copyright © 1986 by Serge A. Zenkovsky and Betty Jean Zenkovsky. Reprinted with the permission of The Darwin Press, Inc.

Chapter 13 Excerpts from *The Black Death,* 14ᵗʰ Century (pp. 16–21, 23, 207, 208, 219–222), translated and edited by Rosemary Horrox. Copyright © 1994. Reprinted with the permission of Manchester University Press.

Excerpts from "Peasant Rebels in London, 1831" (pp. 169–176, 178–181), from *Historia Anglicana* by Thomas Walsingham, in R. B. Dobson, *The Peasants' Revolt of 1381,* 2ⁿᵈ edition. Published by Macmillan Press (1983).

Christine de Pizan. "Laments on the Evils of the Civil War, 1410." Excerpts from *The Epistle of the Prison of Human Life with an Epistle to the Queen of France and Lament on the Evils of the Civil War,* edited and translated by Josette A. Wisman. Copyright © 1984. Reprinted with the permission of Garland Publishing.

Catherine of Siena. "Letters to the Papacy, 1376–1417" (pp. 167, 169, 202, 217–218, 222–223) excerpts from *The Letters of St. Catherine of Siena, Volume I,* translated by Suzanne Noffke, O.P., MRTS vol. 52 (Binghamton, NY, 1988). Copyright © by the Board of Regents for Arizona State University. Reprinted with permission of the publishers. Excerpt from *Medieval Europe: A Short Sourcebook* by Warren Hollister, Joe W. Leedom, Marc A. Meyer, and David S. Spear. Copyright © 1992 by McGraw-Hill, Inc. Reprinted with the permission of the publishers.

Chapter 14 Leonardo Bruni and Giovanni Rucellai. "Florence in the Quattrocento, 1427–1457" (pp. 279–282) from *Major Problems in the History of the Italian Renaissance* by Benjamin G. Kohl and Alison Andrews Smith. Copyright © 1995 by D.C. Heath and Company. Excerpts from *Images of Quattrocento Florence: Selected Writings in Literature, History and Art,* edited by Ugo Baldassarri and Arielle Saiber. Copyright © 2000 by Yale University Press. Both reprinted with the permission of the publishers.

Giovanni Pico della Mirandola. "Oration on the Dignity of Man 1496" (pp. 180–183) from *The Italian Renaissance Reader,* edited by Julia Conaway Bondanella and Mark Musa. Copyright © 1987 by Julia Conaway Bondanella and Mark Musa. Reprinted with the permission of Dutton Signet, a division of Penguin Putnam Inc.

Alessandra. "Letters from a Widow and Matriarch of a Great Family 1450–1465" (pp. 109, 113–117) from *University of Chicago Readings in Western Civilization, 5: The Renaissance,* edited by Eric Cochrane and Julius Kirshner. Copyright © 1986 by The University of Chicago. Reprinted with the permission of The University of Chicago Press.

Bernardino of Siena. "An Italian Preacher: Sins Against Nature 1380–1444" (pp. 119–120, 124–128, 130, 138–139, 147–148, 152) from *the Preacher's Deamons: Bernardino of Siena and the Social Underworld of Early Renaissance Italy* by Franco Mormando. Copyright © 1999 by The University of Chicago. Reprinted with the permission of The University of Chicago Press.

Chapter 15 Desiderius Erasmus. "The Praise of Folly 1514" (pp. 101, 136, 148–150, 153, 155–157, 159, 169, 172–173), edited and translated by John P. Nolan. Copyright © 1964 by John P. Nolan. Reprinted with the permission of Dutton Signet, a division of Penguin Putnam Inc.

Argula von Grumbach and John Hooker. "Women's Actions in the Reformation 1520s–30s" (pp. 164–165) excerpt from *The Dissolution of the Monasteries* by Joyce Youings. Copyright © 1971 by Joyce Youings. Reprinted with the permission of HarperCollins Publishers, Ltd.

Anonymous. "Iconoclasm and Reparations during the Reign of Francis I, 1515–1547" (pp. 290–294) excerpt from *Le journal d'un Bourgeois de Paris sous le Regne de Francois Ier 1515–1536* edited by V. L. Bourrilly (Paris: Alphonse Picard, 1910). Translation by Larissa Taylor. Reprinted with the permission of the translator.

St. Ignatius of Loyola. "A New Kind of Catholicism 1546, 1549, 1553" (pp. 165–166, 230, 233–234, 257, 259, 262–264) from *Saint Ignatius of Loyola: Personal Writings: Reminiscences, Spiritual Diary, Select Letters including the text of The Spiritual Exercises*, edited and translated by Joseph A. Munitiz and Philip Endean. Copyright © 1996 by Joseph A. Munitiz and Philip Endean. Reprinted with the permission of Penguin Books, Ltd.

Chapter 16   Henry IV. "Edict of Nantes, 1598" (pp. 1–16) from "The Great Pressures and Grievances of the Protestants in France," Edmund Everard.

Galileo. Excerpt from "Letter to the Grand Duchess Christina (1615)" from *Discoveries And Opinions of Galileo*, translated by Stillman Drake. Copyright © 1957 by Stillman Drake. Reprinted with the permission of Doubleday, a division of Random House, Inc.

David Pieterzen DeVries. Excerpt (pp. 167–71) from *Voyages from Holland to America* (1655), translated from the Dutch by Henry C. Murphy and privately printed by James Lenox, 1853, pp. 167–71.

Trial Record of Johannes Junius. "The Witch-Persecution at Bamberg, 1628" (pp. 23–28) from *Translations and Reprints from the Original Sources of European History*, translated and edited by George L. Burr, vol. III, no. 4 (University of Pennsylvania, 1912).

Chapter 17   Louis de Rouvroy. Duke of Saint-Simon, *Memoirs* (1648–1690), from *The Memoirs of The Duke of Saint-Simon*, translated by Bayle St. John, vol. II, pp. 363–65.

British Parliament. "The English Bill of Rights (1689)," from *The Statutes: Revised Edition* (1871), vol. II, pp. 10–12.

Ludwig Fabritius. "Account of the Stenka Razin Revolt, 1670" (pp. 120–23) from *Russia under Western Eyes 1517–1825*, edited by Anthony Glenn Cross. Copyright © 1971 by Anthony Glenn Cross. Reprinted with permission.

Marie-Madeleine de Lafayette. "Madame de Lafayette to Joseph Marie de Lescheraine (13 April 1678)" and "Roger de Bussy-Rabutin to Marie de Sevigne (26 June 1678)" (pp. 121–22) from *The Princess of Cleves*, edited and translated by John D. Lyons. Copyright © 1994 by John D. Lyons. Reprinted with the permission of the publishers.

Chapter 18   Olaudah Equiano. Excerpt from "The Slave Ship (1789)" from *Equiano's Travels: His Autobiography*, edited by Paul Edwards (Frederick A. Praeger 1966), pp. 25–32.

Tsar Peter I. "Letter to His Son, Alexei (October 11, 1715)" and "Alexei's Response (October 31, 1715)" from "Correspondence between Peter and Alexis, 1715–1717" in *A Source Book for Russian History from Early Times to 1917*, edited by George Vernadsky, vol. II, pp. 338–39. Copyright © 1972 by Yale University. Reprinted with the permission of Yale University Press.

Montesquieu. Excerpt from "Letter XXXVII, Usbek to Ibben at Smyrna" from *Persian Letters*, translated by John Davidson, vol. I, pp. 85–86.

Mary Astell. Excerpt from *The First English Feminist: Reflections Upon Marriage and Other Writings* (pp. 69–76), edited by Bridget Hill. Copyright © 1986 by Bridget Hill. Reprinted with the permission of St. Martin's Press.